2/20/14

D1574749

GREEN BARONS, FORCE-OF-CIRCUMSTANCE ENTREPRENEURS, IMPOTENT MAYORS

GREEN BARONS, FORCE-OF-CIRCUMSTANCE ENTREPRENEURS, IMPOTENT MAYORS

*Rural Change in the Early Years
of Post-Socialist Capitalist Democracy*

Nigel Swain

CEU PRESS

Central European University Press
Budapest–New York

© 2013 Nigel Swain

Published in 2013 by

Central European University Press

An imprint of the
Central European University Limited Liability Company
Nádor utca 11, H-1051 Budapest, Hungary
Tel: +36-1-327-3138 or 327-3000
Fax: +36-1-327-3183
E-mail: ceupress@ceu.hu
Website: www.ceupress.com

224 West 57th Street, New York NY 10019, USA
Tel: +1-212-547-6932
Fax: +1-646-557-2416
E-mail: martin.greenwald@opensocietyfoundations.org

All rights reserved. No part of this publication may be reproduced,
stored in a retrieval system, or transmitted,
in any form or by any means, without the permission
of the Publisher.

ISBN 978-615-5225-70-3

LIBRARY OF CONGRESS CATALOGING-IN-PUBLICATION DATA

Swain, N. (Nigel)
  Green barons, force-of-circumstance entrepreneurs, impotent mayors : rural change in the early years of post-socialist capitalist democracy / Nigel Swain.
       pages cm
  Includes bibliographical references and index.
  ISBN 978-6155225703 (hardbound)
 1. Agriculture and state—Europe, Eastern.   2. Europe, Eastern—Economic conditions—1989-   3. Europe, Eastern—Economic policy—1989-   4. Post-communism—Europe, Eastern.   5. Democratization—Europe, Eastern. I. Title.
  HD1920.7.Z8S93 2013
  338.10947'091734--dc23

2013023424

Printed in Hungary by Akaprint Kft., Budapest

Table of Contents

List of Tables and Maps xi
Preface xiii
Introduction 1

1. Politics, Policies and Legal Measures 19
    THE NATIONAL POLITICS OF EARLY POST-SOCIALISM 21
        Poland 21
        Hungary 24
        Czechoslovakia and the Czech and Slovak Republics 27
        Bulgaria 30
        Romania 32
    PRIVATISATION AND RESTITUTION POLICIES 36
        Czechoslovakia and the Czech and Slovak Republics 36
        Hungary 39
        Poland 41
        Romania 42
        Bulgaria 43
    CO-OPERATIVE RESTRUCTURING 43
        Co-operative transformation legislation 44
        Legacies of collectivisation and their consequences 50
    CREATING A LOCAL DEMOCRATIC POLITICS 55
        Czechoslovakia and the Czech Republic 55

Slovakia	57
Hungary	58
Poland	60
Romania	63
Bulgaria	64
THE RESEARCH MOMENT	67

2. Common General Findings ... 71

THE RESTRUCTURING OF AGRICULTURE	71
Green barons and others	72
Rural structure in the mid-1990s	85
THE NON-FARM ECONOMY	88
LOCAL GOVERNMENT	98
Inexperience	99
Impotence	102
RURAL COMMUNITIES AND CIVIL SOCIETY	104

3. Bulgaria ... 113

CONTESTED CO-OPERATIVE LIQUIDATION	114
Co-operative livestock farming saved—Pripek	114
Livestock destroyed, a belated successor co-operative and 'elastic' land—Dragana	118
Co-operative livestock retained against the odds—Slivka	123
A successful co-operative on a reduced scale—Kupen	125
Continuity but post-socialist loss of livestock—Breze	126
A spectrum of 'red', 'blue' and family—Venets	127
Problems of a private farmer—Breze	133
LOCAL AUTHORITIES—COPING WITH POST-SOCIALIST RECESSION	134
A commune centre mayor's socialist paternalism—Kupen	134
Salvaging agriculture and its services—*kmetstvo* villages	137
THE DESTRUCTION OF SOCIALIST MOUNTAIN COMMUNITIES—BLAGUN AND CHALA	140
THE NON-FARM ECONOMY—NEW BUSINESSES AND A CUSHION FOR LOCAL EMPLOYMENT	146
BULGARIAN SPECIFICITIES IN SUMMARY	150

4. Czech Republic ... 153

AGRICULTURAL TRANSFORMATIONS—UNCONTESTED, ACRIMONIOUS AND SCANDALOUS ... 154
   Uncontested transformation—Rodáky, Nezávislice, Lesovice, Bárov-Chůzovany ... 155
   A scandalous transformation—Výletnice ... 157
   An acrimonious transformation—Tvrz nad Řekou ... 159

CONTESTED TRANSFORMATION IN AGRICULTURE AND PROTRACTED NON-FARM PRIVATISATION—MĚSTYSOV ... 161

NON-FARM TRANSFORMATIONS—PROTRACTED AND SERENDIPITOUS ... 165
   A glass works, a sawmill and the House of Culture—Nová Huť ... 165
   Serendipitous restitutions and a late-socialist innovation—Lesovice ... 169

INDEPENDENT BUT AT A LOSS—CONTRASTING VILLAGE DEVELOPMENT STRATEGIES ... 171
   A newly independent commuter village—Nezávislice ... 171
   A fuzzy public–private divide—Lesovice ... 174
   A successful business strategy and business *vs* ecology lobbies—Rodáky ... 176
   Traditional rural tourism—Výletnice ... 178

CONTRASTS IN OPTIMISM AND ENVY—BÁROV AND CHŮZOVANY ... 179

CZECH SPECIFICITIES IN SUMMARY ... 191

5. Hungary ... 195

AGRICULTURAL TRANSFORMATION—BANKRUPTCY, SUBTERFUGE AND PATHS TO PRIVATE FARMING ... 196
   Contrived bankruptcy—Korcona ... 196
   'Second economy' to private farming—Szálfa ... 200
   Voluntary liquidation and two successful successors—Pakucs ... 201
   Bankruptcy and subterfuge—Tabar ... 205
   A *modus vivendi* between co-operative and private—Károlyháza ... 207

A Smallholders' policy that failed—Dombház	209
Co-operative continuity—Szálfa	213

THE NON-FARM ECONOMY 215
- Small family businesses—contrasting fates in Pakucs and Tabar 215
- Larger-scale new business success—Károlyháza and Zádorpuszta 218
- 'Socialist personal services gap' family businesses—Korcona 222

LOCAL GOVERNMENT AND LOCAL DEVELOPMENT POLICY 226
- Independence, control of schooling and promoting tourism unsuccessfully—Kissikonda 226
- Ambivalent links with private business—Károlyháza and Kissikonda 229
- The emergence of a business block—Székhely, Korcona, Tabar, Zádorpuszta 232

HUNGARIAN SPECIFICITIES IN SUMMARY 237

6. Poland 241

AGRICULTURAL TRANSFORMATION—STATE FARM PRIVATISATIONS AND SPECIALISTS 243
- From manager to owner—Zalew and Lusowo 243
- Other privatisations—Głaz, Bawełna, Zamek 246
- From socialist specialist to commercial farmer—Zamek and Bawełna 250

LOCAL AUTHORITIES AND REGIME CHANGE 252
- From a clerical to a commercial regime—Bawełna 252
- Clerical influence and intrusion—Pola, Bory and Cukier ... 254
- Continuities, innovations and the PSL—Głaz, Pola, Kanał ... 256
- 'Teachers', 'farmers' and rural tourism—Bory 261

THE NON-FARM ECONOMY 264
- Solidarity-influenced privatisation—Cukier 264
- Insiders and outsiders in the face of disappearing socialist certainties—Kanał 265
- An old new business hostile to the socialist mayor—Głaz .. 268

THE PECULIARITIES OF A NON-EU BORDER COMMUNITY—
SEDNO 269
    State farm privatisation—with a little help from the border 270
    Town and village councils and the border tax 274
    Other border benefits 274
POLISH SPECIFICITIES IN SUMMARY 276

7. Romania 279
    AGRICULTURAL TRANSFORMATION 281
        Smooth progression from co-operative to association—
        Lipova and Purani 281
        A failed association—Colibași 286
        Pre-socialist landholding *vs* machinery—Horia, Lipova and
        Măgura 289
        Agromec as farmer—Măgura 294
        A large-scale private farmer—Remetea 296
    THE NON-FARM ECONOMY—MODEST DEVELOPMENTS . 300
    EXTREME IMPOTENCE AT THE LOCAL LEVEL 305
        The Catholic priest and the doctor—Plopeni 305
        The Reform Church pastor and political patronage—Mica 307
        A vibrant community culture under threat—Măgura 311
        Patronage, incompetence and despair—Bunești, Colibași
        and Horia 314
    ROMANIAN SPECIFICITIES IN SUMMARY 317

8. Slovakia 321
    AGRICULTURAL TRANSFORMATION—VARIATIONS ON THE
    THEME OF CONTINUITY 323
        Co-operative demergers—Hora, Habán, Zurča, Ľupta,
        Bánec 323
        Continuity without demerging—Palina and Krížava 326
        Continuity, secession and one private farmer—Lehota 328
        Client and co-operative privatisation—Klanec 331
    THE NON-FARM ECONOMY 334
        A brand new big business in a village of pensioners and
        Roma—Palina 334

Co-operatives as business parks—Klanec 337
Smaller-scale successful new businesses—Lehota, Ľupta,
Krížava 339
Mixed success plugging the socialist personal services gap—
Zurča and Ľupta 341
Protracted privatisation and commuting to the Czech
Republic—Krížava and Lehota 343
LOCAL AUTHORITY BUSINESSES AND ACCOMMODATIONS
TO CENTRAL POWER 344
Continuity and change—Klanec 344
A new non-market business elite—Krížava 346
Flexible political allegiances—Krížava, Zurča and Ľupta ... 348
Fuzzy ownership and its consequences—Habán 349
Problems of football sponsorship, tourism and promoting
a hotel—Bánec 352
Developing a village 'with no development prospects'—
Hora 355
A change of mayor and perhaps a change of prospects—
Lehota 356
SLOVAK SPECIFICITIES IN SUMMARY 359

Conclusion 361
Bibliography 373
Index of Research Villages 391
General Index 393

List of Tables and Maps

TABLES

2.1. Sector of employment in the 1980s 89
2.2. Sector of employment in 1994–96 89
2.3. Type of work in the 1980s 90
2.4. Type of work in 1994–96 90
2.5. Educational qualifications 91
2.6. Educational qualifications in Western and Eastern Europe .. 92

MAPS

3.1. Research sites, Bulgaria 112
4.1. Research sites, Czech Republic 152
5.1. Research sites, Hungary 194
6.1. Research sites, Poland 240
7.1. Research sites, Romania 278
8.1. Research sites, Slovakia 320

Preface

This book has been a long time coming, but I trust that readers will agree that it was worth the wait. The research on which it is based was conducted in the 1990s and although articles by myself and others based on the project appeared in that decade and immediately after, it has taken a long time to analyse all of the research materials in depth and contextualise them to produce a book-length manuscript which both synthesises all of the findings for all six countries and locates them within the historical moment at which the research took place. This is a book not just about identifying and analysing the rural social change associated with the decollectivisation of agriculture in Eastern Europe, it is also about recovering the historical moment of that change; and in six countries which approached the common project in different ways and from different starting points. It is a work of contemporary comparative history, which began as comparative sociology. I hope that its findings will be of interest to anyone, from whatever academic discipline or none, who is curious about: large-scale social change (including class formation), generally; everyday life (in rural communities) during the early years of post-socialism in Eastern Europe, more specifically; and pathways from socialist to post-socialist agriculture in particular.

Although I am the sole author of the text that follows and bear full responsibility for errors of fact, interpretation and omission, I am deeply indebted to both individuals and institutions without whom it would not have been possible. Above all I owe a debt of gratitude to the following colleagues who carried out the bulk of the interviews and early research: in Bulgaria—Rossitsa Rangelova and Katia Vladimirova; in the Czech Republic—Helena Hudečková, Michal Lošťák, Cyrila Marková and Věra Trnková; in Hungary—Mihály Andor and Tibor Kuczi; in Poland—Andrzej Kaleta, Marzena Sobczak and Grzegorz Zabłocki; in Romania—Ágnes Neményi and Mária Vincze; and in Slovakia—Gejza Blaas, Stanislav Buchta and Iveta Námerová. I am similarly indebted to Katalin Kovács and Ewa Nalewajko who participated in later joint research projects in the region. My ideas would not have crystallised without their labours and the stimulus of discussions with them. Equally important in this respect were discussions with Andrew Cartwright, Chris Hann, Deema Kaneff and Frances Pine, all still or at one time members of the Max Planck Institute for Social Anthropology (Halle-Saale, Germany), and Katherine Verdery (now of the Graduate Center of the City University of New York but then in Berlin).

My second debt of gratitude is to the European and UK funding bodies without which this work would not have been contemplated let alone completed, in particular: the European Commission's awards CIPA-CT92-3022 for project *Rural Employment and Rural Regeneration in Post-Socialist Central Europe* and ACE 94-0598-R for *Agricultural Restructuring and Rural Employment in Bulgaria and Romania*; and the United Kingdom Economic and Social Research Council's awards L 309 25 3037 for *Transitions to Family Farming in Post-Socialist Central Europe* and R 0022 1863 for *Agricultural Protection and Agricultural Interests in Hungary, Poland and Slovakia*.

Thirdly, I am also indebted to the staff and students of the institutions outside Liverpool that have hosted me as a visiting academic while the project was on-going. The Frankfurter Institut für Transformationsstudien and the former chair of Contemporary Economic and Social History at the Europa Universität Viadrina Frankfurt (Oder) held by Helga Schultz welcomed me as a Fellow in 1997–98 and gave me the opportunity to deepen my knowledge of contemporary history on the German and Polish sides of the river Oder. The Slavic Research Center at Hokkaido University (Japan) awarded me a Foreign Visitor Fellowship in 2003–4 and provided a relaxed and congenial environment which allowed me to dig deep into our research materials unencumbered by teaching and administration, while making new friends and exploring a rich and stimulating culture that challenged my eurocentrism. My thanks to them all, and to my family for putting up with my obsession for so long.

Introduction

In the early 1990s, rural communities in East Central Europe and the Balkans underwent the fourth radical restructuring of their production relations of the twentieth century. All had experienced a land reform after the end of World War I, some more radical than others;[1] all had experienced a further land reform at the end of World War II, which, in the eyes of left-of-centre politicians, brought to fruition the possibilities immanent in the earlier reforms which had not focused sufficiently on the needs of the poor peasants;[2] and all had experienced collectivisation, although Poland abandoned it after the failure of Stalinist collectivisation policies in the 1950s.[3] Furthermore, this

---

[1] For discussion of post-WWI land reforms, see Ivan T. Berend, 'Agriculture', in *The Economic History of Eastern Europe 1919–1975. Volume I: Economic Structure and Performance Between the Two Wars*, ed. M.C. Kaser and E.A. Radice (Oxford: Clarendon Press, 1985), 148–209; Wojciech Roszkowski, *Land Reforms in East Central Europe after World War One* (Warsaw: Institute of Political Studies of Polish Academy of Sciences, 1995).

[2] For discussion of post-WWII land reforms, see Berend, 'Agriculture'; Arndt Bauerkämper and Constantin Iordachi, *The Collectivization of Agriculture in Communist Eastern Europe: Comparison and Entanglements* (Budapest: Central European University Press, forthcoming).

[3] For a comparative study of collectivisation in Eastern Europe, see Nigel Swain, 'Eastern European Collectivisations Compared, 1945–62', in Bauerkämper and Iordachi, *The Collectivization of Agriculture*.

fourth restructuring was itself part of an unprecedented historical process of creating capitalism out of communism.[4] These were years of dramatic and large-scale social change: farming structures changed (again!), new classes were formed, and a new politics emerged through which the new classes might operate. Changing production relations and a changing politics provided the opportunities for some to 'seize the time' and radically to alter their life circumstances; for others, the majority, this proved impossible. This is a book about large-scale social change and agency, that is to say, responses to that change. In particular it seeks to document common features of this fourth restructuring of rural Eastern Europe, to identify common scenarios and different trajectories, and to speculate on the conditions (social, economic, cultural) that created 'winners' and 'losers' in the processes of creating post-socialist capitalist democracy in the region's rural communities. It is a book about rural change and the wider transformation (including class formation) of which that change was a part.

The choice of rural communities as a lens through which to investigate processes of post-socialist class formation in Eastern Europe is deliberate. It is easy for citizens of advanced western countries to dismiss the rural sector as irrelevant: such a small proportion of the population is involved, its experience surely cannot be important for the general picture. But there are two counter arguments for selecting rural communities as the locus of research into the genesis of post-socialist capitalist democracy. The first relates to a well-known feature of rural communities: the preponderance of multi-faceted, face-to-face relationships within them. In small-scale, face-to-face societies, relationships are self-evidently complex, overlaid, interwoven; this characteristic cannot be ignored. It is clear to all, to take an invented example, that the shopkeeper is also chairman of the council and organiser of the most important community association in the village, and that he also has a brother who is the biggest farmer in the village. Any investigation of the role of this single individual requires

---

[4] The nature of this post-socialist capitalism is discussed in Nigel Swain, 'A post-socialist capitalism', *Europe-Asia Studies* 63, no. 9 (October 2011): 1671–95. The first two decades of the region's post-socialist history are considered in Geoffrey Swain and Nigel Swain, *Eastern Europe since 1945* (Houndmills: Palgrave Macmillan, 2009, 4th ed.), 233–86.

an examination of the nature of the local economy, the state of local farming, the composition of the local authority and local politics, the nature of local associations, the strength of civil society and so on. It has to be multi-dimensional. The real world of capitalist democracy is similarly interwoven. Market agents are active in politics too. But social science research into large-scale communities tends to focus on a single dimension—the economic, the social, the political. In bigger aggregates this makes sense, but interrelatedness can be lost. Perfectly acceptable results for political science, for example, can be achieved without considering the economic background of the subjects involved. In small-scale communities, the many dimensions in which individuals operate cannot be ignored. The interconnectedness of modern capitalist democracy is thrust centre stage, but on a scale that is relatively easy to grasp. Rural communities thus provide an ideal locus for investigating the complexity of capitalist democracy, the interrelationship of politics, economics, the social and the cultural.

A second reason for insisting on the centrality of rural communities for understanding the nature of the change from socialism to capitalism relates to the status of the major actor in socialist agriculture—the 'collective farm' or agricultural producer co-operative. Not only was this an institution that was unique to the 'actually existing' socialist regimes of the former Eastern Europe, it also embodied within itself two essential features of socialist production relations. These were, first, the unequal powers of labour and management (the ability of managers to manipulate labour inputs to maximise their private benefits), and, second, the institutionalisation of the symbiotic relationship between the 'first' and the 'second' economies.[5] The importance of the 'second economy' to real world socialist economies is well established.[6] What was unique about agricultural producer co-operatives however, especially in the more reformed economies of the

---

[5] Nigel Swain, *Collective Farms which Work?* (Cambridge: Cambridge University Press, 1985), 51–79.
[6] See for example Chris Hann, 'Second economy and civil society', in *Market Economy and Civil Society in Hungary*, ed. Chris Hann (London: Frank Cass and Company, 1990), 21–44; Nigel Swain, *Hungary: The Rise and Fall of Feasible Socialism* (London and New York: Verson, 1992), 171–83.

region, was that both sets of tensions, between 'first' and 'second' economy and between management and labour, were present within the same institution. That is to say, the farms embraced all of the contradictory production relations of 'actually existing' socialism. If collective farms embodied the essence of socialist production relations in this way, it seems plausible that the essence of the changing production relations involved in moving from socialism to capitalism would similarly be encapsulated in the break-up of these quintessentially socialist production organisations. Again, far from being marginal, the key agricultural production entities of the rural economy were central to the transition from socialism to post-socialist capitalism.

This book is a work of comparative contemporary history; it is concerned with both similarity and difference in the process of large-scale social change. The post-socialist regimes of East Central Europe and the Balkans were faced in the 1990s with a broadly similar task of creating the 'market economy' and 'liberal democracy' necessary for 'capitalist democracy', which in the rural context meant breathing real democratic life into structures of local democracy that had never been democratic and recreating farming structures based on private ownership and private enterprise. But, as with the process of collectivisation which began (but was not completed) some four decades previously, they embarked on the project from different starting points, with different resources, and with slightly different ambitions.[7] Identifying these national differences within the common project of creating post-socialist capitalist democracy in rural communities is the structuring theme of this volume.

The interrelated themes of similarity and difference in the processes by which individuals, or groups of individuals, were differentially capable of demonstrating agency, of 'seizing the time' and 'making their own history' at a moment of radical social change recall Marx's famous statement in 'The Eighteenth Brumaire of Louis Napoleon':[8]

> Men make their own history, but they do not make it just as they please; they do not make it under circumstances chosen by them-

---

[7] Bauerkämper and Iordachi, *The Collectivization of Agriculture*.
[8] Karl Marx, 'The Eighteenth Brumaire of Louis Bonaparte', in *Marx Engels: Selected Works in One Volume*, ed. Karl Marx and Friedrich Engels (London: Lawrence and Wishart, 1968), 97.

selves, but under circumstances directly encountered, given and transmitted from the past. The tradition of all the dead generations weighs like a nightmare on the brains of the living.

Marx did not mean these words as a statement of historical philosophy. They follow a few lines after his equally famous statement about history: 'Hegel remarks somewhere that all facts and personages of great importance in world history occur, as it were, twice. He forgot to add: the first time as tragedy, the second as farce.'[9] His focus was on mankind's tendency to seize on imagery from the past to rationalise and justify revolutionary actions in the present. Nevertheless a lot is packed into these few words; they address directly the question of historical agency (the role of individuals in the making of history), and they contain a hint at a realistic (he would say 'materialist') understanding of the influence of the past on the present, which is of relevance when considering explanations in history and the role of comparative history within them.

It is a commonplace, not exclusive to the political Right, that individuals make their own histories. Self-made entrepreneurs who create a business out of nothing, such as Bill Gates, Steve Jobs and Mark Zuckerberg have international renown. But, although they are less well known internationally, there are as many stories of downtrodden workers whose lives are revolutionised by participating in and eventually leading struggle against intransigent employers. In the UK, examples who achieved short-term notoriety are Jimmy Reid (of Upper Clyde Shipbuilders) and Jayaben Desai (of Grunwick). Despite the extensive literature on determinism in history, which usually puts Marxists in the 'determinist' camp,[10] few practitioners of history of any persuasion approach their task in a way that denies that some historical actors 'seize the time' and capitalise on the resources available at given moments in history, while others do not. What historians disagree on more is the weight of 'circumstances directly encountered, given and transmitted from the past'. Just how oppressive is the 'tradition of all the dead generations'? What constraints does it impose on human

---

[9] Ibid.
[10] Niall Ferguson, 'Introduction. Virtual history: Towards a "chaotic" theory of the past', in *Virtual History: Alternatives and Counterfactuals*, ed. Niall Ferguson (London and Basingstoke: Macmillan, 1997), 1–90.

agency? Can individuals swim so powerfully against the tide that they can turn it, or must they ride a wave, itself no easy task?

Both the weight of the 'tradition of all the dead generations' and the importance of comparative history come together in the consideration of counterfactual history. Geoffrey Hawthorn[11] and Niall Ferguson[12] have written of the importance of counterfactuals to explanations in history. Although Ferguson is somewhat dismissive of Hawthorn,[13] who has a more secure standing in the philosophy of the social sciences,[14] both agree that a key aspect of a useful counterfactual argument is that it should be 'plausible'.[15] They do not supply any criteria for selecting, in any given historical context, what to be 'plausible' entails, but it seems reasonable to suggest that 'plausible' counterfactuals should take due account of 'circumstances directly encountered, given and transmitted from the past'. The range and weight of 'plausible' alternative, counterfactual histories from which individuals are free to 'make their own history' is constrained by the 'tradition of all the dead generations' not of their choosing that has gone before. What is more, if assessing the weight of the 'circumstances directly encountered, given and transmitted from the past' is important in order to establish the plausibility of alternative counterfactual accounts, one of the key tools in such analysis is comparative history. Comparing analogous processes in countries undergoing analogous change provides a concrete benchmark, or set of benchmarks, against which the 'plausible' counterfactuals can be compared. Comparative historical analysis can rule out factors that, although plausible as explanations, appear to have played no significant role in an analogous situation. To continue with the surfing analogy, it can help separate out the direction of the wave and the contribution of the surfer.

These abstract considerations can be concretised in terms of the national politics of Hungary in 1989. The scenario of Hungary

---

[11] Geoffrey Hawthorn, *Plausible Worlds: Possibility and Understanding in History and the Social Sciences* (Cambridge: Cambridge University Press, 1991).

[12] Ferguson, 'Introduction'.

[13] Ibid., 18–9.

[14] Geoffrey Hawthorn, *Enlightenment and Despair: A History of Sociology* (Cambridge: Cambridge University Press, 1976).

[15] Hawthorn, *Plausible Worlds*, 16–7.

returning to socialism in that year was impossible. No plausible counterfactual history can be constructed around it. It was fervently desired by certain groups, the Ferenc Münnich Association, for example, and a fleetingly famous Róbert Ribánszky.[16] But they could not overcome the weight of dead generations who had experienced forty years of socialism and rejected it. The public mood was against the socialist restorers however much they exercised their free will and historical agency. By contrast, while the tide of history flowed against the restoration of socialism in 1989, it was the intricate politics of the National Round Table negotiators in the summer of that year that created a characteristic feature of Hungary's post-socialist politics which to an extent determined the entirety of its post-socialist politics: its divided opposition *before* the first free elections. The negotiators rode the anti-socialist wave in the public mood, but, in 'making their own history', they surfed the wave in a manner which steered Hungary's post-socialist trajectory in one of a multitude of 'plausible' post-socialist directions; it was a significantly different trajectory from that followed in neighbouring countries, where anti-communist umbrella organisations survived the first round of post-socialist elections.[17]

This book is not itself an exercise in counterfactual history, nor does it attempt to use history to inform policy-making. It does not use the comparative method to distinguish the causal from the contingent, an essential element in any history-based policy-making. Rather it uses comparative history to identify common and specific features in the experience of six countries responding to a similar historical challenge. It follows the course of smaller-scale, rural actors 'making their own history' against a similar weight of 'tradition of all the dead generations', in nationally similar yet distinct settings, some riding the wave, others fighting against it, most being overtaken by events. It is based on sociological research that was carried out in 1993–94 and 1995–96 in nine villages each in the Czech Republic, Hungary, Poland and Slovakia;

---

[16] The Ferenc Münnich Association is discussed in Nigel Swain, 'Hungary's socialist project in crisis', *New Left Review* I/176 (July–August 1989): 3–29.
[17] For an analysis of the National Round Table negotiations, see Nigel Swain, 'The fog of negotiated revolution', in *Challenging Communism in Eastern Europe: 1956 and Its Legacy*, ed. Terry Cox (London and New York: Routledge, 2008), 159–87.

and in 1995–96 in nine villages each in Romania and Bulgaria. In each country, three villages were located in three regions identified as 'core', 'periphery' (understood conventionally as being geographically remote from the economic centre) and 'industrial periphery' (rural areas where there had been industrial development under socialism which was at risk during the transition to a market economy). Each round of research included both qualitative and quantitative research, the latter in the form of a questionnaire, the former based on semi-structured interviews conducted by a small team of researchers in each village. The selection of villages was left to the country-based researchers who were encouraged to go back to villages where they had worked previously (where this was the case) to maximise the degree of background and contextual information that we could gather. The two-phase Central European research was also preceded by the preparation of background papers on the political, economic and social context of agricultural transformation in each country, but this was not possible for Romania and Bulgaria. This book is based mainly on the qualitative research findings recorded in English-language research reports, although some use is made of the quantitative research and of non-English sources. In order to preserve anonymity, the names of the fifty four research villages and any other villages or proper names used in the text are pseudonyms, some invented, some real, but distant from the actual locations.

Although each team of researchers worked with a common research tool—an *aide memoire*—identifying the general questions to which we required answers, they approached the tasks in their own ways, and qualitative social science methods were not equally well embedded in the research traditions of all countries. In the event, the 'core', 'periphery' and 'industrial periphery' classification did not prove to be as useful as anticipated, perhaps because of the severity of the post-socialist recession throughout the rural economy; neither did an attempt to categorise villages as having a 'pro-agriculture', 'pro-development' or 'laissez-faire' development policy. But fifty-four village studies, thirty-six of them based on two visits to the communities a couple of years apart, have provided a wide range of material for analysis.[18]

---

[18] During the course of the research I visited all but one of the villages and, with the help of my colleagues, conducted interviews in many of them.

The research on which the book is based was thus conceived as comparative sociology, while the book itself attempts to recast the findings as comparative contemporary history. Numerous compromises were inevitable in both processes. Within social enquiry, the standard methodological divide is between the qualitative and quantitative approaches, the former being better suited for recovering intentions, meanings and the irreducible uniqueness of social beings and their actions, the latter for recovering standardised information better suited for statistical manipulation and wider comparison. The two extremes are the social survey and the case study, in particular the detailed long-term participant observation of the ethnographer. There is an inevitable trade-off. The social survey, if representative of the population to which it relates, can tell us something certain not only about the sample but also the wider population; its results are generalisable. The case study might address more complex, subjectively revealing issues, but it only tells us with certainly about the case study.

Our research tried to 'have its cake and eat it too'. We wanted to access the sorts of information that qualitative research is suited to, but we also wanted to produce results that reflected a range of developments in more than one community, hence the selection of nine villages per country. The result was a compromise that purists on either side must necessarily reject. Short village visits conducted by social researchers who were not in the main trained as social anthropologists could not hope to replicate the richness of ethnographic material that professional anthropologists would gather over the course of their normally year-long stay in a community. 'Where is the depth?'—the purist ethnographer will ask. By contrast, nor is statistical representativeness addressed by researching in nine haphazardly selected villages rather than one; for the quantitative methods purist, nine villages is simply compounding the problem of unrepresentativeness nine times. We sought a pragmatic middle way. Researching in nine villages per country rather than one does not address the issue of representativeness, but it does somewhat reduce the possibility of our understanding being skewed because the chosen village is wholly uncharacteristic of the larger community. The purist ethnographer will rightly identify our lack of depth and failure to highlight complexity, but the qualitative method was not chosen to mimic the concerns of ethnography: it was chosen rather to permit the recovery of meanings and intentions. Our pragmatic yardstick of success was to be able to recover this sort of information too (we also have our survey data) from more than one community to give a sense of the range of the early post-socialist, rural experience, so that we could feed that information into an examination of similarity and difference. It was recovering this (not representative) range of post-socialist experience, focused on the key issues of agricultural restructuring, employment and entrepreneurship in the non-farm economy, and local politics that was our orienting goal; we could not begin to recover a rural community in its complexity as ethnographers would. The latter will be disappointed by the thinness of the results; quantitative methods devotees will still say, 'representative of what?' We hope, nevertheless, that we have both recovered meanings and intentions and also identified a range of developments which were characteristic of the rural communities under investigation.

Recasting comparative sociology as comparative contemporary history threw up other methodological considerations. History is an exceedingly broad discipline, yet a single feature differentiates the historical method from all other approaches to social enquiry: historical research design cannot manipulate the present in order to achieve or test desired outcomes. It cannot ask people to fill in a questionnaire or take part in an experiment; it cannot ask people about that they are doing; at most it can interrogate survivors about what they did. Historians are stuck with the debris of the past from which they have to pick as best they can. There is a particular onus in the profession on accumulating knowledge about where that debris might be located (which archives have what information) because experiments or surveys cannot be designed from scratch. From the historian's perspective, our research materials are unusual. They were not official documents from an earlier era, but neither did the standard concerns about oral history obtain, because they are a record of contemporary interviews. The reliability of memory, a central concern for many historians using 'oral testimony', was not a concern, although, of course, all other issues of reliability and the danger of the interviewer and the interview situation itself influencing outcomes were. Furthermore, in converting comparative sociology into comparative contemporary history, it gradually became apparent that the sources were being treated in an historical fashion. As time passed, it was no longer possible to go back and ask further questions, seek further clarification, because the world had moved on. Increasingly our results too constituted debris from the past that had to be accepted as they were and incorporated into a historical narrative. Conventional historians might find the sources unfamiliar and unusual, but they are just another form of debris from the past, a debris constructed within the context of a sociological research design. They should be treated with caution as such.

Beyond concern with agency, continuity and change, perennial themes of the historian, this book is stubbornly non-disciplinary. It poaches from anthropology, economics, sociology and politics, but is not concerned with making a contribution to any of them, nor even to history except in as much as understanding change is central to what history does. It has no ambition to push forward the bounds of individual disciplines within academia, simply to understand better the contours of and possibilities immanent within post-socialist social change. The division of academia into disciplines is generally positive (except when the bounds of one discipline are pushed so far that it enters territory better suited to another), but necessarily constraining and partial. Multi-disciplinary research often founders because the interests of each participant, not to mention their chances for career advancement, are structured around their discipline's understanding of importance, and this is rarely shared by the other participating disciplines. Poaching by an academic with experience in multiple disciplines but a commitment to none is perhaps more fruitful.[19]

This refusal to engage with the theoretical concerns of individual disciplines might irritate their disciples. But equally this book is not atheoretical or empiricist. It is informed by an understanding of the socio-economics of everyday socialism and what the creation of capitalism out of a society of that type entails. It makes use of simple but, it is hoped, powerful concepts (all of which are explained when first encountered), which emerged from the data, such as 'green barons', 'force-of-circumstance entrepreneurs', the 'socialist personal services gap', the 'socialist public services gap', 'full, direct and specific restitution', 'partial, indirect and uniform restitution', the 'inverted

---

[19] I was trained in social and political sciences, was briefly employed in an economics department, regularly teach political science, have taught in a history department for over two decades and can, I hope, claim that some of my best friends are anthropologists.

pyramid of land ownership' and 'ersatz shock therapy'. These concepts structure the analysis. But the book shares the historian's concern with obdurate reality that refuses easily to be categorised. Material is included which does not fit neatly into generalisations, about which there is no discussion in 'the literature' simply because 'that is how it was': in the early-to-mid years of the 1990s in parts of Eastern Europe this was happening. Confounding examples are as important as generalisations when understanding the range and contours of social change.

The preceding paragraphs notwithstanding, in addressing the emergence of post-socialist capitalism, this work touches on the emergence or re-emergence of a particular property type, and it would be inappropriate to ignore the considerable literature that has developed on this subject, particularly the unresolved debate between economists and anthropologists. Economics as a discipline has a tendency towards imperialism. It is incredibly effective at what it does well, which is to analyse the behaviour of economic agents who are self-interested, because company law requires them to be: companies must by law maximise the wealth of their shareholders, and economics is good at analysing and predicting the behaviour of business entities. But some economists want to extend that insight beyond economic agents and claim that all human beings always act in the same way. Thus, even though a minute's consideration of family and small-group dynamics suggests that this is manifestly untrue, economists endeavour to extend their models of individual self-interest maximisers to politics and the social sciences. Anthropologists, who focus on the complexity of social interaction, find such imperialism particularly irritating, and this is reflected in the disagreement over property. For economists, the only true property is the property supported by exclusive ownership rights that underpins capitalist society. This property form has been part of the reason for that system's potential for dynamic growth, not least because the limited liability company with which it is associated allows agents to divest themselves of liabilities if things go wrong. For economists, societies which have not developed such a sense of property have not yet developed 'property', and for the discipline what is of interest is to explain how exclusive property rights contribute to growth. Anthropologists, who historically scarcely engaged with advanced market societies, naturally developed a broader definition of property related to bundles of rights (which include wide-ranging potential liabilities), although more recently legal anthropologists have interpreted it as 'the ways in which the relations between society's members with respect to valuables are given meaning, form and significance'.[20] The Max Planck Institute for Social Anthropology for years had a Property Relations Group which investigated effectively and instructively property issues in the post-socialist transition, and Katherine Verdery, who has produced perhaps the most sustained village ethnography on post-socialist transformation in Romania, is at pains to remind us that there is nothing 'natural' about private property: reintroducing it is a social process that has to be learned.[21]

For anthropologists, the imperialist claims of economics threaten to undermine the fundamentals of their discipline. It is understandable why they might want to go head-to-head with economists concerning *the* definition of property. But to the pragmatic historian cum sceptical sociologist, there is no need to hanker after a perfect definition. For the historian it is self-evident that perceptions of property have changed over time, while for sociologists, systems based on exclusive property rights are part of their bread and butter, and the sceptical sociologist can regard the benefits of high growth but limited liabilities as open to question. This project saw no need to intervene directly in the property debate between economists and anthropologists, yet it is clear that in the early post-socialist years there was a move from one property regime to another and that, as Verdery stresses, this is a process that had to be learned.

Writing on the history of European countries located 'east of the Elbe'[22] since 1989 inevitably involves treading in a terminological minefield. Geographically, what is meant by 'Eastern Europe', 'East Central

---

[20] Chris Hann, *'Not the Horse We Wanted!' Postsocialism, Neoliberalism, and Eurasia* (Münster: LIT Verlag, 2006), 22.
[21] Katherine Verdery, *The Vanishing Hectare: Property and Value in Postsocialist Transylvania* (Ithaca, NY: Cornell University Press, 2003), 4.
[22] For a discussion of the 'second serfdom' which was introduced in Europe 'east of the Elbe' in the fifteenth and sixteenth centuries, see B.H. Slicher van Bath, 'Agriculture in the Vital Revolution', in *The Cambridge Economic History of Europe. Volume V: The Economic Organization of Early Modern Europe*, ed. E.E. Rich (Cambridge: Cambridge University Press, 1977), 42–132; Jerome Blum, 'The rise of serfdom in Eastern Europe', *American Historical Review* 62, no. 4 (1957): 807–36.

Europe', 'the Balkans'? What is meant by 'capitalist', 'socialist', 'state socialist', 'actually existing socialist', 'democratic', what even by more neutral-sounding terms as 'market economy' and 'liberal democracy'? All are inescapably value-laden, and there is little to be gained from rehearsing here the arguments in favour of one rather than another. This book takes an historical approach to geographical terminology. 'Eastern Europe' refers to the countries that came under Soviet domination after 1945 and adopted the Soviet-style planning system. 'The Balkans' refers to regions of Europe that remained under Ottoman rule until some point in the nineteenth century. 'East Central Europe' is a residual category referring to the countries of 'Eastern Europe' that are not part of 'the Balkans'. 'Socialist', 'state socialist', 'communist' and 'actually existing socialist' are used synonymously to denote the systems of governance and economic organisation originally modelled on the Soviet Union that were introduced in Eastern European countries during the period from roughly 1948 until roughly 1989. The questions of whether these systems were 'truly' socialist or not, or whether 'true socialism' is possible at all are both eschewed. 'Capitalism' denotes an economic system based primarily on market competition between privately-owned economic entities. Since the economic reforms introduced into socialist economies created competition but not private ownership in terms of any private responsibility for liabilities, the term is *de facto* synonymous with 'market economy'. 'Democracy' is taken to mean what political scientists would call 'polyarchy', the key feature of which being a system based on competitive political parties which gives the voting public the ability at least to vote out of office a party that it is unhappy with.[23] These are often referred to as 'liberal democracies', for unclear reasons since, by their very nature, they are often dominated by parties with a conservative or social democratic rather than liberal ideology. 'Capitalist democracy' is therefore a democracy which rules a capitalist economy. Finally, 'post-socialist' is used to qualify the nature of 'capitalist democracy' in the region because, as this author has argued elsewhere, the countries concerned retained a number of characteristics from the socialist legacy.[24]

---

[23] Andrew Heywood, *Politics* (Houndmills: Palgrave, 2002, 2nd ed.), 32–4.
[24] For the importance of legacy, see Swain, 'A post-socialist capitalism'.

Chapter 1 of this work addresses key developments in the first, pre-European Union phase of post-socialist capitalist democracy in Eastern Europe, when each country followed its own conception of 'liberal democracy' and 'market economy'. It focuses first on national politics, and issues of privatisation and restitution, and then on issues which directly affected the local rural level, co-operative restructuring and local government reform. Chapter 2 presents the common research findings in terms of agricultural transformation, non-farm employment and new businesses, local government and local democracy, and civil society. The remaining chapters then switch focus more from similarity to difference: they consider in turn post-socialist rural change in Bulgaria, the Czech Republic, Hungary, Poland, Romania and Slovakia, illustrating more fully areas of similarity, but identifying extensively country specificities.

Each country-specific chapter adopts the general structure of considering first the agricultural transformation (what happened to the structures of socialist agriculture and what came next?), then developments in the non-farm economy (employment, unemployment, new business formation) and finally the attempts made by local government actors and others to address village problems and provide some direction for development. One of our central concerns was not to focus on villages as isolated agricultural communities—because we were sufficiently well acquainted with socialist villages to know that villages were integrated into a larger society and agriculture was by no means their only source of livelihood, a point that is developed further in Chapter 2. In the Bulgarian chapter the order of the last two sections is switched, and in the Bulgarian, Czech and Polish chapters some villages are considered outside this structure because of specific features in that the village's response to the post-socialist recession that transcended the constraints of this three-dimensional approach: in Sedno in Poland, in Blagun and Chala in Bulgaria, and in Bárov and Chůzovany, and Městysov in the Czech Republic.

Our focus on these three components of rural life had implications for the structure of the book. Questions concerning the non-farm economy and local government actors and their rural development strategies were central to our research agenda, but relatively little has been written on them that allows fruitful comparison. Agricultural restructuring in the region has been considered extensively and this work engages with its findings, but there has been much less research about both the rural non-farm economy and local government. Chris Hann, for example, has edited and contributed to two excellent volumes on the post-socialist transformation,[25] and has published independently on the theme.[26] Questions of the non-farm economy and the development priorities of local government actors do not figure significantly in these and other volumes, however. The work of Junior Davies represents the 'exception that proves the rule' in terms of a focused analysis of non-farm rural development.[27] There is also an extensive literature on entrepreneurship, but little of it relates to Eastern Europe. In our villages, market conditions were changing so dramatically that the conventional distinctions between push and pull factors or opportunity-driven and unemployment-driven factors were drowned out.[28] On balance there were more push or unemployment-driven factors in the number of force-of-circumstance entrepreneurs than there were pull or opportunity-driven ones, and this is a conclusion that Valchovska comes to on the basis of studying new farming enterprises in Bulgaria.[29] We did not examine our entrepreneurs long enough to contribute to debates about stages in the development of entrepreneurship, although the evidence from our samples tends to concur with Valchovska's argument that entrepreneurship is an experience embedded in the relationship between person, business and family.[30]

In the case of local government, beyond rather formal presentations of levels and competencies, the research agenda changed rapidly over the course of the 1990s as both practitioners and analysts of rural development were obliged to get to grips with the idiosyncrasies

---

[25] Chris Hann (ed.), *Postsocialism: Ideals and Practices in Eurasia* (London and New York: Routledge, 2002); Chris Hann and The 'Property Relations' Group (eds.), *The Postsocialist Agrarian Question: Property Relations and the Rural Condition* (Münster: LIT Verlag, 2003).
[26] Hann, 'Not the Horse'.
[27] Junior Davis, 'Sustainable non-farm rural livelihood diversification in Romania during transition', *Eastern European Countryside* 7 (2001): 51–67.
[28] Stela Valchovska, 'Entrepreneurship among post-socialist agricultural producers: The case of Bulgaria' (PhD diss., University of Gloucestershire, 2010), 33–60, discusses these contrasting approaches to entrepreneurship.
[29] Ibid., 193.
[30] Ibid., 60.

of EU funding, a consequence of the second, EU-dominated phase of post-socialist history. This spawned a large literature, but its contours are very different from the issues of the pre-EU phase when local actors could make plans, perhaps naive plans, without reference to EU funding models. It is only recently that sociological enquiry into local authority powers and how they are used has recommenced.[31] In view of this imbalance in published research relating to our three main subject areas, it was decided not to precede the presentation of our findings in each country chapter with a discussion of 'the literature', but rather to incorporate appropriate reference to the literature where its findings had a bearing on our own.

The book attempts, then, to recreate a moment in the early-to-mid 1990s, in the early stages of the emergence of capitalism from socialism, when wholly privately owned entities had not yet become the norm, when democratic practice was still new and unfamiliar, when local class alliances and local capitalist actors were only just beginning to emerge. It is tempting to ask 'what happened next?' Who was ultimately successful, who was not? Some villages have indeed been revisited, and village websites (which most now have) have been scrutinised. But posing the 'what ultimately happened' question imposes an artificial finality. Change does not stop. Some of the new businesses of the 1990s remained twenty years or so on, while others had disappeared (particularly those related to textiles); key actors in the 1990s were still present, but no longer the central figures that they had been. But history had not ended in 1989, nor did it end in 2012. Even those still successful in 2012 might fail the year after. The 'what happened in the end?' question has not been pursued. This book focuses on non-teleological change: the changes that took place from the 1980s into the early-to-mid 1990s, with their futures thereafter open ended.

---

[31] See, for example, Katalin Kovács, 'Rescuing a small village school in the context of rural change in Hungary', *Journal of Rural Studies* 28, no. 2 (April 2012): 108–17.

CHAPTER 1

Politics, Policies and Legal Measures

In the more than two decades following the collapse of socialism in Eastern Europe a particular kind of post-socialist capitalism has emerged, a capitalism that is extremely dependent on western, mainly European, companies and which retains many traces of its socialist birth.[1] This work insists is that post-socialist capitalism is something new and different, and agrees with Frances Pine when she stresses that the post socialist return to subsistence farming does not represent a return to the structures of an earlier era.[2] Both Steven Sampson[3] and Don Kalb[4] have used the phrase 'comprador bourgeoisie' in the context of the dependence of post-socialist Eastern Europe on the advanced economies. While elements similar to a comprador bourgeoisie are clearly present in the post-socialist world, use of a term

---

[1] See Swain, 'A post-socialist capitalism'.
[2] Frances Pine, 'Retreat to the household? Gendered domains in postsocialist Poland', in *Postsocialism: Ideals and Practices in Eurasia*, ed. Chris Hann (London and New York: Routledge, 2002), 99.
[3] Steven Sampson, 'Beyond transition: Rethinking elite configurations in the Balkans', in *Postsocialism: Ideals and Practices in Eurasia*, ed. Chris Hann (London and New York: Routledge, 2002), 299.
[4] Don Kalb, 'Afterword: Globalism and postsocialist prospects', in *Postsocialism: Ideals and Practices in Eurasia*, ed. Chris Hann (London and New York: Routledge, 2002), 320.

associated with the economics of imperialism tends to draw attention away from what is new and different about post-socialist capitalism.

A crucial dividing line in the post-socialist history of Eastern Europe came towards the end of the 1990s when the European Union began to specify very concretely what its conditions for membership were.[5] Prior to that, the terms of the Copenhagen Criteria of 1993 (democratic institutions and a functioning market economy) had been left vague and countries had adopted their own paths to capitalism. In this, they were constrained by certain common features of the post-socialist economic environment: the absence of a market to establish a universally recognised measure of value; the low level of domestic personal savings with which assets could be purchased; and the socialist economy's lack of international product competitiveness. These three features together created a context for privatisation, the key element in market reform, which Mandelbaum characterised as 'selling assets with no value to people with no money'.[6] There was a fourth determining element in socialism's economic legacy: its disproportionate focus on industry. Sectors which dominated post-industrial, western economies were weak or entirely absent; these gaps were ripe for exploitation. The focus on industry also meant that industrialisation had outstripped urbanisation, resulting in underurbanisation and an unusually rural-based proletariat.[7]

This chapter will focus on policy priorities and techniques adopted for privatisation, restitution, and the creation of democratic politics in

---

[5] See Swain and Swain, *Eastern Europe* (4th edition), 233–5.
[6] Michael Mandelbaum, 'Introduction', in *Making Markets: Economic Transformation in Eastern Europe and the Post-Soviet States*, ed. Safiqul Islam and Michael Mandelbaum (New York: Council on Foreign Relations Press, 1993), 6.
[7] György Konrád and Iván Szelényi, 'Social conflicts of under-urbanisation', in *Urban and Social Economics in Market and Planned Economies: Volume I*, ed. Alan A. Brown, Joseph A. Licari and Egon Neuberger (New York: Praeger, 1974), 206–26; David A. Kideckel, *The Solitude of Collectivism: Romanian Villagers to the Revolution and Beyond* (Ithaca, NY and London: Cornell University Press, 1993), 633–4; Nigel Swain, 'Collective farms as sources of stability and decay in the centrally planned economies of East Central Europe', Rural Transition Series Working Paper no. 30 (Centre for Central and Eastern European Studies, University of Liverpool, 1994), 30–2.

the rural context in the first half dozen or so years immediately following the change of system. But in order to do this, the political climate of those first few post-socialist years in the six countries under consideration must be examined, since this informed much of the direction of what followed, as must the performance of parties which competed for the peasant vote.

THE NATIONAL POLITICS OF EARLY POST-SOCIALISM

In retrospect, the course of both the collapse of socialism and early post-socialist politics can be seen to have been determined significantly by two key factors in late socialist society: the strength of the opposition to socialism, and the strength of a reform communist wing within the socialist party. The former determined where the revolution would take place and who would replace the socialist old guard, the second the nature of the regime that would come to power when, after a period of rather painful post-socialist freedom, the pendulum of democratic politics swung and the socialists returned to power.

Poland

Poland was the first country in the region to form a non-communist government in August-September 1989. It did so after a period of extensive negotiations between Solidarity and the communist party, and on the basis of elections which guaranteed the latter both the majority of the seats in parliament and the presidency. The first genuinely free elections were not held until October 1991, by which time, following around 18 months of 'shock therapy', Solidarity, which had always been an umbrella covering many strands, had split into a number of new parties. A minority, right-of-centre government was formed under Jan Olszewski, but it lasted only half a dozen months before being replaced by a broader right-of-centre coalition under Hanna Suchocka in July 1992. She lost a Solidarity-initiated vote of confidence in May 1993 and early elections were called for in September 1993, which were won by a coalition of the former communists and the Peasant Party (PSL). The latter proved more stable and retained power until September 1997. But the return of the socialists did not signal a return to the past. In fact, the socialists were more committed to radical reform than the peasant party, which was always ready to moderate the impact of market forces in the interests of its peasant constituency.[8]

The Polish post-socialist political system was unique in having as a major political actor an avowedly peasant party (the PSL), with clear pro-peasant and pro-agriculture policies. The PSL had emerged from the socialist-era 'satellite' United Peasant Party, the ZSL, and over the course of the early post-socialist years established itself as *the* peasant party. Early splinter groups and Solidarity-aligned parties which claimed the same name and its original heritage as an anti-Communist peasant party (such as PSL-M and PSL-PL associated with figures like Gabriel Janowski who had represented Rural Solidarity in the Roundtable negotiations) all failed to get above the voting threshold in the second post-socialist parliamentary elections; Samoobrona (Self-defence), which would compete with the PSL later for the peasant and 'victims of transition' vote, was not yet a major political force. Samoobrona's big increase in support came after the PSL's period in government, after which many were dissatisfied with its defence of peasant interests, and the party divided first on whether it should support smaller farmers (Waldemar Pawlak) or larger ones (Roman Jagieliński) and then on whether it should remain a single-constituency party or push for a wider constituency. This issue dogged the party for the rest of the 1990s and much of the 2000s as it lost support to Samoobrona, but it remained a predominantly single-constituency party. In the 2007 elections this policy seemed to be paying off as it entered coalition government with the mainly urban Civic Platform, while Samoobrona's

---

[8] For developments in Poland during this period, see Nigel Swain, 'Negotiated revolution in Poland and Hungary, 1989', in *Revolution and Resistance in Eastern Europe: Challenges to Communist Rule*, ed. Kevin McDermott and Matthew Stibbe (Oxford and New York: Berg, 2006), 139–55; Swain and Swain, *Eastern Europe* (1st edition); Swain and Swain, *Eastern Europe* (2nd edition); David S. Mason, 'Poland', in *Developments in East European Politics*, ed. Stephen White, Judy Batt and Paul G. Lewis (Houndmills: Macmillan, 1993), 36–50; Frances Millard, 'Poland', in *Developments in Central and East European Politics 3*, ed. Stephen White, Judy Batt and Paul G. Lewis (Houndmills: Palgrave Macmillan, 2003), 23–40.

support plummeted after its period of government in coalition with the Law and Justice Party and the League of Polish Families.[9]

More important than its longevity as a significant force in post-socialist politics is the PSL's organisation. Most socialist regimes of Eastern Europe had satellite parties of one form or another, many of them supposedly representing the interests of farmers and peasants. What was unique about Poland was that, because it had not collectivised, that peasant constituency remained and so did the organisational structures that supported it. One of the general themes of post-socialist politics was the organisational advantage that the successors to the communist parties enjoyed because they inherited structures throughout the country (see the discussion of Bulgaria below). In Poland, the countryside remained the bailiwick of the ZSL rather than the communist party, and the PSL inherited all of its assets. Aleks Szczerbiak, who has analysed post-socialist Polish politics extensively, has argued that the PSL is unique, not just in Poland but in the whole region, for having many of the characteristics of a Western European mass party. On the basis of a regional study he concluded that 'the PSL is the only party with a well-developed organisation structure in rural areas',[10] and that 'the PSL is easily the largest party to have emerged in Poland since 1989—some

---

[9] For background on the PSL, see Ewa Nalewajko, 'Political parties and agriculture in Poland', Rural Transition Series Working Paper no. 17 (Centre for Central and Eastern European Studies, University of Liverpool); Katalin Kovács and Nigel Swain, 'Agricultural politics and the "Peasant Revolt" in Hungary', Rural Transition Series Working Paper no. 46 (Centre for Central and Eastern European Studies, University of Liverpool, 1997); Kenneth Ka-Lok Chan, 'Poland at the crossroads: The 1993 general election', *Europe-Asia Studies* 47, no. 1 (January 1995): 123–45; Frances Millard, 'Poland's politics and the travails of transition after 2001: The 2005 elections', *Europe-Asia Studies* 58, no. 7 (November 2006): 1007–30; Aleks Szczerbiak, 'Interests and values: Polish parties and their electorates', *Europe-Asia Studies* 51, no. 8 (December 1999): 1401–32; Aleks Szczerbiak, 'Old and new divisions in Polish politics: Polish parties' electoral strategies and bases of support', *Europe-Asia Studies* 55, no. 5 (July 2003): 729–46; Aleks Szczerbiak, 'The birth of a bipolar party system or a referendum on a polarizing government: The October 2007 Polish party elections', *Journal of Communist Studies and Transition Politics* 24, no. 3 (September 2008): 415–43.

[10] Aleks Szczerbiak, 'Testing party models in East-Central Europe: Local party organization in postcommunist Poland', *Party Politics* 5, no. 4 (October 1999): 528.

way ahead of the communist successor'.[11] It is also important to note that, while the PSL is broadly sympathetic to Christian ethics, it favours the separation of church and state,[12] has always had 'an anti-clerical element in [its] electorate that it has been careful not to alienate',[13] and it identifies with the centre left rather than the centre right,[14] although it has gone into coalitions with both right and left.

Hungary

Hungary's opposition in the late socialist years was not nearly as numerous as Solidarity, but what distinguished the path to post-socialism in Hungary was the fact that the opposition was divided from the start. The Opposition Round Table was established in March 1989 to prevent the Party using divide and rule tactics against it, yet the path of the National Round Table negotiations of the summer was influenced, ultimately, by the success of the Party in achieving just that. The outcome was a commitment to democratic elections to be held in March–April 1990 and an interim socialist government which was dominated by reform communists. The elections were won not by an umbrella organisation which subsequently split, but by a coalition government made up of an already clearly identified right-of-centre strand within the opposition which commanded an absolute majority and implemented a clear programme until its term came to an end. In the second post-socialist elections, the socialists returned to power in a not-strictly-necessary coalition with the liberal strand of the socialist era opposition, and, despite the inevitable tensions in this alliance, it too continued for a full term. As in Poland, the socialists proved themselves committed to continued reforms; it was they who implemented the 'Bokros package', the first really serious package of spending cuts.[15]

---

[11] Aleks Szczerbiak, 'The Polish Peasant Party: A mass party in postcommunist Eastern Europe?" *East European Politics and Societies* 15, no. 3 (2001): 575.
[12] Nalewajko, 'Political parties', 12.
[13] Szczerbiak, 'The Polish Peasant Party', 570.
[14] Brigid Fowler, 'Concentrated orange: Fidesz and the remaking of the Hungarian centre-right, 1994–2002', *Journal of Communist Studies and Transition Politics* 20, no. 3 (September 2004): 99–100; Szczerbiak, 'Old and new divisions', 734.
[15] For developments in Hungary during this period, see Swain, 'Negotiated revolution'; Nigel Swain, 'Hungary', in *Developments in East European*

One party within the first post-socialist governing coalition was the Smallholders' Party which saw itself as the inheritor of the party of the same name that had won the first post-World War II elections and been the main anti-Communist force in Hungary until 1947. Unlike the PSL/ZSL, it had not been incorporated into socialist-era political structures, so had no significant resource base in the countryside. I have argued elsewhere, that one of the characteristics of peasant or agrarian parties in the immediate post-war years was that they tended to shed specifically agrarian and pro-peasant policies in favour of more general right-of-centre and often national and Christian policies as they became the only acceptable representative of non-socialist politics.[16] Its inheritance of a solid and extensive peasant constituency in Poland kept the PSL a peasant party, but most of the parties in the region that claimed the heritage of a peasant party from the post-war era continued that period's trend away from peasant to anti-communist, national and Christian politics.

The Smallholder Party in Hungary followed this trend. Originally formed by an older generation that had links with the pre-socialist past, it split many times until it was taken over by József Torgyán, a lawyer with no links to agriculture or the peasantry who engendered a further split when he took it out of the first post-socialist coalition government because of its disagreement over restitution policy (and also because it was clear that Torgyán would not be offered ministerial office).[17] Torgyán was confirmed as leader in the 1994 elections and the party's identity moved away from that of representing the issues of a single rural constituency.[18] In this respect it is noticeable that the party played no role in the mass peasant demonstrations of 1997, which created a

---

Politics, ed. Stephen White, Judy Batt and Paul G. Lewis (Houndmills: Macmillan, 1993), 66–82; Swain and Swain, *Eastern Europe* (1st edition); Swain and Swain, *Eastern Europe* (2nd edition).

[16] Nigel Swain, 'The fate of peasant parties during socialist transformation', in *Bauerngesellschaften auf dem Weg in die Moderne*, ed. Helga Schultz and Angela Harre (Wiesbaden: Harrassowitz Verlag, 2010), 163–76.

[17] Nigel Swain, 'Political parties and agriculture in Hungary', Rural Transition Series Working Paper no. 24 (Centre for Central and Eastern European Studies, University of Liverpool, 1994); Fowler, 'Concentrated orange', 84.

[18] Fowler, 'Concentrated orange', 99–100.

new, short-lived body to represent radical peasant interests.[19] For a time, the Smallholders looked as if they might become a major force on the national Christian right of politics as its two earlier coalition partners fell apart. But Torgyán was no match for Viktor Orbán as he reshaped the formerly liberal Fidesz into a party of the right. Orbán was willing to rule in coalition with the Smallholders after the 1998 elections, but in the Autumn of 2000 a series of fortuitously timed corruption scandals became public knowledge which resulted ultimately in first another split in the party, then Torgyán's resignation and finally the party's demise. Fidesz took over its electoral support.[20]

Nevertheless, despite its move to a national Christian politics which eventually consumed it, the Smallholders did play an important role in early agricultural and restitution politics. Unlike all other Hungarian parties at the time, the Smallholders advocated re-privatisation and the return of land to its ownership of 1 January 1947.[21] This date was chosen because it pre-dated all collectivisation attempts yet postdated the post-war land reform that the Smallholders had accepted in principle, although their conception of a family farming future was somewhat different to that of the communists.[22] As the Hungarian daily newspaper *Magyar Nemzet* reported on 23 January 1990, grassroots members of the party were registering the intentions of peasants to farm, rent or sell their recovered land in early January 1990, and a year later as reported by the same paper on 17 January 1991 they were 'occupying' land in an attempt (ultimately unsuccessful) to ensure that

---

[19] For a full study of these demonstrations, see Katalin Kovács, 'The 1997 "Peasant Revolt" in Hungary', *Eastern European Countryside* 5 (1999): 43–58.

[20] For more on Hungarian politics in this period, see Barnabas Racz, 'Political pluralisation in Hungary: The 1990 elections', *Soviet Studies* 43, no. 1 (1991): 107–36; Barnabas Racz, 'The Left in Hungary and the 2002 parliamentary elections', *Europe-Asia Studies* 55, no. 5 (July 2003): 747–69; Barnabas Racz and Istvan Kukorelli, 'The "second generation" post-communist elections in Hungary', *Europe-Asia Studies* 47, no. 2 (March 1995): 251–79; Fowler, 'Concentrated orange'.

[21] Swain, 'Political parties'.

[22] Ferenc Donáth, *Reform és forradalom: A magyar mezőgazdaság strukturális átalakulása 1945–1975* [Reform and revolution: The structural transformation of Hungarian agriculture 1945–1975] (Budapest: Akadémiai Kiadó, 1977), 38–45.

it was returned to its previous owners. The party constantly lobbied within the coalition to achieve its goal, and eventually Torgyán split both his party and the coalition on the matter when he walked out in February 1992.[23] Even after the passing of the restitution and co-operative restructuring legislation (see below), the Smallholders engaged in a rearguard guerrilla action against it, insisting on special aid for those who established 'agricultural ventures', widening the scope of those who could have a claim over co-operative assets and proposing (although it ultimately failed) that members could have the right annually to withdraw assets from a co-operative.[24]

Briefly, then, the Smallholders were a significant force in both agricultural politics nationally and early extra-legal attempts at co-operative restructuring. But, their rearguard guerrilla war notwithstanding, their influence was waning as restitution and co-operative restructuring were implemented and Torgyán took them towards national, Christian politics. The other Hungarian agrarian party worthy of brief note was the Agrarian Alliance. Widely viewed as the party of co-operative chairmen and managers, it achieved minimal electoral success (two individually elected members of parliament in 1990).[25] The Christian Democratic People's Party had a very distinctive agricultural policy,[26] but, unlike the Smallholders, it was happy to jettison its own policy when it joined the coalition.

Czechoslovakia and the Czech and Slovak Republics

The socialist-era opposition in Czechoslovakia was well known internationally, but domestically was rather small, in both parts of the republic, and its small support base differed in orientation in the two parts of the federation. The dominant strand in Czech Bohemia

---

[23] Sándor Kurtán, Péter Sándor and László Vass (eds.), *Magyarország politikai évkönyve* [Political yearbook of Hungary] (Budapest: Demokrácia Kutatások Magyar Központja Alapítvány, 1993), 374.
[24] Swain, 'The Smallholders' Party versus the green barons: Class relations in the restructuring of Hungarian agriculture', Rural Transition Series Working Paper no. 8 (Centre for Central and Eastern European Studies, University of Liverpool, 1993).
[25] Swain, 'Political parties', 9–12.
[26] Ibid., 14–42.

and Moravia was liberal, while that in Slovakia was Catholic. Slovak nationalism was at this point not a prominent concern, but it was something which had never gone away since the foundation of the republic. In Czechoslovakia, unlike Poland and Hungary, this small opposition was catapulted into taking a leading role following mass popular demonstrations which had occurred independently of its activity. Perhaps because it had no taint of compromise from having negotiated with the enemy, it could take a fundamentalist line; yet, as in Poland, anti-socialist politics was initially dominated by umbrella groups, Civic Forum in Bohemia and Moravia, Public Against Violence in Slovakia. These groupings stood in the first post-socialist elections in June 1990, but they fared less well in the local government elections of November 1990 and then began to fall apart, and they did so in distinctive ways, which became more acute as politics became dominated by the 'velvet divorce'. Although opinion polls suggested that the majority opinion was against the break-up of the country and would have opposed it if there had been a referendum on the matter,[27] no referendum took place. The Slovakia issue split the federal coalition government and elections were scheduled for June 1992. In these, the Czechs voted just as unambiguously for the extreme liberal rhetoric of Klaus's Civic Democratic Party (ODS), as the Slovaks did for the increasingly dogmatic nationalism of Mečiar's Movement for a Democratic Slovakia (HZDS). All attempts to hold the country together failed and the 'velvet divorce' was complete by the end of December.

In the Czech Republic, the social democrats and communists did well in the local elections of November 1994, despite the fact that local politics proved an important breeding ground for a new generation of ODS politicians.[28] In the 1996 national elections, the social democrats received only three per cent less of the vote than the ODS, but the

---

[27] Jan Rychlík, 'The possibilities for Czech–Slovak compromise, 1989–1992', in *Irreconcilable Differences? Explaining Czechoslovakia's Dissolution*, ed. Michael Kraus and Allison Stanger (Lanham, MD and Oxford: Rowman and Littlefield, 2000), 61.

[28] Tadayuki Hayashi, '"Neo-liberals" and the politics of economic transformation in the post-communist Czech Republic', in *Democracy and Market Economics in Central and Eastern Europe: Are New Institutions Being Consolidated?* ed. Tadayuki Hayashi (Sapporo: Slavic Research Center, Hokkaido University, 2004), 143–4.

Kraus era continued as he succeeded in forming a coalition government. However, the economic crisis of 1997 precipitated his demise and a social democratic-led minority government took power in June 1998. In newly independent Slovakia, Mečiar briefly lost power in March 1994 after he lost a vote of confidence, but he consolidated his dominant position in early elections that October, and, while the HZDS did not fare quite so well in the local elections of November 1994, it was particularly successful in villages.[29] His government then behaved in an increasingly authoritarian manner towards the president and parliament, building up a clientelistic regime which also strengthened economic ties with Russia, but it was voted out of office by Slovakia's democratic silent majority on an 85 per cent turn-out in September 1998.

The two halves of the former Czechoslovakia were unique in the region in that no self-consciously peasant party emerged onto the post-socialist political scene, which was probably not unrelated to the fact that the hugely successful inter-war Agrarian Party had not been permitted to take part in post-war politics because it was deemed to have compromised itself by co-operating with the Nazis. In the Czech lands a Farmers' Movement emerged to protect the interests of co-operatives, and an Agricultural Party was formed which was seen as the party of co-operative managers. It failed to get into parliament in 1991 but then became part of the Liberal Social Union which in 1992 was chaired by František Trnka, the Agricultural Party's leader and former vice-chairman of the Slušovice agricultural co-operative (which had gained a degree of notoriety in the late socialist years).[30] In this alliance it gained eight seats and fought against what it saw as anti-co-operative measures such as the 'sanctions law' which imposed severe penalties for incorrect implementation of restitution and co-operative transfor-

---

[29] Personal communication from Tadayuki Hayashi.
[30] Tadayuki Hayashi, 'Politics of the agricultural transformation in Czechoslovakia: 1990–1991', in *The New Structure of the Rural Economy of Post-Communist Countries*, ed. Osamu Ieda (Sapporo: Slavic Research Center, Hokkaido University, 2001), 26–7. For the importance of Slušovice, see Martin Myant, *The Czechoslovak Economy 1948–1988* (Cambridge: Cambridge University Press, 1989), 200–1; Frederic L. Pryor, *The Red and the Green: The Rise and Fall of Collectivized Agriculture in Marxist Regimes* (Princeton, NJ: Princeton University Press, 1992), 153.

mation legislation discussed below. It saw itself as a Czech agrarian party in the Švehla mould (supporting well-to-do rather than poor peasants).[31] In Slovakia neither the equivalent Farmers' Movement nor the Slovak Agrarian Party got into parliament, but the former in particular was known to exert a strong influence on Mečiar's staunchly pro-co-operative government.[32] In neither country was there any significant political representation of a peasant interest, real or rhetorical.

Bulgaria

Political change in Bulgaria began the day after the Berlin Wall fell, and, from the start, there was a suspicion that the Bulgarian Socialist Party (BSP) was trying to ride the reform wave in order to save itself. The opposition committed a defining error of immediate post-socialist politics and accepted early elections. But free elections are only really free if all parties have an equivalent material base, and the Bulgarian opposition did not give itself time to build one, while the socialists (like socialists elsewhere and the PSL in Poland) had inherited an institutional base in every community. The result was an electoral victory for the socialists in June 1990. But the socialist government did not remain in power for long. Several opposition Union of Democratic Forces (SDS) politicians persuaded themselves that the elections had been fraudulent; the socialist president was forced to resign in July because of remarks made the previous December about bringing in the tanks; and by November a combination of factionalism in the party and strike waves outside it led to the creation, on 20 December, of a coalition (technically 'cohabitation') government which included both BSP and SDS members. This government remained in power until the planned elections in October 1991. These were won by the SDS, although it needed the support of the Movement for Rights and Free-

---

[31] Frantisek Pospisil, 'Czech agricultural political parties and movements 1992', Rural Transition Series Working Paper no. 11 (Centre for Central and Eastern European Studies, University of Liverpool, 1994), 17–21.

[32] Gejza Blaas, Stanislav Buchta and Iveta Námerová, 'The economic, legislative, political and social policy contest of Slovak agriculture', Rural Transition Series Working Paper no. 23 (Centre for Central and Eastern European Studies, University of Liverpool, 1994).

doms (DPS), the party of Bulgaria's ethnic Turks and Pomaks (ethnic Bulgarians of Muslim faith),[33] but the BSP did well in the countryside and was also victorious in the local elections that took place at the same time.

The new government's highest stated priority was the 'decommunisation of the country', and it made many enemies in the process. On 28 October it lost a vote of confidence, mainly because it had lost the support of the DPS, and, after two months of uncertainty, a 'government of national responsibility' was put together under Liuben Berov which struggled on until September 1994 when new elections were called for December. These returned to power an unreformed BSP which, lulled by a return to growth, did not feel further radical reform was necessary. But loss-making state companies were receiving soft loans from banks, so creating a banking crisis (15 collapsed in 1996), followed by an exchange rate crisis (the lev fell from 71 to 3000 to the dollar between early 1996 and early 1997), which triggered inflation (it reached 333 per cent in 1996 and was projected to reach 690 per cent in 1997). As a consequence, the government performed poorly as early as October–November 1995 in the local elections, although in rural areas its popularity increased. The SDS won the presidential elections of 1996, and in early 1997, with violent street disturbances and a further financial crisis, early elections war called for August 1997. These in turn removed the BSP from power.[34]

Bulgaria, like Poland, had retained an originally independent and anti-communist peasant party as a socialist 'satellite' party, the Bulgarian Agrarian National Union (BZNS). But Bulgaria, unlike Poland, had collectivised fully and BZNS had lost its constituency. Bulgarian rural voters

---

[33] For general background on Pomaks, see Mary Neuburger, *The Orient Within: Muslim Minorities and the Negotiation of Nationhood in Modern Bulgaria* (Ithaca, NY and London: Cornell University Press, 2004). For more on recent Pomak–Bulgarian relations, see John Pickles, '"There are no Turks in Bulgaria": Violence, ethnicity, and economic practice in the border regions and Muslim communities of post-socialist Bulgaria', Working Paper no. 25 (Max Planck Institute for Social Anthropology, Halle-Saale, 2001), 2–6.

[34] Emil Giatzidis, *An Introduction to Post-Communist Bulgaria: Political, Economic and Social Transformation* (Manchester and New York: Manchester University Press, 2002), 84–91.

tended to vote socialist[35] and BZNS played only a minor role in post-socialist Bulgarian politics. As early as September 1989, dissidents in BZNS established a breakaway BZNS-Nikola Petkov (BZNS-NP), which became a founding member of the SDS. The old BZNS acted as a 'third force' in Bulgaria's roundtable negotiations in April 1990, but neither branch did well in the first democratic elections. The two branches united in February 1992 under the leadership of the daughter of its interwar and immediate post-war leader GM Dmitrov who had returned from the United States.[36] But in November 1993 a pro-BSP BZNS-Aleksander Stamboliski (AS) group broke away, and the party split many times such that at one point 11 variants were registered. A further split in September 2006 forced the largest BZNS organisation to change its name to BZNS-People's Union, but both joined the SDS in 1997. Thereafter none of its various incarnations was a major force in Bulgarian politics. Nevertheless, the pro-socialist faction provided the Minister of Agriculture for much of the socialist government of the mid-1990s, while a SDS faction provided the same minister from 1997 to 2001.[37] The key parties involved in restitution and co-operative restructuring legislation, however, were the BSP and SDS, as discussed below, although all BZNS parties bar the pro-BSP one favoured the return of land to historic boundaries.[38]

Romania

The irony about immediate post-socialist developments in Romania was that, while this was the country where something close to an

---

[35] Creed sees voting BSP in Bulgaria as a form of resistance, a 'moral economy' vote against the world. See Gerald W. Creed, 'Deconstructing socialism in Bulgaria', in *Uncertain Transition: Ethnographies of Change in the Postsocialist World*, ed. Michael Burawoy and Katherine Verdery (Lanham, MD and Oxford: Rowman and Littlefield, 1999), 234–7.

[36] John D. Bell, 'Populism and pragmatism: The BANU in Bulgarian politics', in *Populism in Eastern Europe: Racism, Nationalism, and Society*, ed. Joseph Held (New York: Boulder East European Monograph, distributed by Columbia University Press, 1996), 52–4.

[37] Janusz Bugajski, *Political Parties of Eastern Europe: A Guide to Politics in the Post-Communist Era* (New York: ME Sharpe Center for Strategic and International Studies, 2002), 802–3.

[38] Bell, 'Populism', 55.

armed insurrection had taken place, the political, economic and social change that followed was the least revolutionary. Debates continue over whether it represented a revolution at all, or whether a slightly more reform-oriented wing of the old regime seized power.[39] But, unlike Bulgaria, the opposition was not sufficiently strong to launch an extra-parliamentary attack, while Iliescu had no qualms about organising the miners twice in 1990 as an extra-parliamentary *force de frappe* to nip opposition in the bud. The politics that followed was messy. Socialist party offshoots and Iliescu dominated, winning elections in 1990 and 1992, but in the latter period they could not form a majority without the support of extreme right-wing, nationalist parties, with whom it was difficult to reach an agreement. The mould of Romanian politics was broken in November 1996 when the Romanian Democratic Convention (CDR) a nominally liberal coalition, a 'coalition of coalitions'[40] was elected, but it too proved incapable of tackling entrenched interests and the status quo. As Gallagher has put it:

> Emil Constantinescu, the new President, failed to become an effective rallying force for change. Capitalists with a background in the old communist *nomenklatura* continued to divert large amounts of state funding for their own private use under the eyes of incompetent and quarrelsome 'reformers' who soon lost the respect or the vast bulk of the Romanian people.[41]

It was only after Iliescu returned to power in 2000, in the era of increased EU influence, that he began implementing policies that were

---

[39] See, for example, Nestor Ratesh, *Romania: The Entangled Revolution* (New York and London: Praeger, with The Center for Strategic and International Studies, Washington DC, 1991); Peter Siani-Davies, *The Romanian Revolution of December 1989* (Ithaca, NY and London: Cornell University Press).

[40] Michael Shafir, 'The Ciorbea Government and democratization: A preliminary assessment', in *Post-Communist Romania: Coming to Terms with Transition*, ed. Duncan Light and David Phinnemore (Houndmills: Palgrave, 2001), 84.

[41] Tom Gallagher, 'The Balkans since 1989: The winding retreat from national communism', in *Developments in Central and East European Politics 3*, ed. Stephen White, Judy Batt and Paul G. Lewis (Houndmills: Palgrave Macmillan, 2003), 79.

in line with those of post-socialist reform communists in Poland and Hungary.

The trend for historical peasant parties to enter the world of post-socialist politics as a national Christian party rather than a specifically peasant or agrarian party is perhaps best exemplified by the Romanian National Peasant Party (PNȚ), which entered that era as the Christian-Democratic National Peasant Party (PNȚ-CD). The elderly leadership of the party, which claimed that it was a 'party of market economy and peasant property',[42] had joined the European Christian Democratic Union extra-legally in February 1987 in the belief that Iuliu Maniu had pursued a Christian morality in the immediate post-war years.[43] The party, the first post-socialist party to be established, was dominated by those who had been the victims of communism following the suppression of the party and arrest Maniu and Ion Mihalache and took an 'uncompromising anti-communist stance'.[44] But only 15 per cent of its members were farmers,[45] and it was better known for its national and nationalist policies than agrarian ones. Although it failed in the 1990 elections, it became the leading force in the CDR electoral alliance which took power in 1996: with 46 per cent of its candidates,[46] it was 'indisputably in command'.[47] It thus has to take much of the responsibility for the alliance's failure, the result in part of 'the unwillingness of the [party] seniors to delegate to experts'.[48] As Elena Stefoi noted, 'many [party] representatives sincerely believe that years spent in

---

[42] Bogdan Szajkowski, 'Romania', in *New Political Parties of Eastern Europe and the Soviet Union*, ed. Bogdan Szajkowski (Harlow: Longman Current Affairs, 1991), 236.

[43] Nicolae Păun, Georgiana Ciceo and Dorin Domuța, 'Religious interactions of the Romanian political parties. Case study: The Christian Democratic connection', *Journal for the Study of Religions and Ideologies* 8, no. 24 (2009): 110–1.

[44] Păun, Ciceo and Domuța, 'Religious interactions', 111.

[45] Ibid.

[46] Tom Gallagher, *Theft of a Nation: Romania since Communism* (London: Hurst, 2005), 105.

[47] Gallagher, *Theft*, 146; Michael Shafir and Dan Ionescu, 'Romania: A nebulous political shift', in *Building Democracy: The OMRI Annual Survey of Eastern Europe and the Former Soviet Union*, ed. Open Media Research Institute (Armonk, NY and London: M.E. Sharpe, 1996), 164.

[48] Gallagher, *Theft*, 157.

prison are an alibi to cover up inefficiency and legislative nonsense.'⁴⁹ The party failed badly in the 2000 elections and split in the summer of 2001.⁵⁰ It re-entered politics in 2005 and re-adopted its old name in 2006, but performed poorly again in the elections of 2008.⁵¹

Although the CDR was responsible for two key agricultural measures, Law 169, which abolished the earlier 10 hectare maximum on the amount of land that could be returned to owners, and the privatisation of remaining nationally owned agricultural assets,⁵² the party is most remembered for the nationalistic opposition of its chair of the Senate Education Committee to the minority rights proposals of the Hungarian Democratic Union of Romania (UDMR) representing Romania's Hungarian minority, which was a fellow coalition partner. Although ultimately expelled from the party because of these views, he was the only party politician whose polling rating increased.⁵³ The Agrarian Democratic Party of Romania (PDAR), which had been part of the brief Stolojan government (1991–92)⁵⁴ and also formed part of the CDR, had an impact on agrarian affairs, but it was not pro-peasant. Under the influence of Triță Fănită, a director of Agroexport which engaged in the international trade in grain, it acted as a major force in delaying the privatisation of state farms until 2001.⁵⁵

The political climate therefore in the countries under consideration in the mid-1990s might be characterised as follows. Poland was dominated by forces committed to post-socialist capitalism, and power had peacefully passed from a Solidarity-inspired but weak coalition of right-of-centre parties to a stronger coalition of former socialists

---

⁴⁹ Ibid.
⁵⁰ Ibid., 257, 305.
⁵¹ Păun, Ciceo and Domuța, 'Religious interactions', 112–3.
⁵² Nigel Swain and Mária Vincze, 'Agricultural restructuring in Transylvania in the post-communist period', in *Post-Communist Romania: Coming to Terms with Transition*, ed. Duncan Light and David Phinnemore (Houndmills: Palgrave, 2001), 178–9.
⁵³ Shafir, 'The Ciorbea Government', 95–7; Tom Gallagher, 'Nationalism and Romanian political culture in the 1990s', in *Post-Communist Romania: Coming to Terms with Transition*, ed. Duncan Light and David Phinnemore (Houndmills: Palgrave, 2001), 113.
⁵⁴ Shafir, 'The Ciorbea Government', 84.
⁵⁵ Verdery, *The Vanishing Hectare*, 279.

and representatives of a peasant party which had mass local support. Hungary had much in common with Poland: socialists were back in power and committed to market reforms, but the Smallholders were beginning their decline. The Czech Republic was dominated by a liberal rhetoric which was beginning to lose some of its appeal, while in Slovakia Mečiarism was at its apogee and the silent majority either remained silent or adapted to his clientelism. In Bulgaria, there was a moment of relative stagnation, when reform measures had stalled and former communists hoped for a 'third way' that might save them from market capitalism, while Romanian politics was still stalling on radical change, retained an authoritarian and clientelistic cast, and was under the influence of extreme nationalism.

PRIVATISATION AND RESTITUTION POLICIES

The strategies for transforming a socialist into a market economy adopted by the countries of Eastern Europe were various and had their origins in late socialist experience.

Czechoslovakia and the Czech and Slovak Republics

For the Czech intelligentsia that was catapulted to the fore at the end of 1989, there was a sense that the socialist era constituted forty entirely wasted years. The priority was root-and-branch reform, and—since the country had minimal debt—it could afford to experiment. This manifested itself in radical (but also radically different) approaches to the issues of restitution and privatisation. As far as restitution was concerned, it was decided to undo forty years literally and return assets to their previous owners. The policy can be described as 'full, direct, and specific'[56] in as much as the full value of the assets (in certain cases net of deductions for socialist improvements) was returned; the

---

[56] See Nigel Swain, 'The ethics of agricultural transition', Rural Transition Series Working Paper no. 31 (Centre for Central and Eastern European Studies, University of Liverpool, 1994); Nigel Swain, 'Agricultural restitution and co-operative transformation in the Czech Republic, Hungary and Slovakia', *Europe-Asia Studies* 51, no. 7 (November 1999): 1199–219.

assets themselves, rather than some sort of monetary equivalent, were returned; and the nature of what was returned differed according to what had been lost: if you (or your forebears) lost a sawmill, you got that sawmill back; if you lost land, you got land back.

Czechoslovakia's approach to privatisation, however required moving away from real individuals (such as those who currently worked in the enterprises concerned) and privatising to the population at large in the form of vouchers. All citizens had suffered under the economic irrationalities of socialism, so all citizens should be able to participate in its transformation towards 'people's capitalism'. Every citizen should be given some sort of share in the private economy, but the size of that share would depend on the prospects of each enterprise and the supply and demand for shares in it, as expressed in a competitive auction. The result was a policy which highlighted 'voucher privatisation', although other approaches were permitted; only 62 per cent of shares in privatised companies at the end of 1992 were owned by voucher-holders, furthermore voucher privatisation tended to be favoured by financially troubled companies and companies where the workers wanted to engineer a worker buy-out.[57]

There was a fundamentalist logic to Czechoslovak people's capitalism, but it required excessively optimistic assumptions about knowledge. Citizens did not have perfect knowledge of the companies in which they were to bid for shares by auction. Interest in them stagnated—until investment privatisation funds entered the fray. The upshot of fundamentalist privatisation was, as commentators subsequently noted, the very opposite of its intent. 'Private' ownership turned out to be exceptionally 'fuzzy'; 'corporate governance' was exceptionally weak.[58] The new owners were not real individuals oper-

---

[57] Lina Takla, 'The relationship between privatization and the reform of the banking sector: The case of the Czech Republic and Slovakia', in *Privatization in Central and Eastern Europe*, ed. Saul Estrin (London and New York: Longman, 1994), 160.

[58] Takla, 'The relationship'; John C. Coffee, Jr, 'Institutional investors in transitional economies: Lessons from the Czech experience', in *Corporate Governance in Central Europe and Russia. Volume 1: Banks, Funds, and Foreign Investors*, ed. Roman Frydman, Cheryl W. Gray and Andrzej Rapaczynski (Budapest, London and New York: Central European University Press, 1996), 111–86.

ating in the context of market constraints; they were rather quasi-private corporations, still ultimately controlled by state-owned banks, operating in the context of weak bankruptcy legislation and a government that, despite the talk of 'shock therapy', was willing to subsidise the banks 'off the books' via the Consolidation Bank.[59] A further consequence of the weak bankruptcy legislation was payments arrears and debts went unpaid. Bezemer notes this as a problem in Czech agriculture.[60] In our villages it was an even more substantial problem in Slovakia. There was little pressure in this context to bite the bullet of sacking labour, so unemployment remained remarkably low. The fuzzy ownership problem came to a head after the economic crisis of 1997; in the mid-1990s, the Czech Republic still operated under the 'ersatz shock therapy' of voucher privatisation, fuzzy ownership and low rates of unemployment.[61]

Slovakia was not an independent country at the time of the first round of voucher privatisation in 1992 and thus took part in the national scheme. But by the second round, which was implemented in the Czech Republic in 1994, Slovakia was independent and voucher privatisation was scrapped in favour of more 'standard methods'. What this meant in the context of Mečiar's increasingly authoritarian and clientelist regime soon became clear. In 1995 voucher privatisation was cancelled altogether and replaced by 'bond privatisation' which converted the vouchers into interest-bearing bonds.[62] By the mid-1990s,

---

[59] Takla, 'The relationship', 169; Francis Harris, 'How Mr Klaus cooked the budget: Black hole', *Business Central Europe* 6, no. 49 (March 1998): 58–9.

[60] Dirk J. Bezemer, 'Micro-economic institutions and the transformation of agribusiness: Evidence from the Czech Republic', *Eastern European Countryside* 5 (1999): 95.

[61] See Swain, 'A post-socialist capitalism', 1681. Martin Myant et al., *Successful Transformations? The Creation of Market Economies in Eastern Germany and the Czech Republic* (Cheltenham and Brookfield: Edward Elgar, 1996), 132, argues that there were other reasons for this low level of unemployment, but the dramatic increase between 1996 and 1999 and the subsequent rates of almost twice the level of the first half decade or so suggests that low levels of unemployment and fuzzy ownership were two sides of the same coin. See also Swain, 'The Visegrad countries of Eastern Europe', in *European Economies since the Second World War*, ed. B.J. Foley (Houndmills: Macmillan, 1998), 195–200.

[62] Swain, 'The Visegrad countries', 199–200.

the Slovak economy was also only a partially market economy, but its non-market elements were openly politicised in a way that the 'ersatz shock-therapy' of the Czech Republic was not. There was also a much higher level of unemployment, which can partly be explained by Slovakia's later, socialist industrialisation, and the Czech Republic's earlier, non-socialist industrialisation, which gave it a structure untypical of the socialist world. Slovakia had more communities wholly dependent on a single industry or plant, some of them based in the Czech Republic, whereas the Czech regions had a variety of industries;[63] furthermore, Slovakia spawned fewer entrepreneurs in the immediate post-socialist years than did the Czech Republic,[64] a fact also explained in part by a less mature and variegated industrial base.

Hungary

In Hungary, which had a twenty-year tradition of reforming its economic institutions and where dissident and party economists were in constant contact, the demand for radical, fundamentalist change was more muted. Economists and politicians alike were conscious of the country's level of debt, a debt that was held predominantly by private institutions rather than sovereign bodies and therefore was not likely to be forgiven. Value-for-money became the watchword of Hungary's privatisation strategy of 1990, and in order to ensure value for money, privatisation was entrusted to a new body, the State Privatisation Agency, which, in collaboration with the international consulting companies was charged with getting the best deal for the national economy. 'Fuzzy' ownership and weak corporate governance did not plague this approach, but speed was a problem here, too; in 1991 new actors were introduced to speed up the process of privatising smaller companies and promoting employee share ownership schemes, but always with external experts playing the dominant role. Although part of the mechanism for financing this included the right to soft credits in order to buy shares, the Hungarians were keen differentiate it from

---

[63] Myant et al., *Successful Transformations?*, 155–8.
[64] Ibid., 135–9.

a Czech-style 'give-away'.[65] The socialist government briefly hesitated on privatisation in 1994 before passing new legislation and a framework for faster sales, including utilities and the energy sector in 1995. Although less fundamentalist in conception, the Hungarian approach created real owners who had the ability to change direction radically in the pursuit of market opportunity.[66]

But if the Hungarians eschewed 'vouchers' for privatisation, they became the centre-piece of Hungarian restitution policy, which was in many ways the mirror image of the Czechoslovak approach. Following two appeals to its constitutional court,[67] Hungary devised an approach to restitution that was 'partial, indirect and uniform'. That is to say, it did not return the full value of what was lost; it returned only a form of financial compensation, and it ensured that all beneficiaries were rewarded in the same way, whatever the object that they lost. In fact, the 'uniform' principle was subverted in a minor way thanks to the Smallholders' guerrilla warfare noted above in that some minor specific benefits, 'credit vouchers'[68] accrued to those who had lost land, but the principle was clear. Nothing physical was returned, only vouchers, whose value was calculated according to a degressive formula that effectively placed a ceiling on the amount that anyone could obtain. Equally, every recipient of vouchers could use them in the same way, irrespective of the nature of their loss: to bid in land auctions, as means of payment for buying state and local authority flats, as an asset to be taken into account at face value when applying for privatisation or certain business promotion credits, or to purchase supplementary pension benefits.[69] For example, the son of a baker

---

[65] Anna Canning and Paul Hare, 'The privatisation process—economic and political aspects of the Hungarian approach', in *Privatization in Central and Eastern Europe*, ed. Saul Estrin (London and New York: Longman, 1994), 209.

[66] Swain, 'The Visegrad countries', 195–201.

[67] Swain, 'Agricultural transformation in Hungary: The context', Rural Transition Series Working Paper no. 7 (Centre for Central and Eastern European Studies, University of Liverpool, 1993).

[68] Swain, 'The Smallholders' Party'.

[69] Swain, 'The legislative framework for agricultural transition in Hungary', Rural Transition Series Working Paper no. 25 (Centre for Central and Eastern European Studies, University of Liverpool, 1994), 5.

whose bakery was nationalised received vouchers to a proportion of the value of the business which he could then use to bid for land, but, unlike his counterpart in the former Czechoslovakia, he had no right to the building itself, even if it was still in existence. Hungary's focus on paper securities both for restitution and, as is discussed below, co-operative shares, led Kovács and Bihari to argue that it was particularly 'market-conform'.[70]

Poland

A distinguishing feature of the Polish approach to restitution and privatisation, certainly up to the end of the 1990s and thus well beyond the period considered in detail below, is that it had no policy on restitution. This seems to be associated with a widespread belief that, in agriculture at least, restitution was unnecessary because Poland was a country of small-scale peasant farms which it had not collectivised. It was also related to widespread anxiety concerning the Pandora's box that might be opened if restitution were countenanced for property lost when the country shifted bodily westwards and Germans were displaced, and this despite the fact that over 100,000 claims had been lodged by around 1992.[71] The Polish approach to privatisation under the communist-dominated government in 1990 focused on value-for-money stock market floatations, but this failed and it switched focus to promote speed-of-sale, introducing a mass privatisation programme in June 1991 which had elements of both the Czechoslovak and Hungarian approaches, but differed in detail. As in Hungary, a government agency was created to oversee the process, the Ministry of Privatisation, but the Poles followed some of the Czechoslovak model in that under the mass privatisation programme, citizens were awarded vouchers for shares at a nominal fee on a citizenship basis. But, after the first free elections of

---

[70] Katalin Kovács and Zsuzsanna Bihari, 'State and co-operative farms in transition: The Hungarian case', in *Rural Societies under Communism and Beyond: Hungarian and Polish Perspectives*, ed. Paweł Starosta, Imre Kovách and Krzystof Gorlach (Łódź: Łódź University Press, 1999), 148.

[71] Roman Frydman, Andrzej Rapaczynski and John S. Earle, *The Privatization Process in Central Europe* (Budapest, London and New York: Central European University Press, 1993), 202–3.

1991, the programme became a political football and was only finally launched in July 1995 (and completed a year later) after the socialists returned to power. Meanwhile, extensive privatisation took place outside the scheme, using the mechanism of 'privatisation through liquidation' which, despite the name did not mean bankruptcy.[72]

Romania

Romania passed an apparently radical privatisation law in August 1991,[73] but was reluctant to implement it, and the precise relationship between the funds involved remained opaque.[74] Only 22 state-owned enterprises were privatised in 1992 and 260 in 1993, nearly all management buy-outs.[75] In 1994, although measures were taken apparently to speed up privatisation, the companies on offer appeared less attractive over night following a compulsory revaluation of state assets that year. Furthermore 151 key companies were excluded and made part of a special rehabilitation plan. By 1995 only eight per cent of state-owned enterprises had been privatised,[76] and the deadline for the new privatisation law of that year had to be extended to May 1996 because people did not understand the process; 80 per cent of its privatisation was in the form of management buy-outs.[77] In September 1997 the new reformist government was obliged to cancel key privatisation because of entrenched political interests.[78] As in Poland, no measures were passed concerning restitution, except in the case of the partial restitution of land discussed below.[79]

---

[72] Swain, 'The Visegrad countries', 197; Stanisław Gomułka and Piotr Jasiński, 'Privatization in Poland 1989–1993: Policies, methods, and results', in *Privatization in Central and Eastern Europe*, ed. Saul Estrin (London and New York: Longman, 1994), 218–51.
[73] Frydman et al., *The Privatization Process*, 239–53.
[74] Steven D. Roper, *Romania: The Unfinished Revolution* (London and New York: Routledge, 2000), 91–2.
[75] Ibid., 95.
[76] Ibid., 97.
[77] Ibid., 98.
[78] Ibid., 101.
[79] Frydman et al. make no mention of restitution measures in Romania in *The Privatization Process*, yet it figures in all their accounts of other countries.

Bulgaria

Bulgaria waited over a year before introducing any reforms, but it got in control of inflation in 1992 and in the same year passed a Law on the Transformation and Privatisation of State-Owned and Municipal enterprises, which established a Privatisation Agency. But the SDS government was more interested in land restitution (see below), and the Berov government was unable to pursue an assertive economic policy, while the socialists hesitated on all reforms, including privatisation. In 1994, 93 per cent of industrial output still came from state-owned companies and, while the privatisation law was amended that year to allow for mass privatisation, it was only scheduled to start in January 1996.[80] Despite this, as in Romania, 'quiet' and 'illegal' privatisation of state companies to their managers was thought to have been extensive, although exact figures remained unknown.[81]

CO-OPERATIVE RESTRUCTURING

If privatisation and restitution policies varied quite dramatically across Eastern Europe, this was less the case with co-operative restructuring legislation. Here measures were more similar, but the outcomes were equally various because of the impact of very different legacies of collectivisation. Before considering this legislation, however, a clarification of the ownership of land under collectivisation is required.

Unlike the Soviet Union, Eastern European regimes had not nationalised the land prior to collectivisation. In all countries under current consideration, with the exception of Hungary, land normally remained in private ownership. In countries which bothered about legal niceties, such as Czechoslovakia, legislation was passed to prioritise the use-rights of the co-operative over the property-rights of the members,[82] but most countries simply *de facto* negated the property

---

[80] Giatzidis, *An Introduction*, 84–91.
[81] Frydman et al., *The Privatization Process*, 34–5.
[82] Jiří Karlík, *Questions of Ownership and Use of Land and Other Agricultural Means* (Prague: Ekonomický Ústav Československé Akademie VĚD, 1991), 9–10.

rights. In Hungary, following its 1967 land law, an increasing proportion of collectively farmed land became owned by co-operatives themselves. The consequence of this was that for every country other than Hungary, land was not generally a restitution issue. It simply had to be returned *de facto* to its *de jure* owner. Restitution in the main only affected land in the case of former kulaks whose land had been confiscated in the class warfare of the early 1950s.

Co-operative transformation legislation

In Poland, co-operative transformation, like restitution, was not a pressing issue. In Czechoslovakia, the early politics of decollectivisation was complex and contradictory, the radical elements being associated with the '3 Ts', Vlastimil Tlustý, Miroslav Tyl and František Tomášek, all of whom had been active on the agrarian committee of the Czech Civic Forum.[83] One of the compromises that emerged was that, despite the emphasis on full, direct and specific restitution, there was no insistence that those who wished to leave the co-operative and farm independently should be returned their land in its 'historic boundaries'. Equivalent land could be substituted. Nevertheless, the co-operative transformation legislation focused on physical assets, favoured former owners, and was somewhat unsophisticated financially.[84] The key features of the procedure were that all movable and immovable property that had been put into the co-operative when originally formed were returned to its original owners or their heirs, and the remainder was distributed as shares to entitled persons in three blocks: 50 per cent in proportion to the amount of land put into the

---

[83] Hayashi, 'Politics', 27. For a fuller account, see Nigel Swain, 'Decollectivization politics and rural change in Bulgaria, Poland and the former Czechoslovakia', *Social History* 32, no. 1 (February 2007): 12–14.

[84] The contents of the Act are fully described in Yohanan Stryjan, 'Czechoslovak agricultural co-operation: The vagaries of institutional transformation', Berliner Heft zum Internationalen Genossenschaftswesen no. 5 (Institut für Genossenschaftswesen an der Humboldt Universität zu Berlin, 1994), 17–8. See also OECD, *Review of Agricultural Policies: Czech Republic* (Paris: Organisation of Economic Co-operation and Development, 1995), 82 and OECD, *Review of Agricultural Policies: Slovak Republic* (Paris: Organisation of Economic Co-operation and Development, 1997), 66.

co-operative; 30 per cent in proportion to the amount of capital put into the co-operative; and 20 per cent in proportion to the number of years worked on the co-operative. Entitled persons who did not, either immediately or within seven years, decide to take out their shares and register as private farmers, were entitled to the full cash value of their shares seven years after transformation. The process thus greatly favoured former owners,[85] reflected the restitution legislation's focus on physical assets, and placed the prospect of a future cash-call on co-operatives seven years after transformation.

In Hungary, the effect of the 1967 land law had been that only 35 per cent of collectively farmed land remained in private hands, while 61 per cent was co-operatively owned and the rest was owned by the state.[86] Those with claims relating to still privately owned land were awarded 'proportionate share land' from a separate co-operative land fund rather than the original land contributed.[87] Because post-1967 land sales to co-operatives were deemed to have been unconstitutional, land owned by co-operatives was covered by the restitution legislation. If members wanted land back they used their vouchers in land auctions like any other voucher holder. A consequence of the system of auctions and perhaps more importantly the unofficial agreements that often preceded them (to keep the price low or to exclude outsiders—see Chapter 5) was a sense of 'everyone should get something' rather than 'I should get mine back'.[88]

Hungarian co-operative transformation legislation was similar in basic conception to Czechoslovak procedures in that it endeavoured to assign real owners to assets in a 'naming' process,[89] but it differed in

---

[85] Stryjan, 'Czechoslovak agricultural co-operation', 16, talks of a 'massive disenfranchisement' of those who did not own land.
[86] István Harcsa, 'Privatisation and reprivatisation in Hungarian agriculture', *Acta Oeconomica* 43, nos. 3–4 (1991): 321–48.
[87] Swain, 'The legislative framework', 20.
[88] For a fuller account of Hungarian land auctions, see Nigel Swain, 'Getting land in Central Europe', in *After Socialism: Land Reform and Social Change in Eastern Europe*, ed. Ray Abrahams (Providence, RI and Oxford: Berghahn Books, 1996), 204–13. See also Swain, 'Agricultural restitution'.
[89] The 'naming process' is described in Nigel Swain, Mihály Andor and Tibor Kuczi, 'The privatization of Hungarian collective farms', *Eastern European Countryside* 1 (1995): 69–80.

matters of detail. There was less of a focus on the original owners—the distribution was 20% land and property originally contributed, 40% service and the remainder to be decided by farms. In Tázlár, Hann reports villagers complaining that the amount based on salaries was too high, which turned the leaders into major shareholders.[90] In the Czech Republic, as will be shown, the feeling was that former land holding was excessively weighted. Another difference from Czechoslovak procedures was that 1992 was an all-or-nothing year (there was no seven-year reconsideration period), and co-operative shares were not physical assets but financial securities that could be exchanged for assets (if the member wanted to leave and farm privately) or traded. They soon changed hands at around 20 per cent of their face value. The Hungarian system, like that in Romania, also ensured that those who had not contributed land to the co-operative could obtain small plots of roughly the same size as the socialist-era household plot.[91]

Co-operative transformation in Bulgaria was highly politicised and had neither Hungary's financial sophistication nor Czechoslovakia's pragmatism. The 'cohabitation' government introduced a Law on the Use and Ownership of Agricultural Land in February–April 1991, which re-established the maximum restrictions on holdings of 1946 (30 hectares in Dobrudzha, 20 hectares elsewhere). But, rather than return to owners the land that they had lost, it permitted, as in Czechoslovakia, the return of alternative, 'equivalent' land. The law on co-operatives of August 1991 was similarly modest in intent, permitting existing co-operatives effectively to re-register as new ones, which differed only from the socialist ones in that membership was voluntary, members were paid a rent for their land, and received dividends on co-operative profits. But in March 1992 the SDS government amended the 'land law' and adopted a much more radical line on co-operatives. The major change in the land law was the new insistence that wherever possible land should be returned in its 'historic boundaries', despite the fact that a survey by the Ministry of Agriculture in 1992 showed

---

[90] Hann, 'Not the Horse', 59.
[91] Katalin Kovács, 'Strengths, controversies and a show-case of failure in Hungarian agricultural restructuring: The case of the Hollóföldje Co-operative', *Replika* (Hungarian Social Science Quarterly) (Special Issue 1998): 176.

that land still intact in former borders amounted to less than 12 per cent of all land nationwide.[92] In the case of co-operatives, the focus switched from 'transformation' to 'liquidation', although 'liquidation' differed from 'transformation' only in terms of the end point: total liquidation. The process for allocating shares to individual members was similar to that adopted in Czechoslovakia and Hungary, being based on the amount of land contributed to the farm, the number of days worked on it, and any other assets contributed to the farm.[93]

But the different end point was significant. County governors were instructed to establish in every district 'liquidating committees' with the contradictory tasks of managing co-operative farm production while at the same time liquidating their assets. New co-operatives which had been established under the earlier legislation were to be wound up, and no one was permitted to join a new co-operative unless they held full legal title to the actual land contributed to the former co-operative; a notional share of formerly collectivised land was insufficient. These restrictions were softened with the fall of the SDS government, and, after the return of the BSP in December 1994, the government moved to protect co-operatives with measures passed in May 1995. These suspended the liquidation committees, replaced them with bodies elected by co-operative members themselves, and allowed co-operatives to accept land from owners 'collectively', that is to say without the need to wait for full formal title.[94] The new slogan was 'new real boundaries', which meant returning land in a single parcel, but basing the allocation on historically owned land rather than simply offering a share of the collectively farmed land.[95] Barbara Cellarius

---

[92] Gerald W. Creed, *Domesticating Revolution: From Socialist Reform to Ambivalent Transition in a Bulgarian Village* (University Park, PA: The Pennsylvania State University Press, 1998), 232.

[93] Ibid., 225. See also John D. Bell, 'Democratization and political participation in "postcommunist" Bulgaria', in *Politics, Power and the Struggle for Democracy in South-East Europe*, ed. Karen Dawisha and Bruce Parrott (Cambridge: Cambridge University Press, 1997), 387.

[94] Creed, *Domesticating Revolution*, 225–6.

[95] Dobrinka Kostova and Christian Giordano, 'The agrarian elite in Bulgaria—adaptation to the transformation', in *Rural Potentials for a Global Tomorrow: 9th World Congress of Rural Sociology*, ed. Veska Kozhuharova (Sofia: Bulgarian Academy of Sciences, Institute of Sociology, 1996), 56–7.

cites 2001 data which reveal that in the event only 26.5 per cent of land was returned on the basis of its historic boundaries.[96]

Agricultural restructuring in the Romanian countryside was structured by four key legal measures: Laws No. 1, 18 and 36 of 1991, and Law No. 16 of 1994.[97] Law 18/1991 on the land stock established the legal framework for liquidating existing co-operatives and distributing their assets to entitled persons and successor units, and permitted the restoration of a maximum of 10 hectares of land per family as partial restitution for the moral injustices of collectivisation. Land was restored in kind to all entitled persons or their heirs irrespective of whether they were employed in agriculture. In addition, Decree No. 42 of 1990 increased the size of personal plots to 0.5 hectares and allowed co-operatives to allocate such plots to agricultural engineers and others associated with the co-operative.[98] Law No. 1 of 1991 affected agricultural restructuring in that it ruled that people whose family had two hectares of productive land in lowland areas, or four hectares in the mountains, should be considered agricultural producers and hence ineligible for unemployment benefit, so turning unemployment into an agricultural problem. Law 36/1991 regulated the agricultural companies and other entities active in agriculture, and Law 16/1994 covered land rental.

However, despite the fact that much of the discussion of Romanian decollectivisation relates to attempts to re-establish historic borders and the problems associated with this (see Chapter 7), Law 18/1991 did not

---

[96] Barbara A. Cellarius, 'Property restitution and natural resource use in the Rhodope Mountains, Bulgaria', in *The Postsocialist Agrarian Question: Property Relations and the Rural Condition*, ed. Chris Hann and the 'Property Relations' Group (Münster: LIT Verlag, 2003), 196.

[97] For a thorough presentation in English of all the legislation associated with Romanian agricultural restructuring and its effects, see Alexander H. Sarris and Dinu Gavrilescu, 'Restructuring of farms and agricultural systems in Romania', in *Agricultural Privatisation, Land Reform and Farm Restructuring in Central and Eastern Europe*, ed. Johan F.M. Swinnen, Allan Buckwell and Erik Mathijs (Aldershot: Ashgate, 1997), 189–228.

[98] Andrew Cartwright, *The Return of the Peasant: Land Reform in Post-Communist Romania* (Aldershot and Burlington, VT: Ashgate, 2001), 108. Verdery, *The Vanishing Hectare*, 96 refers to Law No. 42 with the same provisions.

insist on historic borders. Quite the reverse, the expectation seemed to be for co-operatives to transform seamlessly into associations.[99] The pressure to recreate historic borders came from the grassroots. Citizens appeared to reject everything to do with socialism and wanted to start over again, although this sentiment was perhaps stronger in mountainous areas like Transylvania than the lowland Regat.

As in Bulgaria, liquidation committees were established to oversee the distribution of co-operative property which, because Romanian co-operative farms had not generally owned machinery (mechanical services having been performed by Stalinist state-owned Machine and Tractor Stations—Agromecs),[100] related primarily to animals, stables and other farm buildings. Once outstanding debts had been taken into account, the remaining property was distributed to members and those who had contributed to the foundation of the farm in the ratios of 60 percent based on the amount of labour contributed to co-operative, and 40 per cent on the amount of land originally contributed. If there was no legal successor to the farm, the members took out their shares in the form of physical assets up to the value of their property shares without there being a need for an auction. If a single co-operative successor emerged, that body took over the co-operative's property and also its debts. If, on the other hand, more than one successor organisation emerged, then auctions had to take place in order to determine which successor got hold of the former co-operative's more valuable assets. In fact, however, in many places, animals and anything else that could be easily carried were often removed before these committees had time meet, leaving the co-operative buildings empty and with little purpose in an agriculture based on small-scale farming. Successor organisations to the co-operatives generally took the form of either 'family partnerships' (also known as 'family associations') or 'agricultural companies' (also known as 'agricultural associations'). The former were loose partnerships of farming families which

---

[99] Cartwright, *The Return of the Peasant*, 155–6.
[100] Machine and Tractor Stations remained initially in state hands. Privatisation began in 1993 when 90 of the total of 521 were privatised, the favoured form of privatisation for these bodies being the management–employee buy-out. But privatisation only gathered pace in 1996 and in our surveyed villages most were still in state hands.

registered with the relevant authorities but did not have legal identities of their own. The latter were corporations in that they had separate legal identities, and they usually continued the management structure of the former co-operative, together with the co-operative principle of one member, one vote. In addition, like other corporations, they could not own land in their own right without ministerial permission. They also benefited from a five year exemption from profits tax, provided they continued in operation for ten years. State farms had been converted into State Agricultural Companies by Law 15 of August 1990 and were not affected by Law 18/1991.

Legacies of collectivisation and their consequences

Broadly speaking, there were four distinct experiences of socialist agriculture in Eastern Europe between 1948, when collectivisation came onto the political agenda, and the collapse of socialism some forty years later. These have been characterised as: 'Stalinist collectivisation', 'collectivisation abandoned', 'neo-Stalinist collectivisation', and 'Hungarian collectivisation'.[101]

'Stalinist collectivisation' was the original model for organising life and labour on collective farms and was based on Soviet developments in the 1930s; it was the model used everywhere in the socialist world in the early 1950s. The essence of the model was as follows: co-operative property was inferior and could not be trusted; agricultural purchase prices were low; peasants and co-operatives alike were subjected to oppressive compulsory deliveries; incomes from the co-operative were low, mainly in kind, and based on the 'labour day' rather than a wage; machinery was held in state-owned machine and tractor stations; private household plots were barely tolerated; and there was minimal diversification out of agriculture. In Romania (and Albania), where Stalinism never disappeared from the political system, the essential features of Stalinist collectivisation were also retained, although the 'labour day' was increasingly supplemented by share-cropping arrange-

---

[101] Nigel Swain, 'A framework for comparing social change in the post-socialist countryside', *Eastern European Countryside* 4 (1998): 5–18; Swain, 'Decollectivization politics'.

ments such as the 'accord global system'.[102] Farm agronomists had the status of 'employees' and their salaries were covered by the state because farms had insufficient resources to pay for such professionals themselves. Other white collar staff were also employees, but were paid by the farm.

In Poland, dissatisfaction with the Stalinist model and the forceful methods used to impose it resulted in collectivisation being abandoned in 1956 following Gomułka's successful wresting of some aspects of 'national communism' from Soviet hegemony. But, because private farming was not encouraged and market forces were suppressed, what emerged was something very different from western farming. It was a dual structure of relatively large, very inefficient state sector farms covering roughly 20 per cent of agricultural land and employing mainly elements which had not succeeded in independent farming, and peasant farms which were fossilised in their late 1940s structure. Peasant farms remained an unloved island of private ownership in a sea of socialist institutions, although, as we will see in the account of Sedno (Chapter 6), co-operation between the two sectors could be extensive. In fact, the degree of tolerance towards peasant farmers fluctuated, and there were periods, in the mid-1970s for example, when policy appeared to favour something akin to renewed collectivisation. Persistent doctrinal opposition to private farming meant that private farmers were consistently discriminated against in the provision of state subsidies and restricted in the acquisition of land and machinery, both supervised by the local commune. Initially government policy focused on encouraging the gradual increase of the socialised sector via measure's such as providing pensions to those who handed their land over to the state. In the late 1970s however it switched to encouraging a group of privileged, slightly larger-scale farmers, the 'specialists', who received preferential access to credits and machinery in return for producing under contract to the state. Despite this belated support for some private farmers, average farm size tended to stagnate.[103]

---

[102] Kideckel, *The Solitude*, 109–15.
[103] See Swain, 'Collective farms'; and OECD, *Review of Agricultural Policies: Poland* (Paris: Organisation of Economic Co-operation and Development, 1995), 42.

In Czechoslovakia and Bulgaria (and the GDR), recognition of the limitations of the Stalinist model resulted not in the abandonment of collectivisation, but in its reform. In essence, the state abandoned the notion of co-operatives as second class socialist forms and entrusted them and their members with money, machinery and increased autonomy. Generally this entailed the following measures: agricultural purchase prices were increased; compulsory deliveries were replaced by contract sales; incomes from agriculture took the form of a regular wage;[104] income levels from agriculture approximated those in industry; pension and social security benefits were introduced, and on a par with industry; diversification out of agriculture was encouraged; and an accommodation was reached with the 'household plot', which in Czechoslovakia often became a virtual entity: the right to a share of produce or co-operative income. Bulgaria embraced the neo-Stalinist model, but distinguished itself by, on the one hand, merging large-scale socialist farms to an excessive degree into agro-industrial complexes which removed agricultural machinery from villages into a modified variant of the machine and tractor station, while, on the other, positively encouraging household plot production to an extent which almost matched Hungarian practice (see below). It also failed to increase agricultural wages. The net effect of this, taken together with the extreme size of the farms and the encouragement of household plot farming, was the take-over of day-to-day collective farm work by ethnic Turks who, as newcomers, had little stake in village property, and an aging membership which focused only on their household plots.[105] Extreme centralism was also associated with extensive use of the *akord* system (similar to the Romanian 'accord global') into the 1980s at the local level in non-mechanised branches.[106]

---

[104] To begin with these often took the form of payment of a percentage, often 80 per cent, of the nominal wage every month, supplemented by the outstanding 20 per cent at the end of the year provided targets were met.

[105] Deema Kaneff, *Who Owns the Past? The Politics of Time in a 'Model' Bulgarian Village* (New York and Oxford: Berghahn Books, 2004), 27, describes these processes in her study of Talpa. Stanka Dobreva, 'The family farm in Bulgaria: Traditions and changes', *Sociologia Ruralis* 34, no. 4 (1994): 350 reports the ageing village population.

[106] Creed, *Domesticating Revolution*, 90–3 and 105–7.

Hungarian collectivisation can be considered as a distinct model because, in addition to all the features of the neo-Stalinist model (including extensive diversification out of agriculture), it introduced two more. First, Hungary systematically encouraged household plot, small-scale private farming, and it did so partly by following Poland's 'collectivisation abandoned' model of rewarding with improved social benefits those who fell in line with government priorities. Rather than tacitly encourage the sale of household plot produce to state purchasers, as happened in the GDR and Czechoslovakia, a substantial 'symbiotic' relationship between large-scale socialist and small-scale private agriculture was self-consciously and systematically pursued. On the one hand, the members received extra social benefits for producing privately but marketing via the socialist sector; on the other, collective farm management benefited in the form of bonuses if it encouraged private plot production. In addition, farms benefited from central government investment programmes which encouraged this sort of integration.[107] The second distinguishing feature of the Hungarian model was the impact of Hungary's New Economic Mechanism (introduced in 1968). By 1989 farm managements had operated for twenty years in a quasi market environment where there were no plan targets, considerable real autonomy in decision-making and farm organisation, and genuine competition.

These different socialist legacies impacted differently on rural communities in the period following 1989. Under the Stalinist model, Romanian collective farm members had received no benefits from their co-operative farm membership, only costs. As soon as the possibility arose, many farms were spontaneously broken up; co-operative property was joyously destroyed as members, who had got nothing out of their co-operatives, took what little they could and started farming for themselves. In Poland, there were effectively no collective farms to break up, only State Farms, and little changed initially, although once the government had passed the necessary legislation, state farm managers began taking over parts of their former state farms and running them privately, while some of the socialist-era 'specialists' expanded

---

[107] For a full account of this 'symbiotic' relationship, see Swain, *Collective Farms*, 51–79.

their holdings by buying or renting State Farm land. The 'organic' process whereby slightly richer farmers bought out slightly poorer ones did not take place. Small farmers did not sell their land because it was a vital source of food and security against unemployment. Average farm size increased only slowly.

The impact of transition in the neo-Stalinist countries was initially the reverse of that of Romania. Neo-Stalinist collectivisation had provided very significant benefits to the members of collective farms which they were reluctant to relinquish. There were few spontaneous moves to break-up farms in Czechoslovakia and successor co-operatives tended to persist. The same was initially the case in Bulgaria, but the extreme political pressure discussed above pushed them towards liquidation. Hungarian co-operative farm members had a lot to lose by leaving the collective too, and the majority initial response was to keep them together. However, in Hungary there were both political pressures (government campaigns against co-operatives and their managers, and pressure from the Smallholders to return land to former owners) and economic pressures (assiduous enforcement of bankruptcy legislation which came into effect, as did co-operative transformation legislation, in 1992) to enforce change. Hence, to a greater degree than in the Czech and Slovak Republics, the co-operative transformation process became one of co-operative break-up, often using bankruptcy rather than co-operative transformation legislation. But, unlike Romania and to a lesser extent Bulgaria, assets were not destroyed or abandoned.[108] They were used rather by management as stepping stones in the creation of private, very large-scale successor farms. At the same time, some who had already established significant private farms on the basis of 'second economy' household plot farming in the socialist years followed the model of the Polish 'specialist farmers' of the 1970s and expanded further.

---

[108] For a discussion of Bulgarian co-operative liquidation and the destruction associated with it, see Dobreva, 'The family farm', 344–6.

CREATING A LOCAL DEMOCRATIC POLITICS[109]

Finally some of the legal measures taken to create new democratic local political structures should be considered. Here too socialist legacies and the differing concerns of socialist-era reformers impacted to create radically different situations in the countries under consideration.

Czechoslovakia and the Czech Republic

Following the 'velvet revolution' in Czechoslovakia, the initial concern of the anti-communist forces was to undo the socialist bad. This took three key forms. First, a Co-optation Act was passed, valid for the first months of 1990 only, which allowed for the removal of the personnel of the past, the most distrusted representatives of the old regime on all local and regional National Committees (councils).[110] Second, on an institutional level, the communist era regions of Central Bohemia, Southern Bohemia, Western Bohemia, Northern Bohemia, Eastern Bohemia, Northern Moravia, Southern Moravia and Prague, which had replaced the historic areas of Bohemia, Moravia and Silesia in 1949, were abolished.[111] Third, local authorities began to de-merge

---

[109] In the new millennium a debate arose about regional policy as an example of the European Union imposing structures on candidate countries. See Conor O'Dwyer, 'Reforming regional governance in East Central Europe: Europeanization or domestic politics as usual?' *East European Politics and Societies* 20, no. 2 (May 2006): 219–53; Martin Myant and Simon Smith, Simon Smith, 'Regional development and post-communist politics in a Czech region', *Europe-Asia Studies* 58, no. 2 (March 2006): 147–68 also consider Czech regional policy. The debate does not relate to the period under consideration here.

[110] Jan Kára and Jiří Blažek, 'Czechoslovakia: Regional and local government reform since 1989', in *Local Government in the New Europe*, ed. Robert J. Bennett (London and New York: Belhaven Press, 1993), 248.

[111] Kenneth Davey, 'The Czech and Slovak Republics', in *Local Government in Eastern Europe*, ed. Andrew Coulson (Aldershot and Brookfield, VT: Edward Elgar, 1995), 45; Jiří Blažek and Sjaak Boeckhout, 'Regional policy in the Czech Republic and EU accession', in *Transition, Cohesion and Regional Policy in Central and Eastern Europe*, ed. John Bachtler,

into their constituent parts. From the 1970s onwards, there had been a process of rationalisation, both in the spheres of local government and co-operative farm organisation, which merged previously independent local authorities into larger units. By the 1990s, the formerly independent villages understandably (although naively) interpreted all their woes as stemming from the decision to merge, and therefore demanded autonomy. As a consequence, the number of municipalities increased by 40 per cent between 1989 and 1991, and the process continued at a somewhat reduced rate until at least 1996 by which time there were over 50 per cent more municipalities than there had been when socialism collapsed.[112] Each municipality was run by a council (municipal assembly) which elected a board and a mayor who was both the political and administrative head of the local authority.[113]

But enthusiasm for undoing the socialist past was not matched by policies for a post-socialist future. No measure was passed to regulate local authority finance until January 1993, when the 1993 Act ensured municipalities revenues from: shares of taxes levied by the state (50 per cent of personal income tax and 100 per cent of taxes on unincorporated businesses),[114] grants from the central budget, income from municipal property and municipal funds, local fees and dues, income from entrepreneurial and other activities, and credits and loans and other income fixed by legal provision.[115] Furthermore, rather few responsibilities were devolved to the autonomous municipalities: pre-school education, the maintenance of primary and secondary school buildings, nurseries, health care, social welfare, culture, sport, physical

---

Ruth Downes and Grzegorz Gorzelak (Aldershot and Burlington, VT : Ashgate, 2000), 309; Michael Illner, 'Territorial government in the Czech Republic', in *Decentralisation and Transition in the Visegrad: Poland, Hungary, the Czech Republic and Slovakia*, ed. Emil J. Kirchner (Houndmills: Macmillan, 1999), 80.

[112] Illner, 'Territorial government', 87.
[113] Karel Lacina, 'Basic information on local governments in the Czech Republic', in *Local Governments in the CEE and CIS, 1994: An Anthology of Descriptive Papers*, ed. The Institute for Local Government and Public Services (Budapest: Institute for Local Government and Public Services, 1994), 65–6.
[114] Davey, 'The Czech and Slovak Republics', 42 and 50.
[115] Illner, 'Territorial government', 83.

planning and a number of other similar services.¹¹⁶ The 'deconcentrated state' in the form of District Offices retained responsibility for regulatory and quasi judicial matters, registering births, deaths and marriages, the application of building but not planning regulations, and preparing regional or district economic plans.¹¹⁷ District Offices also created new sub-offices in smaller communities which were somewhat confusingly located in municipal offices and came under the supervision of that municipality's mayor.¹¹⁸ In addition to acting as territorial units of the deconcentrated state, the District Offices also supervised the activities of the municipalities. The District Offices themselves were superintended by district assemblies elected by municipalities in proportion to their population size which also decided about the distribution of state grants between municipalities.¹¹⁹ Central government also continued to be represented by a variety of 'deconcentrated' offices of a variety of ministries from the Ministry of Finance through the Ministry of Agriculture to the Ministries of Health and Education.¹²⁰

Slovakia

The initial stages of local government reform were similar in Slovakia to those in the Czech Republic, although the tendency for municipalities to 'demerge' was less pronounced. The number of municipalities increased by only four percent between 1980 and 1991, and by 5.2 per cent by 1996.¹²¹ In Slovakia too, there was an even greater proliferation of 'deconcentrated' central state offices than in the Czech Republic.¹²² The new sub-district offices were entirely separate from the municipal organisation and not under the supervision of a mayor, which at least removed the conflicting responsibilities of the Czech approach, but at the

---

[116] Lacina, 'Basic information', 63.
[117] Davey, 'The Czech and Slovak Republics', 46.
[118] Ibid.
[119] Illner, 'Territorial government', 91.
[120] For a full list, see Lacina, 'Basic information', 62.
[121] Lubomir Faltan and Vladimir Krivy, 'Slovakia: Changes in public administration', in *Decentralisation and Transition in the Visegrad: Poland, Hungary, the Czech Republic and Slovakia*, ed. Emil J. Kirchner (Houndmills: Macmillan, 1999), 103.
[122] Davey, 'The Czech and Slovak Republics', 46.

expense of greater concentration of state powers.[123] The Slovak municipalities had responsibility for rather little. In addition to the management of municipal property and administering minor local taxes and fees, they had responsibilities for pre-school (but not primary or secondary) education, clubs for pensioners, meals for pensioners, laundries, social care centres (but not health care), local libraries, 'maintaining the local historical record' (archives), local roads and a few others.[124] Slovakia differed from the Czech Republic fundamentally, however, in that the mayor was directly elected at the same time as the assembly members.[125]

Slovakia also differed from the Czech Republic in terms of local authority financing, which also came on stream in January 1993. Sources of revenue were not so different in principle and included tax and non-tax revenues administered by the municipality, shares in state taxes in accordance with the Act on the State Budget for a given year (for example 29.9 per cent of personal income tax, 30 per cent of motor vehicle taxes, 5.87 per cent of corporate profits tax), earnings from bonds and investments, grants from state funds and the state budget, and credits.[126] The big difference concerned the level of funding and its unpredictability, the fact that it could change from year to year. In the Mečiar years in particular, it tended to change in a downward direction. It was estimated that by the mid-1990s only 4 per cent of total tax revenues went to the municipalities and that the local budget share of GDP had fallen from 21.6 per cent in 1990 to 4.3 per cent in 1995.[127]

Hungary

In Hungary in 1989–90, as in Czechoslovakia, the focus was on undoing the 'socialist' mergers of local authorities which began in the 1970s when the 'districts' were abolished and 'centre villages' cre-

---

[123] Ibid.
[124] Sona Capková, 'Basic information on local governments in Slovakia', in *Local Governments in the CEE and CIS, 1994: An Anthology of Descriptive Papers*, ed. The Institute for Local Government and Public Services (Budapest: Institute for Local Government and Public Services, 1994), 193–6.
[125] Ibid. 197.
[126] Davey, 'The Czech and Slovak Republics', 50.
[127] Faltan, and Krivy, 'Slovakia', 108.

ated.[128] The number of municipalities all but doubled from 1,523 in 1989 to 3,039 in 1991;[129] the fragmentation that this dramatic increase in the number of small local authorities created was not addressed at the time, although it continued to haunt policy makers for the next decade.[130] In 1994 settlements with fewer than 300 inhabitants were barred from establishing municipalities.[131] Hungary differed from the former Czechoslovakia in three respects. First, it devolved from the start quite significant areas of responsibility to the municipalities. Second, there was only a rather small 'deconcentrated state' apparatus with no representation at the municipality level. Third, a reasonably transparent method of local authority funding was elaborated as early as 1991,[132] although it increasingly failed to keep up with local authority costs. The main form of state contribution was 'normative' subsidies: per capita or block grants for general purposes, education, social welfare homes, vocational schools, rural theatres, day care for the elderly and so on. In addition, they received a percentage (initially 50 per cent) of personal income tax paid by residents, the car weight tax paid by residents, environmental fines paid by companies operating on their territory, and the site value of companies privatised on local authority land. There were also targeted subsidies which could be applied for and money from the national health system for health care.[133] In municipalities with population under 10,000, both the council and the mayor were elected directly, the number of council seats being determined by the size of the population.

---

[128] Swain, *Collective Farms*, 136.
[129] Andor, 'The terrain of local politics in Hungary', Rural Transition Series Working Paper no. 22 (Centre for Central and Eastern European Studies, University of Liverpool, 1994), 8. Andor was personally involved in local government in the late 1980s and early 1990s.
[130] Éva Fekete et al., 'Size of local governments, local democracy and local service delivery in Hungary', in *Consolidation or Fragmentation? The Size of Local Governments in Central and Eastern Europe*, ed. Paweł Swianiewicz (Budapest: Local Government and Public Reform Initiative, Open Society Institute, 2002), 31–100.
[131] Fekete et al., 'Size of local governments', 38.
[132] Zoltán Hajdú, 'Local government reform in Hungary', in *Local Government in the New Europe*, ed. Robert J. Bennett (London and New York: Belhaven Press, 1993), 240; Davey, 'Local government', 57.
[133] Andor, 'The terrain of local politics', 8–9.

Poland

In Poland, local government had not figured high on the list of priorities of Solidarity and the opposition forces, and de-merger at the municipal level was not an issue. Poland had a long tradition of the lowest level of the administrative hierarchy (since 1973 around 2,400 *gmina* or communes) being responsible for a number of settlements.[134] Below the commune, 'sub-basic' representation took the form of the directly elected *sołtys* or 'headman' in charge of each settlement (*sołectwo*) in the commune. In all, there were around 40,000 of these, the most common number of *sołectwa* per *gmina* being between eleven and twenty.[135] The *sołectwo* was represented on the commune council to the limited extent that it would constitute the electoral ward if the number of *sołectwa* equalled the number of commune council seats available and the *sołtys* was invited to commune council meetings as an observer. Despite the fact that they were a rather recent, socialist creation, nobody questioned the size or composition of the *gmina* when reform came onto the agenda.[136] More important was the middle tier, the *powiat*, which had been abolished in 1975 when the number of *województwo* had also been increased from 17 to 49.[137] The socialist government could thus be accused of having swept away a traditional three-tier structure that stretched back to the Middle Ages,[138] and it was this that fired the opposition's imagination. The focus of reformers was on this socialist sin rather than the autonomy of settlements within

---

[134] Paweł Swianiewicz and Mikołaj Herbst, 'Economies and diseconomies of scale in Polish local governments', in *Consolidation or Fragmentation? The Size of Local Governments in Central and Eastern Europe*, ed. Paweł Swianiewicz (Budapest: Local Government and Public Reform Initiative, Open Society Institute, 2002), 227.

[135] Ibid., 229–30.

[136] Ibid., 230.

[137] Jerzy Regulski, *Local Government Reform in Poland: An Insider's Story* (Budapest: Local Government and Public Service Reform Initiative, Open Society Institute, 2003), 20; Manabu Sengoku, 'Local government and the state: Change and continuity of the local system in Poland', in *The Emerging Local Governments in Eastern Europe and Russia: Historical and Post-Communist Developments*, ed. Osamu Ieda (Hiroshima: Keisuisha, 2000), 59–60.

[138] Regulski, *Local Government Reform*, 20.

gmina; all agreed that the *powiats* had to be re-introduced.[139] Restructuring which included the *powiats* and *województwa* was finally passed in 1998 for introduction in 1999.

Local government remained a low priority after Solidarity came to power: regional reform become a political football, and so too do did the responsibilities of the municipalities and their financial autonomy. As early as 1989, it had been assumed that the municipalities would take over responsibility for primary education. But the date for transferring authority for primary education was pushed back to January 1994,[140] and, with the advent of the socialist government in 1993, it was put back again to January 1996. There was a similarly politically polarised debate about the rights of local authorities to establish commercial ventures. The parties of the political Left supported this right; those on the political Right opposed it. The parties of the right won the day, and measures introduced in November 1992 restricted *gmina* economic activities to 'public services', although the measure only came into effect on 20 June 1994 and failed to specify clearly what 'public services' were.[141]

The 1990 local government legislation gave local authorities a variety of sources of revenue: local taxes on property, motor vehicles, dogs, inheritance, economic activity, fees, municipal property, the agriculture tax where appropriate,[142] specific central government grants, general government grants, and assigned shares of national taxation. These were 5 per cent of the tax on legal entities, 30 per cent of the tax on wages and salaries, and 50 per cent of personal income tax paid only by those with 'independent' sources of income. Following tax reform at the end of 1991, the latter two were abolished, and a new revenue stream of 15 per cent of the new personal income tax (paid by all) was established.[143] Nevertheless, a dedicated local authority finance

---

[139] Ibid., 66.
[140] Ibid., 35, 44, 70, 108–9; Anna Cielecka and John Gibson, 'Local government in Poland', in *Local Government in Eastern Europe*, ed. Andrew Coulson (Aldershot and Brookfield, VT: Edward Elgar, 1995), 25 and 40.
[141] Regulski, *Local Government Reform*, 61, 64–5, 69; Cielecka and Gibson, 'Local government', 38.
[142] As we shall see in Chapter 6, the considerable scope for varying the impact of this tax had a considerable influence in Polish local politics.
[143] Cielecka and Gibson, 'Local government in Poland', 33–4.

act was not passed until December 1993,[144] and even then it did not mean that the municipalities received the funds they required. Zaucha has argued that 'despite greater tasks and responsibilities ... the ratio of their budgets to GDP had remained unchanged', although his data were for 1991–94 only, and the taking over of responsibility for education became compulsory in 1996.[145] The areas of responsibility that had devolved to the municipalities by the mid 1990s included pre-school and primary education, culture and libraries, sport, tourism, parks and cemeteries, land use, roads, water, sewerage, waste disposal and gas supply.[146] The law on public assistance of 1990 also gave *gminas* responsibility to maintain a public assistance office to help those who met the official definition of poverty in the form of minimal cash benefits, hot meals, accommodation, medical expenses, funeral costs and so on.[147]

Councils were elected by universal suffrage, but the Polish mayoralty was an unusual institution. Mayors were appointed by the council and did not have to be council members. They then appointed the clerk to the council and other administrative officers.[148] In the early years, too, there was a problem of intervention from the 'deconcentrated state', in particular by the *wojewoda*, who, until 1992, supervised *gmina* finance. Legislation introduced by the Senate in 1992 created independent Regional Audit Chambers to take over this supervisory role.[149] Legislation at the same time also sought to create more effective local government by making it more difficult for the mayor or the council board to be dismissed on a whim by a minority of councillors, and transferred the power to make decisions about the sale or encumbrance

---

[144] Regulski, *Local Government Reform*, 147.

[145] Jacek Zaucha, 'Regional and local development in Poland', in *Decentralisation and Transition in the Visegrad: Poland, Hungary, the Czech Republic and Slovakia*, ed. Emil J. Kirchner (Houndmills: Macmillan, 1999), 60–1.

[146] Andrzej Kowalczyk, 'Basic information on local governments in Poland', in *Local Governments in the CEE and CIS, 1994: An Anthology of Descriptive Papers*, ed. The Institute for Local Government and Public Services (Budapest: Institute for Local Government and Public Services, 1994), 151.

[147] Louisa Vinton, 'Poland's social safety net: An overview', *RFE/RL Research Report* 2, no. 17 (23 April 1993): 8–9.

[148] Kowalczyk, 'Basic information', 152–3.

[149] Regulski, *Local Government Reform*, 64–5.

of municipal properties to the board rather than the council.[150] The local government act of September 1995 extended some powers to the *sołectwa* and sought to ensure, with no great success, that municipalities always received sufficient funds to cover their new responsibilities.

Romania

In Romania, if there were a 'socialist sin' to be undone, it would have been 'systematisation', but it had scarcely happened.[151] As in Poland, there were no widespread demands to de-merge rural communes which had a long tradition. Indeed, Ceauşescu's local administration reform of 1968 had been popular in that it abolished the Soviet-style regions and recreated the historic counties headed by prefects.[152] Nor was local government reform high on the agenda of the first post-socialist government. The first local government elections did not take place until almost two years after the national ones, in February 1992, after a new constitution had been passed. The NSF performed badly, as governments mid-term often do. The national government therefore adopted a position of hostility to local authorities, preferring rather to strengthen the 'deconcentrated state'.

The basic system of local government introduced by the Law on Local Public Administration in 1991 confirmed 41 counties and 2,948 municipalities. Central government was represented at the county level by the prefect who was appointed by the Department of Local Public Administration within the prime minister's office. The municipality councils and their mayors were directly elected, and municipalities were responsible for public utilities and the maintenance (only) of health care centres, educational facilities, libraries, cultural centres and care homes, and for cultural, sports and some social services. The bulk of local

---

[150] Ibid., 65.
[151] For a discussion of 'systematisation', see Per Ronnas, 'Turning the Romanian peasant into a New Socialist man: An assessment of rural development policy in Romania', *Soviet Studies* 41, no. 4 (October 1989): 543–59; Michael Shafir, *Romania: Politics, Economics and Society* (London: Frances Pinter, 1985), 142–3 and Siani-Davies, *The Romanian Revolution*, 13 and 49–50.
[152] Shafir, *Romania*, 104–5.

authority revenues came from state grants, 84 per cent in 1992, most of the remainder for local taxes on property (houses and other buildings) and vehicles.[153] Local authorities thus did not have extensive responsibilities and were highly dependent on central government for funding. But the real weakness in the system lay with the dependence of the local authorities on the prefect for the distribution of funds: the prefect was the dispenser of all government funds to the locality, and the law on devolving finance downwards that was promised in the 1991 legislation did not appear until 1998. The prefect could also dismiss the head of local public services.[154] Furthermore, villages within a commune initially had no guaranteed form of representation on the commune council. In 1996, following the local authority elections, new provision was made for a village delegate (with observer status) to attend commune council meetings on behalf of commune villages which did not have a representative on the council.[155] Restrictions were also imposed on the powers of the prefect in relation to suspending councils, and a clear definition of local authority powers was elaborated.[156]

Bulgaria

The basic units of the Bulgarian system of local government were the biggest in the region by a significant degree, and they were the only self-government element in the system. Regional (*oblast*) governors represented the 'deconcentrated state', and plans for a district level

---

[153] Mihai Farcas, 'Basic information on local governments in Romania', in *Local Governments in the CEE and CIS, 1994: An Anthology of Descriptive Papers*, ed. The Institute for Local Government and Public Services (Budapest: Institute for Local Government and Public Services, 1994), 163–6 and 168–9.

[154] Adrian Campbell, 'Local government in Romania', in *Local Government in Eastern Europe*, ed. Andrew Coulson (Aldershot and Brookfield, VT: Edward Elgar, 1995), 81–2 and 92–4.

[155] Takafumi Nakajima, 'Local government in Romania', in *The Emerging Local Governments in Eastern Europe and Russia: Historical and Post-Communist Developments*, ed. Osamu Ieda (Hiroshima: Keisuisha, 2000) 221–3.

[156] Pena Coman et al., 'Local government in Romania', in *Stabilization of Local Governments*, ed. Emilia Kandeva (Budapest: Central European University Press, 2001), 355.

(*okolia*) were abandoned. In 1993 there were 279 municipalities, 3,913 mayor-governed (see below) settlements and 5,335 settlements in Bulgaria.[157] The number had been further reduced by the end of the 1990s to 263, when their average population was 30,000 and the average number of settlements per municipality was 20.[158] The average population of Polish communes, by contrast, was 15,000, while the figures for Hungary, the Czech Republic and Slovakia were 3,300, 1,800 and 1,850 respectively.[159] Like Poland, Bulgaria had introduced a 'sub-basic' institution to cope with this greater size: the *kmetstvo*, or mayor-governed settlement. But its position was weak. No central regulations governed *kmetstvo* funding, so that municipal centres could retain as much as 97 per cent of available funds for themselves;[160] nor was there provision for the individual settlements that made up the municipality be represented on the municipal council. The *kmetstva* heads were invited as observers only to council meetings, but because the electoral system was strict proportional representation, they could not rely on Poland's electoral ward provision for partial representation. Often 90 per cent of councillors came from the biggest settlement in the commune.[161] There had been no discussion of local government

---

[157] Stephan Kyutchukov, 'Basic information on local governments in Bulgaria', in *Local Governments in the CEE and CIS, 1994: An Anthology of Descriptive Papers*, ed. The Institute for Local Government and Public Services (Budapest: Institute for Local Government and Public Services, 1994), 40.

[158] Stefan Ivanov et al., 'Does larger mean more effective? Size and the function of local governments in Bulgaria', in *Consolidation or Fragmentation? The Size of Local Governments in Central and Eastern Europe*, ed. Paweł Swianiewicz (Budapest: Local Government and Public Reform Initiative, Open Society Institute, 2002) 176 and 179.

[159] Harald Baldersheim et al., 'New institutions of local government: A comparison', in *Local Democracy and the Process of Transformation in East-Central Europe*, ed. Harald Baldersheim, Michal Illner, Audun Offerdal, Lawrence Rose and Paweł Swianiewicz (Boulder, CO and Oxford: Westview Press, 1996), 25.

[160] Ivanov et al., 'Does larger mean more effective?', 197.

[161] Paweł Swianiewicz, 'Is there a third way between small yet ineffective and big yet less democratic? Comparative conclusions and lessons learned', in *Consolidation or Fragmentation? The Size of Local Governments in Central and Eastern Europe*, ed. Paweł Swianiewicz (Budapest: Local Government and Public Reform Initiative, Open Society Institute, 2002), 315–7.

reform prior to the collapse of socialism; there was no popular pressure to eradicate the socialist local government structures, despite the fact that the socialist government had restructured the system of local government considerably. A three-tier system had been reduced to a two-tier one in 1959, and municipalities had been merged constantly, particularly after the introduction of the *kmetstvo* in 1978; indeed, as late as 1987, the socialist government had reduced the number of regional bodies, now with the pre-war name *oblast* from 27 to 9.[162]

The interim government elected in October 1991 drew up a Self-government and Local Administration Act in 1991. This turned municipalities into autonomous juridical bodies with their own budgets, but the extent to which responsibilities were devolved to the municipalities was rather small. Bulgarian municipalities in the early-to-mid 1990s had responsibility for kindergartens and school buildings, the infrastructure, welfare for the unemployed and socially vulnerable, water supply and sewerage and health care, although the latter was coordinated by central government.[163] Local government finance reform started in practice in 1993 with the introduction of an intergovernmental transfer formula and a system of state grants and incomes raised locally through taxes (50 per cent of personal income tax and 10 per cent of corporate income tax), fees and charges on certain trading activities, and income from rent and sale of municipal property. Commentators at the time reported that local sources represented 53 per cent of their funds. Retrospective data suggested, however, that local sources of revenue never made up more than 20 per cent of the total, and that central funding provided between 80 and 90 per cent of local authority funds for the whole of the 1990s. Further, while the share of government expenditure within GDP between 1991 and 2000 fell by 9 per cent, the reduction in local government expenditure was 28 per cent suggesting a transfer of financial problems from central to local government.[164] In the mid 1990s, state

---

[162] Makoto Kimura, 'An analysis of local government in Bulgaria', in *The Emerging Local Governments in Eastern Europe and Russia: Historical and Post-Communist Developments*, ed. Osamu Ieda (Hiroshima: Keisuisha, 2000) 340–1.
[163] Kyutchukov, 'Basic information', 45.
[164] Ivanov et al., 'Does larger mean more effective?', 172, 175 and 189.

funding was provided on the basis of historical criteria rather than current need, and even the taxes collected locally had to be sent to the central government for redistribution from the centre back to the municipalities.[165] The effect of the Local Taxes and Fees Act of 1998 was to increase the significance of local sources (to nearer 20 per cent than ten per cent), but municipalities still did not have the means to influence the size of their local tax revenues.[166] Meanwhile, amendments to the local government act in 1995, amongst other things, placed minimum sizes on the *obshtina* (6,000) and *kmetstvo* (500), and ratified the European Charter of Local Self-Government, even though its structures scarcely conformed to the latter's requirements. The size limitation on the *kmetstvo* reduced their number by more than a half, from 3,907 in 1995 to 1,688 in 1999.[167]

THE RESEARCH MOMENT

This review of the different regimes in power in the first decade or so of post-socialist history in the six countries under consideration and of key policy measures taken in the fields of privatisation and restitution, co-operative restructuring, and local government reform concludes with an identification of the research moment in each country.

Our first round of interviews in the Czech Republic took place after the process of local authority demergers had taken place, not long after the formal completion of co-operative restructuring, just after the introduction of the first legislation on local authority finance on 1 January 1993, and shortly before the second round of local authority elections in November 1994. They thus reflected the local political situation of the 1990s prior to the break-up of Civic Forum, whilst nationally the ODS had become predominant. The second round of interviews took place two or more years into post-restructuring agriculture, a year or so into the third local government term,

---

[165] David Jepson, Valerie McDonnell and Belin Mollov, 'Local government in Bulgaria', in *Local Government in Eastern Europe*, ed. Andrew Coulson (Aldershot and Brookfield, VT: Edward Elgar, 1995) 107 and 113.
[166] Ivanov et al., 'Does larger mean more effective?', 174 and 190.
[167] Kimura, 'An analysis of local government', 349–52 and 360.

but before the June 1996 parliamentary elections which presaged the end of the Klaus era. Both, then, were periods when the dominant political force was the ODS, but in the later period its supremacy, both nationally and locally, was beginning to wane; economically, 'ersatz shock therapy' had not yet been dislodged by the financial crisis of 1997.

Our first Slovak interviews took place not long after the completion of co-operative restructuring, in the latter half of the first year of the independent Slovakia, before Moravčik briefly ousted Mečiar, and towards the end of the first term of post socialist local governments. They thus reflected the local politics of the 1990s prior to the break-up of Public Against Violence in which the Christian Democrats (KDH) had also performed well. The second round of interviews took place well into Mečiar's clientelistic authoritarianism after winning the 1994 national and local elections, when much political support swung from the KDH to his HZDS. It was a period too when agricultural co-operatives were being lauded by Mečiar as part of Slovakia's 'third way' path to the future.

The first round of interviews in Hungary took place after village demergers, not long after the completion of co-operative restructuring and the passage of the bankruptcy law, and towards the end of the first term of post-socialist local authorities, but before both the parliamentary and local government elections of the Spring and Autumn of 1994 respectively. Despite holding the agriculture portfolio, the Smallholders had failed to see their vision of restitution implemented, as noted above, and their influence was on the wane. The second round of interviews took place two years into post-restructuring agriculture, well into the Socialist-Free Democratic coalition government. Although the socialist party was successful in the 1994 local elections,[168] the Hungarian Democratic Forum had not repeated its national success in the local elections of the Autumn of 1990, so there was less of a Right–Left shift in local politics in 1994.

---

[168] Osamu Ieda, 'Local government in Hungary', in *The Emerging Local Governments in Eastern Europe and Russia: Historical and Post-Communist Developments*, ed. Osamu Ieda (Hiroshima: Keisuisha, 2000), 126.

Our first Polish interviews took place not long after the commencement of state farm privatisation,[169] in the period between president Wałęsa's dismissal of parliament in May 1993 following the Solidarity-inspired vote of no confidence in the Suchocka government and the victory of the socialist and peasant parties in the September 1993 parliamentary elections. They were also before the passing of the December 1993 law on *gmina* finance. Local authorities still reflected the conditions of May 1990, when Civic Committees dominated local politics. The second round took place well into the socialist-PSL administration, when state farms had formally ceased to exist,[170] and a year or so into a second generation of local government administrations following the October 1994 local elections at which there was no clear winner, but where the government coalition partners did well, and the PSL did particularly well in rural areas. They also took place before the date on which devolution of responsibility for education would become mandatory, although it was optional by this time.

In Romania, the single round of interviews took place, with minor exceptions, in the last years of Iliescu's second presidency, prior to local government elections in June 1996 and the victory of the reformist parties in the national parliamentary elections in November 1996. Co-operatives had already been broken up, associations—mostly—had been formed, and land had been re-allocated, although full legal title had not been awarded, and would not be for some time. The interviews thus also preceded the July 1996 measures which reformed local government and public administration and restricted the powers of the prefects, and pre-dated the removal of the 10 hectare maximum on holdings imposed by the 1991 law. They took place, that is, when a clientelistic regime with a rather questionable commitment to reform still held sway.

In Bulgaria, our research took place during the incumbency of the 'unreforming' BSP government of the mid-decade, a regime which was attempting, in a politically charged climate, to reverse some of the

---

[169] Elżbieta Psyk-Piotrowska, 'State-owned and co-operative farms in Poland during the transformation process', in *Rural Societies under Communism and Beyond: Hungarian and Polish Perspectives*, ed. Paweł Starosta, Imre Kovách and Krzysztof Gorlach (Łódź: Łódź University Press, 1999), 157.
[170] Ibid.

extreme anti-co-operative measures of the earlier SDS government. Although the BSP was effectively forced out of power by extra-parliamentary pressure in January 1997, it performed well in the October–November 1995 local government elections, especially in rural areas, and it was in the run-up to and immediately following these that our interviews took place—at a high-point for BSP support.

Our research did not take place in a political vacuum. The differing political environments in each country inevitably shaped the context within which our research took place. They influenced the matters of the moment which neither interviewees nor interviewers could entirely ignore.

CHAPTER 2

Common General Findings

This chapter presents some of the general findings of our research. Its focus is on common and general elements in rural change in the period under consideration and will consider in turn the restructuring of agriculture, the non-farm economy, local government, and rural communities and civil society. The country-specific chapters that follow will provide greater depth and switch attention rather to specific phenomena in each country.

THE RESTRUCTURING OF AGRICULTURE

It is difficult to question the justice of restoring real land ownership rights to those who had lost them *de facto* if not, technically, *de jure*. But doing so ignored two processes that had taken place during the forty years of socialist industrialisation that the Hungarian land law of 1967 had sought to address (see Chapter 1). These processes were that fewer and fewer people were making their living from agriculture, and that more and more were moving to towns, even if, as also noted in Chapter 1, Eastern Europe was relatively underurbanised. The consequence of this for post-socialist agriculture was twofold. First, much agricultural land was owned by people who had long ceased to live in the villages where their land was located, the 'outside owners' as they were usually termed.¹ Second, the amount of land that anyone under normal circumstances had the right to, though it was rather more than was necessary for simple subsistence, was far too little to constitute the basis of a viable farm in the conditions of the late twentieth century (with the exception of 'residual estates' discussed below).² The world had changed during the forty and more years following the post-war land reforms. A prosperous farm in 1945 would be hopelessly uncompetitive almost half a century later. These fundamentals of farming economics could not be changed by restitution, however well intentioned. For most beneficiaries, therefore, not just the 'outside owners' but villagers as well, commercial farming was not a realistic option and the easiest solution to this sudden windfall of land was to maintain some of the land for self-supply and rent the rest to whatever larger unit emerged from co-operative transformation process.

Green barons and others

The consequence of this combination of widespread, fragmented ownership and rental was a pattern of land holding that was historically unique and the mirror image of traditional structures. Post-socialism

---

¹ For a discussion of the significance of outside owners in the Hungarian transformation see Katalin Kovács, 'The transition in Hungarian agriculture 1990–1993: General tendenceis, background factors and the case of the "Golden Age"', in *After Socialism: Land Reform and Social Change in Eastern Europe*, ed. Ray Abrahams (Providence and Oxford: Berghahn Books, 1996), 51–84. For the situation in Czechoslovakia, see Helena Hudečková, Michal Lošťák and Sandie Rikoon, 'Reflections of "late modernity" in land ownership in the Czech Republic', *Eastern European Countryside* 6 (2000): 93–110; Stryjan, 'Czechoslovak agricultural co-operation', 19–20, and Axel Woltz et al., *Agricultural Transformation in Slovakia: The Change of Institutions and Organisations* (Heidelberg Studies in Applied Economics and Rural Institutions, Publications of the Research Centre for International Agrarian and Economic Development no. 29, Saarbrücken: Verlag für Entwicklungspolitik, 1998), 69. The contemporary literature was less concerned about 'outside owners' as an issue in Bulgaria and Romania, perhaps because it was just one of many problems related to restoring 'historical boundaries'.
² Hann, '*Not the Horse*', 66 notes in his discussion of Tázlár the tiny number of viable family farms in Hungary. Czechoslovak 'residual estates' are discussed in Swain 'Decollectivization politics', 12–9.

became characterised by a system under which many owned land, but only a few rented it, the direct opposite of traditional patterns whereby an elite few owned large tracts of land which they rented out to more numerous tenants. The rental of land by Western European farmers to complement the amount that they own is not unusual. But the scale of the rental from tiny owners in post-socialist Eastern Europe was unprecedented. Successor farms could have as many as two thousand rental contracts with landowners, a bureaucratic nightmare simply to maintain and an additional cost over the essentially free use of land that co-operatives had enjoyed previously. More tellingly, using rented land as security for raising loans remained an unresolved issue, as did (and does) the question of land mortgage schemes generally. Such a system of land-tenure could entail further unanticipated costs. In the case of Noble Grape village in Western Hungary, the successor company to the co-operative had to pay out 10 million forints in damages in 1994 because it had ploughed the wrong land.[3]

This 'inverted pyramid' of land ownership—'many owners, few renters'[4]—had a further consequence. Land is generally seen as important in farming success: those who get the most land tend to become the most successful farmers. But in the post-socialist context, everybody had land, but only a little of it, and they did not know what do to with it. As Chris Hann has put it, land was a 'dubious asset'.[5] What determined success was access to capital and machinery, for without them, land could not be farmed. The only partial exception to this was in contexts where all socialist-era assets disappeared, as they did in some Romania villagers (as discussed in Chapter 7). In these cases, where no new farms approximated the socialist-era dimensions, the size of the pre-socialist era land holding was of more determining importance; children of middle-to-large peasants fared better. It should be noted in this respect too that machinery was not so readily acces-

---

[3] Bettina van Hoven (ed.), *Europe: Lives in Transition* (Harlow: Pearson Education, 2004), 105.
[4] Katherine Verdery and I seem to have hit on this characterisation quite independently of one another. She uses it in *The Vanishing Hectare*, 364. The 'inverted pyramid' image comes from the inhabitant of a country whose landholding structure still retains feudal elements.
[5] Hann, *'Not the Horse'*, 86.

sible either in Romania (because of the persistence of the state-owned machine and tractor stations) or in Bulgaria (where a recentralisation of more complex equipment had accompanied the creation of the agro-industrial complexes). The opportunities for using the socialist legacy as a springboard for success in these two countries were more limited.

To note the small and dispersed size of the land parcels created by the post-socialist reforms and the prevalence of rental arrangements that accompanied them begs the question of the nature of the post-socialist, large-scale successor farms and the social background of those who dominated them. One of the clearest social consequences of co-operative transformation (which mirrored developments in privatisation generally) was that the former co-operative management, or rather sections within it, tended to win out—the 'green barons' of the title. This was hardly surprising; it could hardly have been otherwise. These were the people with the necessary human, social and cultural resources to capitalise on the new opportunities. They had the human capital of their professional expertise required to begin a career in socialist management and the social and cultural capital gained from pursuing a socialist career in this milieu.

To give some examples. A credentialist system had operated in Hungary since the 1970s which imposed the highest standards of educational qualification on co-operative farm managements.[6] All the protagonists from co-operative management had the human capital advantage of university qualifications. Not all shared the same social capital advantages, however; but they could be significant. Personal contacts could guarantee credits, as KGy from Korcona recounted in the following anecdote:

> It was very interesting. This year the director [of the Paks canning factory] did not want to sign the credit agreement [for cash advances], because they gave him the paper and it was headed with the name of the new company, because, as you know, we had established the new limited liability company. However, the com-

---

[6] Nigel Swain, 'Co-operative elites in Hungary after 1945', in *Agrarismus und Agrareliten in Mittel- und Ostmitteleuropa*, ed. Eduard Kubů, Torsten Lorenz, Uwe Müller and Jiří Šouša (Berlin–Prague, 2013); Swain, *Collective Farms*, 114–29.

mercial director then pointed out that in fact this company was Gyuri, that is to say me; and after that, he signed it immediately.

Analogous forces were at play in Rodáky in the Czech Republic. The horticulture section of the socialist-era agricultural co-operative had developed a successful cut flowers business. But in the course of the agricultural transition, the manager of the business had left and set up an entirely independent business. The co-operative responded by appointing a new manager to the cut flower unit and going into competition with its former employee. But the former manager had the customer list, the contacts and the business nous; the co-operative unit floundered and was ultimately closed down. The former manager's business by contrast flourished initially, although by 1999 there were reports that he was suffering in the face of Dutch competition. Bezemer explains how a private farmer in one of the villages that he investigated managed to acquire a loan because of his personal acquaintance with the bank manager.[7] Giordano and Kostova also stress the importance of Nedko's social network at both the national and local levels when accessing credits and recruiting technicians and workers to his extensive farming business in Bulgaria,[8] and personal connections were central to the successful Bulgarian farm described by Kovela.[9]

Socialist managers also enjoyed advantages of cultural capital over the ordinary member. They were familiar with large-scale operations and at ease managing the work of others and taking on debt. As the former chairman of the Pakucs co-operative said:

> Those of us who used to work as leaders in the agrarian sector in the previous system are used to thinking in millions and to taking

---

[7] Bezemer, 'Micro-economic institutions', 94.
[8] Christian Giordano and Dobrinka Kostova, 'Social production of mistrust', in *Postsocialism: Ideals and Practices in Eurasia*, ed. Chris Hann (London and New York: Routledge, 2002), 85.
[9] Galina Kovela, 'How to be an entrepreneur in a village', *Eastern European Countryside* 7 (2001): 91–100; Mieke Meurs, *The Evolution of Agrarian Institutions: A Comparative Study of Post-Socialist Hungary and Bulgaria* (Ann Arbor, MI: The University of Michigan Press, 2001), 17–8, also reports the importance of social capital for obtaining credit, the 'old boy network'.

out loans. Now we apply these principles in our lives as private farmers and can cope with things better than the ordinary villagers who do not borrow, because their mothers taught them not to.

Thus, 'green barons' generally won out, but they did so in slightly different ways. Where co-operatives stayed together, as they did in the Czech Republic and especially Slovakia, the management remained in place, although those too closely associated with the old regime might be replaced. Where liquidation was the primary goal, whether it was Bulgaria's formally, politically driven liquidation or the spontaneous reaction against a hated system as in Romania, it was the former management that created the successor co-operatives or associations if they emerged at all, and their competitor private units even if, in the case of Bulgaria's 'blue co-operatives', they retained the title 'co-operative'. In Hungary, it was more common for co-operatives to transmogrify into a number of new entities, but it was the former management which led each new successor company.[10] Even in Poland, where socialist large-scale agriculture was represented by the state farms, it was generally former state farm managers who took over their successors.

In conflicts over the future of socialist large-scale farming, whether co-operative or state, it was difficult for ordinary members to counter the transformation proposals forwarded by top management. The latter had a virtual monopoly of information about the economics of the farm. Furthermore top management did not feel that it was its job to inform members fully of the paragraphs of the relevant laws in their respective countries that might counter its interests.[11] This is illustrated more fully below.

In Slovakia, co-operatives continued in all of our nine villages and continued to be dominated by their managers. In one case, a breakaway co-operative was formed, also by a former manager. Parallel research revealed other cases of co-operative break-up, but in all cases the successor(s) were run by previous managers, and they all termed

---

[10] Nigel Swain, 'From kolkhoz to holding company: A Hungarian agricultural producer co-operative in transition', *Journal of Historical Sociology* 13, no. 2 (June 2000): 142–71.
[11] Ibid.

themselves 'co-operatives'.¹² The situation in the Czech Republic was broadly similar. The co-operative remained in five villages (two of them covered by the same co-operative); it disappeared entirely in another, and in two others it was broken up into private companies dominated by socialist-era managers.

There was somewhat more variation in the picture of socialist management take-over in our nine Hungarian villages. In the case of three farms, the collectives broke up into a number of private companies all headed by representatives of the former management. In another, there was a similar break-up, but the new dominant figures were a lower-level leader on the one hand and an outsider who had influence with the farm chairman on the other. Two co-operatives remained intact, still dominated by the old leadership. In one case the farm fell apart but its former chairman became the owner of its rather successful non-agricultural venture. In two villages, both with marginal agricultural conditions and located a long way away from where the collective farm was centred, co-operative farming was simply abandoned. Parallel research into the Noble Grape co-operative revealed a complex corporate (holding company) structure with a parallel co-operative, but with all subsidiaries headed by members of the former management.[13]

In five of the Polish communes where we conducted research, state farms or other state-owned farming entities were successfully privatised to former managers. This was also the case in another Polish village included in parallel research. In another commune, the state farm was still under the supervision of the State Treasury, which meant that it was still being run by its old management. Two communes had not had a state farm at all, and in a third the state farm was based in one of the other communes covered by the research. On the other hand, many of the co-operatives which engaged in agricultural production, the very few classic agricultural producer co-operatives which had survived since the 1950s and some of the Co-operatives of Agricultural Circles (see Chapter 6) which had extended into production in the 1970s, ceased operations entirely in the early transition years.

---

[12] Iveta Námerová and Nigel Swain, 'Co-operative transformation and co-operative survival in Slovakia', *Replika* (Hungarian Social Science Quarterly) (Special Issue 1998): 207–21.

[13] Swain, 'From kolkhoz to holding company'.

In Romania, in one commune a large-scale private farm, run by the former co-operative chairman, constituted the major private successor farm. Katherine Verdery refers to such farmers as 'supertenants'.[14] In four of our eight Romanian communes that had formerly had collective farms (one had never been collectivised), post-socialist associations of differing sizes, all dominated by the former collective farm management, were established, but in two cases the associations ultimately failed, and they all operated on a smaller-scale than their socialist predecessors. All farming ventures in Romania suffered because, as noted above, machinery had remained with Agromecs under socialism and remained there (legally at least) rather than become dispersed amongst the new producers. Failure of successor entities was marginally less common in Bulgaria. There successor 'red' co-operatives grew from the ashes of liquidation in seven of the nine villages to operate on a more modest scale. In four of these villages one or more alternative 'blue' co-operatives also emerged,[15] although in one it ultimately failed. In two villages no common entity survived liquidation. But where large-scale farming survived, it was dominated by socialist-era managers.

There was no case in our Bulgarian villages of socialist era managers taking over former co-operatives to create large-scale private farms of equivalent dimensions to socialist-era farms. Such cases figure in the Bulgarian literature, where the new farmers are usually referred to as *arendatori*. Giordano, mostly in collaboration with Kostova, has described in numerous publications the way in which co-operative farm managers, in particular Nedko, suddenly out of a job in 1992 when the liquidation committees took over, underwent a rapid conversion and became private agricultural entrepreneurs renting huge farms of up to 15,000 hectares.[16] Lee-Ann Small has referred to farms

---

[14] Verdery, *The Vanishing Hectare*, 310–45. I have not adopted this terminology, although it has the merit of stressing that the land farmed is rented and not owned.

[15] These terms are considered fully in Chapter 3.

[16] Their *arendatori* are discussed in papers from 1995 to 2010. See Dobrinka Kostova and Christian Giordano, 'Reprivatization without peasants', *Eastern European Countryside* 1 (1995): 99–112; Kostova and Giordano, 'The agrarian elite'; Christian Giordano and Dobrinka Kostova, 'The unexpected effects of the land reform in post-socialist Bulgaria', *Eastern*

of 3,500 hectares also in the Dobrudzha region,[17] and Stela Valchovska's work included a farmer of 4,000 hectares,[18] while, writing a little earlier, Draganova talks of farms of hundreds of hectares.[19] Draganova also provides survey evidence showing that over two thirds of 'agribusinessmen' came from either a management or an agricultural professional background (although almost a quarter had never worked in agriculture at all)[20] and Ramchev and Keliyan refer to large-scale agricultural contractors and the success of sections of the former *nomenklatura*.[21] Our village interviews too were replete with stories of big farms run by former *nomenklatura* individuals. But what was striking in our accounts was how imprecise the stories were. They were always outsiders to the village; they did not have names; no one could provide details on who they were; where, precisely, they had worked previously; how, precisely, they had manipulated the system to come out winners. This was perhaps in part explained by a degree of reticence to talk about a process which was more highly politicised in Bulgaria than elsewhere, but it was also a reflection of aspects of Bulgaria's late socialist history. Giordano and Kostova got to the heart of the problem when they noted:

European Countryside 7 (1999): 5–18; Giordano and Kostova, 'Social production'; Christian Giordano, 'Multiple modernities in Bulgaria: Social strategies of capitalist entrepreneurs in the agrarian sector', *Eastern European Countryside* 16 (2010): 5–24.

[17] Lee-Ann Small, 'Agriculture-based livelihood strategies in Bulgaria and Southern Russia: Implications for agrarian change' (PhD diss., University of Aberdeen, 2005), 123, 155 and 211.

[18] Valchovska, 'Entrepreneurship', 230.

[19] Marianna Draganova, 'New social actors in Bulgarian private sector agriculture', in *The Bulgarian Village and Globalisation Processes: XVIIth Congress of the European Society of Rural Sociology*, ed. Veska Kozhuharova (Sofia: Bulgarian Society of Rural Sociology, Institute of Sociology, 1997), 48.

[20] Ibid., 52–3.

[21] Kolio Ramchev, 'The personality split as a factor towards market development of the Bulgarian village', in *The Bulgarian Village and Globalisation Processes: XVIIth Congress of the European Society of Rural Sociology*, ed. Veska Kozhuharova (Sofia: Bulgarian Society of Rural Sociology, Institute of Sociology, 1997), 89; Maya Keliyan, 'Agriculture and rural development in Bulgaria and Japan: A comparative perspective', in *Rural Potentials for a Global Tomorrow: 9th World Congress of Rural Sociology*, ed. Veska Kozhuharova (Sofia: Bulgarian Academy of Sciences, Institute of Sociology, 1996), 32.

> If the research had focused on the rural and local reality, centred on one or more villages of Dobrudzha, the population would have largely limited to old and/or lowly qualified people, a statistically small proportion of the agricultural sector. Most of the entrepreneurs presently doing business in Dobrudzha's agriculture are not to be found in the villages.[22]

Our research did indeed focus on villages only, and did indeed interview a lot of elderly and poorly qualified people. We focused on villages too in the former Czechoslovakia, Hungary, Romania and Poland and successfully identified all of the key actors in collective or state farm privatisation. But Bulgaria's extreme socialist centralisation meant that the village was too small an arena in which to investigate all aspects of post-socialist transformation.

Within this general picture of the managers dominating the co-operative transformation process, the task of managers was easiest when the co-operative had been economically successful prior to transformation. Managers of successful farms had the authority and prestige to persuade members to accept their proposals, whether their proposal entailed radical restructuring into a joint stock company or retaining the co-operative in a more or less traditional form. Additional factors which affected the fate of co-operatives were the social and demographic profile of the membership (it was generally the case that older, more feminised memberships were more likely to fall in with management's plans, especially if management argued its case in terms of providing them with better security) and whether or not the village retained the co-operative farm management centre following the farm mergers which characterised all countries in the 1970s. If the co-operative centre was located outside the village, interest in it and knowledge about it inevitably declined, and villagers were less well placed to counter managerial claims or get access to co-operative assets. This was particularly the case in Bulgaria where, as discussed in Chapter 1, socialist centralisation had been taken to an unprecedented degree. Whether or not top managers opted for private farming or strove to retain the co-operative form depended in part on the extent to which

---

[22] Giordano and Kostova, 'Social production', 77.

the management was tied existentially to the co-operative. Those with an alternative, either outside the agricultural sector or as a private farmer might cut and run, while management with only weak claims in its own right to land or machinery, was more likely to see its future in the co-operative than in private farming.

Those who, despite the odds, managed to take their land out of co-operatives and begin farming privately found it difficult to succeed with the amount of land and equipment available. Aspirant farmers (in Hungary and the neo-Stalinist countries) who had built new houses during the prosperous days of late socialism rued the day, because they no longer had the out-buildings and stables that they needed. Given that most of the region had been fully collectivised for thirty years by the 1990s, the only people in a position to reclaim land that they had actually farmed in the past were pensioners; others reclaimed it out of respect for dead or elderly relatives. It was difficult for such pensioners and 'nostalgia' farmers who accumulated land on the basis of historical family property to compete with the professionals from socialist agriculture. Even those who made a reasonable go of smaller-scale, 'nostalgia' farming worried that their children would not continue, echoing the views of a member of the 'Red Flag' co-operative interviewed in 1976 who said that while he would be happy to go back to the old way of farming, he could only do so with family help, and there was no one in the family to help him.

There were exceptions, of course. In Hungary, as Iván Szelényi's book on socialist era agricultural entrepreneurs makes clear,[23] there were growing numbers of rural dwellers, especially those who focused on horticulture, who had turned what had started off as a second-economy specialisation into thriving businesses by the 1990s. Some of these were able to compete as full-time farmers, as could some in the former Czechoslovakia who benefited from the pro-family farming measures of the early post-socialist years and used the new credits available (see below) to build on second-economy ventures that had already reached sizeable proportions. In Romania, where post-socialist successor farms included smaller-scale family associations and much

---

[23] Ivan Szelenyi, *Socialist Entrepreneurs: Embourgeoisement in Rural Hungary* (Cambridge: Polity Press, 1988).

of the equipment that larger associations might have enjoyed had been destroyed or was locked up in Agromecs, smaller-scale private farms could be reasonably successful. In Poland, of course, some of the 'specialists' of the 1970s already had farms viable by Western European standards and were able to benefit from State Farm privatisation to increase them further.

A unique feature of both the Czech and Slovak countryside was farms put together by those lucky enough to have a restitution claim on a 'residual estate'. The latter were the creation of the land reform that followed the World War I. Larger estates, located around the former manor house, had been created out of the 'residue' of the land reform and were awarded to either proven good farmers or those who had loyally served the formation of the first Czechoslovak republic. Farms of over 100 hectares, as these generally were, were more than viable in the late twentieth century; those who restituted them uniquely acquired a potentially prosperous farm.[24]

A further common feature of the co-operative transformation process was that the year of transformation (1992) was a 'window of opportunity' as far as starting private family farming was concerned. This was particularly true in Hungary, where the legislation prevented the withdrawal of assets from the co-operatives after that date, but it was also the clear norm in the Czech and Slovak Republics and in Romania and Bulgaria. In Valchovska's study, only two out of 18 'opportunity-driven agricultural entrepreneurs began their businesses outside the immediate post-transition years';[25] and Verdery notes that 'an early start on acquiring the basic infrastructure ... was crucial'.[26] Very few embarked on private farming after the completion of co-operative transformation or liquidation projects. Co-operatives and corporate farms did continue to change their form in the years following transformation (especially in Hungary where private companies gradually cut their ties from 'holding co-operatives'),[27] but, generally, if new private family farms missed the window of opportunity of 1992, then they were too late.

---

[24] See also Swain, 'Decollectivization politics', 12–9.
[25] Valchovska, 'Entrepreneurship', 132.
[26] Verdery, *The Vanishing Hectare*, 341.
[27] Kovács, 'Strengths'.

In Hungary and the former Czechoslovakia (but not Romania or Bulgaria),[28] this window of opportunity was also connected with the introduction, but ultimate failure, of overtly pro-family farm support policies in the early post transformation years. Until 1993–94 in the two former halves of Czechoslovakia and in Hungary rather generous aid packages were offered to new private farmers. In Hungary, those who registered as farmers received additional 'credit vouchers' for use in restitution land auctions and 'reorganisation credit' was initially directed at new private farmers and other new entities emerging from transformed co-operatives, although it was extended at the end of 1993 to include internal co-operative restructurings.[29] Kovács and Bihari subsequently reported that subsidies went to export trading companies rather than producers.[30] Generous support (such as tax-free status for the first five years and generous access to loans) continued while Czechoslovakia remained together. But, after the 'velvet divorce', in Slovakia, pro-private farming support was gradually removed as part of Mečiar's vision of a uniquely Slovak third way based on co-operatives.[31] Non-commercial criteria were introduced. Credit became dependent on the 'bona fides' of applicants,[32] and the State Support Fund for Agriculture and the Food Industry had the right to override

---

[28] The OECD reports on Romanian and Bulgarian agriculture mention no such support. See OECD, *Review of Agricultural Policies: Romania* (Paris: Organisation of Economic Co-operation and Development, 2000); OECD, *Review of Agricultural Policies: Bulgaria* (Paris: Organisation of Economic Co-operation and Development, 2000).

[29] OECD, *Review of Agricultural Policies: Hungary* (Paris: Organisation of Economic Co-operation and Development, 1994), 128. For the change in policy towards co-operative restructuring compare 173/1991 (XII.27) Korm. rendelet and 182/1993 (XII.30) Korm. rendelet. Support for family farmers peaked in 1994, while the reorganisation credit continued to rise. See Hungarian Ministry of Agriculture, *Vidékfejlesztési politika: Strukturális és környezetvédelmi intézkedések* [Rural development policy: Structural and environmental measures] (Budapest: Hungarian Ministry of Agriculture, May 1996), 22–3. I am grateful to Katalin Kovács for this information.

[30] Kovács and Bihari, 'State and co-operative farms', 132–3.

[31] Iveta Námerová, 'Private farmers in Slovakia: Genesis, composition, conflict', *Eastern European Countryside* 5 (1999): 59–74.

[32] OECD, *Review of Agricultural Policies: Slovak Republic*, 99.

the decisions of the banks.³³ In the Czech Republic, the introduction of more rigorous financial criteria for support in 1994 effectively discriminated against smaller farmer,³⁴ prompting Dirk Bezemer to wonder whether

> the link between a large or professional farm status and access to credit is best explained in terms of rational credit allocation (based on track records, farm prospects, liquidity backing etc.), or perhaps more appropriately seen in terms of integration into an economic system where connections based on political leverage or personal considerations are vital to favourable allocation of resources.³⁵

He noted in other research the reluctance of banks to lend generally because of problems with collateral.³⁶ Námerová also notes how it was easier in Slovakia for larger farms in the know to get access to credit.³⁷ Private farmers in all three countries saw the pre-1993–94 period as a 'golden age', but governments had been obliged to abandon pro-family farm support both because it was too expensive and because it could not easily be supervised. In all three countries stories of supposed farmers using soft loans in order to buy cars or improve their houses rather than invest in agricultural buildings and machinery were legion.

In all six of the Eastern European countries covered by this research, socialist sector (state and co-operative) farms had been merged into larger units over the socialist years, in particular in the 1970s,³⁸ and it was only in the excessively centralised Bulgaria that measures had been taken in the late 1980s to undo some of this

---

³³ Dirk J. Bezemer, *Structural Change in the Post-Socialist Transformation of Central European Agriculture: Studies from the Czech and Slovak Republics* (Amsterdam: University of Amsterdam, Tinbergen Institute, 2001), 133.
³⁴ OECD, *Review of Agricultural Policies: Czech Republic*, 149.
³⁵ Bezemer, *Structural Change*, 116–7.
³⁶ Bezemer, 'Micro-economic institutions', 93–5.
³⁷ Námerová, 'Private farmers', 72.
³⁸ See Swain, 'Collective farms'; Swain, 'The evolution of Hungary's agricultural system since 1967', in *Hungary: A Decade of Economic Reform*, ed. Paul Hare, Hugo Radice and Nigel Swain (London: George Allen & Unwin, 1981), 225–51; Swain, 'Decollectivization politics'.

process. After 1989 it was possible for all now genuinely autonomous co-operative organisations to undo these socialist-era interventions and demerge farms if they so wished, just as local authorities were demerged extensively in Hungary and Czechoslovakia as discussed in Chapter 1. Yet, certainly in the villages covered by our project, it was only in Slovakia that demerging co-operatives into their pre-1970s component parts was a common demand. Many in Hungary felt that the late 1960s model of one co-operative per village had been a golden era,[39] but returning to that era was no longer realistic given the extent to which activities had been integrated in the larger unit.

Rural structure in the mid-1990s

The net result of post-socialist agricultural restructuring by the mid-1990s was a dual model of agriculture rather than the Western European model of family farming, but with slightly different patterns of dualism in each country, and different again from the dual structure that had characterised socialist agriculture. In Poland, average farm size had increased somewhat from 6.6 hectares in 1990 to 7.9 hectares in 1996.[40] The state farm sector which, in 1990, consisted of 1,658 farms of an average 1,057 hectares on 18.7 per cent of arable land had, by mid-decade, technically disappeared to be replaced by 3,000 farms of an average 523 hectares which in the main rented their leased their land from the state.[41] By the end of the millennium, 8.6 per cent of units farmed 40 per cent of the land and produced 73.5 per cent of commercial output, while 56.4 per cent of farms were under five hectares and made up 19.5 per cent of land, and 70 per cent of farms produced only 4.7 per cent of commercial output.[42]

---

[39] This verdict emerged in numerous interviews conducted with former collective farm members and managers in Hungary.
[40] Andrzej Pilichowski, 'Land in the Polish Agrarian System', in *Rural Societies under Communism and Beyond: Hungarian and Polish Perspectives*, ed. Paweł Starosta, Imre Kovách and Krzystof Gorlach (Łódź: Łódź University Press, 1999), 170.
[41] Psyk-Piotrowska, 'State-owned and co-operative farms', 156–60.
[42] Andrew Cartwright and Nigel Swain, 'Finding farmers in Eastern Europe: Some issues', Rural Transition Series Working Paper no. 60 (Centre for Central and Eastern European Studies, University of Liverpool, 2002), 22.

By 1994 co-operatives farmed 47.7 per cent of agricultural land in the Czech Republic and 69.9 per cent in Slovakia. Other corporate bodies (successor companies to collective farms) farmed 25.7 per cent and 4.6 per cent respectively, and private individual farms accounted for 23.2 per cent of land in the Czech Republic and 5.2 per cent in Slovakia. In the Czech Republic over 80 per cent of private individual farms were of less than 10 hectares. In Slovakia 76 per cent of the fewer farms were under 10 hectares. On the other hand, in both countries, around two per cent of individual private farms were over 100 hectares in size.[43]

In Hungary by the end of 1994, 31.7 per cent of land was farmed by co-operatives, 35.9 per cent by private corporate farms and 32.4 per cent by individual farmers. Of individual farms larger than one hectare, 90.6 per cent were smaller than ten hectares. The general picture at the village level was of from one to ten families per village with farms that covered more than subsistence, and three to four families at most which were embarking on large-scale commercial farming. For the remainder, the vast majority, the plot was for self-supply.[44]

In Bulgaria by 1996, some 66 per cent of cultivated land was farmed by 3,500 large-scale farms, while 14.4 per cent of land was farmed by 1.5 million small farms, 72 per cent of which were under 0.5 hectares and 51.5 per cent under 0.2 hectares in size. In 1995, the post liquidation co-operatives, either 'red' ('successor co-operatives') or 'blue' (entirely new ones rewarding land and capital input more fully; see Chapter 3), were on average a fifth of the size of the socialist co-operatives, three and a half times more numerous, and with an average

---

[43] See OECD, *Review of Agricultural Policies: Czech Republic*, 91; Námerová, 'Private farmers', 3; and OECD, *Review of Agricultural Policies: Slovak Republic*, 71.

[44] For a full account in English of Hungarian agricultural privatisation, see Swain, 'Agricultural privatisation in Hungary', Rural Transition Series Working Paper no. 32 (Centre for Central and Eastern European Studies, University of Liverpool, 1994). The figures come from *Az élelmiszergazdaság 1994. évi fejlődése* [The development of the food economy in 1994] (Budapest: Central Statistical Office, 1995), 43 and 47; and *A mezőgazdaság 1996. évi fejlődése* [The development of agriculture in 1996] (Budapest: Central Statistical Office, 1997), 22.

membership of 244. In 83 per cent of villages, however, there was only one co-operative.⁴⁵

By the end of 1995, agricultural associations farmed 15.23 per cent of non-state agricultural land in Romania, simple associations farmed 14.02 per cent, and the remaining 70.75 per cent was farmed by over 3.5 million individual households, on plots of an average 2.24 hectares. Of these, 31.3 per cent were between 0.5 and one hectare, and a further 32.6 per cent between one and three hectares.⁴⁶

The four key players within these structures were:
1. Small-scale, pluriactive, often benefit-dependent (either unemployment benefit or old-age pension) self-supply-oriented producers;
2. Small to medium scale private family farmers;
3. Large-scale private corporate farms, 'successor' farms to socialist production units; and
4. 'Socialist type' post socialist transformed co-operatives.

All four were present in the countries under consideration in the first half of the 1990s, and everywhere the first group was by far the most numerous. The proportions of the other groups varied somewhat from country to country, depending as we have seen on the pattern of collectivised agriculture that it had experienced and factors inherent in the co-operative transformation legislation, in particular the extent to which liquidation was prioritised over transformation, but also the balance of a focus on restituting the past or providing a basis for the future. While in Central Europe the general picture was of building post-socialist agriculture on the achievements of the socialist past, in Bulgaria and Romania, the task was more to build post-socialist agri-

---

⁴⁵ See OECD, *Review of Agricultural Policies: Bulgaria*, 79; and Sophia Davidova, Allan Buckwell and Diana Kopeva, 'Bulgaria: Economics and politics of post-reform farm structures', in *Agricultural Privatisation, Land Reform and Farm Restructuring in Central and Eastern Europe*, ed. Johan F.M. Swinnen, Allan Buckwell and Erik Mathijs (Aldershot: Ashgate, 1997), 23–62.

⁴⁶ See Sarris and Gavrilescu, 'Restructuring farms', 191–3 and 201; and Ágnes Neményi, *Erdélyi falvak—gazdasági, szociális struktúrák és folyamatok* [Transylvanian villages—economic and social structures and processes] (Cluj-Napoca: Alsand, 1997), 13.

culture from the ruins of the past, from socialist structures that had been destroyed, albeit for very different reasons.

THE NON-FARM ECONOMY

A consequence of socialism's underurbanisation (Chapter 1) and the high levels of commuting associated with it, taken together with the growth of non-agricultural jobs and the persistence of extensive non-agricultural units within co-operatives in some countries (especially Hungary and the former Czechoslovakia), was that high levels of education and experience of non-farm work existed in the Eastern European countryside. Rural populations were unusually well qualified for a future based on non-farm employment. While it might have been expected that large-scale economic restructuring would be associated with a skills gap, this was not the case.

This can be illustrated by some quantitative data on employment in the 1980s and 1994–96 that was collected as part of the research. Respondents were asked both about their current (1994 in Central Europe, 1996 in Bulgaria and Romania) employment and their longest job in the 1980s. These figures (Tables 2.1 and 2.2), based on samples of the rural population,[47] clearly indicate that, in the 1980s, agriculture was a minority activity, even for the rural population. Agricultural employment declined further with the collapse of socialism, as did employment outside agriculture (except in the Czech Republic and to a lesser extent Poland), such that the highest figure for agricultural employment amongst the rural population was Poland's 24 per cent. Although only Slovak villages recorded really high levels of unemployment in 1993–94, the increase everywhere from almost zero was significant. Not quite so dramatic, but still significant, was the increase in pensioners, especially in Hungary, Romania and Bulgaria. To some

---

[47] In Hungary and Slovakia the samples were representative of the country as a whole, in the remaining countries they were representative of the three types of rural area noted in the Introduction: the economic core (close to a prosperous regional centre), the periphery (remote geographically), and the 'industrial periphery' (areas with 'socialist' heavy industry which were in decline).

extent this reflects the numbers responding to reduced employment options by taking early retirement. The vast majority of these pensioners, of course, did not give up agricultural activity to meet their family needs, but they were no longer employed as part of a commercial agricultural venture.

Sector	ECE6	Cz	Hu	Pl	Sk	Bg	Ro
In agriculture	24.5	15.9	16.8	31.8	27.9	30.0	24.6
Outside agriculture	50.3	55.0	54.4	33.9	55.2	54.2	49.1
Unemployed	0.5	0.8	0.2	0.4	1.2	0.5	0.1
Pensioner or other	24.7	28.2	28.6	34.0	15.8	15.3	26.3
Total	100.0	100.0	100.0	100.0	100.0	100.0	100.0

Table 2.1. Sector of employment in the 1980s

Sector	ECE6	Cz	Hu	Pl	Sk	Bg	Ro
In agriculture	14.6	10.8	3.9	24.1	18.2	22.7	8.1
Outside agriculture	40.8	62.1	35.7	33.1	42.5	39.0	32.1
Unemployed	7.8	2.0	8.5	8.7	17.0	6.0	4.7
Pensioner or other	36.8	25.1	51.9	34.1	22.4	32.3	55.0
Total	100.0	100.0	100.0	100.0	100.0	100.0	100.0

Table 2.2. Sector of employment in 1994–96

Tables 2.3 and 2.4 attempt to quantify the extent to which the rural population not only had experience of non-agricultural employment, but possessed skills and capacities which might be transferred to new and changing economic environments. It makes the assumption that the sorts of skills required by professional, managerial and white collar jobs, and the ability to decide to become an entrepreneur (even a 'force-of-circumstance entrepreneur') indicate human capacities that can respond and adjust to changing circumstances. In our sample, the percentage of the rural population that was 'professional, managerial or an entrepreneur' or white collar was quite high. The exceptions were Poland (not collectivising was associated with not creating the skilled white and blue-collar labour force required by collectivised agriculture) and Romania (with its Stalinist model of collectivisation), and, more surprisingly Hungary (perhaps reflecting its more streamlined organisation of agricultural co-operatives, an interpretation supported by the extremely low figure for those employed in manual labour in agriculture). In both the 1980s and in 1993–94, between just over a third and just under two thirds of the rural population in our villages either were manual workers outside agriculture or workers in sectors with transferable skills.

Sector	ECE6	Cz	Hu	Pl	Sk	Bg	Ro
a) Professional, managerial & entrepreneur	12.1	18.0	6.6	2.9	18.2	19.2	7.4
b) White collar	7.7	11.5	8.0	2.2	10.7	9.1	4.4
c) Manual outside agriculture	34.9	31.2	41.1	29.4	32.5	35.5	39.4
a + b + c (transferable)	54.5	60.7	55.7	34.5	61.4	63.8	51.2
d) Manual in agriculture	20.3	10.3	15.5	31.1	21.8	20.4	22.4
e) Unemployed	0.5	0.8	0.2	0.4	1.2	0.5	0.1
f) Pensioner or other	24.7	28.2	28.6	34.0	15.8	15.3	26.3
Total	100.0	100.0	100.0	100.0	100.0	100.0	100.0

Table 2.3. Type of work in the 1980s

Sector	ECE6	Cz	Hu	Pl	Sk	Bg	Ro
a) Professional, managerial & entrepreneur	14.0	26.1	7.9	4.1	19.0	18.0	8.8
b) White collar	6.6	12.7	6.0	1.1	7.5	9.2	3.3
c) Manual outside agriculture	22.6	26.2	22.2	28.1	20.2	18.0	20.7
a + b + c (transferable)	43.2	65.0	36.1	33.3	46.7	45.2	32.8
d) Manual in agriculture	12.2	7.9	3.5	23.9	13.9	16.5	7.3
e) Unemployed	7.8	2.0	8.5	8.7	17.0	6.0	4.7
f) Pensioner or other	36.8	25.1	51.9	34.1	22.4	32.3	55.0
Total	100.0	100.0	100.0	100.0	100.0	100.0	100.0

Table 2.4. Type of work in 1994–96

The figures for education (Table 2.5) are also revealing, although the very high figures for university or higher vocational education in some countries suggest a degree of inconsistency in defining higher education, and countries with an older rural population recorded greater numbers with basic education only. All countries, even Poland, which had the lowest share of university graduates (again, not unrelated to the absence of a collective farm élite), had a solid mass of people with either vocational secondary (leading to a university entrance exam) or skilled worker or craft training. The lowest figure for these two categories taken together was Romania, at 24.9 per cent, Hungary coming next with 31.7 per cent. The figures for those who have completed secondary education or craft training were more impressive, over 50 per cent for the region as a whole.

Sector	ECE6	Cz	Hu	Pl	Sk	Bg	Ro
a) 8 yrs elementary or less	35.0	6.2	51.8	42.5	35.3	20.0	53.2
b) Skilled worker or craft training	23.7	28.8	24.3	34.4	29.5	7.1	18.1
c) Academic secondary	11.4	13.0	5.0	8.7	7.3	22.2	12.4
d) Vocational secondary	16.4	33.7	7.4	9.7	15.6	25.6	6.8
b + c + d	51.5	75.5	36.7	52.8	52.4	54.9	37.3
e) Post secondary technical	3.8	2.4	5.3	2.1	1.5	6.1	5.2
f) University or higher vocational	8.6	13.9	6.2	2.6	9.3	15.5	4.2
e + f	12.4	16.3	11.5	4.7	10.8	21.6	9.4
No answer	1.2	2.0	0.0	0.0	1.5	3.5	0.1
Total	100.0	100.0	100.0	100.0	100.0	100.0	100.0

Table 2.5. Educational qualifications

These figures were particularly impressive when compared to roughly similar figures from Western Europe analysed by van den Bor, Bryden and Fuller.[48] Their findings for farm operators in their Western European research sites (rather than the rural population generally) were that 61 per cent had primary education or no fulltime education, 32 per cent had secondary education, and 7 per cent had tertiary education. Our consolidated findings for all six Eastern European countries (Table 2.6) show 35.0 per cent with basic education or less, 51.5 per cent with secondary, and 12.4 per cent with post secondary vocational

---

[48] W. van den Bor, J.M. Bryden and A.M. Fuller, 'Rethinking rural human resource management: The impact of globalisation and rural restructuring on rural education and training in Western Europe', Mansholt Studies no. 10 (The Graduate School Mansholt Institute, Wageningen Agricultural University, 1998), 93–5.

or university and higher vocational education. It goes without saying that these data are not directly comparable, and it is interesting that the share of tertiary education in the two halves of Europe is not so very different. Nevertheless, the data would seem to suggest that the share of rural dwellers with a completed secondary education and the transferable skills that went with it was higher in Eastern Europe than it was in Western Europe.

Education level	Western Europe	ECE6
Primary education	61.0	35.0
Secondary education	32.0	51.5
Tertiary education	7.0	12.4
No answer	0.0	1.2
Total	100.0	100.0

Table 2.6. *Educational qualifications in Western and Eastern Europe*[49]

Much of this potential was wasted as enterprises reduced their commuting work force and post-socialist co-operatives shed jobs, no longer obliged as their socialist predecessors had been to provide members with employment. The extent of this job-shedding varied from country to country, but where market forces came quickly into operation, such as Hungary and in Poland, state sector, labour forces were slashed by from around 50 to 70 per cent.[50] Interestingly, a collective farm manager interviewed by the Hungarian rural sociologist Pál Juhász in the 1970s expressed the opinion that, if he were operating under market conditions, he would sack two-thirds of the work force and take a lease on the land that he was currently farming for the co-operative.[51]

---

[49] Western European data is for Farm Operators in selected regions in 1991. See van den Bor, Bryden and Fuller, 'Rethinking', 94.
[50] For Poland, see Psyk-Piotrowska, 'State-owned and co-operative farms', 163. Bezemer, 'Micro-economic institutions', 87, also reports dramatic reductions in agricultural co-operative labour forces.
[51] Pál Juhász, 'Az agrárértelmiség meghasonlása' [Discord within the agrarian intelligentsia], in *Juhász Pál—Emberek és intézmények: Két zsákutca az agráriumban* [Pál Juhász—Men and institutions: Two dead-ends in the agrarian sphere], ed. József Marelyin Kiss and Tibor Kuczi (Budapest: Új Mandátum Könyvkiadó, 2006), 192.

This is more or less exactly what happened everywhere two decades or so later.

Those who lost their jobs retreated into subsistence agriculture, juggled incomes from formal and informal economies, or became self-employed. In the euphoric climate of post-socialism, anyone who was not an employee tended to become labelled as an 'entrepreneur', which results in a degree of ambiguity. Some, but very few private sector businessmen in our villages qualified as 'entrepreneurs' in the normal sense of this word. They had used their native wit and resourcefulness to create larger businesses employing many others. But most who were active in the private sector were not there because they chose to be but simply because there was no other option; they were 'force-of-circumstance entrepreneurs'. Unlike in the developing world, however, those who lost jobs did not drift towards the peripheral shanty towns (with the exception of Albania); indeed, the direction of migration tended to be from towns to villages, as first-generation town dwellers who had been made redundant retreated to villages where they hoped to be able to make a go of subsistence farming. In the Hungarian case this is confirmed statistically by Schafft.[52]

Near subsistence farmers, as noted above, were the most significant players numerically in the post-socialist rural transition. They do not figure prominently in this account, however, because they represented the 'silent majority', the residue in the post-peasant world of the peasant capacity for survival in the most adverse conditions (see discussion below), who survived but were neither significant winners or losers. The means by which such a 'silent majority' survived is well illustrated in the account of a Hungarian pensioner couple from Tabar. Regular purchases from shops were restricted to bread, cooking oil, spices, sugar, flour, matches and soda siphons (not a luxury in Hungary where everyday drinks include syrups and wine diluted with soda). Rarer purchases included dairy products such as butter and sour cream. Almost everything else necessary for their relatively restricted diet came from their holding. They killed a pig twice a year for pork and sausages etc.; they kept 80–100 chickens for meat and eggs, and regularly sold some

---

[52] Kai A. Schafft, 'A network approach to understanding post-socialist rural inequality in the 1990s', *Eastern European Countryside* 6 (2000): 30–3.

of the eggs to supplement their income. The husband was an angler and they cleaned and froze the fish that he caught. They grew potatoes, cabbage, peas and beans, some of which were frozen, the remainder stored dry. They also grew lettuce, carrots, tomatoes, paprikas and cucumbers (some of them forced in a small greenhouse) some of which were eaten fresh, the remainder pickled for the winter. Their fruit (strawberries, raspberries, apricots peaches, grapes, pears, melons and plums) was turned into either conserves or syrups. They purchased most of their clothes and the majority of utensils, cutlery, crockery and so on second hand from the so-called 'Polish market', where private individuals—including tourists from impoverished Poland—offered their goods. On one occasion the wife bought up material from the nearby textile plant that had gone bankrupt and had a woman from the village sew them into clothes for a fraction of the shop price. They also managed to buy various items of kitchen furniture (cupboards and so on, a gas cooker) from an agricultural co-operative that was closing down. For the first third of the winter they could usually heat their boiler from maize husks and other combustible waste matter.

This survival strategy was very similar to that of middle-aged couple who were made unemployed in Pripek in Bulgaria when the local chicken processing unit closed down. They too only spent cash regularly only on bread, salt, clothes, shoes, transport, coal for the winter, electricity, water and the telephone (the provision of telephones to Bulgarian rural communities was much higher than elsewhere in the region).[53] Similarly almost invisible in this account are the Roma, the group which probably suffered most from the post-socialist recession. Their extreme social exclusion is noted in Hora and Palina in Slovakia, a budding entrepreneur is encountered in Remetea (Romania) as is a successful post-socialist businessman in Krížava (Slovakia), and concern with their interests becomes an issue in the unseating of a mayor in Hungary's Székhely.

New 'force-of-circumstance entrepreneurs' discovered that there was one element of the socialist legacy that provided an opportunity: the 'socialist personal services gap'. Stalinist socialism had invested in

---

[53] For a much fuller account of survival strategies in the early post-socialist years, see Sue Bridger and Frances Pine (eds.), *Surviving Post-Socialism: Local Strategies and Regional Responses in Eastern Europe and the Former Soviet Union* (London and New York: Routledge, 1998).

industry at the expense of agriculture and the services, and on heavy industry within the industrial sector. Although these priorities changed to some extent as socialist economies were reformed, as Chapter 1 notes, a bias against the services was retained, as was a reluctance to invest extensively, either publicly or by promoting private investment, in villages. Rural communities thus entered the post-socialist world with a gap in the personal services sector, which budding entrepreneurs were anxious to plug. In almost every village in Eastern Europe, there was scope for new bars, new shops, new hairdressers, new providers of agricultural services, new car repair facilities and so on, despite the fact that the economy was entering a decade-long recession; because socialism had never provided them. The number of new businesses that emerged in our Eastern European villages was surprising large given the depth of the recession and the collapse of agricultural production, but the vast majority plugged the gaps of socialism's legacy and employed only the operators themselves and their family members.

As the country-specific chapters that follow will illustrate, some new post-socialist businesses did manage to develop beyond 'force-of-circumstance entrepreneurship' to become successful small-to-medium businesses. Although our research could not investigate the life-histories of new entrepreneurs in the same systematic fashion as was the case in Hungarian research reported by Laki and Szallai,[54] our findings do not contradict their categorisation. Central to successful entrepreneurs was human, social and cultural capital accumulated over years of socialist sector employment: knowledge about businesses, business processes and the acquisition of a network of contacts associated with that business. This was true both of those who established an entirely new business in the post socialist period, and the rather fewer who had already established a private business under late socialism, which was more common in Poland and Hungary than elsewhere. But human, social and cultural capital alone were not enough. Many villagers enjoyed such advantages. Successful entrepreneurs were motivated by some sort of psychological drive which Laki and Szalai identified as motivating the 'upwardly mobile', 'status convergers', 'status restorers'

---

[54] Mihály Laki and Júlia Szalai, 'The puzzle of success: Hungarian entrepreneurs at the turn of the millennium', *Europe-Asia Studies* 58, no. 3 (May 2006): 317–45.

and 'self-made men'. Some of the new rural entrepreneurs encountered in our research for whom we have significant life-history data shared the characteristics identified by Laki and Szalai, and will be encountered in later chapters. Our more general findings on the origins of entrepreneurship relate to two factors only: elements in an individual's life-history that could provide a wider perspective than the local community and thus provide them with an opportunity to spot a wider market opportunity; and the sorts of family resources that could be mobilised to support entrepreneurial projects in the absence of institutional support. Although business development agencies were active everywhere, in only one case in all of our villages was a new business founded thanks to the support of such an agency.

Our research identified three sub-types of individuals whose life-histories had given them experience of the wider world and the opportunity to develop a vision which might include the pull or opportunity-driven factors necessary for entrepreneurship: 'returnees'—villagers who had left the village for education and early employment, but had then decided to return to the village; 'incomers'—people who moved into the village from outside, perhaps because they married into the village; and 'outsiders'—people who had never lived in the village community, but for some fortuitous reason had some familiarity with it, perhaps because they had once holidayed there. More ambitious investors, and those with the necessary human, social and cultural capital were able to acquire financial backing, but most budding entrepreneurs, especially those near the 'force-of-circumstance entrepreneur' end of the spectrum, could only rely on the family. Extended families pooled resources, either to obtain loans or provide loans directly. Very often at least one family member would retain a secure job, or at least some sort of state benefit, so as to avoid putting all eggs into the entrepreneurial basket. Family members could provide social capital too. The wife's or a parent's social networks proved to be very important sources of social capital in some of the cases considered in following chapters. The role of the family in supporting the self-employed and budding business people was a major finding in Valchovska's study of farming businesses;[55] it is stressed by both Andor and

---

[55] Valchovska, 'Entrepreneurship', 195.

Kuczi[56] and Brown et al.,[57] and is clearly reflected in the chapters that follow.

Given the context for Eastern European privatisation discussed in Chapter 1, it is not surprising that access to foreign funds proved to be a further significant factor in rural entrepreneurship. In particular, what might be termed the 'border effect' was significant. Villages located close to an EU border benefited from the interest of EU-based countries. They did not necessarily invest directly, but they stimulated employment based on the low cost of Eastern European labour and lower environmental standards. This was the case along the western borders of Poland, Hungary and the Czech Republic and the southern border of Bulgaria, a phenomenon that has been investigated in depth by John Pickles and Robert Begg, who note the emergence of Greek and Turkish investors in the region, especially employing women, in the apparel industry.[58] Social capital networks which extended across national borders could also be significant, as could the poor man's source of foreign funds—remittances from employment abroad. This was very common in the proximity of EU borders, but far from unknown elsewhere. Nevertheless, our cases also suggest that only a minority of those working abroad used their resources to invest in a business; for most it was just an alternative source of income. The experience of Sedno in Poland (Chapter 6) reflects a very different, less optimistic non-EU border effect.

Restitution of non-agricultural assets from the pre-socialist world only formed the basis of post-socialist non-agricultural businesses in the Czech Republic, and this constitutes a sub-theme in Chapter 4. This uniquely Czech phenomenon was a consequence of the focus of Czechoslovak legislation on full, direct and specific restitution, and the greater level of industrial development in pre-socialist Bohemia and

---

[56] Mihály Andor and Tibor Kuczi, 'What happened in Hungarian agriculture after 1990?', *Eastern European Countryside* 4 (1998): 91–3.

[57] David L. Brown and László Kulcsár, 'Rural families and rural development in Central and Eastern Europe', *Eastern European Countryside* 6 (2000): 5–23.

[58] See John Pickles and Robert Begg, 'Ethnicity, state violence, and neo-liberal transitions in post-communist Bulgaria', *Growth and Change* 31, no. 2 (Spring 2000): 179–210; and Pickles, 'There are no Turks'.

Moravia where there were many more businesses that could be restituted than in Slovakia, where the same legislation obtained.

LOCAL GOVERNMENT

As the latter sections of Chapter 1 revealed, there were differences between the six Eastern European countries in their enthusiasm for local government reform and the issues which each country considered most pressing. Undoing socialist centralisation was a key demand of the Hungarians, a slightly lower priority for the Czechs, and a much lower priority for the Slovaks. The Poles, with a long tradition of communes encompassing many settlements, were more exercised by reforming the middle levels of local government; for the Romanians and Bulgarians, where late-socialist reform movements had been much weaker and there were fewer local activists, local government reform scarcely figured on the political agenda. The differing structures of local government in each country also had an impact on the salience of local political issues in our rural communities. In Hungary and the former Czechoslovakia, where each village had its own council, local politics had a more immediate impact. All of our Polish communities were also commune centres and local political issues were thus closer to local citizens. In Romania, seven of the nine villages were communal centres and at the time when the research was conducted, sub-basic units did not even have the right of observer status on commune councils. In the extremely centralised Bulgaria, only one village had the status of a commune centre, although a second had aspirations to become one. With such differing structures, the degree of coverage of local political issues could not be uniform, and it was inevitably thinnest in Bulgaria. Despite these differences, the experiences of those involved in local government in the early post-socialist years had much in common, which can be grouped under the very general headings of 'inexperience' and 'impotence'.[59]

---

[59] For a fuller discussion, see Nigel Swain, 'Inexperienced and impotent: Rural local government in an Eastern European meso-Area *in Statu Nascendi*', *Acta Slavica Iaponica* 22 (2005): 1–24; and Nigel Swain, 'Changing dynamics in the East European meso-area: A rural, grass-roots perspective', in *Reconstruction and Interaction of Slavic Eurasia and Its Neigh-*

Inexperience

After forty years of single-party rule and no tradition of local democracy in the inter-war period (except in the case of Czechoslovakia), the inexperience of local people responding to the challenge of influencing local events for themselves was manifest in a number of ways. The first was continuity or inertia: the old leaders often became the new leaders. In a number of cases, despite their association with the old regime, mayors who had served their communities well in the socialist years were frequently re-elected. There were three such cases in our sample in Hungary and one each in the Czech Republic, Slovakia and Poland.[60]

This willingness, in the case of loyal servants of the community, to disregard the politics of the past was in some respects a manifestation of a more general characteristic of local politics in the first post-socialist decade, namely the relative unimportance of party labels. Most local politicians felt that party affiliation did not matter much at the local level, where the issues of importance were so divorced from those of the national arena, even in countries where the differences between the national parties were extreme. This unimportance of party labels is confirmed in the Czech case for the years 1991–97 by Ryšavý.[61] Whatever their party labels, local activists felt able to collaborate on the mundane issues facing rural communities. This relative insignificance of party labels manifested itself differently in different countries. In Hungary there was a tendency for local politicians to stand as 'independents'; even well-known party figures would suddenly declare themselves independent. In the first local elections in the autumn of 1990, country-wide between 73 and 89 per cent of mayors who were elected stood as independents.[62]

---

bouring Worlds, ed. Osamu Ieda and Tomohiko Uyama (Sapporo: Slavic Research Center, Hokkaido University, 2006), 43–60.

[60] This question was not specifically asked in Bulgaria and Romania.
[61] Dan Ryšavý, 'Changes in the local political elite in small towns and rural areas: Does revolution devour its children?' *Eastern European Countryside* 12 (2006): 58.
[62] Antal Bőhm and György Szoboszlai, Önkormányzati választások 1990 [Local government elections 1990] (Budapest: Magyar Tudományos Akadémia Politikai Tudományok Intézete, 1992).

In the Czech Republic we encountered unlikely coalitions between extreme left Communists and extreme right Republicans, whereas, in Slovakia, local politicians changed affiliation as the KDH declined in popularity at the expense of the HZDS. In Romania the UDMR totally dominated ethnically Hungarian villages, even if people did not agree with its policies. Elsewhere, there was also a tendency to switch parties, not so much reflecting party popularity as structures of power and patronage. A process that the EU critically labelled 'political migration'[63] took place so that local politicians belonged to the same party as the county prefect (appointed as noted in Chapter 1 by the national government), because only he had financial largesse to dispense, and he tended to favour his own party. This kind of systematic patronage was a Romanian specificity, but there were analogous developments everywhere — individual cases of political patronage thanks to some figure or other on the local scene having influential contacts at the national level.

The situation in Poland differed somewhat from other countries because of the existence of a party, the PSL, which both identified as a peasant party and was the off-shoot (in part) of a socialist-era satellite party. As noted in Chapter 1, it was the only party in the region to become a 'mass party' of the western type. Because of its peasant constituency and long-standing mass roots in rural communities, it could uniquely be at the same time both pro-private farming and a potentially conservative part of the old-order establishment. It dominated politics in four of our Polish communes, but independents dominated two others, while party representation in the remaining three was mixed.

A further manifestation of inexperience might be labelled by purists as 'corruption', but 'corruption' implies malicious intent, and the sense that we gained from interviewing those concerned was that this was often not the case. This aspect of inexperience relates to the 'fuzziness' of the distinction between private interests and public service. After forty years during which the private was essentially reduced to the personal and everything else was public (socialist), it is not surprising that some found it hard to learn to adjust to a new regime where there were both public and private economic and commercial interests that had to

---

[63] Swain, 'Changing dynamics', 60.

be separated. Mayors, exasperated by what they saw as the passivity of the population and its reluctance to get things moving, might use (and pay) their own private company to implement council works. Their interpretation of this behaviour was that this was a laudable initiative to overcome communal torpor; they did not recognise the conflict of interest that is self-evident to those with experience of more established democracies. Or, as a part of a general strategy of promoting business, they might provide just a little more than average assistance to the business of a relative, without sensing that a conflict of interest was involved. Paraphrasing Verdery's point discussed in the Introduction, the *mores* of a new regime have to be learned; they are not natural.

Attributing such minor corruption to a 'fuzziness' concerning private interests and public service might reflect naivety on our part, but it is consonant with other of our general findings, in particular the fact that at this relatively early point in the post-socialist era, when, as it can be argued in the light of works by Szelényi and others,[64] a 'fuzziness' concerning ownership was in the process of transforming itself into clear private ownership, there was only embryonic evidence of the emergence of a business interest in local politics. Conflicting private interests did find their ways onto the local agendas in many of our villages, as will be seen in later chapters, but it was only in some villages, and in the Central European cases only after the second post-socialist local elections, that evidence of a new private business elite endeavouring to influence the local political scene to their advantage began to emerge.

As discussed in Chapter 1, most local authorities in the post-socialist era were offered a new role in distributing certain sorts of discretionary benefits for the extremely poor. A certain type of inexperience was manifest here too in so far as these admittedly very limited resources tended to be dispensed on the basis of conventional and common-sense understandings of who the 'deserving' poor were, rather than reflecting views informed by social-policy professionals and welfare experts. Our research confirms Ferge's findings in this respect.[65]

---

[64] Szelényi's work on the new elites and capitalism without capitalists is discussed in Swain, 'A post-socialist capitalism', 1678–9.
[65] Zsuzsa Ferge, 'Welfare and "ill-fare" systems in Central-Eastern Europe', in *Globalization and European Welfare States: Challenges and Change*, ed. R. Sykes, B. Palier and P.M. Prior (Houndmills: Palgrave Macmillan, 2001), 146.

Impotence

The second common characteristic of local authority activity was 'impotence' in the face of a challenging new world. Not all countries had imposed new legal responsibilities on local councils. As discussed in Chapter 1, this was only the case in Hungary and Poland in relation to education, and in Poland it was only compulsory after the end of our research. Nevertheless, all local authorities experienced a *de facto* increase in responsibilities because of the collapse of the socialist system. The local collective farm, or other significant socialist enterprise, had experienced in the past at least a moral obligation to help its local community, to differing extents in the different countries under consideration. This support had disappeared, and new private companies were generally slow to step in to fill the gap. Local authorities thus experienced a form of 'fiscal stress' brought about by increased responsibilities but, in the declining economic climate of the post-socialist depression, decreasing resources. In Romania, the 'fiscal stress' was so extreme that some communities were dependent on foreign charities, whose activities were often directed only towards sub-communities of confessional kin.

In such straightened circumstances, local authorities and local political representatives could do little more than address the legacy of the socialist past that they experienced most acutely: the underdevelopment of the infrastructure and public services. If socialism's prioritisation of industry and the productive economy had provided opportunities for an embryonic private sector to plug the 'personal services gap', local authorities, with few resources at their disposal, faced the burden of plugging the 'socialist public services gap' with regard to infrastructural and communal services. When considering the development paths for their villages, few local authorities could think much beyond this. In poorer regions, some turned to agriculture and measures which would help the poor survive by resorting to subsistence agriculture. This was particularly the case in Bulgaria, where local *kmetstvo* mayors had little power and the local infrastructure included irrigation systems for agriculture for which no one was responsible if co-operatives were liquidated.[66] In

---

[66] For an interesting study of water syndicates in Bulgaria, see Insa Theesfeld and Ivan Boevsky, 'Pre-socialist cooperative traditions: The case of water syndicates in Bulgaria', *Sociologia Ruralis* 43, no. 3 (2005): 171–86.

richer regions, some leaders developed non-agricultural strategies based on turning the village into a dormitory community for nearby towns, or promoting rural tourism for the benefit of more distant urban communities. It was rare for villages to think beyond these alternatives, although, as the following chapters illustrate, some did. Rural tourism figured higher on the agenda in Poland than in other countries, perhaps because, with a non-collectivised agriculture of which they were ashamed, planners had long been looking for alternative development strategies for the countryside.

It was most unusual for local authorities to see direct engagement in economic activities as a way to resolve problems and stimulate the local economy. This solution was only adopted in a few cases in Mečiar's 'third way' Slovakia, and not at all in the poorer Balkan villages, perhaps because of their fewer resources rather than a doctrinal unwillingness to intervene directly. This is perhaps not surprising given the trajectory towards post-socialist capitalism; the Poles, as noted in Chapter 1, prohibited local authorities from engaging in such activity in the spirit of prioritising private over public. Yet it is worthy of note nevertheless, given the extensive literature on 'Town and Village Enterprises' (TVEs) at a certain phase in the Chinese 'transition'. This failure of municipality-owned enterprises to emerge in post-socialist Eastern Europe tends to suggest that the TVE form was indeed one associated with the conditions of 'fuzzy ownership' under late socialism rather than the increasingly clear-cut and exclusive property claims of post-socialist capitalism. There is a large literature on this topic.[67] Cer-

---

[67] See, for example, Chun Chang and Yijiang Wang, 'The nature of the township-village enterprise', *Journal of Comparative Economics* 19, no. 3 (December 1994): 434–52; Jiahua Che and Yingyi Qian, 'Insecure property rights and government ownership of firms', *The Quarterly Journal of Economics* 113, no. 2 (May 1998): 467–96; Che and Qian, "Insecure Property."; Hehui Jin and Yingyi Qian, 'Public versus private ownership of firms: Evidence from rural China', *The Quarterly Journal of Economics* 113, no. 3 (August 1998): 773–808; David D. Li, 'A theory of ambiguous property rights in transition economies: The case of the Chinese non-state sector', *Journal of Comparative Economics* 23, no. 1 (August 1996): 1–19; and William A. Bird and Lin Qingsong (eds.), *China's Rural Industry: Structure, Development and Reform* (Oxford: Oxford University Press for the World Bank), 1990.

tainly the TVEs were beginning to wane in importance in China in the 1990s as the balance of private and public sector enterprises swung towards the former; by the new millennium, they had been replaced by fully privatised companies.[68]

RURAL COMMUNITIES AND CIVIL SOCIETY

During the socialist era, Eastern European villages lost their physical and social isolation of the years before World War II. Then, the peasant village was a separate world, and the latifundium of the estate workers a different community again. Developing Robert Redfield's earlier categorisation of peasants as 'part-societies with part-cultures'[69] and Eric Wolf's emphasis on the 'underdog' position of the peasantry,[70] Teodor Shanin stresses both partial exclusion and the 'underdog position of the peasantry' in the second edition of his best-selling collection on peasants and peasant societies.[71] Ferenc Erdei, writing on Hungary in the 1940s, made similar points about separation and subordination,[72] while the further separation of the estate workers from the world of the independent peasant is lyrically described by Gyula

---

[68] For the waning of the TVEs in favour of genuine private ownership in the 1990s, see Laixiang Sun, 'Ownership reform in the absence of crisis: China's township, village and private enterprises', in *Small and Medium Enterprises in Transitional Economies*, ed. Robert J. McIntyre and Bruno Dallago (Houndmills: Palgrave Macmillan, 2003), 134–52. When this author visited rural China in April 2004, all local authorities consulted reported the complete privatisation of the sector.

[69] Robert Redfield, 'The part-societies with part-cultures', in *Peasants and Peasant Societies: Selected Readings*, ed. Teodor Shanin (Oxford and New York: Basil Blackwell, 1987, 2nd ed.), 60.

[70] Eric R. Wolf, *Peasants* (Englewood Cliffs, NJ: Prentice Hall, 1966), 3–4, 11 and 13. On p. 13, he talks about the peasantry being defined 'primarily in terms of its subordinate relationships to a group of controlling outsiders'.

[71] Teodor Shanin, 'Introduction: Peasantry as a concept', in *Peasants and Peasant Societies: Selected Readings*, ed. Teodor Shanin (Oxford and New York: Basil Blackwell, 1987, 2nd ed.), 4.

[72] Ferenc Erdei, *A magyar társadalomról* [On Hungarian society] (Budapest: Akadémiai Kiadó, 1980), 237.

Illyés in his memoirs.[73] Socialism had ended such isolation by pulling villagers into the larger labour market and by revolutionising its contacts with the outside world. Lenin's slogan that socialism equalled Soviet power and the electrification of the countryside was perhaps a distortion of the truth, but socialism did bring electrification, and with it radio, television and later deep-freezes; and it constructed an impressive network of public transport. Villagers could physically move from their homes to the wider community, and they could hear and watch the debates and concerns of the wider community through the media of television and radio. Villagers might not share the values of the wider community, but they impinged on them in ways that had not been possible decades before. But it worked both ways. Being no longer communities based around independent subsistence farming, they were no longer so autonomous. They depended on the wider world for jobs, and for the electricity to power radios, TVs, lights and deep freezes. Villages remained an alien world for the urban middle classes; there was minimal western-style suburbanisation of villages near urban centres because of the low level of infrastructural development (that would come with post-socialism),[74] but they were no longer outside society as traditional peasant societies had been.

In our village studies we addressed the question of isolation in terms of transport connections and telecommunications. The results were unsurprising and do not warrant extensive analysis. Although transport links were being reduced in the early post-socialist years with the decline of commuting and pressure to reduce costs in all areas, they remained reasonably good. Telephone provision remained

---

[73] Gyula Illyés, *Puszták népe* [People of the puszta] (Budapest: Szépirodalmi Könyvkiadó, 1967), 5 and 8.

[74] For studies of post-socialist suburbanisation see Katalin Kovács, 'Szuburbanizációs folyamatok a fővárosban és a budapesti agglomerációban' [Suburbanisation processes in the capital and in the Budapest agglomeration], in *Társadalmi-gazdasági átakalukás a budapesti agglomerációban* [Socioeconomic transformation in the Budapest agglomeration], ed. Gy. Bartha and P. Beluszky (Budapest: Magyar Tudományos Akadémia Regionális Kutatások Központja, 1999), 91–114; and Judit Tímár and Mónika Mária Váradi, 'The uneven development of suburbanization during transition in Hungary', *European Urban and Regional Studies* 8, no. 4 (October 2001): 349–60.

poor, but figured high on the local authority to-do agenda—part of the 'socialist public services gap'. Nearly all houses had televisions; satellite television was not uncommon in both Central Europe and the Balkans, even in remote regions, and many Central European villages (and some Balkan ones) provided cable TV services to the community. We also asked about computers and modems, but unsurprisingly, in the early-to-mid 1990s, these were uncommon.

We were also interested in changing casts of mind (*mentalité*) as socialist paternalism was replaced by the 'cash nexus' of market capitalism, and the impact of this on civil society. In order to investigate this, a number of questions were formulated about community activity and village associations. The results were not clear cut. Most village mayors complained about the inability to find volunteers any more, and bemoaned the selfishness that they saw becoming increasingly common. But this has to be set against the fact that much 'voluntary' activity under socialism had not been voluntary at all; it was rather the result of intense moral pressure to contribute to the community. Yet even compulsory volunteering can create group cohesion, the loss of which can be sincerely mourned. Something had changed, although whether it was detrimental to long-term community identify was unclear. In many communities, key individuals kept community activities alive, in others new activities were created, despite reductions in local authority funding; furthermore the provision of alternative funding for them from the private sector (the market solution) was by no means uncommon.

Numerous interviewees, not just mayors, used words which translate best as 'envy' to describe the attitude of many early post-socialist rural citizens. They disliked, distrusted, despised, 'envied', and did not seek to emulate (in fact encouraged to fail), all those who had somehow succeeded in escaping poverty and making a success. 'Envy' certainly played a part, but it is perhaps better to see this as a residual sense of the 'moral economy' of socialism, which rejected (and made almost impossible) all forms of unearned income. Income under socialism was based on labour; anyone engaged in what might be described as 'arbitrage' was transgressing a socialist norm that had been engrained in citizens over 40 years of lived socialism. Furthermore the socialist experience came on top of generations of peasant society which equally valued hard work above all else. Gaining money from anything other than hard work was tantamount to theft, and could only be explained as such; Hudečková and Lošťák for example discovered strong negative attitudes to the possibility of unearned profit.[75] The attitudes that many of our villagers expressed about 'middlemen' and 'traders', people who offered to buy their crops but then did not, or enforced 'low' (that is to say market) prices echoed in many respects those described by E.P. Thompson when English eighteenth century peasants were suddenly confronted with the 'cash nexus' of an emerging capitalism.[76] Hann has explored such parallels both explicitly[77] and more discursively.[78] This residual moral economy of socialism is clearly related to the fuzziness over the public-private divide described above.

In this context, the results of some of our survey questions about attitudes to entrepreneurs are instructive. Overall in 1996 in the six countries covered by the research 27 per cent of respondents thought entrepreneurs were 'capable people', a figure identical (except for rounding) to the four Central European countries where research also took place in 1994. But 15.7 per cent of respondents thought that entrepreneurs were 'predatory beasts' in 1996, compared with 14.3 per cent in the Central European four countries in 1994. Attitudes to entrepreneurs were most negative in Slovakia and Romania where post-socialist regimes were least committed to the liberal market economy: 24 per cent and 23 per cent respectively chose the 'predatory beasts' option in 1996. But they were also strong in Poland (19 per cent of respondents in 1996, 21 per cent in 1994). Attitudes in Hungary and the Czech Republic were more positive: the 'predatory beasts' option was only chosen by 5 per cent of Hungarian and 11 per cent of Czech respondents in 1996. The Hungarian figure had declined from 8 per cent in 1994, whereas the Czech figure had

---

[75] Helena Hudečková and Michal Lošťák, 'Privatization in Czechoslovak agriculture: Results of a 1990 sociological survey', *Sociologia Ruralis* 32, nos. 2–3 (1992): 295.
[76] E. P. Thompson, *Customs in Common* (London: Penguin, 1993).
[77] Hann, *'Not the Horse'*, 27–31.
[78] Chris Hann, 'Introduction: Decollectivisation and the moral economy', in *The Postsocialist Agrarian Question: Property Relations and the Rural Condition*, ed. Chris Hann and The 'Property Relations' Group (Münster: LIT Verlag, 2003), 1–46.

increased from 8 per cent in that same year. Poles were consistently reluctant to recognise entrepreneurs as 'capable people' (18 per cent of respondents in both 1994 and 1996); the Slovaks were somewhat more likely to (22 per cent in 1996, 24 per cent in 1994); but the Romanians were unusual in that they were as likely as the Czechs and Hungarians to view them as 'capable' people (32 per cent of respondents in 1996 compared with 34 per cent for Czechs and 31 per cent for Hungarians—the 1994 figures for the latter two being very similar, 34 per cent and 32 per cent respectively), yet they were also most likely to view them as 'predatory beasts'. The data are not unambiguous, but it is telling that less than a third of the sample viewed entrepreneurs in positive light and one in sixth had views so negative as to warrant the term 'predatory beasts'.

Questions about the numbers of community associations and clubs in our villages were equally inconclusive. Hann is generally negative about the impact of post-socialism on cohesion and community spirit in Tázlár,[79] although in the case of one of the associations that he describes, the loss of a key *animatrice* seems to be the issue rather than the demise of the association. In many ways the experience in our villages said more about different national histories than about the impact of the 'cash nexus' on socialist paternalism and civil society. The former Czechoslovakia had many more such associations, a function presumably of its higher level of economic development and more developed civil society prior to the socialist era. In Hungary, the cynicism and exhaustion engendered by working fulltime in the first economy and almost fulltime in the second during the final decades of socialism seem to have had a negative impact on all forms of community life, and far fewer associations were noted than in Poland, which in this respect too was characterised by greater (but not universal) continuity. There was a clear tendency for those associations most linked to the party and its satellite organisations to decline at the expense of organisations with no political affiliation. But many associations had had an economic function too, and some of these continued despite links with the past. Other societies had an importance greater than their name implied. Hunting associations in both the Czech Republic

---

[79] Hann, *'Not the Horse'*, 83.

and Hungary (Korcona) both provided recreation for the local political elite and in doing so constituted an important locale for exchanging social capital in the post-socialist era. Furthermore, in some villages, some activities just happened to be more popular in others. In Městysov in the Czech Republic, for example, most associations were in decline, but the sports club flourished. In Czech Rodáky, however, after a dip, community life prospered; in Slovak Lehota interwar traditions of amateur dramatics were resurrected; and in Mica and Măgura in Romania, as will be considered more fully in Chapter 7, vibrant ethnic minority community organisations developed, even though, as in Hann's Tázlár, they were also somewhat dependent on individual initiatives for their survival.

On balance, despite the conflicting strands, the evidence seems to point to changing forms of community association: from those associated with the institutions of socialism to independent ones, backed by private business sponsors or with links to a variety of political parties. In the depth of the post-socialist recession, there was some overall decline and retreat into the household, but as the economy picked up, so too did manifestations of community identity. Some continued to bemoan the 'dumbing-down' associated with cultural facilities being used for low-brow but financially rewarding activities such as discos for the young, and it is certainly true that in the absence of central finance, local community associations were dependent on chance factors such as a local businessman's enthusiasm for football rather than theatre. Yet Výletnice attracted sponsorship from a holiday home owner, and many of the new businesses of significant dimensions in the Czech Republic provided sponsorship of one kind or another. In the longer term community life proved resilient despite the disappearance of socialist-era support. Our Bulgarian research did not address these issues, but Deema Kaneff has considered the topic at length. After presenting Talpa's extensive socialist-era cultural activities, she notes first a decline in volunteering, but then a slow birth of new activities and festivities supported by new sponsors, although most of this happened later that our study, from 2004 onwards.[80]

---

[80] Kaneff, *Who Owns the Past?*, 161–6, 179, 183–5 and 190–4.

The Church, of course, was a special form of association which regained a genuinely autonomous status after 1989. The general picture, however, is that this new autonomy was not associated with churches taking on dramatically new roles in rural communities. In Hungary and the former Czechoslovakia, there were occasional instances of clerics taking on a short-lived political role, but in general all that was reported was a slight increase in congregation size, renewed vigour celebrating traditional festivals, a shortage of clerics and the introduction of religious instruction in schools. It was the same for predominantly Catholic Slovakia as for the multi-confessional Czech Republic (Catholic, Evangelical, Hussite)[81] and Hungary (Catholic, Reform, Greek Catholic). In the much more extensively multi-confessional Romania (Orthodox, Greek Orthodox, Catholic, Reform, Unitarian, Pentecostalist),[82] as some of the case studies will reveal, local clerics played a very significant role, but this was more to do with the man than the institution. The general picture was similarly of slightly bigger congregations and a somewhat greater role in social life. The situation was essentially the same in multi-confessional Bulgaria (Orthodox Christianity, Islam), but more new churches and mosques were being built, reflecting perhaps the greater success that Bulgarian socialists had achieved replacing religious rituals with secular ones.[83] A partial exception to this pattern was Poland, where the Catholic Church had been uniquely strong in the socialist period and had had ties with Solidarity and the opposition. In Poland, some congregations were reported to be falling rather than increasing; in many communities there was a sense that the Church was being too demanding reclaiming land and buildings, and too interfering in terms of public morality. Examples of such interventions are presented in Chapter 6.

---

[81] These are the faiths found in our villages, not the countries as a whole.

[82] For a discussion of Pentecostalism as a church for 'marginalised elements' in Romania, see Monica Heintz, 'Romanian orthodoxy between the urban and the rural', Working Paper no. 67 (Max Planck Institute for Social Anthropology, Halle-Saale, 2004), 6.

[83] For the popularity of secular burials in Bulgaria, see Deema Kaneff, 'Why don't people die "naturally" any more? Changing Relations between "the individual" and "the state" in post-socialist Bulgaria', *Journal of the Royal Anthropological Institute* 8, no. 1 (March 2002): 89–105.

Map 3.1. Research sites, Bulgaria

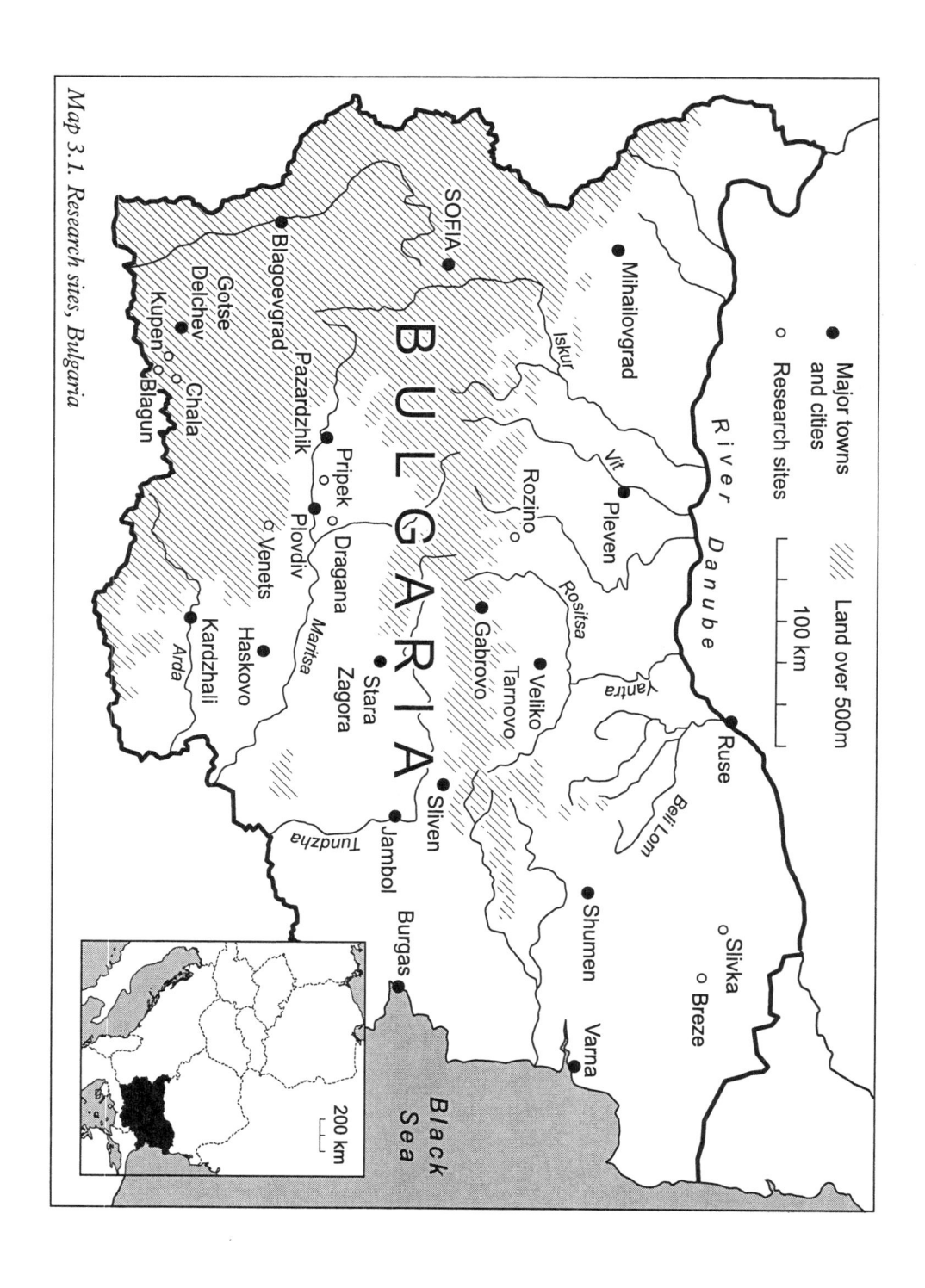

CHAPTER 3

Bulgaria

Rural Bulgaria in the early-to-mid 1990s had been on the receiving end of one of the defining policy differences between the main actors in post-socialist national politics. Bulgaria had been one of the true 'gradualists' in the early post socialist years, although unemployment levels were amongst the highest in the region; it was only after the political and financial crisis of 1997 that all strands of political opinion became convinced of the need for radical reform. But agriculture had dominated the national political debate in the early part of the 1990s, and the essence of that debate was reflected in its terminology. Co-operative 'transformation' was not on the agenda, as it had been everywhere else; what was demanded, when the socialists were removed from power, was co-operative 'liquidation'. The process was politicised to an unusual degree, enflaming passions and hardening positions. For those who ran the co-operatives, the focus was on 'saving' from destruction socialist institutions of which many were exceedingly proud, for their mainly pensioner members and themselves. For those who opposed them, all vestiges of socialist large-scale farming were anathema and had to be destroyed. Meanwhile anonymous individuals, external to the village, like Giordano and Kostova's Nedko (see Chapter 2), established post-socialist large-scale farms, while others, better known in the community established 'blue' co-operatives or smaller, family farms. In the sphere of local government, perhaps the defining characteristic of the Bulgarian countryside at this time was the extreme centralisation of power; Bulgaria's extra-large communes had experienced no post-socialist increase in autonomy, neither had the sub-commune units.

CONTESTED CO-OPERATIVE LIQUIDATION

Co-operative livestock farming saved—Pripek

The politics of co-operative liquidation reached boiling point in the village of Pripek; indeed the village made the national news. Pripek was a unit of the 'Rodopi' commune of Plovdiv city, located some 18 kilometres west of Plovdiv with, in the mid-1990s, a population of 6,500, primarily ethnic Bulgarians, in 1,800 dwellings. The village had already established a reputation for exporting grapes, red peppers, wine and rice in pre-socialist times, when it benefitted from the services of a number of consumer co-operatives, one of which established its own dairy; and in 1938, the Water Syndicate Maritsa was established to provide irrigation for the small-scale and dispersed plots. Collectivisation came early. By 1948, roughly two per cent of the total village population, predominantly from the rural poor, had established the village's first agricultural producer co-operative, and by 1951 it had expanded to cover 1,362 families covering 5,700 hectares and 83 cows. Ever in the vanguard, the farm joined an Agrarian and Production Complex together with two other villages as early as 1970, when their local authorities were also amalgamated; in 1973, both local authority and farm were expanded further to include another village, while in 1978, they all joined a Research and Production Complex of Fruit Culture.

Although there had been opposition to collectivisation at first, the 1970s were viewed locally as the decade when the farm prospered. Gross agricultural production increased from around 160,000 leva in the early 1950s to 4.2 million leva in 1960, and 7.8 million leva in 1970; the cattle herd expanded from 83 cows in 1951 to 550 in 1970. By this time, the co-operative possessed 105 tractors, 10 threshing machines, 14 combine harvesters, 25 automobiles, and it had built (in 1979) a new refrigerated store for 5,000 tons of fruit in a neighbouring settlement four kilometres away, using the expertise of Research and Production Institute. It also had a new dairy farm and a poultry unit. The outlook of the village was also transformed in this decade by the construction of approximately 1,100 brick houses.

By the 1980s, the co-operative had expanded further and was highly profitable, cultivating 3,600 hectares of land with a membership of around 2000 (with as many as 1,500 working as field workers, 90 with livestock, 30–40 as tractor drivers and 30–40 as machinery operators) ten engineers, 30 agronomists and numerous accountants and economists, and a computer centre. Its 2,400 hectares of rice fields were irrigated, as was the bulk of its arable land. There was a dairy farm (600 cows), a sheep farm (4500 sheep), a pig farm (500 pigs) and a poultry farm (15,000 birds). On the cropping side, in addition to rice, it specialised in maize and market gardening, and in 1984 invested further in vineyards and fruit growing. The co-operative also had holiday accommodation for its members in three locations. Its private household plot ('subsidiary farm') sector, which sold through official state purchase stations, was equally well developed. Farm managers reported that members could earn between 15–20 per cent of their monthly income from their plots (almost certainly an under estimate), growing beans, peppers and cucumbers, many of which went for export, and also milk and meat. The private sector alone produced 2,000 tons of tomatoes, 3,000 tons of cucumbers, 3,400 tons of peppers and 500 tons of meat. In sum, agriculture in Pripek represented Bulgarian socialist agriculture at its apogee.

'Unfortunately, then came democracy.' This was the verdict of the co-operative chairman in Pripek on the co-operative liquidation process in his village. But, in the end, 'local conditions', that is to say, the nature and composition of the local authority and its willingness to intervene, allowed them to 'protect' some of the assets, such as orchards, buildings, some of the machines; and it was the only village in the area where co-operative livestock farming continued after liquidation.

The liquidation committee, established in 1992, had a membership made up of 'mid-wives, teachers, and nurses', none with a background in agriculture.[1] Thus for some, they understood nothing about

---

[1] This description of the committee might have to be taken with a pinch of salt. The equivalent in Dragana is described as including a hairdresser (see below). The committee which implemented collectivisation in our Czech village Rodáky decades earlier also reportedly included a hairdresser according to one account. It might be that whenever the *status quo* in agri-

agriculture, while for others, they did not have a vested interest in maintaining the status quo. At a Co-operative General Meeting prior to liquidation, the members voted not to give the liquidation committee access to the co-operative. The government sent 100 police officers with dogs to enforce their access (and thus the co-operative's destruction), but the members were true to their resolve and did not let the committee in. The result was a two-month stand-off until June 1992, when a compromise of sorts was reached. A new liquidation committee was established, this one elected by the village rather than being appointed by the district as was the norm. But the liquidation process could not be stopped and many combines were reputedly sold at knock-down prices to Greeks. The return of land, unlike liquidation, proceeded relatively smoothly on the other hand, because the village had kept exhaustive documentation of land ownership and transfers.

A successor co-operative emerged from the ashes. Its statutes allowed for three types of member: those who had land in the co-operative and also worked for it, the majority, about 50 per cent of the membership; those who worked in the co-operative, but had no land in it; and those who had land in the co-operative, but did not work for it,[2] the majority of whom were local pensioners. A number of villagers were initially attracted by the idea of private farming and took their land out, only to think better of it a year later and put it back in again. The successor co-operative had 2,046 members, cultivated 4,100 hectares of land that was still irrigated, and employed 600. All contributed 55,000 leva as initial capital, which was used to help buy many of the machines, livestock and buildings of the socialist co-operative, including the holiday homes and the refrigerated fruit store. The five-strong top management consisted of the chairman (a member of the BSP), his deputy, a lawyer, an accountant and an engineer. Co-operative members continued to receive subsidised produce (rice, cheese, flour, meat) and benefited from concessionary rates at

---

culture is under threat, those involved in the old world see the new world as being determined by hairdressers, a stereotypical job unconnected with agriculture.

[2] Danka Dobreva, 'The farm production co-operative as a support for the rural household in Bulgaria', *Eastern European Countryside* 7 (2001): 84, reports on the potential conflicts between these groups.

the co-operative's holiday centres in the mountains and by the sea;[3] furthermore, the co-operative continued to support the local community extensively. Although its initial business strategy was to maintain as much as possible of the socialist legacy and prevent it from being destroyed, its working style did change to adapt to market ways. Management was decentralised and 'under financial control'. Only 14 worked in administration, compared with 50 previously, although nine agronomists remained. By the mid-1990s, the co-operative was profitable and able to repay its debts, producing wheat, grapes, apples, plums, cherries and peaches. Its yields were (it claimed) three times those of the private sector which, inevitably, had fewer technical and material inputs at its disposal. It was also beginning to invest. It had bought a potato production line from the Netherlands and had begun work building a new dairy. In 1994 it negotiated a contract with a firm from Finland to grow potatoes, and in both 1994 and 1995 it made a similar deal with a firm from Greece to grow onions. Succession from socialist co-operative to post-socialist co-operative was thus ultimately quite smooth, despite the tensions of the early years.

This successor co-operative was not the only entity in Pripek's post-liquidation agriculture. Three other new co-operatives were also established in the year of co-operative liquidation, but they survived for less than a year. They had land, but no one to work it. Many of members of these three failed co-operatives tried to join the successor co-operative, but, mainly because of individual personal antagonisms, only 30 families were allowed in. There were others who were happy to remain in the private sector. In all, by the mid-1990s, there were 300 private farmers in Pripek with farms averaging five hectares. Yet the fact that they had between them only 15 tractors and 50 packhorses (plus 10 cars according to one pensioner) suggested a low level of mechanisation. The co-operative was in fact willing to perform agricultural services for outsiders as well as co-operative members, so it was possible to leave the co-operative and still benefit its additional resources, although on a commercial basis. But the majority preferred to rent their land (or most of it) back to the co-operative and reap the rewards of membership. In the view of a former mayor, the majority

---

[3] Ibid., 86, reports similar kinds of benefit.

of the private farmers were pensioners, often people who had returned to the village from the town. They struggled with individual farming because they had no inputs or materials, were reliant on the co-operative to perform services for them and purchase their production, and valued their subsidised rice, cheese, flour, meat.[4]

Despite the numerical predominance of small-scale, under-mechanised farms in the private sector, villagers, including the chairman of the successor co-operative, reported the existence of 'new kulaks': former co-operative managers and managers from the towns who had experience and contacts in the food industry (social capital), who had acquired machinery (material capital) and were used to taking risks (cultural capital), who were in a position to produce on a large scale under contract to the food industry. The small-scale, private farmers, with no such contacts or contracts, suffered from the disappearance of socialist market channels for their produce. They were obliged to sell at the local authority-supported informal wholesale market by the side of the main road. Dobreva also noted the breakdown of marketing channels in post-socialist villages,[5] while Giordano and Kostova linked the phenomenon to the activities of the *akuli* (sharks) who controlled the major food markets (Sofia, Plovdiv, Varna).[6]

Livestock destroyed, a belated successor co-operative and 'elastic' land—Dragana

The experience of nearby Dragana was similar in many respects, but the formation of a post-socialist co-operative was delayed, there was rather more destruction of communal resources; and land reallocation was more contested. Dragana, in the mid-1990s, was a village of some 2,180 people and 800 households, mainly ethnic Bulgarians, living in 730 separate dwellings located in a rich farming area some 15 kilometres north of Plovdiv. In the mayor's perhaps partisan view, the land was so fertile that it could produce three crops per year. Like Pripek, it

---

[4] Dobreva, 'The family farm', 348–9, has noted the poor levels of equipment enjoyed by those who embark on private farming, seeing them more as successors to private plots rather than commercial farms.
[5] Ibid., 351.
[6] Giordano and Kostova, 'Social production', 87–8.

had established a Credit and Consumer Co-operative early on, in this case 1912, which continued, in one guise or another, until the mid-1990s, later supplemented by the Regional Consumer Co-operative. In addition, between the two world wars, seventeen families had collaborated to buy a threshing machine, whilst others had built a co-operative dairy. It too was in the vanguard of collectivisation, beginning in 1948, and mass collectivisation had been achieved by 1956. The farm was then merged with those in two villages a little closer to Plovdiv in 1971, and in 1973 it became part of an Agricultural Industrial Complex which specialised in field crops and livestock (cows, buffaloes, sheep and pigs), but also engaged in vegetable production. In 1978, concentration was taken a step further, and it became part of a Research and Production Complex, which developed a strong line in horticulture and fruit production in addition to livestock.

In the 1970s in particular, the pattern of agriculture and village life generally was transformed by mechanisation. By this time the Complex had 60 tractors, 10 combines, 7 threshing machines and made extensive use of selected seeds and fertilizers to boost yields; it even made use of 'agricultural aviation' for crop spraying. All aspects of production were supervised by professionals from the institutes of the Research and Production Complex, and it employed 10 economists, 8 engineers, 23 agronomists, 30 specialists and 390 manual workers. The latter were for the most part middle-aged or pensioners. The farm also developed irrigation schemes for its fields; indeed, all 2,000 hectares of Dragana village land was eventually irrigated by system of underground piping. In addition to rice, the farm produced barley, maize and lucerne, and cultivated 100 hectares of Virginia tobacco for which it also built drying facilities. It also grew new potatoes, mint and morello cherries, which were exported to Belgium, Czechoslovakia and the Soviet Union. Livestock farming too was developed and brought up-to-date. Cattle sheds and a dairy were built for its 300 cows and 180 buffaloes; and 2,500-head sheep farm was established, in addition to a pig farm and a poultry farm. The value of total agricultural output towards the end of the socialist era reached four million leva.

Autonomy in decision-making reverted to the co-operative in about 1981 as the era of the Agro-Industrial Complexes came to an end. In addition to its agricultural activities, the co-operative had several non-agricultural workshops (a bakery, machinery repair shop and so on) in Dragana itself (the majority) and in a nearby village, but all were related to agriculture in some way. By the 1980s, the co-operative had between 7–800 members. In addition to the industrial workers, 130 worked in livestock, 200 in horticulture and cropping, and 280 in auxiliary production. The co-operative also employed six economists, five engineers, seven zoo-technicians, two agronomists and a vet. Thus, even after the gigantomania of the Agro-Industrial Complexes, the co-operative farmed on a considerable scale, with sophisticated equipment and at a high technological level.

In 1992, the Dragana co-operative underwent liquidation, under the supervision of a Liquidating Committee appointed by district officials and made up of a 'railway worker, a trade unionist and a hairdresser'.[7] There followed a period of private farming until late 1996, when some 500 villagers signed up for the formation of a new co-operative. Thus, although a 'successor co-operative' did emerge eventually, it was only after considerable delay. During the liquidation process, co-operative livestock was distributed to members such that each village family received approximately two cows and some sheep, goats and pigs. Needless to say, many were simply slaughtered, because the members did not have the facilities to keep them. The machinery and equipment was sold at auction, and at very low prices, 'almost free of charge'—according to the school headmistress. Furthermore, before even the auctions could take place, much of the equipment was stolen or swapped for old machines, and there were enduring suspicions that all of the tractor drivers simply took possession of the good tractors for themselves. There was also considerable loss of, and damage to, property, particularly in relation to the rice cultivation. Tobacco cultivation, once a staple, ceased entirely; horticulture was abandoned. Legally the Liquidation Committee was under an obligation to look after the large-scale apple orchard that the co-operative had owned, but it did not. The trees were not irrigated and the orchard (which used to export 8,000 tonnes of apples) was destroyed. Co-operative liquidation also meant that the former co-operative specialists such as agronomists lost their jobs. Some found work as consultants for companies related to agriculture, such as fertiliser firms; others became policemen or body-

---

[7] See note above.

guards, yet others, even people with higher education, were reduced to taking cleaning jobs.

Despite the legal requirement for full, direct and specific restitution within historic boundaries, those in charge of land reallocation bent the rules. Owners were allocated plots where possible, or perhaps when it suited influential people most, on contiguous areas of land, rather than regaining their actual patrimony in its historical boundaries. This had the consequence of greatly speeding up the process because the 'historical boundaries' clause was proving exceptionally difficult to implement nationally. Ministry of Agriculture estimates cited by Creed suggested that only 12 per cent of land nationally could be redistributed directly in the approved way.[8] But there was always an element of discretion in the decisions concerning land allocation. Although it was the Land Commission that made the final decisions, our interviewees felt that this power of discretion lay with the Liquidation Committee. As one of them reported, 'Whether or not you get land in one place depends on the Liquidation Committee'. This discretion operated in the interests of the local establishment. The mayor, for example, received in a single location the 12 hectares of rice paddy that he inherited through his wife, and he became a relatively successful farmer. Others were not so lucky. One interviewee had six hectares of land in 11 different locations, with the result that he cultivated only 30 per cent of it because it was inefficient to cultivate more. In all, roughly one third of the land remained uncultivated. Barbara Cellarius refers to disagreements over land allocation neutrally as the difference between real and mental maps in her discussion of land restitution in Chepelare in the central Rhodope mountains,[9] but the disagreements mirror Verdery's claims about the 'elasticity' of land in Romania,[10] which takes centre stage in much writing on Romanian agricultural restructuring (see Chapter 7). Self-interest as well as poor memory played a role.

---

[8] Gerald W. Creed, 'An old song in a new voice: Decollectivization in Bulgaria', in *Eastern European Communities: The Struggle for Balance in Turbulent Times*, ed. David A. Kideckel (Boulder, CO and Oxford: Westview Press, 1995), 30.

[9] Cellarius, 'Property restitution', 198.

[10] Verdery, 'The elasticity of land: Problems of property restitution in Transylvania', *Slavic Review* 53, no. 4 (Winter, 1994): 1071–109.

'The only good result of liquidation was that people learned what they actually had, which was very little.' So said the former chairman of the co-operative who, with the enthusiastic encouragement of the mayor, for whom this was a major priority, was, in the more pro-co-operative climate of 1996, actively trying to create a successor co-operative to assist those who were incapable of farming their newly acquired land. The founding General Meeting had decided to contribute the minimal sum of 2,000 leva as initial capital, and established an equally minimal membership fee of 500 leva. It planned to operate on half of the land previously farmed by the socialist co-operative, and, because all equipment and machinery had been lost during the liquidation process, it was seeking to find replacements, either new or second hand; and there were no plans to re-enter livestock production. The organisers were looking to PHARE and the Ministry of Agriculture for financial support. But its prospects were uncertain, a fact reflected in the difficulties that it experienced finding an agronomist; most people approached were afraid of the risk and the responsibility. Furthermore, local enthusiasm for the project was ambivalent. The organisers recognised that for most members, commitment to the co-operative would only be partial. They expected that the members would keep some private land, certainly their best land, for themselves. They knew and accepted that people would devote less time to the common and more to the private, to their vegetable production in particular; over 50 per cent of villagers used poly tunnels for vegetable growing. They knew it, and did not like it: 'It is difficult to work with people who will not be personally committed to the farm'—commented the former socialist co-operative chairman. But they accepted it and continued their plans in a spirit of socialist paternalism and the likelihood of at least some income for themselves from the venture.[11]

While most villagers focused on small-scale farming and were glad to join a co-operative that would take over responsibility for the land that they were unable to farm themselves, there were six larger farms in the village which had amassed more than 15 hectares—the 'more enterprising farmers' who took a risk and acquired machinery early on

---

[11] A similar lack of commitment to the commons is reflected in the attitudes of many Romanian villagers to associations, as in Colibaşi. See Chapter 7 and references cited there.

and then negotiated with relatives in order to increase the size of their holding. Most of the really big agriculture-related businesses, however, as in Pripek, were owned by former managers, who had left the village long ago (although maintained contacts with it) as their careers progressed in socialist Bulgaria's highly concentrated agro-food industry. Such people could exploit both food industry contacts to secure marketing channels, and their earlier links with the co-operative to obtain machinery at 'realistic' prices.

Co-operative livestock retained against the odds—Slivka

Co-operative traditions in Slivka, which in the mid-1990s was an ethnically Bulgarian community with a population of 561, also had a long co-operative pedigree, going back to the co-operative of 1905 which supplied the villagers with industrial products, seeds and machinery. Post-socialist co-operative liquidation was also a fraught affair. The co-operative underwent liquidation in 1992 and was succeeded by three new ones, which jointly leased about 90 per cent of village land. Two were rather small, 600 and 100 hectares respectively, and the third is considered in more detail below. The Liquidation Committee took the word 'liquidation' seriously, under intense pressure from district officials. It began with co-operative's flock of 1,300 sheep. Events followed a pattern similar to those described by Radost Ivanova in Panaretovo.[12] All entitled persons received vouchers with numbers on them. The sheep were similarly numbered, and the members then wandered through the flock searching for the animal with their number on its back, before dragging it off. The animals were panicked and bleated incessantly. The same procedure was used to 'liquidate' the 700 cattle, but, in this case, outsiders turned up to buy up stock at knock-down prices from members who did not want to keep their animals.

Even while 'liquidation' was taking place, the wife of the chairman of the co-operative, the future mayor of the mid 1990s, began to orga-

---

[12] Radost Ivanova, 'Social change as reflected in the lives of Bulgarian villagers', in *Eastern European Communities: The Struggle for Balance in Turbulent Times*, ed. David A. Kideckel (Boulder, CO and Oxford: Westview Press, 1995), 219.

nise a successor co-operative, because many villagers had nowhere to keep the animals and, if no communal solution could be found, there would be little alternative but to slaughter the animals. They succeeded and the co-operative became the biggest of the three post-socialist co-operatives. But, in the view of those involved, the Liquidation Committee sabotaged their endeavour at every stage. It refused to allow them to inherit co-operative machinery, something that they claimed (and events in Breze tended to confirm) was common practice elsewhere; and there was even a period when it sent letters to the utilities companies urging them disconnect the embryonic co-operative's electricity and water. In addition, there were accusations that the Liquidation Committee did not determine the distribution of co-operative shares properly, and that animals were given to people who did not even have shares. Further, the Liquidation Committee, or so it was claimed, even manipulated the auctions at which former co-operative's machinery and equipment was sold. Unusually for such auctions, prices were pushed up by people with 'suitcases full of money', so that it was difficult for the new co-operative to acquire the machinery that it needed and had been prevented from inheriting. It did buy machinery at the auction, but it was obliged to take out loans at 50 per cent interest rates to cover the purchases.

By 1996, this successor co-operative was in its third year of operation and was farming profitably on 1,300 hectares. Despite the poor relations with the Liquidation Committee, it had succeeded in purchasing the former co-operative's bakery, and it had started collecting milk from its members and had acquired a building which it hoped to convert into a small dairy for the production of cheese and perhaps butter. It further had schemes to can fruit juices and make preserves, and to build a mill, although there were no plans to move beyond agriculture-related activities. The triumph of this co-operative, in its leaders' eyes, was that, despite the difficulties at the time of transformation, they had succeeded in saving the large-scale animal sheds from devastation and thus had kept their livestock together. In addition to co-operative participation, almost all households were engaged in small-scale vegetable production or livestock farming; some 136 families used poly tunnels, and there were seven privately owned tractors. Most of those who left the co-operative voluntarily did so with 'obsolete equipment', to use the mayor's description. Only a handful of people farmed on a scale for which the designation 'private farmer' was appropriate, mostly former co-operative farm managers who were not based in the village.

A successful co-operative on a reduced scale—Kupen

The transformed co-operative in the relatively remote village of Kupen (which will be introduced more fully below) also managed to preserve its predecessor's livestock production, but on a significantly reduced scale. Collectivisation there began rather late, in 1956, but it was completed within a year in 1957, when 80 per cent of the village population had joined the farm. In 1974 it merged with surrounding villages (including Blagun and Chala, see below), and in 1978 an Agrarian and Industrial Complex was founded on the basis of all of the villages of the Kupen commune. In 1980, this Complex then merged with another based in Gotse Delchev. The 1970s, when the co-operative had 455 members, was remembered here too as a golden age. It produced high quality tobacco, grapes, apples, plums, tomatoes and quinces, while on the livestock side it reared both pigs and cattle and maintained a dairy herd. Although the original co-operative leaders only had elementary schooling, by the 1970s a new generation of university-educated management had been introduced. As one pensioner member remembered fondly: 'Every year we got high incomes selling grapes, plums, apples, quinces, wheat.' Almost every house in the village dated from the socialist era; the village was effectively rebuilt with co-operative wealth.

Given the importance of the co-operative to village wealth, it is not surprising that in 1991, before the liquidation legislation was passed, a General Meeting of the co-operative voted unanimously for the co-operative to stay together; the only change that members wanted was a new management. But the SDS liquidation legislation made this impossible, and in 1992 the co-operative was liquidated. In the process its machinery and equipment was either stolen or sold 'almost free of charge' in the words of a pensioner member. A successor co-operative emerged, but it operated in Kupen only, with 300 owners and a greatly reduced managerial staff: only three employed fulltime and seven working on a percentage basis. It concentrated on livestock, mainly cattle, but 300 hectares of the land tilled by its predecessor remained uncultivated, mostly in areas where industry still offered alternative employment.[13]

Continuity but post-socialist loss of livestock—Breze

In Breze, which in the mid-1990s was a predominantly Bulgarian village of 751 inhabitants located near Silistra in the northeast of Southern Dobrudja, the co-operative also failed to retain its livestock production, but this was a result of the economics of post-socialist agriculture rather than destruction at the time of liquidation. The first producer co-operative had been established in 1954, and mass collectivisation followed in 1956. The co-operative had joined a Complex in 1976, but this was demerged in the 1980s and it subsequently operated across four villages, each a separate budgetary unit, with Breze at its centre.

There were many elements of continuity in the farm's liquidation. The head of the new co-operative, which was the only one in the village and farmed 95 per cent of its land, was the same as the head of the old one. It farmed 1,300 hectares, roughly the same amount as at its formation in 1956, and it retained a total membership of around 1000. Furthermore, the co-operative management, aided by local officials, managed to retain much of the machinery and successfully prevented those who wanted to take their land, leave the co-operative and farm privately from getting access to it. The new co-operative, however, was not simply a continuation of the old one. Management, other than the chairman, was new, and there was a new management style: 'there is financial control'. The latter impacted negatively on employment. Only an estimated 52 people worked in the new co-operative as manual 'field workers'; ten individuals were classified as unskilled and a further 10 classified as semi-skilled.

The co-operative had initially managed to keep hold of its 250 cows and 1,000 sheep, but, in the spirit of 'financial control', it felt that it could not afford to employ people to look after them full time on

---

[13] Dobreva, 'The farm', 84, reported that co-operatives have problems finding managerial staff. The more successful transformations from within our villages suggest this was not a universal problem.

a large-scale production basis. The management expected rather the individual co-operative members to look after the animals on their own plots. But this did not happen: members did not want to bother with more livestock than was necessary for their immediate needs. Furthermore, a halfway-house solution of employing Roma on a casual basis to look after the herds had not been a success. Over time, the animals were either slaughtered or sold and the material infrastructure for livestock farming disappeared, despite the fact that the management was of the view that successful co-operatives were those that retained livestock farming and the regular income it produced.

A spectrum of 'red', 'blue' and family—Venets

Venets in the mid-1990s was a village of just over 2,000 inhabitants, mainly ethnic Bulgarians, and 550 dwellings, less than ten miles south of Plovdiv and roughly equidistant from Asenovgrad. There, post-socialist co-operative liquidation was also associated with the destruction of livestock, and its largest private farmers were outsiders to the village and unknown by villagers. But there was perhaps more variety in the composition of post-socialist in the village.

Like the other villages in the Plovdiv area, Venets was endowed with good agricultural land and had benefited from an extensive co-operative network in the pre-socialist years. The village had indeed acquired the nickname 'little America' because of its wealth and it boasted credit co-operatives, cereals and fodder co-operatives, consumer co-operatives, a wine-growers' co-operative and, briefly, a tobacco co-operative in pre-socialist times. The first agricultural producer co-operative was established in 1951, and mass collectivisation followed in 1957, to be completed in 1958. In 1970, the co-operative was integrated with those in two neighbouring villages, and in 1972 it was reconstituted as an Agrarian-Industrial Complex. In 1978, a third, more distant village was added, and the farm and local research facilities were integrated into a larger National Research and Production Complex focusing on fruit and vines. The Complex was later expanded by a Centre for Agricultural Machinery (Machine and Tractor Station), a Chemical Services Laboratory and a refrigerated storage facility located in other, more distant villages. As elsewhere, the 1970s were seen by most villagers as a decade of progress: agricultural output increased twenty fold, fixed assets five fold, tractors and combine harvesters by a factor of ten, and a significant proportion of the crop was exported. Co-operative management was made up of qualified professionals, workers were taken to the plants owned by the Complex by bus, and ate their lunch in the plant canteen. Here too, 'agricultural aviation' was used for both spraying and transportation. By the 1980s, the co-operative was a front-runner in the region, and towards the end of the decade was building on that success by beginning work to construct a new fruit store. Post-socialist agricultural restructuring in Venets witnessed the liquidation of the socialist co-operative and its replacement by a 'red', post-socialist successor co-operative. But this was no longer the sole agricultural force in the village. The socialist co-operative was also succeeded by another, 'blue' co-operative, a private corporate farm, and an array of private family farms.

The views of these private farmers were radically different from the opinions of those wedded to the co-operative form. While the people behind the successor co-operative in Slivka, for example, accused the Liquidation Committee of behaving aggressively towards the co-operative, in Venets the accusation was that it favoured the co-operative. The most telling point that they made was that the Liquidation Committee had approved the creation of the successor co-operative before the Land Commission had determined land ownership. That is to say, it handed over most of the equipment and buildings to the successor co-operative before villagers had received title to their land and were in a position to farm privately. The available machinery thus was either 'plundered' (in the words of a village teacher) by the successor co-operative or those of its former managers who became large-scale farmers, or left unused and rusting, while the villagers waited for the Land Commission to complete its task. In the view of one young man forced by unemployment to become a private farmer, the Liquidation Committee was a 'mafia structure' which gave all the good land and equipment to its friends, and the rest to the co-operative: it 'destroyed everything', it 'stole everything' and sold it to the handful of villagers who were prospering. He had wanted to get machinery out of the process, but had failed.

The consequence of co-operative liquidation for land use in the village was that a third of the land previously farmed was left uncultivated, while a half was rented from either absentee owners, now resident in towns, or pensioners who were unable to farm the land themselves. Despite supposed favouritism in respect of the co-operative, the irrigation system was abandoned entirely and left to be destroyed and pilfered, and livestock farming was abandoned completely, as in so many villages. Most village families ended up with 2–3 goats; some 80 per cent of them received one cow or more; and roughly half of villagers gained some sheep. By 1995, the 'red' socialist successor co-operative had 260 members, and found employment for 130 according to the farm chairman, although the mayor put the figure at 70. The farm cultivated 650 hectares, including 22.8 hectares of vineyard and eight hectares of maize, with the help of four tractors and a threshing machine. In addition to agricultural jobs, the co-operative provided some employment for security guards, machine operators and book-keepers; despite a reduction in administrative jobs, the co-operative retained eight managers. It had paid off its debts and was holding its head above water commercially, with an income of 392,000 leva and crops of 1.3 million tons of grain, 170 tons of maize, 45 tons of cherries (of which 30 tons were exported), 150 tons of grapes, 45 tons of apples. But overall its yields in 1994 were a fraction of those for the last socialist years, not surprising given the destruction of the irrigation system. The best, lucerne, was only a third of previous levels. The management had successfully persuaded members to pool resources and invest in spraying and transportation equipment, and, in 1995, it was planning to invest in the completion of the fruit store that had been planned in the 1980s.

The other co-operative in the village, the 'blue co-operative', had enjoyed no privileged status at the time of liquidation; indeed it was only established in 1995. Despite the political resonance of the labels 'red' and 'blue', in interviews those concerned insisted that the differences were based as much on personal friendships and antagonisms as on ideological commitment. Kaneff's fieldwork in Talpa suggests, however, that the villagers interviewed in Venets were being somewhat disingenuous. Blue was the SDS's colour after all, while red is traditionally associated with communism and socialism in Bulgaria as elsewhere. In Talpa, no BSP members joined the 'blue' co-operative (they had also been excluded from the Liquidation Council),[14] while those who owned larger holdings and saw themselves as the victims of socialism were more likely to join it.[15] Although the 'blue co-operative' leaders, who lived in a nearby town,[16] had the classic background in co-operative leadership,[17] they had been active in the formation of anti-communist political parties.[18] In the socialist-dominated mid-1990s, its leaders continued to term it a co-operative because of the negative associations with the word 'firm',[19] but by 2000 they had lost these inhibitions and it was referred to as a 'firm'; landowners who used it complained that the leaders had forgotten that they were farming 'our land'.[20] Talpa's 'red co-operative', by contrast, continued to provide cheap grain for its members,[21] and echoed an earlier socialist past by choosing the name 'Progress', the one used by the village co-operative in pre-socialist times.[22]

In Venets, whatever the reasons behind its genesis, the 'blue' co-operative operated on a different basis from the 'red' one. It had 235 members with 600 hectares of land, and employed around 70, although the mayor suggested a more pessimistic 35. The members had been obliged to use the shares that they acquired from the old co-operative to buy equipment because it had inherited nothing from it. Both management and financial control were decentralised. Members were paid no rent for their land, and the co-operative provided them with no social benefits; on the other hand, it did pay them a dividend

---

[14] Deema Kaneff, 'Responses to "democratic" land reform in a Bulgarian village', in *After Socialism: Land Reform and Social Change in Eastern Europe*, ed. Ray Abrahams (Providence and Oxford: Berghahn Books, 1996), 89.
[15] Ibid., 106–7.
[16] Deema Kaneff, 'Private co-operatives and local property relations in rural Bulgaria', *Replika* (Hungarian Social Science Quarterly) (Special Issue 1998): 166.
[17] Kaneff, 'Responses', 106.
[18] Kaneff, 'Private co-operatives', 168.
[19] Ibid., 167.
[20] Deema Kaneff, 'Property, work and local identity', Working Paper no. 15 (Max Planck Institute for Social Anthropology, Halle-Saale, 2000), 13.
[21] Kaneff, 'Private co-operatives', 168.
[22] Kaneff, 'Responses', 109–10.

from its profits. The 'blue' co-operative that emerged in Rozino was likewise more commercial in orientation and did not offer agricultural services to its members.

In addition to the two co-operatives, a farming company was also formed in 1995 with 550 hectares of land, owned by 200 individuals; it found employment for between 35 and 40. The people responsible for this company were remarkably anonymous, however. They were described by villagers as being former co-operative managers who managed to acquire machinery and enjoyed long-established contacts, especially with food industry companies, and even with foreign firms. They were not their immediate bosses in the village co-operative structure, but more distant individuals with influence from the earlier era of highly concentrated farming. Interviewees varied in their estimates for the number of private farmers in the village. Some put their number as low as 50, others as high as 200, and almost every villager had some sort of income from agriculture. The number of dairy farmers was put at two or three only; 18 people had tractors, and only seven or eight villagers had as much as 10 hectares of land. Most village landowners however rented some or all of their land to one or other of the co-operatives, because they did not have the means to farm it alone. In the estimation of one farmer, one in ten farmers had machinery that they were in a position to rent to others.

RA was characteristic of pensioner-farmers. His 1.2 hectares were returned to him by the Land Commission and he originally put them into the 'red' co-operative. But, in 1994, he and his wife decided to leave the co-operative, because, despite his generally positive disposition towards it, he felt that it was unfair of it to charge him for wheat grown on what was his land. They became private farmers with 0.5 hectares of relatively easy-to-maintain cherry orchard, 0.2 hectares of vineyards, 0.2 hectares of maize. He rented 0.3 hectares back to the co-operative despite not being a member. In addition to the income that he gained from his land, he had a pension of 5,600 leva (the maximum) from his employment as a tractor driver in the socialist years. Only his wife helped with the farm from his immediate family. His son had a business repairing cars that were insurance write-offs and lived separately. His daughter also lived away from home. But two of his grandchildren did help on the farm and were planning to build a house nearby.

PF farmed on a larger scale, but still on a part-time basis. He owned seven hectares, (two hectares of orchards and five hectares maize) and rented an extra three hectares of maize from the co-operative. He was young and keen to take up the farming challenge, despite having been obliged by force of circumstance to adopt this lifestyle. He had previously worked on the co-operative as an assistant in the spare parts machinery shop. He had acquired most of the machinery that he needed, but it was second hand, purchased from an intermediary who had bought machinery in bulk at a co-operative liquidation auction. He carried out the farm work with the help of his wife, although they hired occasional labour. His other job was with the water supply company, which operated in three nearby villages, and which offered him the possibility of flexible working hours. Although he had been careful to avoid debt and had not taken out any bank loans, he confessed to finding life as a private farmer difficult.

UN was another young man possibly on his way to becoming a medium-sized family farmer. He farmed fulltime, but that was more through force of circumstance than because it was justified by the size of his farm. UN had never previously been gainfully employed. He went from school, to military service, to unemployment; and because he had never worked, did not qualify for unemployment benefit. Farming was the only possible option, although it was not one that he had ever anticipated. Asked if, in his youth, he had ever expected to become a farmer, he said that the idea was absurd. He planned to farm a total of 8 hectares of inherited land together with his uncle, who also worked in agriculture fulltime. They lived in separate households, but farmed the land together, employing occasional additional seasonal labour. However, because the ownership situation had not been finally clarified, they only cultivated half of this area at the time of interview, which included 1.2 hectares of vineyards, the remainder being maize, wheat and orchards. They had no equipment of their own and were obliged to rent everything, either from one of the co-operatives or from neighbouring farmers. He acknowledged a degree of resentment at paying in rental a sum equivalent to the amount the person was likely to have paid for the machinery, which in any case had probably once been co-operative property and hence was in a sense partly 'his own'. Like all small-scale private farmers in the village, he had no chance of contract production or of securing partial payment in advance, and felt himself to be at the mercy of 'middlemen' who offered the benefit of paying in cash, but would either turn up or not depending on market conditions.

Problems of a private farmer—Breze

A former *kmetstvo* mayor of Breze faced similar problems when he attempted to embark on private farming. Until 1976, he had worked in the Breze co-operative as an accountant responsible for livestock. Then, when the Complex was formed, he became president of the co-operative's control commission, the body which, in theory, supervised the management's behaviour in the interests of the membership. In 1979, he was suggested as mayor in the neighbouring village, and two years later he returned to Breze as mayor. Under his tenure, electricity came to the village and the complex of council buildings that dominated the centre of the village was designed and built. In 1985, however, he was urged to leave because of personal conflicts, and he went to work in the light engineering works in the village. With the collapse of socialism, he had to change career again, and, since 1991, he had worked as a caretaker in the local school. But all the while he had also been engaging in part-time farming. He was unable to take out of the co-operative all of the land to which he was entitled because he had no one to help him farm it; and he was unable to get any machinery from the co-operative, because the management successfully manipulated events to keep it *in situ*. So he took out a single hectare only, together with some livestock, mainly goats, and farmed it with the help of his large family, mainly his daughters and sons-in-law. Although he was disappointed by his inability to acquire machinery, he expressed his pleasure that the equipment had stayed in the village: it had not been wasted or gone to outsiders. Despite the part-time nature of his endeavour, by 1995 he saw himself as a farmer and hoped that one of his grandchildren would continue the farm; he felt that he had created the basics for them to develop further.

Local Authorities—Coping with Post-Socialist Recession

A commune centre mayor's socialist paternalism—Kupen

As was discussed in Chapter One, what distinguished the structure of local government in Bulgaria in the 1990s was its extreme centralisation.[23] While there had been moves in the 1980s to break up the extreme centralisation of agricultural production, no such pressures had emerged in terms of local government, and neither had the reform of local government become a demand of the political forces that triggered the 'change of system'. The consequence of this extreme centralisation was that only one of the nine villages covered in our research had the status of a commune centre, whose mayor, unlike a *kmetstvo* mayor, who had a budget and powers to influence the direction of commune development. That commune-centre village was Kupen.

Kupen in the mid-1990s was a predominantly Bulgarian and Orthodox village of 3,600 inhabitants situated some 15 kilometres south-east of Gotse Delchev, near Bulgaria's border with Greece. The village also had a Roma population estimated at between 50 and 60. Approximately 80 per cent of its population claimed descent from Bulgarians who were resettled from Greece in the population transfers of the 1920s. Kupen formally came into being as late as 1959, the amalgamation of two smaller villages. One of these had been named after a Bulgarian general who was remembered locally as having been instrumental in keeping their village within Bulgaria after World War I. This was a misremembering. The general concerned had been active in the Balkan Wars and was present at the Treaty of London which ended the first of them, but he had died in 1916. Furthermore, the location of Kupen within Bulgaria after World War I had never been in serious dispute. The Pirin mountain peaks to the south constituted an obvious border to even the most politically motivated cartog-

---

[23] Kaneff's Talpa, for example, formed part of a commune that covered 19 villages.

rapher; the disputed areas between Greece and Bulgaria lay further to the east.[24]

The Kupen commune council had, in the words of the mayor, total autonomy concerning how it spent its budget, which, as he correctly explained, was collected from 50 percent of individual income tax and 10 per cent of business taxes in the area (see Chapter 1). But, as he also ruefully noted, most went on the salaries of council workers, and social and health care. By the mid-1990s, Kupen itself was responsible for a general school with 392 pupils, a kindergarten with 140 children, a crèche with 22 children and a secondary school with 154 children; not to mention the health centre and two pensioners' clubs. Kupen's financial situation was made worse by a specific local measure, the abolition of special border-region subsidies. Despite its restricted means, the commune continued to make use of its discretionary social welfare budget to offer financial support to the village poor for the purchase of medicines, something that the nearby town of Gotse Delchev (or so it was claimed) had given up two years previously. Socialist industrialisation and its status as a commune centre meant that Kupen itself suffered little from the 'socialist public services gap'. The vast majority of streets were paved (most interviewees hazarded the figure 80 per cent), the whole of the village was provided with mains drainage and running water, 90 per cent of houses had bathrooms and there were as many telephones in the village as there were houses. A digital telephone exchange was even promised for 1997. The role and significance of the church was reported not to have increased since 1989, although new churches were being built throughout the commune and the mayor maintained cordial relations with the Orthodox Church.

The mayor of Kupen, a former chemical engineer and member of the BSP, was, in the eyes of the co-operative accountant, 'the most educated and influential person in the village'. He exuded dynamism and enthused listeners with his vision for the community. His goal

---

[24] See Henry Robert Wilkinson, *Maps and Politics: A Review of the Ethnographic Cartography of Macedonia* (Liverpool: Liverpool University Press, 1951), 234; and Stephen P. Ladas, *The Exchange of Minorities: Bulgaria, Greece and Turkey* (New York: Harvard University and Radcliffe College, Bureau of International Research, 1932), 122–3 and 592–617.

was to see his village achieve the status of a town,[25] and the means by which he sought to achieve this was by developing non-agricultural jobs. He could see no future in basing a development strategy on agriculture in a remote region like his. Rural areas needed industry in his view; indeed, his calculations showed that, despite its peripheral location, by the mid-1990s, 60 per cent of village's GDP came from manufacturing. He expressed irritation at the fact that land-use regulations assumed that rural land would be used for agriculture and placed restrictions on other forms of development. His strategy relied very much on his personal authority, however; he had established no body charged with the tasks of developing an industrial strategy or achieving the goal of urban status, although the council organised informal consulting services to support such new businesses. His enthusiasm rubbed off on the population all the same. One pensioner interviewed was of the opinion that things were going well in the village and that 'we shall be a town soon'. Beyond the ambition of achieving urban status, the mayor had faith in the expected improvements in cross-border communications to promote business and tourism from Greece and the Mediterranean. He claimed that the Greeks thought that Bulgaria had many advantages over Greece as a place for investing in the kinds of light industry that socialism had created in the region.[26] More defensively, and in a spirit of socialist paternalism that complemented his developmental vision,[27] the mayor strove informally to ensure that at least one person in every household had some form of employment, so that all households had a source of regular income, however small. In addition the mayor's office organised a job-creation, public works programme that benefited 52 people per year. The temporary employment that this created allowed them to re-qualify for unemployment benefit.

---

[25] Kaneff, *Who Owns the Past?*, 41, notes the importance of a town-village discourse in Bulgarian socialist policies and the desire for villages to become 'more like towns'.

[26] Pickles and Begg, 'Ethnicity'; and Pickles, '"There are No Turks"' examine Turkish interest in the post-socialist apparel industry further along the mountains.

[27] Kaneff, *Who Owns the Past?*, 174, uses the same term in the context of local government in Talpa.

Salvaging agriculture and its services—*kmetstvo* villages

In all of the other villages in the study, the only organ of local government was the *kmetstvo* whose powers, as described in Chapter 1, were severely limited. They could attend council meetings as observers only, and were entirely dependent on the commune mayor for finance. It is not surprising, therefore, that their vision was somewhat restricted, rarely extending beyond agriculture, such as the fate of the co-operative or the maintenance of the irrigation system for which the socialist-era co-operatives had been responsible.

As a *kmetstvo* village within a Plovid-based commune, Pripek had extremely limited abilities to influence its own fate, although the 'socialist public services gap' was not especially wide. Two thirds of village streets were paved, mains drainage was supplied to part of the village, all households had bathrooms; and the vast majority had phones. But if the co-operative continued to provide members with vegetable oil, rice, meat, poultry and cheese at reduced prices, it could no longer provide school dinners free of charge, bread for pensioners free of charge and subsidise the cost of meals in the kindergarten by 60 per cent. One pensioner was resigned to a period in the immediate future when 'one cannot think about social policy'. The horizons of the local politicians did not, and could not, stretch far beyond salvaging something from what they saw as the chaos of post-socialist agriculture (both the mayor and president of the co-operative were members of the BSP). In the Pripek case this meant supporting the co-operative in its attempt to keep control of the fruit store. The co-operative in Rozino had similarly succeeded in building the buffalo shed that its socialist predecessor had planned. Village development strategy to the extent that there could be one thus focused on the co-operative and its agricultural activities; but key individuals were aware that agricultural production in itself was not enough, that successful co-operatives needed to process and market what they produced. One of Pripek's former *kmetstvo* mayors used the example of rice: they should produce ready-packaged rice, not just the bulk commodity. Beyond recreating a more viable agriculture, local politicians pinned their hopes for some amelioration of opportunities and prospects on the achievement of the status of an independent commune, and this was a declared goal of village development policy.

Dragana, like Pripek, did not suffer from a dramatic 'socialist public services gap', thanks to its proximity to Plovdiv. Mains drainage was under construction and almost complete; the vast majority of houses had running water and baths; perhaps a third of the streets were paved, and two thirds of households had telephones. The energies of the mayor, a member of BANU and himself a farmer, were devoted to agriculture and the consequences of the liquidation of socialist agriculture. When asked what his most pressing problems were, he focused on: the creation of the new co-operative, his major concern, the need for cheap credits for agriculture, and the need to promote the 'agricultural exchange', which, as in Pripek, had developed informally at the side of the main road through the village. The latter provided a market outlet for small-scale producers whom the still or former state purchasing companies ignored, even if the producers complained about the prices that such 'middlemen' offered. Not all villagers were content with such priorities. Some felt that the focus on agriculture was a knee-jerk reaction which reflected a lack of direction. In the view of the school headmistress, 'local policy is developing spontaneously, according to the principle of "let things drift"'. One pensioner was more condemnatory, describing the mayor as a person who 'had returned to the village only recently from the town and was intent on merely feathering his own nest'. The mayor, like many of our mayors throughout the region, complained rather about the estrangement of most of the village population from community life, and of the new climate of self-interestedness that had emerged.

In Venets, the mayor's view was that the village was totally dependent on inadequate central finances from which to support a general school with 200 pupils and 12 teachers, a kindergarten with 60 youngsters (to which parents made additional financial contributions), a health centre employing one doctor, two dentists, a nurse and a midwife, and a pharmacy. Luckily, because of its location in the vicinity of Plovdiv, infrastructural provision was relatively good. There was no mains drainage, but all houses had running water and baths, most roads were paved and an estimated 90–95 per cent of households had telephones. The collapse of socialist agriculture nevertheless had created new responsibilities. Crucially, the village had fallen heir to the irrigation system that had been abandoned by the co-operative, and had to use some of its meagre funds to help recreate it. The mayor, like his counterpart in Pripek, was interested in saving the co-operative's fruit store from destruction, for it was expected that it would use a third of its capacity for village rather than co-operative needs.

Breze had been a commune centre until local government reform of 1979 when that role was taken over by a neighbouring larger settlement situated closer to Silistra. Perhaps because of that diminished status, its socialist legacy was one of underinvestment. Many streets remained unpaved and there was no mains drainage, although 190 houses had bathrooms, and almost all had running water and telephones. It too gained responsibility for the co-operative farm's irrigation system. But the *kmetstvo*'s concerns were of a different nature. Unusually in Breze, the 'change of system' had been associated with net migration out of the village. The school roll was falling and some 20 households had abandoned the village entirely and gone to the towns to look for work. He was worried that the village would eventually die out.

The concerns of the *kmetstvo* of Slivka, located not far from Breze, were similar. The 'socialist public services gap' in his village was relatively large. All village roads in the central part of the village were paved, but there was no mains drainage, around a third of the houses lacked running water, and only 54 of them bathrooms, yet almost all had telephones. The mayor tended to dwell on the perceived injustices of the Liquidation Committee, and this was understandable, given the emotionally charged nature of the proceedings and his family background. His father had been the co-operative accountant, and his grandfather had been a founder member. Yet it was his duty to oversee the destruction of the body that his father and grandfather had helped create. He was very conscious of his inability to meet needs in the social sphere, particularly in relation to health care and the kindergarten, which was threatened with closure, because it already had fewer than the permissible minimum number of children. He worried about the village's ageing population and the preference of the young for life in Silistra, and he was obliged to turn down the fifteen families who, a teacher reported, had approached the local council for additional municipal aid in 1994. He spoke of the general need for 'economic buildings', tangible evidence of economic development, and he was particularly proud that budgetary funds had been made available to build a new Orthodox church, which the village had previously lacked. This represented the most concrete evidence to support the claim of some, like the co-operative economist, that the role of the church had increased since 1989.

THE DESTRUCTION OF SOCIALIST MOUNTAIN COMMUNITIES—BLAGUN AND CHALA

The cases discussed above, mainly from the Plovdiv area and from the vicinity of Silistra, have included accounts from many who mourned the passing of the socialist way of live, focusing on the 'senseless' destruction of technologically advanced, capital-intensive systems of agricultural production. Those involved in managing large-scale farming saw no logic in destroying such investment which extended to 'agricultural aviation' in order to recreate inefficient peasant farming. Post-socialist developments in Chala and Blagun in the Pirin Mountains of the far south of the country almost on the border with Greece witnessed the destruction of a rather different type of socialist community, one based on traditional farming on a much more modest scale, but one equally made possible by socialist Bulgaria's generous levels of agricultural support. It was a region particularly badly hit by the post-socialist recession.[28]

Chala in the mid-1990s was a predominantly Pomak (see Chapter 1) village of 478 inhabitants and 99 households, located about eight miles south-east of Kupen and within two miles of the border with Greece. It was part of the Kupen commune, but had had its own mayor since 1950. Unlike its counterparts in traditional agricultural areas, the village had no pre-war experience of co-operation; the first consumer co-operative, the Selcop shop was opened at the beginning of the 1950s. Prior to that, villagers had baked their own bread and been dependent on two private traders in Kupen for other supplies.

Collectivisation in this era of marginal agricultural production came late, in 1959 in the case of Chala. Convinced, with some justification, that there was little future in large-scale co-operative farming

---

[28] Pickles, "'There are No Turks'", 7.

in such a hilly region, the authorities decided in 1960, after the first co-operative harvest, that the whole village should be moved to the region of the Northern Bulgarian town of Rasgrad. Abandoning the project of collectivised agriculture was politically impossible, so the villagers had to be moved to a geographical region where large-scale communal agriculture was possible. Most village houses were razed to the ground; only a few with stone-roofs were left standing. The villagers, however, opposed this drastic solution. They drafted a petition and sent it together with a delegation to the government; and they finally received permission to move back to their mountain home. They began cultivating the land again, and in 1974 became the Chala brigade of the Kupen co-operative, headed by a leader who had only general secondary educational qualifications, unlike the majority of co-operative managers. It farmed 150 hectares, provided employment for 220 villagers and was profitable, the main crop being 50 hectares of tobacco which, they farmed both communally as the co-operative brigade and on their household plots. Some villagers privately produced meat and milk which they sold to the state purchasing company, Rhodopa, but the two sheep sheds in the village both belonged to the main Kupen farm. Over the course of the 1970s and 1980s the Chala villagers built new houses and recreated their lives, although socialist investment in infrastructure was low. By the 1990s, there were no paved streets; there was no mains drainage, although all houses had running water and 70 per cent had bathrooms; and there were only four telephones in the whole village. Their brigade constituted an essentially single-crop, relatively unimportant, underdeveloped outpost of the larger farm.

Blagun, located further along the road from Kupen but further away from the winding border with Greece, experienced the socialist era similarly, but without the drama of having been forcibly abandoned. It was, in the mid-1990s, a village of 738 inhabitants and 170 households, which had developed out of what had originally been a temporary shepherding settlement high in the hills. Its citizens too were overwhelmingly Pomaks, although one former mayor was a lone voice in estimating that the village was 70 per cent Orthodox and 30 per cent Muslim. Before the socialist period its inhabitants lived almost entirely from agriculture, but with plots averaging only 1–2 hectares, theirs was essentially subsistence farming; they produced their own seeds and fertilizer (manure) and used animal traction, donkey or mule.

The first co-operative activity in Blagun was established in 1948, somewhat earlier than Chala, when Selcop opened a shop in the village. Collectivisation also arrived marginally earlier than its neighbour, in 1958. There were doubts in Blagun too about the merits of collectivising such an isolated village, but the solution was less dramatic than in Chala. Villagers were encouraged to move away from the village to more favourable living conditions, and about 350 villagers abandoned their mountain isolation for a lowland village near Rousse in Northeast Bulgaria.[29] But the village remained, as did the Blagun co-operative brigade with approximately 400 members and 600 hectares of village land. Only about 200 members were active, and they concentrated their attention on 130 hectares of tobacco (including that allocated for their 0.2 hectare household plots). The Blagun co-operative too was merged into the Kupen co-operative and then Complex in the 1970s, and operated thereafter as a small, isolated tobacco-growing brigade with its own leader and accountant. It relied on Kupen for the services of an agronomist and other experts, and all marketing was organised by Kupen via Bulgartabak. Its plan targets were set at relatively modest levels and it regularly over fulfilled them threefold, and even fivefold in 1985. Thus the socialist sector incomes of villagers, complemented by social security benefits, pensions, and the proceeds of their household plots (which were also marketed via the co-operative), were high. In addition to tobacco, the brigade grew some rye as fodder for the oxen that they used for ploughing, and the members grew vegetables and kept smaller livestock for their own consumption. As the co-operative developed, cattle sheds and water tanks were built, and this resulted in the creation of a second brigade in 1988. Villagers used their high incomes to build new houses, although, as in Chala, socialist infrastructural investment in the village was low. In the 1990s, almost all houses had running water, but it was supplied from wells; there was no mains drainage, the telephone situation was poor (only four in the village according to the postman, none at all according to a former mayor), and bus services had been reduced by a third, although, unlike Chala, more than 80 per cent of the streets were

---

[29] The migration of Pomaks and ethnic Turks from the mountains to more fertile lowlands was a common phenomenon. Kaneff's Talpa included a population of relocated Pomaks, Kaneff, *Who Owns the Past?*, 168.

paved. Nevertheless, for those who could put up with the remoteness of the area and the rigour of predominantly manual labour on the soil, life in Blagun as in Chala was good and uncomplicated.

The co-operative in Chala was liquidated against the wishes of its members. They initially resolved to continue to produce communally despite the liquidation proceedings, but this only lasted for a year. After this they gave up and moved to farming on a wholly private basis. Their judgement was that co-operative farming was possible only with state support; without it, private self-interests became paramount and insurmountable. Nothing of the co-operative remained. The sheep sheds, which were the responsibility of Kuplen not Chala, were destroyed and abandoned as an empty shell; the fittings of the cattle sheds were sold or plundered; and the oxen were sold, as was the only tractor. Farming returned to its pre-war conditions and all villagers engaged in it, but on a tiny scale. All used poly-tunnels to dry tobacco and grow vegetables, but no one provided them with agricultural services. The fact that the village's stock of tractors doubled from the single one of the socialist era, which could work on about a third of the co-operative land, to two, complemented by a truck, did not signify a flourishing agriculture. Most villagers relied for the bulk of their ploughing and other field work on mules, donkeys, and horses, whatever they could obtain to replace the co-operative's oxen. In 1993 and 1994 they continued to concentrate mainly on tobacco, but, given the uncertain market conditions, by 1995 most villagers had cut back heavily and were looking for alternative crops.

The era of socialist plenty came to an end in Blagun too at the beginning of 1992. Both brigades were liquidated. All villagers returned, as the postman bemoaned, to the small-scale farming that had existed before World War II: tiny, excessively 'parcelled out' plots of land, cultivated with the help of horses, mules or donkeys, with no institutional help to market their produce. The fact that there were no more than two tractors in the village was less of a problem because, as in Chala, oxen were the preferred means of traction in this hilly landscape. Nevertheless, the communal cattle sheds stood in ruins, machinery disappeared, and the oxen were 'liquidated' as a co-operative asset, which is to say, they were distributed to members who then kept, slaughtered or sold them, as they saw fit. None of the village co-operative members had agreed with the liquidation, and the majority would have liked to have recreated a successor, but, unlike Chala, they did not even attempt to keep co-operative farming going. As a former mayor stated, 'it cannot be done in the old way; there is no machinery, because everything is destroyed; members no longer have any money, because it has already been spent'. By the mid 1990s, farming in the village was in the hands of about 200 private farmers, including the former co-operative leaders; but the average holding was still little more than a hectare. The Blagun villagers too suffered from the diminishing market for tobacco, and complained that in 1995, they had yet to be paid for their 1993 crops. As in Chala, nearly all villagers grew vegetables in addition to tobacco for their own use, mostly with the help of poly tunnels, but it was difficult to develop vegetable production as an alternative cash crop because of the village's isolation. The villagers felt abandoned. 'Everyone has to take care of everything himself—seeds, fertilisers, and above all markets for his production'— complained the same postman, although some of the older villagers reported that at least they felt that they understood agriculture and could solve their own problems.

Socialism had also produced opportunities for non-agricultural employment for both Chala and Blagun villagers from the 1970s onwards, when younger people sought out unskilled labour in Kupen and beyond (even as far as Sofia). Women, and later some men, were employed especially in a unit of a shoe-manufacturing production co-operative which was established in Kupen. This co-operative subcontracted to a state factory in a distant town near the Macedonian border, which produced mainly for the Soviet market. Young men began to commute to Gotse Delchev also in the 1970s to work in the construction industry, and, by the end of the 1980s, people from both villages commuted to the state sector to work in construction or as fitters and drivers in a state automobile enterprise, or in the Complex's Machine and Tractor Station which was located near Gotse Delchev.

All this changed after 1989, although the shoe factory in Kupen continued in operation. By 1995, some 50 villagers in Blagun were officially registered as unemployed and in receipt of benefit, but village sources estimated the number looking for work and unable to find it was nearer 100. In Chala, a total of 83 villagers were officially listed as unemployed, roughly half of whom received unemployment benefit. But unofficial estimates put the figure much higher, as high as 50 per cent of the population of working age in the view of one pensioner, who added: 'People are desperate. They do not see any perspective for development, no way out from unemployment. We are located at the end of Bulgaria, closer to Greece. Nobody sees us, nobody hears us.'

Neither post-socialist Chala nor post-socialist Blagun developed new businesses of any scale, but the number of family businesses that emerged was appreciable given the small size of the villages and their remote geographical location. There were perhaps seven or eight new businesses in Chala all told, all plugging the 'socialist personal services gap', including a carpenter, a baker and two or three pubs *cum* snack bars. All but the bakery were located in the houses of their owners; none offered the prospect of providing employment beyond the family circle. In Blagun the new businesses were made up of a private bakery and four pubs. All were family businesses and plugged some of the 'socialist personal services gap', but none had plans to expand employment beyond the family circle.

Despite this image of villages where a hard but cushioned socialist way of life had been destroyed and replaced by a world which offered little for those not accustomed to the toil of peasant agriculture with limited consumer demands that could be met on the basis of subsistence farming, neither mayor was a member of the BSP. The mayor of Blagun was a retired teacher and a member of the SDS. His counterpart in Chala was a local man, born and bred, also university educated, and a member of the BZNS-NP (see Chapter 1). He had been a manager in a textile factory within the Kupen commune during the socialist years, but had 'seized the time' and become a private entrepreneur in the same field, running a business which produced to order, mainly for Italian companies. His presence amongst the village and commune leadership represented, perhaps, the merest hint that a business elite was beginning to exert an influence on the local political stage. Yet there was little concrete evidence of this, beyond the negative impressions that villagers had of their elected representatives. In Chala, one pensioner complained that the mayor was no longer interested in the social needs of the population. The kindergarten had to close in 1994; there was no club for pensioners, and discretionary social welfare expenditure had been reduced. In Blagun, there was a general view that elected representatives were more interested in serving their own interests than devoting themselves to the needs of the villagers, that they stood for election simply to achieve power, but had no conception of how the village economy might be developed. Despite this uncertainty and insecurity, and despite the fact that most interviewees were of the opinion that the impact of religion on village life had not increased, villagers in Chala, mirroring the drive that had seen them recreate their village in the 1960s, had found the resources necessary to build a new mosque after 1989. This evidence of village solidarity notwithstanding, one pensioner noted, 'there is hatred between individual families and this makes me think that we cannot work for common ideas'.

THE NON-FARM ECONOMY—NEW BUSINESSES AND A CUSHION FOR LOCAL EMPLOYMENT

Although unemployment rates in Bulgaria were generally high, the experience of many of our villages was that it was commuting jobs in particular that had been cut, and local employment opportunities remained more buoyant. In Pripek, for example, the number of jobs in the village itself did not decline too dramatically in the early socialist years, but those offered by commuting did. Opportunities for non-farm employment in Pripek had emerged early in the socialist era. The Red Star Producer Co-operative started operations as early as 1948, and by the end of the 1980s it was engaged in 22 different activities including woodworking, house-painting, barber and hairdresser services, car repair, repairs of electric appliances; it employed a total of 150. Subsidiary factories of two state enterprises were also located in the village, the Industrial Firm 'Bulgaria' and the Vasov's Plants, which both employed as many as 80 at one time. The Napreduk credit co-operative continued its activities in the village from the pre-socialist to the socialist years, and between 1964 and 1970 it increased its turnover from 1.3 to 1.8 million leva. In 1971 it constructed a new restaurant and department store building. Established under the auspices of the Agro-Industrial Complex and subsequently run independently, there was also a dairy which employed 40 people and a specialist chicken farm and slaughter house which employed 75. There was also a small firm manufacturing grain and fodder which employed 17. Many more villagers, of course, more than half of those of working age, were employed in the booming socialist industry of Plovdiv and Pazardjik, both were located an easy commute away.

After 1989, the employment situation changed radically, but the net loss of jobs located in the village itself was not dramatic. The two state subsidiaries closed down, shedding a total of 90 jobs (both had slimmed down in the interim), and the chicken slaughter house also eventually went bankrupt because of a shortage of feed. Creed reports the closure of many socialist sector industries in the 1990s,[30] and a non-agricultural socialist era business closed in Talpa during the same period.[31] Nevertheless, in Pripek, the producer co-operative and credit co-operative continued their operations, and at more or less their former employment levels, as did the small grain and fodder company. To complement this, about 45 new businesses (100 according to one pensioner) were created in the village, many located in owners' houses, and concentrating on plugging the socialist personal services gap—shops, pubs, coffee-shops, carpenters and so on. In addition, fifty privately owned trucks and six privately owned buses were reported by the mayor. In addition to these primarily family ventures, some foreign investors had created a not insignificant number of new jobs. Biggest amongst these was the dressmaking and tailoring factory opened in collaboration with an Italian company, which employed 80, almost compensating for the 90 jobs lost when the two state subsidiaries closed down. In addition, a Greek firm participated in the construction and running of a petrol station, which employed 22. The relative affluence of the village was reflected in the fact that branches of three banks had opened there, despite the fact that entrepreneurs claimed that they were reluctant to take out loans because of the high rates of interest.

The number of villagers commuting to work outside Pripek fell by half, however, according to the president of the co-operative, although a local builder estimated that they still numbered between three and four hundred, and the president maintained that employers continued to provide them with free transport to work. The lost commuting jobs had an impact on unemployment. The co-operative president

---

[30] Gerald W. Creed, 'Economic crisis and ritual decline in Eastern Europe', in *Postsocialism: Ideals and Practices in Eurasia*, ed. Chris Hann (London and New York: Routledge, 2002), 63.

[31] Kaneff, *Who Owns the Past?*, 178.

estimated that 300 were unemployed, while others put the figures at nearer 4–500 to take into account the fact that many young people did not register. Where local businesses found success, and when foreign companies saw an investment opportunity, it seemed the job-loss of the early socialist years could be parried.

The situation for non-farm employment in Rozino was somewhat different in that there had been no investment in non-agricultural jobs in the village itself under socialism, yet opportunities to commute to work outside the village remained stable. Dragana, by contrast, was similar in many ways to Pripek: commuting jobs in particular were lost, but village job-loss was relatively modest. In addition, the new entrepreneurs were the beneficiaries of socialist-era social and cultural capital. Opportunities for non-farm employment in Dragana had been established from the 1960s onwards. An early example was a subsidiary branch of the First of May textile producer co-operative which employed around 80. Later on, an engineering works with 100 workers was established, a branch of the large-scale state industrial plant based in the town of Sopot, and, in 1972, a plastics moulding works was also established which employed around 60 workers. In addition, some 60 to 70 people worked in the nearby air base, mostly in its workshop, 30 were employed in a road building works, and 25 in construction works. The 'Edinstvo' co-operative and the Regional Consumer Co-operative 'Trakia' also provided non-agricultural jobs in the village, and the former had established a coffee and pastry shop. Beyond the village boundaries, non-agricultural employment was further expanded in the 1980s in the fields of road construction and electrical services, providing around 600 new jobs. In total, more than half of Dragana's active population commuted to work in nearby towns, their travel costs subsidised by the companies, at the end of the socialist era.

Non-farm employment decreased after 1989, but not catastrophically. Commuting jobs fell from a half to a third of the economically active village population. In the village itself, the light engineering works closed down, the air base workshop reduced its staff to 15, and the employment capacity of the 'Edinstvo' and 'Trakia' co-operatives decreased, although the latter continued to employ carpenters, milling machine operators and shop assistants, while the former was planning further new developments. On the other hand, the textile co-operative continued to operate with the same number of employees, as did the plastics works. The mayor also reported 60 people working as security guards and watchmen. Responding to these changing labour market conditions, between 80 and 100 new 'force-of-circumstance-entrepreneurs' emerged in Dragana, mostly self-employed or family businesses in the service sector—shops, coffee shops, pubs and restaurants. Traders in products related to the food industry were also significant, not surprising given the agricultural potential of the land and its (former at least) importance to the local economy, as were intermediaries and service-providers in the food industry. The more significant employers amongst these new businesses were the new 24-hour petrol station, which employed six; a carpentry firm, which employed 15; a mirror factory, which employed eight; and a light engineering firm which employed ten and exported as far afield as Italy and the UK. The premises for some of these businesses had formerly housed the non-agricultural ventures of the co-operative, its repair workshops and a distillery. According to one informant at least, an electrician, the most successful of these entrepreneurs shared a common social background: they were all former managers in the socialist sector who knew 'how to seize the time and take risks'.

New family businesses in Bulgaria as elsewhere tended, as we have seen, to plug the socialist personal services gap. One such business in the village of Slivka was the planned restaurant of Vanya, her husband and their three children. In 1996, Vanya's husband was in Israel working as a builder in order to earn the money necessary to set the business up. He had already worked for three years in Russia, and then had been unemployed for a period. Vanya worked in a bank, lived in a flat in Silistra, and dressed like an elegant urbanite. But once her husband had returned, they planned to buy a house in Slivka, move back to the village where she had family connections and open a restaurant. The village already had many pubs and a disco, but Vanya had a conception of a family restaurant of a type that did not exist locally. Of course, like all villagers, alongside the restaurant, they would keep livestock and engage in part-time farming. Indeed, Vanya, despite her urban appearance, already kept animals in the village, which were looked after by a friend. The local teacher might have had her in mind when he observed pointedly that the new entrepreneurial class in the village was made up of outsiders. But Vanya did not belong to the group that the teacher was most critical of, namely the woman who had chaired of the Liquidation Committee (the wife of a police officer) and her relatives.

In Venets too, family businesses plugging the socialist communal services gap were the norm, although here the most common sector was agriculture-related activities. There were almost 70 dealers in agricultural products, including livestock and machinery. Nevertheless, trading generally, shop keeping and coffee-houses were also common. The businesses consisted of at most the founder and a few family members or friends. None of them provide extensive new employment opportunities. In addition to those engaged in commerce, there were 50–60 self-employed craftsmen—carpenters, electricians and mechanics. In Kupen, the mayor claimed that there were 60 private firms in manufacturing and the services in his village, and, 'unlike elsewhere in Bulgaria, they pay their taxes'. However, the number of new businesses run by new entrepreneurs was probably only 20, and the majority were self-employed or family businesses, bakers, confectioners, shops, coffee shops, bars and craftsmen of various types. In addition, two of the buses on the route to Gotse Delchev were privately operated.

BULGARIAN SPECIFICITIES IN SUMMARY

The agricultural transformation in Bulgaria was highly politicised. It became a major theme in national politics and divided nearly all rural communities and resulted in the destruction of many socialist assets of which managers and members alike had been proud. The new farming was to be built on the ruins of socialist agriculture rather than its achievements. Communal livestock farming in particular struggled to survive into the post-socialist era. The biggest winners in the process, the *arendatori*, were invisible in our villages, although 'red co-operatives', 'blue co-operatives' and struggling private farmers figured prominently. A particular aspect of their struggle was access to markets which in Pripek and Dragana resulted in the formation of unofficial roadside markets.

There were no examples in our sample of successful new non-agricultural businesses created from scratch that employed significant numbers and did more than plug the 'socialist personal services gap', but an impressive number of force-of-circumstance family businesses did emerge in this field, even in remote areas, and the EU 'border effect' was a factor in that Greek companies were interested in investing. The villagers of Chala and Blagun represented dramatic losers in the post-socialist transition in that a tough but rewarding way of life, made possible by the subsidy system of the socialist era, was destroyed. The only alternative was subsistence farming, in the most difficult of conditions. The mayor of the only village included in the study that had the status of a commune centre impressed with his clear socialist-paternalist vision for his community. He wanted it to develop to gain the status of a town; but he also operated an informal employment policy which aimed to ensure that at least one family member retained a job. The vision of *kmetstvo* mayors, for understandable reasons, rarely extended beyond agriculture and the pressing consequences of agricultural transformation. The local political sphere was not dominated entirely by socialists. The mayor of Chala, a member of BANU-NP who had gained control of a local textiles company under privatisation, hinted at the emergence in local politics of a business elite. Despite the conventional complaint expressed by the mayor of Dragana that villagers were becoming estranged from community life, there was sufficient community cohesion and identity amongst believers for new churches to be built in Kupen and Slivka and a new mosque in Chala.

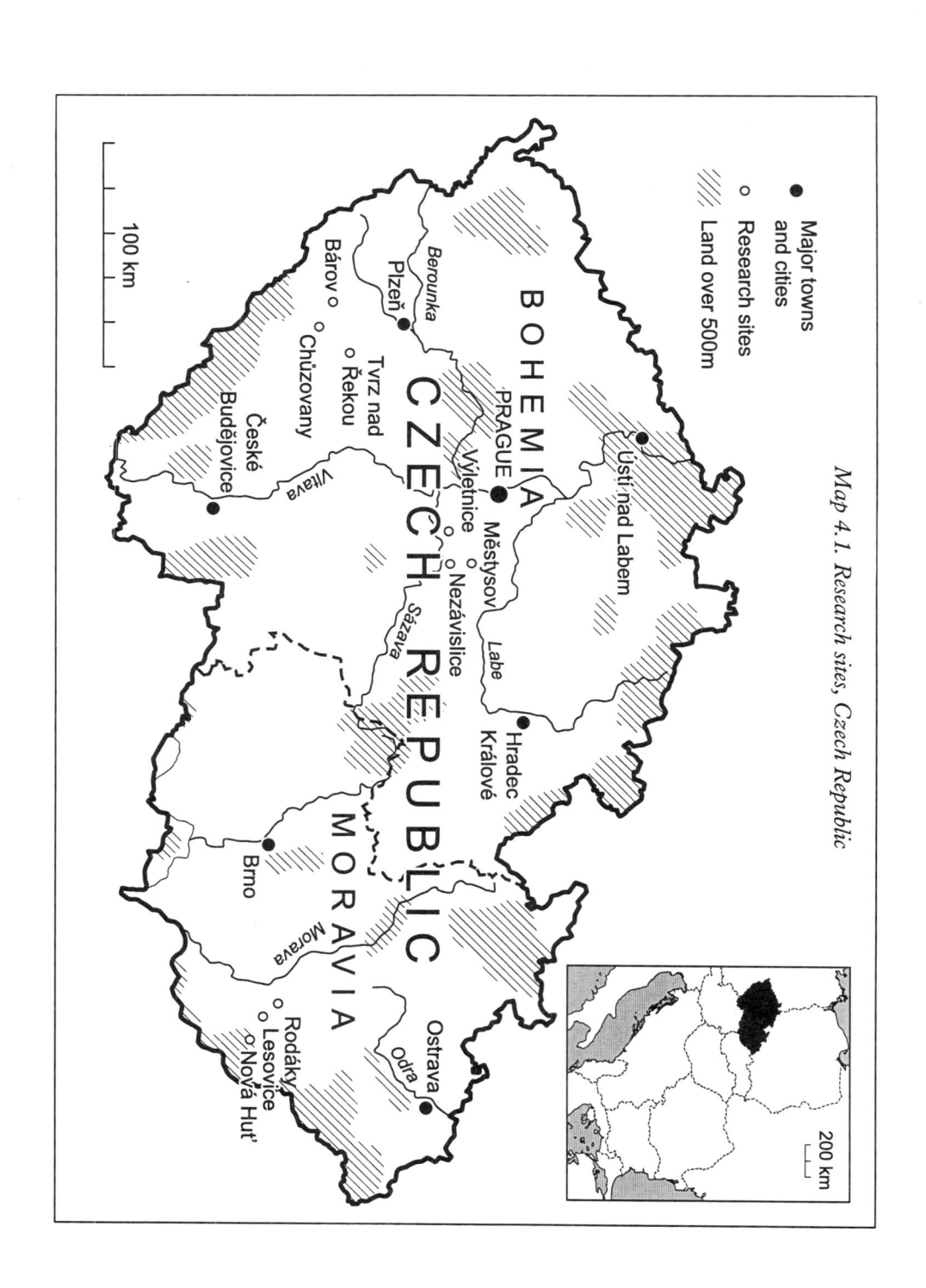

Map 4.1. Research sites, Czech Republic

CHAPTER 4

Czech Republic

As was discussed in Chapter 1, the co-operative transformation and restitution legislation of the still unified Czechoslovakia was somewhat backward-looking, when compared to Hungary at least, and financially unsophisticated. Restitution was physical and direct, rather than denominated in tradable securities, and the value of the compensation that the transformed co-operative had to pay to outside owners (who did not begin private farming) for their assets seven years after transformation was fixed at their 1992 face value. The backward-looking emphasis tended to make membership expensive for all other than those from wealthier landed backgrounds, and the seven-year cash-call placed a considerable burden on co-operative management. Nevertheless, very few in the soon-to-be Czech Republic took their assets out of co-operatives to embark on private farming, and 'transformation' for the most part was not associated with break-up and the formation of new entities, but simply with continuity under the changed conditions. The Unified Agricultural Co-operatives of socialism lost the 'Unified' element of the title and became simply Agricultural Co-operatives.[1] This general lack of enthusiasm for private farming in the

---

[1] Bezemer, 'Micro-economic institutions', 86, reports on the basis of 30 interviews carried out in southern and central Moravia in 1997 that the majority of farms retained their traditional organisation.

Czech Republic is reflected in Hudečková and Lošťák's path-breaking research from 1990,[2] although private farming was not unknown of course. Vera Majerová reports basic demographic and holding data from early in the transition process.[3]

In the non-farm sectors of the rural economy, unemployment remained relatively low thanks to the 'ersatz shock therapy' discussed in Chapter 1. Similarly, despite the attractive simplicity of the voucher approach, privatisation often proved to be a protracted affair. On the other hand, 'full, direct and specific' restitution of non-agricultural assets could lead to dramatic and unexpected changes of ownership. The new local authorities, which had increased in number (although not quite so dramatically as in Hungary), remained centralised in terms of funding, suffered from the loss of support from socialist-era institutions, and were characterised by inexperience.

AGRICULTURAL TRANSFORMATIONS—UNCONTESTED, ACRIMONIOUS AND SCANDALOUS

There were eight agricultural co-operatives in the nine villages included in our study: Bárov and Chůzovany shared the same farm. Of these, Nová Huť, the co-operative which was managed from a neighbouring village by the late socialist years, simply fell apart at the time of transformation. Some owners took their land back, sufficient to make access to the remaining co-operative fields difficult, and labour discipline deteriorated. The management, faced by constant tension between 'inside' and 'outside' owners, and persistent blame from the membership, lost heart at the prospects of trying to keep together a farm which, because of its geographical location, would always be marginal. The co-operative went into voluntary liquidation in 1993, and, during the course of 1994, it was formally wound up. Of the seven

---

[2] Hudečková and Lošťák, 'Privatization'.

[3] Věra Majerová, 'Reconstitution of private farm family households in the Czech Republic', in *Economic Behaviour of Family Households in an International Context*, ed. James Cécora (Bonn: Society for Agricultural Policy Research and Rural Sociology, 1993), 100–1.

that survived transformation, the process was uncontested in four: the transformation project proposed by management was unopposed, and post-socialist co-operative succeeded socialist co-operative seamlessly, although with some differences in the issues relating to cost of membership and the seven-year financial commitment to outside-owners.

Uncontested transformation—Rodáky, Nezávislice, Lesovice, Bárov-Chůzovany

Uncontested transformation from socialist to post-socialist co-operative is well illustrated by developments in Rodáky. Only one co-operative transformation project was submitted to the membership, the one drafted by management; and only two people voted against it, both external entitled persons. Only four co-operative members opted to take their property out of the co-operative and farm privately full time; none of them was based in Rodáky itself, and only the former co-operative member with 20 hectares in the nearby village of N approximated commercial farming. Membership in the new co-operative was rather expensive however: 10–15,000 crowns, for those who had contributed no property and little labour. About 100 members of the old co-operative could not afford the new membership fee and became co-operative employees instead. Thus the net reduction in the active labour force was around 50 per cent to approximately 220. Despite predictions in 1994 that the co-operative might break up into a number of village-based ventures, this did not happen—for mundane organisational reasons: only the centre at Rodáky had the necessary infrastructure. All the other units in other villages were product-specific and could not constitute the basis for an independent mixed farm. The management remained stable (when the chairman retired he was replaced by his economic deputy) and the farm slowly began to give greater autonomy to its divisions and restructure production: 'trimming production and the labour force', as the economist put it; employment by 1995 was a third of its 1989 level. Rather than wait the full seven years until 1999 that the legislation prescribed, the farm began settling outside owners' claims in 1995, hoping to spread it over the decade to 2005.

The co-operative which farmed in Nezávislice was based in its immediately neighbouring village, Podhrad. Although in the end this co-operative too received only one transformation proposal, the farm's economist, a native of Nezávislice who was to become its mayor, had had ambitious plans to transform it into a limited liability company and then restructure it into essentially a holding company with all the production units as subsidiaries. But he was ahead of membership sentiment. The single transformation proposal that was put to the membership entailed converting to an Agricultural Trading Co-operative in which there would be nine independent accounting units with relative autonomy from the centre. The co-operative cut its labour force and management team dramatically, mostly by axing the non-agricultural units. By 1995 it had slimmed down its workforce further to 180, partly by an increase in the use of subcontracting, but had also made substantial investments, around 22–25 million crowns in tractors, grain storage facilities and a piggery. A year later it was beginning to make inroads towards vertical integration. In its own name it had had shares since 1991 in Unikom, a joint stock company which provided services and materials for farmers. It was also a member of the Farmers' Investment Fund which had been set up by a number of former collective farms in the region, and via this it had holdings in Obila (a grain elevator company in Kutná Hora) and Cukrspol (a sugar beet factory in Kolin) with representatives on the boards of both companies. No one from Nezávislice left the co-operative to begin farming privately; indeed co-operative-wide there were only twelve such cases, and only four of them farmed on anything like a commercial scale: a partnership (which included a lecturer from the agricultural university in Prague) on 110–20 hectares, two farms run by pensioners, and one by a former state farm director.

Transformation in Lesovice was equally uneventful and based on the management's single transformation proposal. The successor co-operative had a smaller membership because the fee was expensive for those with no land in the farm. The membership fee was 20,000 crowns, and the contribution of one hectare of land was valued at 14,000 crowns, while a year's labour on the previous co-operative merited only 1,570 crowns. Thus those who had contributed as little as 1.5 hectares automatically became members, while those who had contributed only their labour had to have worked for 13 years to do so. Here too there was little interest amongst the membership in embarking on fulltime farming. Co-operative-wide only seven became farmers of any scale, while in Lesovice itself, there were only two fulltime family farmers, both elderly men who had continued to farm privately for the whole of the socialist period. Both were scarcely commercial in terms of the size of their operation (8.4 and 9 hectares of land plus four hectares of forest respectively), although the younger son of the latter had given up his veterinary studies to help his father on the farm. Nevertheless as many as 70 members registered their intention to take their land out. They generally took out only a part of it, for supplementary subsistence farming. Others insisted on taking it out just to sell it, or in the vain hope that they could speculate with the land and build a petrol station or something similar on it.

Membership of the Bárov-Chůzovany co-operative was similarly expensive. The fee was 20,000 crowns, the value of one hectare 13,803 crowns and each year worked 1716 crowns. There was also a new member fee of 60,000 crowns and, in this relatively prosperous western region, 18 people were willing to pay it. Here too, although there was only one formal transformation proposal, key figures had floated alternative ideas. A former agronomist had been elected chairman in April 1991 and in addition to cutting eleven management posts, opening all management jobs to competition, and introducing budget centres in each village, he proposed transforming the co-operative into a limited liability company. He was opposed by the co-operative economist, however, and the co-operative structure was retained. The co-operative received over 1,000 claims from persons eligible under the co-operative transformation legislation, but only 60 people requested land back, a total of only 60 hectares, the largest single claim being 8.5 hectares.

A scandalous transformation—Výletnice

By the end of the socialist years, socialist agriculture in Výletnice took the form of a unit of the state farm that was based nearby. In early 1992, Mr V, the son of the owner of one of the two former 'residual estates' (see Chapter 2) located in the village, who had had a career in co-operative agriculture and had run a fur farm with his wife and son, asked to get the farm back. He planned to farm it in conjunction with 260–330 hectares of rented land, a significant portion of the state farm's holding in the village; and the state farm was in agreement. However, after the June 1992 elections, the Czech Minister of Agriculture (always a republican rather than a federal post) Bohumil Kubát, who had entrusted the 'three Ts' to produce the radical federal co-operative transformation legislation (see Chapter 1), was replaced by Josef Lux of the Christian Democrats, a former co-operative manager.[4] Following this ministerial change, which was interpreted by many at the local level as a green light for the continuation of existing structures, the state farm changed its mind. Arguing that Mr V kept on changing his plans, it opted rather to rent the additional land that he wanted to a company called Agroco. The latter had been established in the Autumn of 1992 by four managers of the co-operative in a villager nearer Čáslav, who were well connected to the local, Kutná Hora office of the Ministry of Agriculture. With the help of many former state farm managers, they began to farm most of the land of the former state farm that operated in Výletnice in addition to part of the land of the former state farm of Čáslav. None of the villagers objected, even though an alternative option would have been to establish their own co-operative; the larger land owners in the village had a very negative view of the work discipline of the state farm workers and did not want to set up a co-operative with them. Furthermore, neither the mayor in office in 1992 nor his successor from 1994 was anxious to challenge the existing structures of the agricultural administration. The first mayor had been head of a glass-blowing unit in the nearby glass works and was not involved in agriculture; the second appeared to have no link with agriculture either. He was a local teacher and former member of the 'satellite' Czech Socialist Party, who remained the only village member of the Liberal Party National Socialist (one of its successors). But his party had formed an electoral alliance with the Farmers' Party and he had strong personal ties to the management of the state farm: it had sold him his house (built at state expense), and he, like many of them, was a member of the hunters' association. He stood at the margins of the post-socialist agricultural elite.

The owners of Agroco needed capital for a venture of this size, and went into partnership with, and became a subsidiary of, the Golden Lion company, which was owned by an individual who had many businesses, mainly in restaurants and the hospitality industry in the Kutná Hora region, and was rumoured to have good links with

---

[4] Achim Schülter, 'Institutional change in transition: Restitution, transformation and privatisation in Czech agriculture' (Paper presented at the KATO Symposium, Berlin, Germany, 2–4 November 2000), 25.

the Young Communist League. Although Mr V's retrospective judgement was that Agroco had never intended to farm the land properly ('They never cared for the crops and never harvested them'), they did appear to be serious when interviewed in 1993–94, and their reduction of the staff to one third of its previous level was a normal response to the changed economic circumstances, although they did already owe the council 9,000 crowns in unpaid taxes. But Golden Lion, either because of financial difficulties elsewhere in its businesses, or because it felt that the Agroco owners were not particularly good farmers, lost confidence in the venture. Indeed, the suspicion was expressed that its initial interest had not been in farming at all, but in the future tourist potential of the land. Whatever the reason, Golden Lion decided to cut its losses; it sold everything and ceased its operation, by then owing the council 19,000 crowns in unpaid taxes. 'By 1994 all the property had disappeared', and the owner of Golden Lion decamped to Thailand.

At this point, June 1994, Mr V was informed that if he could not take over his property and start farming, then farming in Výletnice would disappear altogether. He accepted the challenge and established a limited liability company with three partners to run the farm of 500 hectares extending over five villages, with a labour force of only 12 and 100 dairy cows, 150 beef cattle and 40 heifers. In 1995–96 the farm made no profit and was living from one day to the next, suffering from the bad reputation that Agroco had won for itself during its brief period of operation.

An acrimonious transformation—Tvrz nad Řekou

The biggest 'issue' in post-socialist transformation in Tvrz nad Řekou was the case of Mr T and his family, and it well illustrates the essentially contested nature of Czechoslovak 'full, direct and specific' restitution. Mr T was the husband of the granddaughter of one of the four kulaks who were first imprisoned in 1952–53 for failure to meet compulsory deliveries and then expelled from the village (a common fate for kulaks in socialist Czechoslovakia).[5] Neither of the young couple

---

[5] Swain, 'Eastern European Collectivisations' in Bauerkämper and Iordachi, *Collectivization of Agriculture*.

had a background in farming. The husband had worked as deputy director of a theatre in Plzeň, and his wife had been a nuclear engineer. But the husband had become director of the regional office of the Ministry of Agriculture, where he was seen as a promoter of the interests of private farmers.

The conflict was acrimonious because neither side was willing to compromise; and it became protracted because the T family did not have the necessary documentation to win their case easily. They could not prove unambiguously that all of the grandfather's land and property had been taken over by the co-operative while he was in jail. That is to say, the family claimed restitution on the basis of more land than the co-operative thought it had a right to. Additional contested issues were the valuation of the tractor and house that they received in recompense, the unwillingness of the co-operative to give them access to the one hectare of land that would have joined the two parts of their farm, and competition over the rental of land from other families who had been expropriated in the 1950s. The T family needed more land than they owned in order to farm profitably, but rental agreements were hard to organise initially because most owners had not yet received official notification of exactly where their land was located. The co-operative feared, by contrast, that it would not be able to farm profitably if it lost more land. The obduracy of both parties had negative consequences for both. Mr T was bogged down in protracted law suits (which had not been resolved in 1995), while the co-operative had no access to subsidies because one of the conditions of the then-current system of subsidies was that only farms where there were no outstanding restitution issues were eligible.

In 1993, the T family farmed 20 hectares of their own land and rented a further 10 hectares from a former member of the co-operative who had insisted on taking out his 15 hectares just so that he could rent ten of them to Mr T, to punish the co-operative in its chairman's eyes. The latter also felt that the former larger landowners preferred to rent to those of similar backgrounds rather than the co-operative. The T family aspired to 150–200 hectares at this time and had achieved 120 hectares by 1995. In addition to the tractor obtained through co-operative transformation they bought another one second hand. They concentrated on pigs, although the pig market was volatile, and invested heavily in a German-made feeding system. Their biggest problem in 1995 was their shortage of machinery and reliance on private service providers because of their refusal, except in extreme need, to do business with the co-operative. Relations with the co-operative worsened again after Mr T insisted on exercising his prior claim as a private farmer over state land, when the co-operative had already entered into a contract to farm it. The co-operative was obliged to give Mr T contiguous land in exchange, even though the original state land had not been a single parcel. This was further complicated by the fact that many owners in the co-operative refused to let their land be farmed by the T family which was becoming increasingly unpopular. They had also opened a shop in the village, but most villagers boycotted it.

CONTESTED TRANSFORMATION IN AGRICULTURE AND PROTRACTED NON-FARM PRIVATISATION—MĚSTYSOV

Post-socialist developments in Městysov pulled together a number of agricultural and non-agricultural themes: highly contested agricultural transformation, the serendipity of 'full, direct and specific' restitution, the protracted nature of the Czech Republic's privatisation processes and the positive effect of relative proximity to a border. They were all loosely connected by a brick kiln.

In 1987 the Městysov co-operative had established a unit, employing 15, to manufacture fruit drinks to complement its extensive fruit-growing operations. But it had hardly got going before the Soviet bloc market collapsed and western firms entered the domestic market. By 1991, all of the farm's 12 million crown loss was attributable to the fruit drinks business; the co-operative stood on the verge of bankruptcy as it entered transformation, even after it managed to sell off this drain on its resources. At a General Meeting held before transformation, the agronomist (who was elected mayor in 1994) suggested a plan whereby the co-operative would be broken up into three smaller co-operatives, one in each of its key component villages, so returning the farms to their size before the amalgamations of the 1970s. Many members were attracted by this idea, but the chairman opposed it and invited a lawyer to the meeting to convince the membership that it was the wrong solution. His major argument was the following: 'our experience is that the division of co-operative into smaller units is impossible in practice because of the problems associated with dividing up large barns and other buildings'. But it soon became clear that the chairman was following a self-interested agenda. With the help of the same lawyer, within a year he had set about dismantling the co-operative and transferring its assets to his own private company. He got away with this because he had previously packed with his cronies the Co-operative Board (the body that had the right to take all decisions between General Meetings). He finally left the co-operative, but not before he had convinced the inhabitants of Přídolí to put their lands—the orchards which constituted the best part of the co-operative—into his private farm. When other managers saw what was happening, they pursued similar policies. Losses were concentrated in the co-operative and profits in the private farms, while machinery moved from co-operative to private farms at knock-down prices.

As a result, the co-operative finally collapsed, without settling all the property claims against it, and in its place emerged three large-scale corporate farms, three partnerships and five commercial-scale family farms, an outcome that was closer to Hungarian than the normal Czech experience. The former co-operative chairman and four others from the co-operative's top management owned the approximately 500 hectare Orchards Přídolí Ltd. The director who followed him set up Přídolí Ltd, but only in the autumn of 1994, which gradually took over remaining parts of former cooperative. Orchards Starov Ltd had three owners, one of them a former head of the orchards within the co-operative, and it too farmed about 500 hectares of orchards and arable land. Agromeno Hřídelec, a partnership of two individuals from the cooperative management, farmed about 320 hectares of arable land and had a poultry venture. Agrounion Městysov, another two-person partnership of former co-operative managers ran a traditional mixed farm of 718 hectares, and a similar partnership of former managers farmed 560 hectares of arable land. Its head, Mr S, owner of 14 hectares, was the first person to leave the co-operative. The five family farms that emerged from this transformation were: Mr T on 300 hectares, farmed with his son; Mr C on 100 hectares; Mr V on a similar extent; Mr V on 66 hectares, supplemented by a non-agricultural job; and Mr P on 35 hectares.

Mr C, one of the bigger family farmers, was the grandson of an imprisoned and then expelled kulak who had owned a brick kiln in Dolní Bohdíkov, one of the villages where the co-operative operated and which had become part of Městysov administratively; the kiln had been nationalised after his father's arrest. Neither of his parents had lived from agriculture, and he had studied in the army academy in Brno before reclaiming the family land aged 25. His wife had no interest in becoming a farmer, and in the end they divorced. His parents, however, provided support: his father had left his job to work on the farm, and his mother changed jobs to be nearer the farm. By 1995 he worked with two permanently employed agricultural labourers and owned all the machinery that he needed: he had sold all the machines that he had received under restitution in order to buy new ones. He was quick to capitalise on the generous loans and subsidies for purchasing machinery in 1991, and in 1993 he received an interest-free loan for the purchase of a tractor. Both father and son owned new western cars, prompting gossip in the village that he was not above acting on the wrong side of the law and was involved in murky fuel dealings with the nearby Czech air force base.

The restitution of Mr C's property became enmeshed with the privatisation of Prefab, a producer of iron and concrete pre-fabricates for construction, which had employed between 150 and 200 mainly semi-skilled men and women. Also located in Dolní Bohdíkov, it had taken over the staff and facilities of the brick kiln when it closed down in the 1980s. In 1993, restitution and privatisation issues were still unresolved. By 1995, Mr C had abandoned his idea of using the brick kiln and associated buildings as a base for trading in metal and given up his restitution claim. He preferred to focus on agriculture, in particular suckling pigs which he saw as more profitable than dealing in scrap metal, although he still used the clay pit as a dump. The Dolní Bohdíkov unit of Prefab was privatised independently of its parent company and became a private company with two owners. The first was the 35-year-old PJ who had spent all his working life in Prefab, first as a technician, then as marketing director and finally, in 1992, as director. The second, with the bigger share, was the German owner of the business which was Prefab's major business partner. PJ provided the social and cultural capital necessary to run the new firm, the German partner provided the finance, but he valued local knowledge so highly that he had loaned PJ the money to buy his share. The company employed 170, 100 from either Dolní Bohdíkov or Městysov. Because of the labour shortage still manifest in the Czech Republic, this also included 35 workers from Prešov in Slovakia, where the local branch of the Prefab parent company had closed down.

The privatisation of Kolovis, which produced semi-manufactured items and finally brakes for the construction of railway carriages, was also affected by restitution issues. The process was slowed down because of a restitution claim lodged by a descendant of the original owner resident in the United States. The legal proceedings both delayed the process and discouraged potential investors. The court eventually ruled that post-war confiscation had in fact taken place legally under the provisions of the Beneš Decrees, but by 1995 privatisation had still not taken place, although there were three parties interested in the factory, one of them the factory's own economist. The future was equally unclear for the shoe producer located in the village; its fate depended on the not-yet-realised privatisation of its parent company. It had increased employment somewhat after 1991, but, by 1995, its staff had fallen to 50 again. The fate of the village's sugar refinery was also unclear. It had been privatised under voucher privatisation and the diffuse ownership that was the consequence offered no clear strategy other than somehow preserving jobs. Employment possibilities in the local area remained similarly buoyant in 1993 and 1995, the consequence of 'ersatz shock-therapy'. There were some redundancies in the engineering firms of Čáslav and Kutná Hora, but other sectors were unaffected, and the chemical company in Čáslav, although in the process of privatisation, was prospering.

The following comments, by PJ, the Czech owner of the privatised Prefab (speaking in 1995), and the mayor (speaking in 1993) respectively, well reflect the contradictory picture for new businesses:

> (PJ) There are no entrepreneurs in the true sense in Městysov... There are small businessmen and traders who maintain their businesses but do not expand them. Their goal is to have money for their family and consumption... (Mayor) Two years ago there were only two shops in the village. Now it has all the shops that it needs.

Villagers moved quickly to plug a quite extensive 'socialist personal services gap', but most of the new businesses were family affairs which preserved employment rather than creating new jobs. According to the official register in 1993, Městysov had sixty entrepreneurs (excluding shopkeepers) which included: thirteen in building and building-related trades, eleven in textile trades, six hauliers, six consultants (legal, financial, engineering, construction technology), five in knitting, a barber, a hairdresser, a beautician, a carpet cleaner, three pubs, three wood-workers, one car repairer, one household equipment repairer, one electrician, one sign-painter, and one gardener. These sixty created six jobs in catering, six in transport and two in gardening. The 17 totally new shops included three grocers, two butchers, two hardware stores, one coal merchant, and a baker, and created eight new jobs.

NON-FARM TRANSFORMATIONS—PROTRACTED AND SERENDIPITOUS

A glass works, a sawmill and the House of Culture—Nová Huť

Developments in Nová Huť, located in the mountains near the newly international border with Slovakia, also revealed contrasting stories of restitution and privatisation; and neither was characterised by speed or clarity. Nová Huť in fact only became an independent village administratively in the socialist period, having earlier been the industrial zone of its neighbouring village down the valley. The key elements in this industrial zone were the glassworks (dating back to 1861 which had employed 350–400 between the wars) and the sawmill (owned by the O family). This industrial past was associated with a focus on 'red' politics in the socialist years; no church was built in the independent village and, when it was established in February 1949, its agricultural co-operative was one of the first in the region (although it was merged into a state farm in 1956, only to be allocated to a co-operative based in its former mother village in 1977).

The privatisation of the glass-works was a protracted and politicised affair, characteristic of 'ersatz shock therapy'. In 1990 it was taken under the direct control of the company headquarters in

Northern Bohemia and a new director was appointed. But the person acknowledged locally to be best qualified for the job was passed over because of his communist past. VO was chosen instead, a former manager of the company with technical rather than business skills, the son of a glass-blower in the factory who had been forced to leave his post in 1968. The new management continued investment schemes begun in 1989, which freed up labour, transferring it elsewhere in the company rather than creating redundancies. By 1993 the factory continued to produce profitably, but was gradually reducing its labour force (from 705 in 1991 to 669). It had further divested itself of non-economic activities; its house of culture had been returned to Mr O under restitution (of which more below); it had (temporarily) wound up its sponsorship fund; and its eight company flats had been sold—to the new border police. By January 1994 the legal status of the company was of a majority state-owned (in the form of the National Property Fund) joint-stock company awaiting the sale of 42 per cent of its shares. Two years later, little had changed. There had been an attempt to sell the 42 per cent of shares using 'envelope privatisation' (whereby state administrators assessed sealed bids and chose a winner), but none of the bids had been successful, for reasons which the works director could not or would not explain. Workers and managers awaited their fate, trusting that no one would close down a factory with a 135-year-old tradition. A further three years later, privatisation issues had been settled and the works continued to operate, still a part of the same company with its headquarters in Northern Bohemia.

If the Czech Republic's 'ersatz shock therapy' could result in procrastination and the protracted privatisation of some state companies, its pursuance of 'full, direct and specific' restitution could result in serendipitous changes of ownership which put property into the hands of people with no expertise to run them. This was the case of the sawmill, which had also been an early victim of policies aimed at reducing the Czechoslovak armaments industry, which suddenly needed fewer wooden crates; the labour force was reduced to 80. In 1992, the wife of the pre-socialist owner, Mr O, restituted the mill and immediately sold it to her son. Mr O junior had no background in the business. He had been pressured to leave his job in the mill many years before because he was son of the previous owner, and had worked first in a furniture factory and then in the glass works as a quality controller. But he was conscious of his inexperience both in the industry and as a businessman, and he hired two key managers to train him in the business and take on its day-to-day running. The first of these was a director of a wood processing company in Vsetin; the second was the economist whom the glass works refused to appoint as director because of his communist past.

Mr O thus successfully resolved one of the pitfalls of full, direct and specific restitution, but he was immediately faced with another: a charge of 11 million crowns for the improvements to the company made by the state between its nationalisation in 1948 and its return to him. Because of this financial burden he reduced staff to 60, paid minimum wages and tried to reorient production towards exports. He nevertheless retained the works canteen and continued to sponsor the local fire brigade and retirement home. The mill still employed 60 people two years later and, in the mayor's view, was relatively successful, largely, in the view of the head of the tax office, because of Mr O's recognition of his limitations and readiness to work with the existing management and maximise its networks inherited from the socialist years. Financial problems clearly persisted, however, and in 1999 the local council minutes reported that it had 'again' voted to reschedule the mills debts to the council.

As noted above, in addition to the sawmill, Mr O also claimed the House of Culture under restitution. His claim was morally weak, but legally clear. The building had been owned before the war by either the Social Democratic Party or the Sokol physical education movement, older village residents no longer remembered. But during the war, as a means of preventing it falling under Nazi control when the Nazis started to confiscate buildings owned by associations of which they disapproved, it was sold to Mr O senior for a nominal fee, on the verbal understanding that it would be returned when the political situation improved. The building had not been returned after the war, and during the socialist years it had been operated by the glass works. Mr O junior now insisted on asserting his legal title to it, in the expectation that he would be able to sell it to the village for seven million crowns, because he was friendly with the first post-socialist village mayor. But he did not count on the vicissitudes of local politics.

The first post-socialist mayor was a doctor and committed Catholic. He had moved to the village from Bohemia some twenty years earlier in order to be able to attend church openly while continuing in this semi-public profession. When local party members had pressured him to stop going to church, he had replied by calling their bluff: if they wanted a local doctor, they would have to put up with him going to church. With the change of system, he became active in the Christian Democratic Party and Catholic charities for the elderly and stood for mayor, trading on his past disagreements with the party over religion. As soon as he was elected, he promoted the building of a church in this 'communist' village. But things changed radically after the 1994 elections; his successor refused to do business with Mr O. He felt that there were better ways of spending seven million crowns, and the House of Culture remained closed. Paradoxically the amateur dramatic club, of which Mr O had been an active member during the socialist years (he even won awards), now had nowhere to perform and, as the leader of the communists in the village complained, 'All cultural activity in the village has stopped'. The completion of the new church in 1996 partly substituted for the lost House of Culture by providing a venue for village functions, but Mr O's standing in the village was much reduced.

Perhaps because of what the Christian Democrats and supporters of private farming in the village saw as its 'proletarian' ethos, no significant, entirely new private sector business emerged in the village. Companies in the traditional commuting area also cut back on staff and village unemployment reached 6.4 per cent of its economically active population, a very high figure for the Czech Republic at this time. Nevertheless, a number of successful family businesses developed to fill the 'socialist personal services gap'. There were eighteen new shops, thirteen groceries, a cosmetics shop, a bookshop, a petrol station, a butcher (who also processed meat) and a photographer. Outside retailing, by 1993, the village had 52 fulltime entrepreneurs, including 11 engaged in wood processing, five self-employed builders (carpenters, brick-layers, plumber, painters etc), five hauliers, five dress-makers, five restaurants, five other services, three car repairers, three foresters, a cobbler and a hairdresser, two glass cutters, two electrical repairers, one locksmith, a baker, and a manufacturer of pasta. Two years later, the baker had closed, but the pasta business was successful. The couple had been forced into business by redundancy. The wife, a graduate of the textiles industry high school, had previously been an accountant with the council's workshop unit which was one of the first victims of the end of socialism. They used resources gained through restitution and a network of contacts partly obtained via the wife's father, who had been chairman of the local council in the socialist years, to establish a prospering business which even survived a fire in the premises.

Serendipitous restitutions and a late-socialist innovation—Lesovice

In Lesocive there was one successful and one unsuccessful restitution claim, no major privatisations, and a late-socialist innovation was sold off to new owners. The object of restitution was the sawmill which before World War II had employed up to 20 villagers and boasted international exports in the early 1940s. Its owner, the father of the mayor in the post-socialist years, had been active in the anti-Nazi resistance during the war and had been sentenced to death. Luckily, in the chaos of the end-of-war months, the sentence was not carried out and he returned to run the mill; but it was nationalised in 1948. Thereafter he spent most of his working life as head of the construction department of the agricultural co-operative. He designed and built many of its buildings and also wrote the co-operative chronicle. The sawmill itself had functioned for a time as a machinery station employing 25–28. The former owner began negotiations for the return of the mill under restitution in 1989, and by 1992 the mill had recommenced operations employing his four grandsons. It was still functioning in 1996, but the market was rather uncertain and it had taken on no new employees.

The failed restitution claim concerned a small furniture workshop in Lesovice which a Vsetin-based firm had operated until the Great Depression of the 1930s. In addition to producing directly, it had run a home production operation for the manufacture of wicker furniture and knives, rakes and scythes which were sold both nationally and internationally. It began operations again after the war and was nationalised in 1948, becoming part of the Walachian furniture co-operative based in Valašské Meziříčí and employed 15–20 producing hand-made furniture for export to West Germany. After the failure of the restitution claim, the workshop was purchased by a man in Prague whose plans initially were unclear, to the locals at least, for all negotiations took place in Valašské Meziříčí where the co-operative was based. In the end, the unit did begin operations again, under the name Atelier Fain; but it only employed ten and experienced problems from the start.

The privatisation of Lesovice's late-socialist innovation was little more successful at creating jobs. In 1986 the council had introduced an initiative to encourage part-time employment by building and leasing out 'small workshops'. Some 22 different types of service activity were set up employing 16 fulltime and 51 part-time. Between 1990 and 1992, both these 'small workshops' (which operated under council supervision) and the council's own economic activities were all privatised, closed down or otherwise disposed of. To a degree, Lesovice did not so much have to plug a 'socialist personal services gap' in the early post-socialist years as transform a socialist solution for that gap into a more market-oriented one. The council nevertheless retained ownership of key resources. These included a garage and repair workshop run by a man who had worked all of his life in the industry, the building operated by the Union for Collaboration with the Army which contained a small pub and workshop (both run down), the fire station, the school, the kindergarten and a restaurant cum grocer's shop. The latter had been received under restitution because it had been built partly with council money. (The council conveniently forgot to repay to the Ministry of Privatisation the proportion funded by the state.) By 1993, there were, in all, 69 new entrepreneurs in the village, which included: 19 businesses involved in wood processing (sawmills, furniture making), 19 builders, seven metal-workers, six pubs or restaurants, five hauliers, three providers of architectural and engineering services, three tanners, two car repairers, two dressmakers and milliners, two financial advisers, and one baker. As elsewhere, the number of jobs per new business was not so large as to have a major impact on unemployment, which stood at a high 7.3 per cent of the economically active population.

There were in addition three entirely new but rather modest businesses in the village. The first was a motel that was built on the western edge of the village in 1995. The owner, who had worked in the catering industry and had previously rented a hotel elsewhere in the region, married into the village. He bought land for his motel with the help of the council on a site which, according to the village's Development Plan, should develop some form of commercial activity. Initially this plan had envisaged a shop, but the council decided that a hotel was acceptable as the village already had plenty of shops and the hotel would give the village a place which served hot food and the plan had identified this as something the village lacked. But opposition from residents in the neighbourhood prevented the addition of a petrol station next to it, which both the mayor and the entrepreneur had seen as an attractive proposition. The owner had incurred considerable debts building the hotel, but the mayor had faith in him as a businessman, a faith that seems to have been repaid in that the business appeared to be flourishing in 1999. The second new business was a deer farm, owned by a Lesovice resident whose background was entirely in business rather than agriculture or hunting. Initially he got into conflict with his neighbours who complained to the Ministry of Agriculture about the smell, but he weathered the storm by promising to address the problem. The third was Mr C, a saddle-maker, whose business was mainly making harnesses. He had worked all of his life in the agricultural co-operative's unit in the neighbouring village to the west, but in the post-socialist world decided to work from his home in Lesovice. He worked for himself and provided occasional employment for outsiders.

INDEPENDENT BUT AT A LOSS—CONTRASTING VILLAGE DEVELOPMENT STRATEGIES

A newly independent commuter village—Nezávislice

As discussed in Chapter 1, in the Czech Republic there was a considerable increase in the number of local authorities, as councils that had been merged in the socialist years took the opportunity to demerge. Nezávislice was an extreme example of this trend in that it had never been an independent community at all. The rivalry between Nezávislice and neighbouring Podhrad was long-standing and intense, and was reflected, for example, in inhabitants of one village refusing to play football for the other. To this was added the sense that the former had been neglected by the latter during the socialist years, particularly in relation to the infrastructure. Despite the opposition of the former co-operative economist and deputy mayor (later mayor), the population of Nezávislice voted, with 83 per cent of the poll, in favour of independence from Podhrad. Because independence was totally new, its problems were slightly different from elsewhere. Rather than the norm of trying to maintain socialist services on a diminished budget, it suffered from not having facilities at all. Partly for this reason, all of its local office-holders worked part-time, to maximise the proportion of the budget that could be spent on improving the village. There was no school or health centre in the village, although there was a small library run by the ubiquitous co-operative economist in return for small honorarium.

Given the village's poor infrastructural legacy, it is not surprising that this should have figured at the heart of its development plans. The developmental priorities for 1993 were laying water pipes for all (some houses still relied on wells), building a new electrical power generator for the new part of the village which experienced temporary losses of power, re-surfacing the streets and tidying up in places where the sewer pipes had been laid. The pipe laying was fully completed by 1994, as was the electrical work by 1995, by which time negotiations were underway concerning further sewerage work (only 60 per cent of villages had mains sewerage), a water treatment plant, and the laying of gas pipes. Power cables had also been buried as part of the electrical works, so the village looked neater, and more villagers were heating using electricity, which improved the environment, despite the increased expense. Like other villages in the Czech Republic, it had a spatial plan in place which covered the period until 2020 and assumed continued population growth because of Nezávislice's good location from the point of view of transport. It envisaged, classically, three zones for the village, one for family housing, one for industry, and one for recreation. But the emphasis of the council was on a future as a dormitory village for the surrounding area and focused more on the construction of family housing on the 7–8 hectares of land that it was expected the village would own once village boundaries had finally been clarified.

Local politics in Nezávislice was an essentially non-party affair, in fact, to a considerable extent, it was a one-person affair. The mayor elected in 1990 as a representative of Civic Forum was a pensioner (over 70 years old) and part-time guard at a local sawmill, but he had cast iron anti-communist credentials in that he had been imprisoned in the Czech 'gulag' camp of Jáchymov in the 1950s. But the key figure was the deputy mayor, the economist of the Podhrad agricultural co-operative, who also had a private business as an economic consultant. Not only was he active locally, he also played a role in national politics in that he was a representative of Liberal and Social Union, which was closely linked to the Agricultural Party (see Chapter 1), in the House of Nations of the then still Czechoslovak national parliament. On the council he led a three-person block for the Movement of Farmers, the other two being an employee and pensioner of the co-operative.

The first mayor stood down at the 1994 election which the Movement of Farmers won unopposed, and the former deputy mayor and co-operative economist became mayor. Because, in the interim, he had accepted a job in Prague in the equivalent of the Audit Commission and was only in the village from Friday evenings to Monday mornings, the village had to be run on a part-time basis. Two deputy mayors were appointed, a woman who had office hours on Tuesday afternoons, and a man who had office hours on Friday afternoons. The mayor's own office hours were on Sunday mornings. Despite this inconvenience, the mayor felt that there were numerous advantages to his presence in Prague during the working week. As a (by this time) former member of the national parliament, he had built up an extensive network of contacts, and, being in Prague, he could maximise those contacts to obtain information and advice. He shared the view of many that there was no point consulting in the district offices: you had to go higher, and a job in Prague facilitated going higher.

Under the new mayor's tenure perhaps more so than that of his predecessor, policy focused on turning the village into a pleasant, neat, trim village that people would want to live in, a satellite settlement for Čáslav and Kutná Hora area. It was concern for maintaining a habitable village, rather than business development, that prompted the council's interventionist policy regarding the village shop. There was a general feeling in the village, supported by the mayor, that it needed another food shop, after the socialist-era Jednota co-operative closed down. The council agreed therefore to grant a four-year interest-free loan (using the shop itself as collateral) to a husband and wife team to buy the shop and keep the business going. Despite his caution, the mayor was persuaded that the shop was sufficient collateral for a direct investment of scarce communal funds to be safe.

A fuzzy public–private divide—Lesovice

Mid-1990s developments in Lesovice perhaps best illustrated the inexperience of some new local politicians and the fuzziness of the line between public and private interests, that is to say the extent to which they still had to learn the *mores* of a market economy and liberal polity. The mayor throughout this period was a committed Christian in the village's protestant tradition who had been elected for Civic Forum in 1990. More problematically, as noted above, he was one of the sons of the person who had restituted the sawmill. He had followed his father's second career to some extent and worked in the construction projects office of one of the local state companies. He continued to run a private business in the same field alongside his fulltime employment as mayor. To some in the village he was a self-interested man who headed a business clan involved in building-design, construction, wood processing, and forestry (even the village forester was a relative). He was even accused of stealing wood from the forest for the family sawmill. The mayor, however, saw himself rather as a self-sacrificing servant of the community with energy and drive in the face of communal torpor: none of the villagers was prepared any more to do voluntary work for the village, so, following the demise of the direct labour unit, the only way to get things done was for him to establish a company for the purpose. This was his reasoning when he used his own company to lay sewerage pipes (the grant conditions had stipulated that local labour should be used), and when the council employed his son's company to put up wooden railings in front of some houses. Family interests also played a role in a plan that he had, but did not realise, to set up a council-run company to convert sawdust into briquettes; the supplier of the sawdust would, naturally enough, be his father's sawmill.

Although the mayor stated in 1994 that the council did not have a policy of giving loans to businesses that it wanted to attract to the village, it did in fact get its fingers very badly burned by doing the nearest thing to that, namely guaranteeing a loan to an investor in the village. A man from the neighbouring village, whose mother lived in Lesovice, approached the council with the idea of setting up a business trading in food industry products. For this he needed a loan of 35 million crowns, and the bank required some form of security. The budding entrepreneur proposed to the mayor that he guarantee the loan using the village-owned grocery shop and the 90 hectares of council forest as collateral. The mayor, with the support of the council, went ahead with the deal. But the budding entrepreneur defaulted on his debt and left the council responsible for 20 million crowns and a further 6 million accruing in interest charges.

The entrepreneur ended up in gaol for tax fraud, but this did not help the village which feared that its forests would be auctioned off to recover the debt. The mayor engaged in numerous appeals to obtain the money and publicise the affair. He wrote to Václav Klaus, the head of 'his' party (the ODS), to famous émigré Czechs such as Martina Navratilova and Ivan Lendl, and even to the Soros Foundation, but (unsurprisingly) all to no avail. Finally, the threat of publicity and the suspicion that a key bank employee had not been entirely innocent in the matter was effective. The bank suspended interest payments and reduced the debt to 60 per cent of its original value, half of which the council had in cash, the remainder it initially estimated it could provide either by selling the shop or by re-channelling temporarily the government subsidy for providing gas to the village. In the event neither source was used and it was covered from the village's general budget. The solution proposed by the mayor earlier on in the protracted negotiations further reflected his fuzziness over the dividing line between public and private. His idea had been to establish a family business together with his son, to work the forest and generate income specifically to pay off the debt. The firm would rent the forest from the council and take over the debts so that they could be set against the company's tax.

A second, much bigger, potential investment in the village also faltered, partly reflecting naïve expectations of the complex game of local authority 'planning gain' in a market economy. In the autumn of 1993 the village was excited about the prospects of the construction of a medical infusions plant which would employ over 200 on a site in the village. The project seemed a near certainty. Production was to start in autumn 1994, equipment had been ordered from Italy, the company, from Zlín, had a certificate for European production. The issues under discussion were how many villagers from Lesovice might find work on the construction of the site, and later in the plant itself, for there were some concerns that the company would need skilled workers which it would not recruit locally. The mayor was inundated with queries about employment prospects, even though it had nothing to do with him. To add icing to the cake, the deal that had been struck included the company paying for the provision of a water purification plant as 'planning gain' for both Lesovice and the village further up the valley. This was all the more welcome because the State Environmental Fund, to which they had also applied, promised funds only in 1995 even if their application in 1993 were successful.

It seemed too good to be true; and so it turned out. The plant was built, although using rather less local labour than the mayor had hoped, on a site provided by the council, and the council helped with some of the infrastructure and smoothed over dealings with the Land Office, because, in the mayor's words, 'we know people there'. But then the plan was moth-balled, and with it the plans for the water-treatment plant. The mayor never received an adequate explanation, or at least not one that he was prepared to pass on to others; and, while he remained in office, he was optimistic that something would come of it in the end. Finance was clearly an element, for he blamed the banks and described the project as having simply 'run out of money'. The likelihood is that the costs of paying for the 'planning gain' were not irrelevant. When, in 1999, it became clear that there was a pre-accession development project (SAPARD) to fund water purification in the area, the word was also that there was still interest in investing in the infusion plant.

A successful business strategy and business *vs* ecology lobbies—Rodáky

Rodáky's mayor shared the Christian commitment of his counterpart in Lesovice, but he was the opposite of inexperienced. For the whole of the first post-socialist decade he combined socialist-era contacts with post-socialist ideological acceptability: he had unrivalled social capital. He was a well known Christian, and hence was unambiguously uncontaminated by the old regime, but he had served as a member of the Civil Board of the socialist council, and had been a member of the 'satellite' Czechoslovak People's Party since 1983, becoming its chairman in 1990 following its rapid transformation into an independent party and its entry into an electoral alliance with the Christian Democrats. He was also the conductor of the village's brass band. In order to attract businesses to Rodáky, not least to compensate for the jobs lost in the privatisation of the light engineering unit which a Valašské Meziříčí-based enterprise had established in the village in 1960, he developed a simple yet effective strategy for turning disadvantage into advantage. The village was equidistant from a number of commercial centres, but not conveniently close to any of them. He made a selling point of this geographical isolation, reminding potential investors that, because villagers who commuted to work had to build into their personal budgets the costs of travelling away from Rodáky (the socialist custom of subsidising commuting costs had died with socialism), businesses which located in the village could offer relatively low wages. They could discount the commuting costs to local centres and still offer their workforce a net income that would be attractive.

This low-wage incentive became part of a package which included reduced taxes, especially if new facilities were built, the lowest possible rents on premises which the council controlled, free assistance with tax returns, and as much aid as possible in winning contracts with national and local government agencies. The council was not in a position to offer business loans, nor could it offer land because the council-owned land was located mostly in the middle of fields and was rented to the agricultural co-operative. This business package was not without success. A Valašské Meziříčí-based company which made components for the car industry and employed ten was attracted, as was a branch of an Ostrava-based firm which employed 17; a further company established an expanding warehousing operation in the village. The mayor was also very aware of the value of social capital in addition to developing attractive business packages: 'All issues in which we were successful are based on informal personal contacts.' In developing this business development strategy, the mayor demonstrated rather more business acumen than the authors of the village's spatial plan, a company which identified its geographical isolation, but proposed no solution other than recreation and tourism and the possibilities offered for these by local rivers.

Rodáky had always had a strong sense of its identity and difference from surrounding villages, its remoteness, its different dialect, its separateness from surrounding Wallachia, but in 1993 this had little concrete manifestation, and the leader of the local environmentalists bemoaned the decline of community activity even since the socialist period. But gradually the mayor's endeavours to reverse this change were successful. Slowly teachers established a school amateur dramatic group and computer club, the boy scouts were recreated by people who had been members in 1968–69 when, as part of the 'Prague Spring', the boy scouts had briefly been a permitted organisation again, and a Catholic Association had been re-established. Christian Democrat influence made itself felt more by such community activities than as a force in local politics where local issues dominated for all parties. By mid-decade traditional May Day celebrations involving a large May pole (which had continued in a diluted form through the socialist years) were celebrated with renewed vigour, a parade and much Catholic symbolism. The community had been granted the status of a town by this time, a source of considerable pride for the mayor and his colleagues, which further reinforced local identity.

The village spatial plan also stipulated, with an eye to the tourist potential but also fuelled by environmental concerns, that the small petrol station and a statue dating from the 1970s should be removed from the village's central square; one was an architectural eyesore, the other a political one. The idea of removing both was uncontroversial, but the decision about where to relocate the petrol station was not. What was seen as the 'ecology interest', which held seats on the first post-socialist council and claimed good contacts in the regional centre, wanted it removed to the outskirts of down, while the 'business lobby' wanted to keep it near the centre of town, so that local shops would not suffer from a loss in trade. In the end the 'business lobby' won, and the petrol station was relocated to just beyond the central square. This 'business lobby' grew in strength after the 1998 elections when five independents, all business people, were elected to the council.

Traditional rural tourism—Výletnice

If Nezávislice had a strategy of becoming a dormitory village and Rodáky perfected a simple strategy for attracting industrial investment, Výletnice returned somewhat reluctantly to its traditional inter-war strength of tourism. The village's development strategy, on which all parties agreed, despite an apparently dramatic change in the composition of the council and an increase in the number of independents in 1994, was essentially to improve the infrastructure and develop tourism. This included converting the school's boiler from coal to gas or electricity, improving the electrical power generation situation, and improving the water treatment works, the roads, and street lighting. In the early 1990s, under the first mayor, it had helped entrepreneurs by reducing their taxes, but by 1994 it was questioning this policy since few new entrepreneurs had emerged and it looked as if those who did would have done so without the tax breaks. It had also provided small-scale material support: in 1993 it had promised to anyone starting a joiner's business that it would receive free wood from the village's 37 hectares of forest, and it reconstructed the road leading to the sawmill as a form of aid to that business.

Relations between the villagers and the week-end visitors who owned over 100 properties in the village could be tense. It was felt that they fostered businesses, run by outsiders, which did not cater for the basic needs of the village, and that the pressure that the week-end and holiday visitors placed on the village's already stretched infrastructure was unsupportable. The electrical power generator, dating from 1915, could scarcely cope. The village's solution was to increase the taxes on summer cottages by 50 per cent. Former socialist institutions, particularly the state farm, had reduced their levels of commitment to the community, but some progress had been made finding alternative sponsors, including from amongst the week-end visitors. The footballers and hunters were sponsored by entrepreneurs, including Prague-based entrepreneurs with only a cottage in the village and a self-employed lorry driver, and the Children's Day was sponsored by local businesses, as was the kindergarten. In addition to supporting the summer cinema, the council was still able to fund the local library which operated one day a week, establish a new cultural centre under the guidance of a teacher from the local grammar school, and subsidise lunches for pensioners.

Contrasts in Optimism and Envy— Bárov and Chůzovany

Bárov and Chůzovany, neighbouring villages located only a couple of kilometres apart in the Domažlice region of the Southwest, shared (since 1975) an agricultural co-operative which, as noted above, transformed itself in a formally uncontested manner into a post-socialist co-operative. The successor farm proved to be remarkably successful, in particular because it focused on non-agricultural activities, which by 1995 brought in about 50 per cent of its income. It continued to produce wooden pallets, mainly employing men, in Bárov, and initiated the manufacture of metal ones for Škoda and VW Audi in the regional centre, Domažlice, in the unit where it had previously manufactured agricultural equipment for flax harvesting. In addition, it began the production of small electrical motors for fans in Bárov for a German company, employing a mainly female labour force of fifteen. Seventeen women, mostly from an unprofitable mushroom growing unit in Chůzovany, were also employed in 1993 in a business making plaster hand-painted gnomes for export to Germany. In addition, the construction unit employed nine; there were eight lorry drivers, and fourteen mechanics in the repair workshop.

Between 1993 and late 1995 some changes took place in its non-agricultural activities. The manufacture of plaster gnomes closed with the German purchaser owing them a substantial sum; wooden pallet production stagnated because there was no market, but production of fan motors developed substantially and there were plans to increase its staff to 40. The German partner had contemplated, but rejected, setting up a green field site of its own in Bárov; its threat of going it alone persuaded the co-operative not to push for higher wages for its staff. The co-operative had also embarked on two new ventures: the assembly of fork-lift trucks, and the production of staples for the telecoms industry. In the former case, key workers in a nearby company manufacturing fork lift trucks had begun collaborating with a German company behind the backs of their management. They were sacked and moved en bloc to Bárov bringing with them first design, and then production to the co-operative. The German partner provided the engines and did the marketing, the co-operative supplied the bodywork and assembled the final product. The second new activity did not depend on Germany. The unit in Domazlice converted to the manufacture of staples for use in telephone exchanges for the Czech firm Telecom. The co-operative chairman was confident that his contracts with the German companies were secure and that the co-operative had staff with the required skills; nevertheless, he had diversified into the three major lines to avoid dependence on a single contract.

By 1995, three structural issues were emerging. First, there was a view amongst some in the Chůzovany unit that the co-operative was too interested in non-agricultural production and that it, which had no such activity, might survive better on its own. Second, the possibility of transforming the co-operative into a joint stock company had been raised again. The chairman planned to raise the issue after the next round of elections to the co-operative leadership, although he was also aware that there was a danger that if a joint stock company were created, many shares would go to Germany. The third issue related to decentralising co-operative assets. The chairman was interested in developing a more decentralised, sub-contracting approach in all sectors. It became clear, however, that none of the unit managers was interested in sub-contracting the agricultural businesses; they wanted the profitable non-agricultural ones and saw decentralisation as a prelude to privatisation. The chairman was adamant that this was not an option, and the managers left. The chairman regretted their loss, but felt that they would probably have left in any case.

This contrast between an agriculture-dependent Chůzovany unit and an industry-oriented Bárov branch within the co-operative was in some way characteristic of more general differences between the two villages. Superficially, certainly as expressed in the personalities of their respective mayors, Chůzovany was characterised by uncertainty, risk aversion and torpor tinged with envy, while Bárov, whose location was somewhat more advantageous being on a main road to Bavaria (indeed on the historic coach road from Prague to Regensburg before the railway had been built), was forward-looking, dynamic and responded in a positive manner to the changed realities of the post-socialist era. On deeper analysis, while there was certainly something of this contrast in the tone of discussions with the inhabitants of the two communities, the realities were not so stark; and both betrayed signs of the envy and beggar-my-neighbour attitudes that characterised the early post-socialist years (see Chapter 2).

Partly because of its location on a major trade route, trade and commerce had always played a greater role in Bárov than in Chůzovany which, although it was not itself an estate or industrial village was located just across the railway line from Trhovky in which there had been an agricultural estate and a large sawmill, as well as a weaving mill, a factory for the production of wooden boxes and a gravel pit.

Trhovky had been merged with Chůzovany in the 1960s, but had regained its independence after 1989. Both Bárov and Chůzovany had a tradition of commuting construction workers who worked in Bavaria during the Habsburg Monarchy and Prague under the First Republic, yet Bárov before World War II boasted 72 craftsmen or private businesses, including manufactures of traditional pottery, and six pubs, while Chůzovany recorded more commuting to industrial employment in Domazlice and the engineering industry in Plzeň. Extremely crudely put, Chůzovany had something of a proletarian tradition, while Bárov's tradition was somewhat more commercial.

These different traditions could be seen to a limited extent in non-agricultural employment and new business formation: new businesses were of a somewhat larger scale and more diversified in Bárov than in Chůzovany, although Bárov also benefited from a stroke of good fortune as far as restructuring existing businesses was concerned. In the era of early post-socialist transition, the electrical ceramics factory that had existed in this guise since 1942, but whose origins extended even further back, experienced a windfall. A change in German standards regulations offered a ready market for technologically less sophisticated products no longer manufactured in Germany. To this secure market, they added exports to Australia, the UK and Turkey, permitting them to increase their staff in 1992 almost to the level of the late socialist years. In 1993 the company had not yet been privatised; two years later, the management-buyout type solution under consideration in 1993 had been implemented, although the management remained essentially unchanged.

The restructuring of the co-operative which manufactured traditional ceramics was more protracted and painful. The Bárov unit eventually gained independence from the group of which it had been a part, attracting some managers from the Domažlice branch in the process, and it shed its unprofitable unit in a neighbouring village and its sawmill and other surplus buildings in Bárov. Despite these organisational changes, production remained much as before, although it focused its marketing more on smaller local companies than the former socialist wholesalers through which it had traditionally sold. Non-agricultural employment beyond the village enjoyed the cushioning effect of proximity to the German border and 'ersatz shock therapy'. In total, 235 of Bárov's economically active population of 579 commuted to work, the main destinations remaining Domažlice (the engineering industry for men and a shirt factory for women). Women also commuted to new textile factories which had been created locally to produce for the German market at the expense of the German textile factory in Waldmünchen on the other side of the border which had closed down. High levels of commuting in fact meant that there was a shortage of labour locally in most trades and personal services: the kindergarten, for example, could not find a cook, and the mayor claimed that there were only four unemployed people in the whole village. This scale of commuting surprisingly provided an unexpected source of income to the village's sports club, 'Spartak'. In the socialist years the council had helped it modernise and then passed it ownership of a building in one of the remote hamlets under its administration near the border that been abandoned after the expulsion of the Germans in 1945. Because of its proximity to the border, the club could generate income by renting the building out as temporary accommodation for workers who commuted daily to Germany.

The three larger new businesses in Bárov were created by Mr H, Mr M and Mr P respectively. The 59-year-old Mr H, a father of five, had worked as a lorry driver during the socialist years. In 1989 he immediately set himself up as a private haulage contractor and by 1992 not only did he have four lorries but he had expanded his activities into construction and building supplies. In 1992 he rented a building from the ceramics co-operative for storage purposes; in 1993 he reported six employees, four drivers and two bookkeepers; but by 1995 the business was employing over 35. Mr M, a Social Democratic member of the local council, took over the sawmill previously owned by the ceramics co-operative and began running it as an essentially family business together with a friend and his wife, selling mainly in Germany. He had been employed in the mill all his working life and was the obvious person to take it over. In 1993 the business employed between 10 and 15 people depending on demand; by 1995 this had stabilised at 25.

The third new business that provided new jobs of any significance was the construction company managed by Mr P, a resident of a neighbouring village and graduate of a construction industry secondary school. Mr P was the leading figure, although technically it was a limited liability company established by two men and their wives. Although the firm provided significant work opportunities locally, depending on demand (60 in 1993, 25 in 1995), it did not actually employ anyone, operating what in the UK used to be called the 'lump' and what was known locally as the 'Svarc' system the expression coming from the German word *schwarz* (black) and relating to *Schwarzarbeit* (moonlighting): all the construction workers were technically self-employed, so saving employer's social security contributions and any other labour-related tax payments. The system, was as illegal in the Czech Republic as it is in the UK, but Mr P was able to get away with it. By 1995 the company had diversified somewhat in that he had built and owned the first petrol station in the village. Its prospects were to be overshadowed by the opening of a second petrol station operated by the biggest petrol company in the country, and, as his reduced level of staffing suggests, his shady business practices were not paying off. Local businesses and certainly the local council had refused to have dealings with him.

Other new businesses offered less employment than these three, but were numerous and diverse. Outside of retailing and catering, the only other fulltime businesses in 1993 were five workshops, all essentially one-person businesses, producing traditional ceramics. In the retail sector, the former Jednota co-operative was sold under Small Privatisation for 2.3 million crowns to a limited liability company based in a nearby small town. It retained the former staff and continued both the butcher's and grocery business. The vegetable business which had operated in the former House of Recreation was not so easily privatised. The first purchaser could not pay the price he offered at auction and the sale was annulled. Eventually it was acquired by the man who bought the central hotel. A second small food shop was also established by a Mrs K who ran it by herself, while the electrical ceramics factory retained its own food shop that was open to the public, and the agricultural co-operative opened a butcher's, although it was located a long way from the centre of the village.

In addition to the food shops, there was a shoe-shop located in the House of Services and owned by a woman from a nearby town who employed one sales assistant and whose daughter ran a kiosk selling refreshments in the holiday season. In the same building there was also a hairdresser cum barber's, owned by a woman from the same town, who employed one woman. Another kiosk, selling newspapers and magazines was owned by a man from neighbouring Pomeznice who had a string of such kiosks in the area and employed two disabled people from Bárov to run it. There was also a boutique run by a 58-year-old woman who retained her job in the agricultural co-operative, a music shop (both instruments and records), an electrical goods shop, a clothes shop, and a shop which made candle-sticks and similar products from horn and antlers for, mainly German, tourists. A new souvenir shop was to have opened, but one of the partners committed suicide and the plan was abandoned.

In the hospitality sector, in 1993, the only possibility for overnight accommodation was a small bed and breakfast hotel owned by an inhabitant of Pomeznice (who had a washing machine repair business in Chůzovany) and his wife, a Czech émigré to Germany who also owned a small hotel outside the village on the road leading to the German border. The hotel in the centre of the village was under the process of restitution and reconstruction in 1993. This had been completed by 1995, and a second hotel with sports facilities had been opened by a tennis fan from Domažlice, giving the village two three-star hotels, mainly catering for foreign tourists.

In addition to these conventional businesses, Bárov's proximity to Germany attracted two new more out-of-the-ordinary businesses. Two Vietnamese street-vendors set themselves up selling cigarettes and drinks to the passing German traffic, and between three and five prostitutes began to offer their services to the transient, again mainly German, trade. The council succeeded in regulating the former somewhat by renting them space for either a kiosk or a tent for 160 crowns per day. The prostitute trade became a matter of some disagreement between the local council, which was anxious to stop it, and the state authorities which were unwilling to act. Both problems were resolved two years later. The Vietnamese street vendors had moved up to the actual border crossing with Germany, having realised that Bárov was not the best location for their business. Prostitution had disappeared from the streets, to be replaced by two 'erotic clubs', one of them owned by a German with a Czech wife who was learning Czech and was anxious to become part of the community: he contributed to the up-keep of the kindergarten.

New businesses in Chůzovany followed the norm of plugging the socialist personal services gap; but little else. One of the more significant businesses was that of the mayor's 32-year-old son. Although most villagers who worked in Germany used their high German incomes for consumption, the mayor's son used his to accumulate capital for a car body repair and spraying business. He had begun as early as 1990 under the previous council, so rumours of nepotism and a 'family mafia' which circulated were not entirely accurate. The business provided employment for two fulltime staff in 1993 and two years later this had been increased by the addition of two 15-year-old apprentices. Other private businesses were generally even more modest in conception. Mr M, an economist by training ran his own private accountancy business and a tiny wooden toy manufacturing business which he had inherited from his father. It employed two women only and supplied exclusively one German company. Another 45-year-old villager with a background working with electrical equipment made use of capital provided by his wife who had emigrated to Germany to establish a business repairing washing machines, employing one other person to help service them. A catering business (preparing sandwiches, cakes, pies and so on for local businesses) was established by a forty-year-old woman with qualifications as a cook. She did the baking and her husband gave up his job with Czech Railways to take responsibility for deliveries. They went through a difficult period when a major customer in Domažlice went bankrupt, but weathered the storm and found new customers. The village also had a seamstress (a woman of 35) and a cobbler, the latter, a 47 year old man, had trained at the Bata enterprise in Zlín but then never worked in the industry. When the political situation changed in 1990 he set himself up in business, with considerable success. A pensioner set up a small-scale transport business, but immediately antagonised council and neighbours alike. He operated without the appropriate licence and blocked the street by parking his lorry in front of his house. Between 1993 and 1995, two small-scale joinery businesses were started, both finding plenty of work in the local community and in Germany. The first, run by the son of a carpenter who had previously worked in the Trhovky mill, started in his garage but he then built a workshop in his garden and took on two employees. The council had offered him a lot away from inhabited areas, but there was no technical infrastructure there, so it agreed to the business being run from his home after receiving assurances that the neighbours did not object. The other worked from his home and employed only the services of a relative who was in receipt of a disability pension. Although the official statistics recorded a high number of self-employed bricklayers, these were nearly all de facto employees of Mr P's business in Bárov.

Chůzovany's mayor felt that the village could support six food shops, but not that many materialised. The two socialist Jednota co-operatives continued into the 1990s, providing employment for five, but there were rumours of imminent closure by 1995. In addition, there was a private food shop run by a 35-year-old woman from a room in her house who employed a single sales assistant. A former shop assistant in Domažlice, a 28-year-old man, opened a shop selling drinks in his parents' house with the help of his mother. For a time he had had plans to expand the business with a former bricklayer but he then abandoned them. The bricklayer nevertheless went ahead alone and by 1995 had bought the building formerly occupied by the Czech Savings Bank (and before that by the Raiffeisen Bank), and converted it into a grocery. In addition to this, the wife of the cobbler, who had previously worked in a shop in Bárov, opened a clothes shop in the council building. The village also boasted one private pub, the 'upper pub', rented by a 40-year-old outsider to the village who was assisted by her husband. By 1995 it was losing business to the other pub, owned by the agricultural co-operative and located in the House of Culture, also rented to a non-villager.

The combination Czech 'ersatz shock therapy' and the proximity of Germany meant that employment levels in Chůzovany in the early transition period remained buoyant. The workforce of the Trhovky saw-mill, the biggest local employer, remained stable (in 1993 it was still employing 120 people, 40 of them from Chůzovany). Two years later the business was fifty per cent owned by Germans and producing on a scale much as in the past, with similar employment levels. In fact the labour market was so tight that it had to employ a gang of Ukrainians, some very highly educated. But a new production line which required the use of high levels of formaldehyde suggested that laxer environmental standards in the Czech Republic complemented cheap labour in making the country an attractive investment location. Commuting to the engineering industry in Domazlice continued, but some had been put on enforced holiday leave and there was an expectation that the first redundancies would follow soon. The number of women who commuted to the textile factory in nearby Kdyne had fallen to five, but most had found alternative employment in the same industry in villages closer to home.

In the accounts of village developments in Chůzovany, notions of 'greed' and 'envy' abound, and Mr K, a former agronomist in the agricultural co-operative and member of the Chůzovany local council was perhaps a victim of both. His business ambitions were broadly based—manufacturing boilers, construction, building design (carried out by his wife) and even shoe manufacture—although he and his partner from Trhovky only employed two people in 1993. His first attempt to find a location for the business failed because of what seemed to the mayor and others to be the short-term greed of the villagers. A German businessman had approached the mayor with the idea of buying some village land on which to build houses and some commercial premises, thereby providing new jobs for the village. It was understood that Mr K would occupy one of these. The scheme failed however because, in the mayor's estimation, the villagers insisted on an unrealistically high price for the land and were envious of the proposed council financial assistance to an outsider. Meanwhile the German entrepreneur had second thoughts when he realised just how much infrastructural work would be necessary to make the project viable. Mr K's next idea was to buy the former agricultural estate in Trhovky as a base for his new proposed businesses. But this too proved a rather protracted affair. The agricultural co-operative, with which Mr K was not on good terms after his decision to go into business, claimed the 'castle' as its own. It took a court case to establish that the co-operative had only ever rented the estate; its owner had always been the state.

The mayor of Chůzovany was a former lorry driver who had married into the village and worked for the local forestry company for 34 years. He had originally stood for Civic Forum but joined none of its successor parties, preferring to be seen as an independent. He was very conscious of the link between infrastructure and business, and this framed his attitude to village development. He wanted the village to develop crafts, services, even light industry; but the infrastructure was inadequate and, in his view at least, entrepreneurs could not be expected to invest in it themselves. The infrastructure had been a central issue in the failed German investment. Yet, in his view, revenue from its share of income tax and the property tax barely covered the village's basic expenses and provided nothing for further development;

the council was reluctant to raise too much from entrepreneurs, since, in the mayor's words, the tax 'can be expensive for newly created businesses'. The council's only other source of significant income came from renting out rooms in the council building.

Whether the mayor was correct to use words such as 'envy' and 'greed' to describe his villagers in the early-to-mid-1990s, the village did appear to have been characterised by high levels of 'risk aversion' and cynicism. In the mayor's view, in 1993, there was not a single person with plans to set up a new business, hence his reliance on an outside (German) investor. When he did try to bring local entrepreneurs together in a village association, the initiative failed; they were not interested in co-operating. Furthermore, when the council improved roads or the phone network in a particular area, the uniform assumption was that this was thanks to a bribe. Faced with this rather negative climate, which was as strong in 1995 as it was in 1993, the mayor was dispirited and shared the village's low ambitions and aspirations. He hoped that the German might return and renegotiate a deal; and he complained about the poor and worsening level of service, for both councillors and entrepreneurs, provided by the district authorities; but he did nothing about it.

Bárov, by contrast, had big plans for economic development. The slightly more picturesque upper village, together with outlying hamlets, were to be preserved for tourism, while the lower village, in the region of the railway line, was to benefit from the creation of a business park. This ambitious idea came from a professor at the Prague School of Economics whom the mayor had commissioned to develop a village development plan as an addendum to its conventional spatial plan. Two such parks already existed in the region, and Bárov, on a main Czech–Bavarian communications axis, seemed to be well located to benefit from German companies anxious to make use of cheap Czech labour. The project failed to develop in quite the grand way that the plan envisaged, however. This was partly because there was still some lack of clarity concerning who had title to certain parcels of land, but also because of a similar 'greed' to that manifest in Chůzovany. The council did not have enough land of its own for such a venture, but villagers would only sell for inflated, 'German' prices. A German company which manufactured pre-fabricated houses had expressed an interest in locating in the village, but had not yet committed itself.

Bárov's mayor, a member of Social Democratic Party, was, like his counterpart in Chůzovany, an outsider who had essentially married into the village; but he came from a professional background. He had been born in Plžen, but decided with his wife to move to Bárov from Plžen in the late socialist years to escape urban pollution. Although his original profession had been in the building industry, his final job before taking up his post was in the investment department of a state farm in Domažlice. He was very aware of how few resources were available to a local council for business development, and was keen to support it, despite ruefully acknowledging that businesses contributed relatively little in return because they always sought to minimise their tax liabilities. In 1993 he had tried to persuade the local entrepreneurs to form an association, but, as in Chůzovany, it had come to nothing: there was no interest in co-operation, despite there being a strong sense of regional identity reflected in the local dialect, its pottery designs and musical instruments. But his pro-business strategy did not extend to giving loans or guaranteeing loans to potential investors in the village: 'that would be like putting your head in a noose'. Nor did it permit even minor corruption. When the contract for the building work for the home for the elderly was out to tender, the councillor responsible, a member of the ODS, opted for the bid from a company over 150 kilometres away which happened to be owned by his brother. The rest of the council opposed such manifest nepotism, and despite the councillor concerned mobilising a campaign against the council in the ODS-controlled media, the contract eventually went to a local firm.

The mayor was also aware that a village like Bárov could not rely on agriculture, and in this he concurred with the strategy of the agricultural co-operative. He saw collectivisation as the only 'Bolshevik' success in that it had created big farms employing relatively few people. He was also conscious that Czech villages and communes were too small to be effective, citing German evidence that a population of 2,500 was the minimum possible size for an effective local authority. With this in mind, he was an enthusiastic supporter of the Chodska League, which had begun as an informal link between some of the fulltime mayors in the region but had subsequently developed into a formal organisation covering 17 villages by 1995. In his view, associations of this type could even compete with Domažlice for resources.

There were then real differences of tone between 'risk-averse', proletarian Chůzovany and neighbouring entrepreneurial, commercial Bárov; but the reality of developments in Bárov did not quite match the mayor's grand ambitions.

CZECH SPECIFICITIES IN SUMMARY

In the agricultural transformation of the Czech Republic, despite the bias towards former landowners in the regulations, the clear winners were 'green barons': the heads of the re-branded co-operatives, and the former co-operative managers who created the post-socialist successor companies such as those in Městysov. A new and not so different (except for employment levels) model of agriculture was built on the achievements of the socialist era. In the non-agricultural rural economy, no entirely new, big businesses emerged; most were small-scale and plugged the 'socialist personal services gap' as reflected in Nová Huť, Městysov, Lesovice, Bárov and Chůzovany. Privatisation of larger state assets was protracted, while there was an element of serendipity in those who benefited from 'full, direct and specific' restitution of the many more numerous smaller village industries that had existed in Bohemia and Moravia in the pre-socialist years. The physicality of Czech restitution and co-operative restructuring procedures tended to rekindle old wounds—ambiguous attitudes towards the heirs of kulaks in Tvrz nad Řekou, Catholics against 'reds' in Nová Huť.

Thanks to 'ersatz shock therapy', rural unemployment was not high, despite dramatic job losses in agriculture. As might be expected in the highly ordered and in many respects 'bourgeois' society that was the Czech Republic of the 1990s, driving figures in the countryside came from the public sector. The contrast in the way that individual mayors played the cards that history had dealt them was perhaps most apparent in the neighbouring villages of Bárov and Chůzovany. The mayor of 'optimistic' Bárov had been dealt a slightly better hand in that Bárov's location on a trade route was somewhat advantageous, but his personal drive, supported amply by human, social and cultural capital advantage, provided a positive vision for his community (not entirely realised) that contrasted dramatically with his counterpart in 'envious' Chůzovany who was daunted and impotent in the face of the challenge. The mayors of Nezávislice and Rodáky also had clear, but very different visions of their communities (the former as a dormitory village, the latter as a locus of small-scale industry), and both had human, social and cultural capital resources from the past. The latter also had impeccable political capital. As a member of the 'satellite', Czechoslovak People's Party during the socialist years, he had been near to the centre of local power, yet, as a well-known Christian, he also had excellent opposition credentials. Under his rule the 'business lobby' slowly took over the council. By contrast, the behaviour of the mayor of Lesovice demonstrated, in both his fuzziness concerning private and public interests and his naivety regarding a swindler, that he had yet to learn the *mores* associated with a market economy and liberal polity.

Map 5.1. Research sites, Hungary

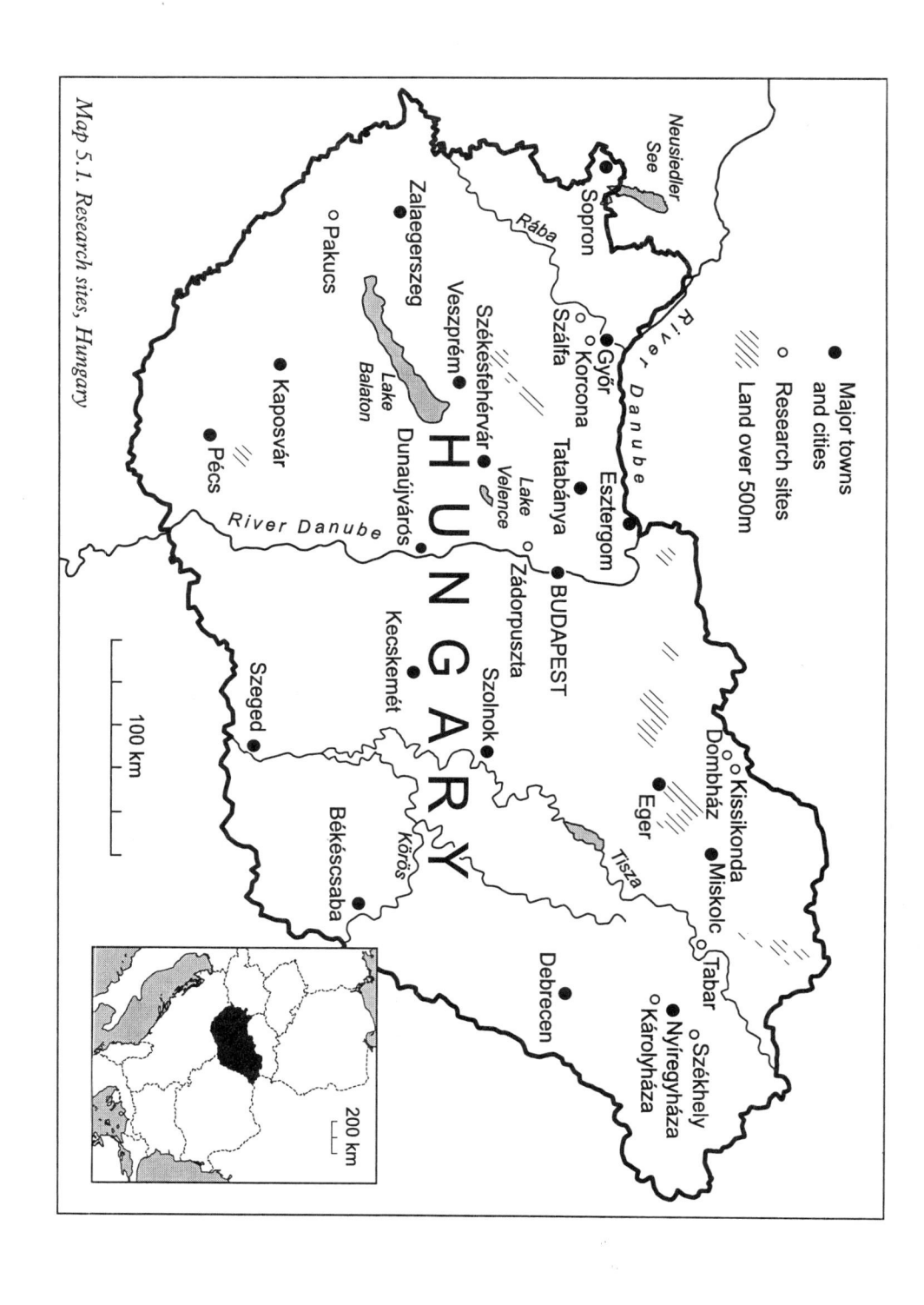

CHAPTER 5

Hungary

As discussed in Chapter 2, despite being considered a 'gradualist' by many commentators, Hungary was committed to rather radical economic reforms in the immediate post-socialist years. In particular it was the only country in the region to pass tough bankruptcy legislation in the first years of the first post-socialist decade, legislation which took effect in 1992, the same year as the co-operative restructuring legislation. Furthermore, the government was not prepared to forgive socialist-era co-operative debts. As a consequence, the transformation of many co-operatives took place in the context of bankruptcy, and canny managers manipulated co-operative transformation and bankruptcy legislation to their advantage. Hungary's reformist policies of the late socialist decades also offered an alternative path to commercial private farming in that some of those who had created flourishing private 'second economy' ventures during this era could build on their success. The combination of 'second economy' and 'first economy' paths to commercial success was also visible in the non-farm economy, although in many instances this concerned the non-agricultural subsidiary enterprises of agricultural co-operatives. In the sphere of local government too, as discussed in Chapter 1, Hungary had been in the vanguard of reform. A vast array of new local authorities were established as socialist era bodies were demerged; and these authorities had some, albeit quite limited, genuine autonomy. Furthermore, in a number of local authorities by 1996, local entrepreneurs were beginning to take a dominant role.[1]

AGRICULTURAL TRANSFORMATION—BANKRUPTCY, SUBTERFUGE AND PATHS TO PRIVATE FARMING

Contrived bankruptcy—Korcona

Korcona, a Catholic village in Western Hungary in the vicinity of Győr, had succeeded against the national trend in retaining and even increasing its population after World War II, and it retained its administrative independence throughout the socialist years. Furthermore, apart from a brief period in the mid-1970s, the agricultural co-operative unusually remained a single-village entity for most of the socialist era. By 1990, it had 162 active members, 40 employees, and members' household plot production was well integrated into co-operative activities: some 400–500 hectares of co-operative land (roughly a quarter of the total) was set aside for members to grow cucumbers, cabbage and tomatoes which they then sold via the co-operative. The agricultural transformation in Korcona resulted in the disappearance of the co-operative and its replacement by a corporate entity which farmed the bulk of the co-operative's land, and a private farm, owned by the former co-operative chairman, which farmed a significant part of the rest. In addition, a number of private farmers with sizeable holdings emerged from the 'second economy'.

An important part of the background to the events in Korcona was the strong suggestion that the co-operative management had been operating on the borders of legality for a number of years. The key figure in this was KGy who had been in charge of the farm's commercial and trading operations.[2] KGy started work on the Korcona co-operative in 1969, and from 1978 until the co-operative's demise

---

[1] Early reports on some of our findings are given in Andor and Kuczi, 'What happened'; and Swain, Andor and Kuczi, 'The privatization'.

[2] The cases of KGy in Korcona, RA in Károlyháza and KB in Kissikonda are also considered in Nigel Swain, 'Social capital and its uses', *Archives Européennes de Sociologie* 44, no. 2 (August 2003): 185–212.

he headed the joint horticultural and commercial department which was responsible for all co-operative sales and purchases from sub-contracting producers. The co-operative chairman, SGy, also joined the Korcona co-operative in 1969, and by 1972 was deputy chairman. He opposed the merger of the mid-1970s and left to work for the cereals trading company, but was invited back to take over the newly independent farm in 1978. He and KGy appear to have used their positions of power to engage in activities normally labelled 'shrinkage'. With an extensive network of trading contacts and a high volume of trade, it was very easy for the odd pig or the odd load of vegetables to disappear. KGy, as the commercial manager, was the key figure in this, but the co-operation of the chairman was necessary for it to work successfully; and they also brought in the party secretary, who did not profit directly, but received an essentially sinecure job in return for turning a blind eye.

The course of politics in 1989–92 convinced SGy and KGy that they no longer needed each other or the co-operative. SGy decided to establish his own private farm and simply resigned in April 1992 without serving any notice or claiming severance pay. KGy, with fewer resources of his own, opted for creating a corporate farm out of the transformed co-operative. It was decided that co-operative transformation should take place in the context of bankruptcy, even though its debts were rather small (around 20 million forints). In the view of a receiver involved in another bankruptcy proceeding, this was a trivial sum: bankruptcy could only be used in such a case, 'if that is what the management wanted'. The receiver in Korcona shared this view. Although management always stressed the size of the debt, and it certainly was failure to come to an agreement with its creditors that triggered the co-operative's declaration of bankruptcy, subsequent developments suggested that bankruptcy was orchestrated.

The advantage of declaring bankruptcy was that the co-operative transformation process and its attendant 'naming' of co-operative property could be circumvented. Assets could be sold to meet debts at auctions which were not as tightly controlled as those organised under the co-operative restructuring legislation; and participation could be restricted to active members rather than all 'entitled persons'. When a transformation auction could not be avoided, the management resorted to manipulation. Members were circulated with a paper indicating the equipment on offer and inviting them to state what equipment they were interested in. If more than one person wanted the same thing, they were called into the co-operative office to 'bid' for it in private negotiations. The outcome of these private bids was that SGy paid 200,000 forints for his combine, while an equivalent machine was sold to another member for 1.4 million forints.

The disadvantage of bankruptcy auctions was that payment had to be made predominantly in cash rather than co-operative shares, because the value of co-operative shares would not be established until the bankruptcy proceedings had been completed. But, especially in the light of the cheap prices paid, this was not a great problem for SGy (who had cash) and KGy (who, as we shall see, did not need it). The bulk of the co-operative's assets were sold at the bankruptcy auction, and most of them were bought by the company that KGy was in the process of establishing, and much of it not in return for cash but in the form of a restructured debt. KGy's company took over co-operative debts, but only the cheap loans to the Co-operative Support Fund, not the expensive debts to the bank.

KGy's company, KZZ Ltd, was set up with KM, the former cropping manager of the farm, and an outsider who supplied capital only. Each partner invested 500,000 forints into the business; and, mainly thanks to KGy's personal contacts, they succeeded in gaining access to the government's Reorganisation Credit. They paid off 50 per cent of the debt that they had taken over from the co-operative and then swapped the balance for cheaper Reorganisation Credit. They then took out a further 1 million forint Reorganisation Credit loan (making a total of around 5 million forints) to buy new equipment in addition to the machinery, buildings and petrol pump that they had already acquired from the co-operative. KGy owned only 16 hectares of land himself and KM only 6 hectares, but the farm began renting roughly 700 hectares of the land formerly farmed by the co-operative. Like the co-operative before it, the company, which employed only 12, was involved in both commerce and farming; and KGy brought with him his network of customers (from wholesale markets to frozen food companies) and suppliers (mainly vegetables and berried fruits). By 1996, they continued to farm on much the same scale, had repaid the Reorganisation Credit, and were gradually replacing their equipment stock.

After he abandoned the co-operative, SGy had a private part-time 'second economy' business to fall back on. He had started growing vegetables in polythene greenhouses as early as 1972 because he was building a house and needed extra money, and he had continued the business throughout his period as chairman. With the help of his own restitution vouchers, his own 'proportionate share land' (see Chapter 1) and 'proportionate share land' purchased from 15 other people, he acquired some 70 hectares of his own, 22 hectares of it near to his house. He also obtained, as we have seen, machinery from the co-operative and one of the co-operative buildings, which he first used to keep equipment in, but then converted into a pickling plant producing both barrels and jars of pickles, a business that was functioning successfully by 1996. By 1996 he had also expanded his specialist vegetable growing to five hectares, although it remained a family farm.

A more conventional 'second economy' path to more modest private farming was that of NFJ. NFJ, the son of a village school teacher, accepted the offer of the post as secretary to the council in Korcona because accommodation was provided and he wanted to get married. (He later built a house with a cheap loan available to council members.) He continued with the job until 1974, when he went to work for the same retail co-operative for which SGy, a friend since childhood, had worked briefly before becoming co-operative chairman. Once chairman, SGy invited NFJ to be transport manager in the co-operative, a post he filled until 1988, when, he was forced to resign after attempting to expose the suspected underhand dealings of SGy and KGy.

At this point NFJ decided to start farming privately and secured a loan from the state Meat Industry Enterprise to build a unit for 150 pigs. These gave him a reasonable income, but he supplemented it with some polythene green houses, 90 per cent devoted to vegetables, 10 per cent to cut flowers. In 1993, NFJ had acquired some 13 hectares of land only through restitution, including some using vouchers bought from his brother at face value in order to avoid family difficulties. But he let KZZ cultivate it because he had no machinery: he had not been able use his property share to buy machinery from the co-operative because the bankruptcy auction had been for 'active owners' only, and he had ceased to be an active member in 1988.

'Second economy' to private farming—Szálfa

In nearby Szálfa, whose co-operative history will be considered more fully below, there were further examples of 'second economy' paths to private farming success. LO was from 1975 onwards head of the Szálfa co-operative's pig unit. But he always had a subsidiary income. By the 1990s he was raising annually six cycles each of 11,000 chickens and 3,000 turkeys. LO was one of the few people to ask to take his land out of the co-operative, a move which precipitated his sacking in October 1993. Using his own restitution vouchers and others bought from neighbours, he acquired some 25 hectares at the village land auctions (three in all). In addition to that, he used his right to 'proportionate share land' (and bought a neighbour's mother's rights to 'proportionate share land') to acquire a small outlying farm building (*tanya*) and its surrounding land, making a total of 38 hectares; in addition to which he rented a further 15 hectares. By 1996 he was operating on 58 hectares, 44 hectares of which were owned, but the chicken business was barely profitable and he saw his future in terms of developing the arable farm.

VL followed a different path. He had worked as a tractor driver and then as a maintenance man in the pig unit. His wife also worked on the co-operative as a bookkeeper. As early as 1991 he had acquired some pieces of agricultural machinery and started a subsidiary business in farming services, and in 1992 he developed the business further by acquiring new and bigger machinery. He even travelled to Austria to buy a second hand baler. In tandem with this he fattened as many as 100 pigs a year. In 1992, both husband and wife left the co-operative. VL immediately concentrated on the business, while his wife made use of a period in receipt of unemployment benefit to study as an accountant and tax advisor. They gave up the pigs in 1993, partly because, once they had left the co-operative, they no longer benefited from feed cereals at cost price. The co-operative withheld 25 per cent of the 900,000 forints worth of property shares that they had claimed, and they lost their case when they took it to court. VL had to content himself with the reduced value, with which he obtained a trailer, a combine and four smaller pieces of machinery. They obtained 13 hectares of 'proportionate share land', both their own and some that they bought, and rented a further 14 hectares. Vegetables (tomatoes, cucumber and paprika) were grown on 2.6 hectares immediately surrounding the house, the remainder of the land grew cereals (sold on contract to the main national wheat purchaser) and alfalfa (sold to a private purchaser who also cut it for him). His agricultural services business provided a solid income, but most of it was outside the village, as were the clients of his wife's accountancy business. Their ambition remained to rent around 70 hectares and live from farming.

Voluntary liquidation and two successful successors—Pakucs

Pakucs, in southwest Hungary not far from the Slovenian border, was a village with a strong craft tradition and history as an administrative centre, with a relatively small percentage of its population working in agriculture, the bulk of them small peasants. Its administrative importance was reflected in the fact that, until 1990, it was responsible for itself and three other villages. In the 1970s the co-operative became part of a larger one which united a total of eight villages, and whose centre was in a village two and a half miles away. At the end of the 1980s the co-operative farmed a total of 3,900 hectares and employed 70 fulltime members with 230 pensioner members; it had converted its sewing workshop into a joint venture with its main German customer with the legal status of a limited liability company, and it ran an upholstery unit which employed seven; and a unit based in Budapest engaged in tool-making and plastic die casting.

Co-operative transformation in Pakucs took place in the context of a voluntary liquidation in the face of bankruptcy. It was replaced by a number of successor companies and two large-scale private farmers. The background to the transformation was the poor management of the co-operative following a change of chairman in 1990. During his 18 month reign, a manageable 30 million forint debt was doubled to an unmanageable one of 60 million forints, as he sold to its management the Budapest-based ancillary enterprise, closed down the construction unit and wound up the German joint venture. In September 1992 he was replaced by SzI who had become Chief Accountant in early 1992 after serving for many years as Chief Agronomist.[3]

---

[3] Hann, 'Not the Horse', 60 describes to hiving off and privatisation of the Tázlár co-operative's plastics factory.

SzI determined that the debts incurred by his predecessor were unmanageable and the only way to avoid bankruptcy and preserve the employment for the majority of the members was to put the co-operative into voluntary liquidation and set up a number of new successor companies with the help of the government's generous Reorganisation Credit (which took over 70 per cent of the debt). The value of the co-operative's assets more or less covered its liabilities, and the new units would benefit from cheap credit. Four successor units were established: Csagro a cereals and forestry farm, Csetej a dairy farm, Csesza a book-keeping and office services company, and Cseta the co-operative's former upholstery workshop. By establishing the successor organisations first and either putting co-operative property into them or renting them assets, the units had the right of first refusal to buy the assets from the co-operative; there was no need to hold a formal auction. The successor units together employed 52 of the 70 active co-operative members at the time of transformation.

The latter two successor companies were not successful. Csesza, made up of six of the co-operative's clerical workers, had no clear market. The members fell out with one another, and the unit soon closed. Cseta could not find its feet independently either and ended up relying wholly on subcontracting to a local furniture company which provided employment for only four of the ten who had worked there when the partnership was established. Csagro, by contrast, prospered. Initially TR, the co-operative plant protection officer, and BA, the co-operative's former forestry section head, were full partners (with full liability); there were thirteen other partners and seven simple employees. TR was in his late twenties at the time of transformation, had had disagreements with the local party bosses in his youth, and had joined Fidesz (the Young Democrats) in 1990, standing for them unsuccessfully in the local elections. He had already started working a side business in 1990 when he rented three hectares of co-operative land. In 1991 this had increased to 21 hectares, and by 1992 he was renting 100 hectares. His interest was clearly in creating a business that was not only a successor to the co-operative, but one that would complement his existing private venture. SzI, the chairman, was not happy with this idea, because he too had designs on the cereals part of the co-operative. In the end he agreed, but only on condition that Csagro also take over the forestry section; hence the inclusion of the forestry chief as a full partner. This proved to be something of a blessing in disguise, however. It gave the partnership the possibility to swap labour between the branches at slack periods, and forestry provided an income in the spring when crop farming had none. Csagro farmed 1,000 hectares of land and 400 hectares of forest from the majority of the 1,300 individuals who ended up as owners of the land formerly farmed by the co-operative. TR himself was immediately active in the land market, although most purchases were so-called 'pocket contracts' whereby the land was paid for, but formal transfer of title would only take place in three years time (oppressive tax penalties effectively made sale of land impossible within three years of receiving it under restitution). He already 'owned' around 100 hectares in 1993 and by 1994 his personal holding was up to almost 400 hectares.

A process of concentration also took place in relation to the ownership of the partnership. Roughly a year after its foundation, it proved necessary to increase Csagro's capital to increase its borrowing potential so that it could buy former co-operative buildings. All members were asked to contribute a minimum of 10,000 forints, but some were not in a position to do so and had to leave. Although at the time TR regretted that few people put additional money into the venture, he later recognised that it was easier to operate with two partners rather than five or six. The business was still operating with a total staff of 22 at this time, but TR recognised that it only really needed six or seven full time. By 1994 staffing levels were down to ten and the full partners owned 88 per cent of the business. Two years later the size of the business was effectively the same, but there were only eight employees and TR complained that labour discipline had got worse.

Csetej rented 400 hectares of arable land and 800 hectares of pasture from former co-operative members and other eligible persons. This meant that not only could it grow its own fodder but it could subsidise the livestock with more profitable cereals farming. The company was headed by SF, the manager of the former dairy unit who owned 80 per cent of the business. It owned 150 cows, four buildings (cow sheds and a workshop), seven tractors, a combine, and, in 1993, was 17 million forints in debt. SF maintained all the 17 staff from the co-operative. It had been part of the original plan that the dairy farm should have access to land that was conveniently near to the farm itself. But in 1994, SF (who had 10 hectares of his own) acknowledged that there was an intense struggle to maintain their land rental contracts, and that this took up as much as 50 per cent of his time. Staff levels remained constant into 1996. One employee left, but he was replaced a man who had been made redundant by Csagro.

The big problem that emerged in 1994, which affected the whole of the village but especially Csetej, was the emergence of an Austrian player on the land market. In the months before the 1994 Land Act which prohibited the purchase of land by corporate entities, a private company which acted as a front for the Austrian was aggressively buying land at premium prices, including a crucial 200 hectares which Csetej had rented for pasture. The then head of the village land distribution committee was believed to be deeply implicated in these manoeuvres, and the farming interests in the village mobilised to have him replaced by TR.

In addition to the two major co-operative successor companies, both of which were essentially one-man businesses, two private commercial farmers also emerged from co-operative transformation. The largest of these was SzI, the co-operative chairman. SzI had no involvement with any of the successor companies, but his family had been active in small-scale agriculture during the socialist years using his wife's name (who had worked as an unqualified nursery nurse but had lost her job by the time of co-operative transformation). SzI carefully stuck to the legal niceties of keeping his wife's business and his own job separate, and through 1994 dutifully acted as one of the two employees of the residual co-operative finding purchasers for the hard-to-sell co-operative assets such as the office building, some service accommodation and some of the animal sheds. Meanwhile his wife bought, with the help of Reorganisation Credit, the animal sheds conveniently located in the centre of the village which she had rented from the co-operative to keep the turkeys in during the socialist years; he set about acquiring land. By 1994 he had 120 hectares of his own and rented a further 200 hectares, and he had bought two tractors and most of the other equipment that he needed. The business (his wife's) was run with the help of two employees and his son who used to be a fitter in the oil industry. It benefited considerably from the contacts that he had established during his chief agronomist years with such bodies as the main grain purchasing company. By 1996, the co-operative had been sold off and closed down, and SzI was officially registered as an agricultural entrepreneur. He planned to build a house next to the farm buildings in the centre of the village; he owned 200 hectares and rented 100 hectares, and he had plans to build a slaughterhouse for the turkeys in order to move up the food chain and benefit from higher prices. This success was reflected in his ownership of a Japanese sports utility vehicle.

Bankruptcy and subterfuge—Tabar

The socialist agricultural co-operative based in Tabar, a predominantly Protestant (Reform Church) village located on the borders of Hungary's north-central industrial area, a longish commute from Miskolc and close to the wine centre of Tokaj, covered two others and concentrated on livestock but also arable, maize, sugar beet and vines. Their household plots were always more important to villagers than communal work, because most cultivated a vineyard from which they could gain a sizeable income. As in Korcona and Pakucs, co-operative transformation took place in the context of bankruptcy, but it was spiced here as in Korcona with an element of subterfuge. The process began in 1989 when, in the spirit of economic reform and liberalisation, the co-operative restructured itself on the basis of individual budget centres. This structure continued until the end of 1990, when the chairman decided to adopt a variant of the much-talked-about 'holding co-operative' model with each of the five major divisions constituted as a one-person limited liability company.[4] This experiment in Tabar, however, was seen by all concerned to have been a disastrous failure, although this was probably less to do with the organisational change itself as the changing economic climate, for the reorganisation coincided with the full impact of price liberalisation and, as some later acknowledged, the change was scarcely radical enough. No staff were shed, and everything went on as before, but within a new organisational structure.

By the end of 1991, all of the limited liability companies were dissolved and a General Meeting was held to elect a new chairman. The membership voted in a certain TM who had been chairman in the past

---

[4] The 'holding co-operative' model was given as an example in the co-operative transformation legislation, see Swain, 'The legislative framework'. Its use and demise figures in Kovács, 'Strengths'.

but had recently returned from a spell in jail and was deeply involved in other private businesses. If some of the members expected wonders from him (as it is reported they did), then they were to be sadly disappointed. He felt he had inherited a farm that could not be saved. The only solutions were winding it up totally or declaring it bankrupt. They chose the latter.

The course of events thereafter becomes a little cloudy. The person in charge of the viticulture section machinery park suggested to TI, a former manager of the viticulture section, that they set up a limited liability company. TI's wife was a qualified agronomist who had worked on the financial side of the co-operative since returning from maternity leave and was increasingly involved in its economic policy. The plan was to take over the co-operative's arable farming, and, in their version of events, the chairman had agreed to this, that is to say to his company taking over the whole cropping activity on the former co-operative, the full 1,800 hectares. With this in mind they planned the establishment of a limited liability company with 23 shareholders, half the number employed in that activity at the time. But at some point during the negotiations, other people put in requests for land, including a certain DJ (whose business activities will be discussed below) who had had no links with the co-operative. The chairman acceded to these requests and told TI that his company could rent only 600 hectares, effectively annulling the agreement that TI claimed had been made with him. This prompted uncertainty and the number of those committed to the venture fell to ten. It soon fell further to eight when one left for personal reasons and another had to be sacked for drunkenness; by 1995, the number had fallen to seven and the farm's acreage had fallen to 500 hectares, 79 owned and the rest rented from 200 villagers.

Getting machinery out of the co-operative proved problematic too because of the chairman's reluctance to bend the rules, a reluctance born perhaps more out of self interest than a commitment to legal norms. TM refused to let TI and his colleagues exchange their property shares in the co-operative for equipment, because the co-operative was undergoing bankruptcy proceedings and the actual value of the shares would only be known once that procedure had been completed. TI could not wait that long and was obliged to buy his equipment from the co-operative at the price determined by the liquidator. By

1993 they had approximately 4.5 million forints worth of machinery (four tractors, three combines, assorted trailers and fixtures for harvesting and ploughing) and a farmstead valued at 2.9 million forints, the basics that they needed for their venture. In 1994 they invested in further equipment and second-hand machinery. The company relied heavily on the commercial contacts that TI and his wife had developed during the socialist years. They had little trouble getting bank loans, for example, because they knew the people in the bank from the old days; and they had plenty of contacts for marketing. By 1995, TI's business had grown steadily and they had even been able to treat themselves to a foreign holiday. It no longer had to hire machinery from the neighbouring farms, but they still had insufficient reserves and could not survive without taking on loans to tide them over the agricultural cycle.

The remainder of the co-operative's land was rented to an individual and a partnership. The partnership was relatively short-lived. It had been established by two former tractor drivers, L and C, but by 1995 it had been dissolved following an argument and each partner carried on separately. DJ, who had no background in farming, did not stay in it for long. It turned out that he was acting as a front for the co-operative chairman who ultimately set up his own operation in the form of a limited partnership, while not abandoning his other business interests which included the petrol station. Using the residual authority that he had as co-operative chairman he succeeded in acquiring the better land around Tabar for himself, forcing TI and his company to make do with land in the neighbouring village.

A *modus vivendi* between co-operative and private—Károlyháza

In Károlyháza, in eastern Hungary, co-operative transformation was not threatened by bankruptcy and secessionists came not from the co-operative top management, but from middle management and a significant number of ordinary members. By mid-decade, the co-operative and these medium-sized private farmers appeared to have developed a reasonable *modus vivendi*. The Károlyháza co-operative entered transformation in crisis, however. In 1992 it had debts of 5.2 million forints and it had already had had to lay off thirty of its active members including most of its administrative staff since 1990; in 1991 it sold off its sewing workshop and closed down its crate-making unit. Originally between 115 and 120 of its 400 membership announced their intention to leave the co-operative and begin private farming. But, once they realised how little they would actually get as their property share, and perhaps influenced by the threat of the sack if they did leave, the number fell significantly to 68, still quite a large number, who jointly accounted for some 14 per cent of co-operative assets. Of these, only 19 were active members, and they were immediately sacked from their co-operative jobs.

The majority of these 19 were colleagues of GyL, the head of the co-operative's equipment unit and repair shop, who had begun a sideline business providing agricultural services for villagers in the 1980s. He persuaded 13 of his 15 colleagues to secede with him to maximise what they obtained from the co-operative. After acrimonious negotiations, they received two combines, a tractor, other machinery, a part of the former co-operative workshop and part of the fruit orchard. But the secessionists did not farm jointly, except for GyL and four others, all relatives. After successful bidding in the restitution Land Auctions, this group farmed around 25 hectares, with an ambition to increase this to nearer one hundred hectares. But the majority of the secessionists took out only two-three hectares of land and used it as an enlarged household plot to meet household food supply needs; indeed, most had been amongst the most active in household plot farming in the socialist years.

The other relatively large-scale farmers in the village had not been active co-operative members. Three came from families which had owned farms of around 40–50 hectares in the past. Mr H, who retired as chairman in 1980, started farming on seven hectares, but soon gave up because his children would not help. KJ's family was more helpful because both of his sons-in-law were unemployed; he established a family farm on 20 hectares. MG, a butcher, pub landlord, restaurant-owner and active member of the Smallholders Party, set up a 29 hectare farm and had himself elected as chairman of the Land Committee. NJ, a former fitter and a brother-in-law of the lady mayor of the village, qualified for 600,000 forints worth of co-operative shares when his wife's and mother-in-law's shares were included. They took them in the form of a fruit orchard and agricultural machinery and also acquired jointly some 40 hectares of land. With two combines, tractors and lorries, they had the equipment necessary to farm on a family basis.

In the years between 1993 and 1996 the co-operative weathered the storm: there were no further serious redundancies, it was reducing its debts, and it expected to be in a position to invest again in two-three years. The chairman persevered for essentially sentimental reasons: he did not want to abandon the 29 years of his life that he had worked in the co-operative sector. In his perception, a division of labour had developed between the co-operative and the private farmers. The latter grew maize, wheat and tobacco commercially, and potatoes and fruit for their own use. The former focused on livestock (which in 1993 had been its main source of income) and horticulture, which was organised as a semi-autonomous unit of subcontracting private farmers.

Developments in Károlyháza were not unlike those in Varsány reported by Hann and Sárkány, where the co-operative was badly depleted during transformation but nevertheless survived.[5] The *modus vivendi* in Károlyháza reminds us forcefully that not all smaller-scale private farms established by co-operative workers rather than managers failed. Kelemen, Megyesi and Kalamász also report a couple who left their co-operative in 1992, bought a tractor, worked in farming services and built up a family farm of 250 hectares, although by then it was dependent on an 'integrator' (a phenomenon of later post-socialist agriculture in Hungary) who persuaded them to establish a producers' group.[6]

A Smallholders' policy that failed—Dombház

Developments in Dombház were radically different from those considered so far, although co-operative transformation took place in a context of bankruptcy here too. Situated in the northern hills close

---

[5] Chris Hann and Mihály Sárkány, 'The great transformation in rural Hungary: Property, life strategies and living standards', in *The Postsocialist Agrarian Question: Property Relations and the Rural Condition*, ed. Chris Hann and The 'Property Relations' Group (Münster: LIT Verlag, 2003), 117–41.

[6] Eszter Kelemen, Boldizsár Megyesi and Ildikó Nagy Kalamász, 'Knowledge dynamics and sustainability in rural livelihood strategies: Two case studies from Hungary', *Sociologia Ruralis* 48, no. 3 (July 2008): 262–4.

to the historic iron-works centre of Ózd, it had become a dormitory village for commuters to socialist industry and a rather unimportant branch of an agricultural co-operative whose centre lay some twenty miles by road beyond Ózd. None of the Dombház leadership was included in the management of the merged co-operative, and all co-operative machinery and animals disappeared from the village. The villagers worked in Ózd and focused on their household plots. Most members kept one or two cows, and the co-operative marketed their milk.

In 1991, the chairman simply announced that this 'is the end of the co-operative in Dombház'. The co-operative was no longer interested in farming its marginal lands and the chairman suggested that they try to reconstitute the previous property relations. Egged on by the local Smallholders Party, which, as discussed in Chapter 1, had advocated this approach to restitution in its national programme, this is what the villagers attempted to do. Smallholder influence at the local level was not unusual. Hann and Sárkány report the influence of an independent but pro-Smallholder mayor in Varsány.[7] Hann does not report the party as an institution playing a significant role in Tázlár,[8] although as in Dombház it was influential nevertheless. In Tázlár it was the biggest party in the village;[9] in Dombház's near neighbour Kissikonda, the socialist mayor had beaten the Smallholder candidate by a mere two votes.

Identifying plots in Dombház proved relatively easy despite contrary experience elsewhere, because everyone remembered who owned what land, and little land had been lost to either private housing or co-operative farm buildings during the socialist years because of its declining population and its marginal status in the co-operative. But, in order return to the pre-socialist property structure, it was crucial to manipulate the land auction system. Villagers prepared for this carefully. Although some 'outsiders' did appear at the first auction, moral pressure was put on them not to participate in the second. Each round of voting was preceded by 'agreement forums' at which the land on offer was apportioned to its former owners who agreed to submit the

---

[7] Hann and Sárkány, 'The great transformation', 171.
[8] Hann, 'Not the Horse', 43–90.
[9] Hann and Sárkány, 'The great transformation', 128.

minimum 500 forint bid which no one else would contest. Despite these precautions, the villagers were not entirely successful. At the third land auction in 1993, two villagers broke ranks and pushed up the bidding to 5,000 forints per golden crown value of land, mainly for forest land. Despite this setback, the villagers estimated that some 90 per cent of land was eventually returned to its previous owners.

It should be noted here, perhaps, that despite the legislative focus on auctions and indirect restitution, such manipulations were not uncommon.[10] In areas like the Lake Balaton coast, where demand for land was extreme, villagers mobilised to minimise the influence of outsiders,[11] although they could not insist on return to historic boundaries. But away from such areas, it was far from unknown. In Tabar, Uncle L (whom we will meet below) managed to manipulate the auctions to ensure he was the only person interested in voting for the better part of his patrimony. In Tázlár, a village with a 'specialist co-operative' where less land had been under communal cultivation, Hann explains that, 'auctions did not play a big role ... overall'.[12] The consequence in Tázlár, but not in Dombház, was that the sorts of disputes that characterised the Romanian agricultural transformation were present in Tázlár too (see Chapter 7 and the references therein). The measurements of the Land Office officials conflicted with the mental maps of villagers; 72 claims were filed for only 130 hectares of land.[13]

In Dombház, the marginality of the village worked against villagers in the co-operative transformation process. They were excluded from the 'naming' of co-operative property. They should have received letters indicating that they would receive a certain share of the property, but they did not arrive. Villagers later discovered that co-operative assets of value in the village had already been sold off to people from

---

[10] These are discussed in Swain, Andor and Kuczi, 'The privatization', 72–3. The events of a single auction are described in Nigel Swain, 'Getting land in Central Europe', in *After Socialism: Land Reform and Social Change in Eastern Europe*, ed. Ray Abrahams (Providence and Oxford: Berghahn Books, 1996), 204–10.
[11] Swain, 'Getting land', 210–3.
[12] Hann, *'Not the Horse'*, 62–3.
[13] Ibid.

outside it. By the time the villagers realised what was happening, it was too late. The co-operative was declared bankrupt in February 1993. In 1996 the majority of the villages were still waiting for the bankrupt co-operative to distribute the 1–1.5 hectares or so each that the villagers were due as their 'proportionate share' land and lived from approximately 0.5 hectares each. As a result the village was dominated by small-scale, near subsistence farmers, all struggling with virtually no agricultural machinery. Only one family farmed on anything approaching a large-scale, with a herd of 30 cows; a further 5–6 families had 15–20 cows. Most of the 90 families in the village kept only two or three.

In order to support a village which appeared to consist of small-scale dairy farmers, the local council proposed a village dairy—Dombmilk. The mayor supported the idea, but it was the brainchild of a member of the local council who was president of the local branch of the Smallholders Party. The council submitted grant applications to the Ministry of Welfare and to the Labour Office, because of the new jobs that it promised. Both applications were successful; this good fortune was not perhaps unrelated to the fact that elder brother of the Smallholder clerk of the council was a member of parliament for the Smallholders Party and had served as a Minister of State in the Antall government. The dairy company was 85 per cent owned by the council and 15 per cent by 8–9 villagers, mainly those employed in the company, who contributed 100,000 forints each. The council also contributed a building, the old school building, which had once belonged to the church; the latter was happy to pass it into the hands of the local authority rather than take it back.

When it began its operations Dombmilk employed 12–13 people, 4–5 of them women. At first they supplied schools, kindergartens and works canteens in the district. They found it difficult to break into the retail market because shops preferred a single supplier for all their dairy products, but got around it by buying their own outlet on Ózd market which immediately doubled the demand for their products. By 1994 they were operating profitably, although they had not repaid their loans. But the economics of the dairy industry was against them. Having solved the marketing problem and established a demand, they could not produce the supply. They had too little milk, and could not persuade villagers to produce more, at least, not at the price that they were obliged to charge if they were to remain in business. All of the villagers, even the head of the Smallholders whose idea Dombmilk was, complained that the purchase price of the milk was too low. But the Dombmilk could not increase the price it paid for their milk because it had to compete on the open market. The farmers, on the other hand, could only get a financial return on their milk if either the price were higher or they farmed more efficiently, and the latter was impossible because they had few cows and antiquated equipment. The council had expected milk production to increase once it had provided the facilities for purchasing and processing; but this did not happen. Dombmilk went out of business.

In retrospect, the collapse of Dombmilk was not surprising. The flaw in the project was not so much that it was conceived primarily as a social service to farmers (somewhere for them to sell their milk) with an inadequate assessment of market conditions, as it was the wrong product. Traditional, inefficient farming methods cannot be competitive in the production of a bulk commodity like milk. A rural development advisor would have suggested concentrating on local, specialty, niche products with high value-added, but there were none, and no other advisors were consulted. The grants came from the welfare and labour ministries, and the conception from a member of the Smallholder's Party with a rather romanticised vision of the future of small-scale family farming in Hungary.

Co-operative continuity—Szálfa

In a stark contrast to all of the preceding cases, the co-operative in Szálfa survived and remained aggressively dominant like its counterparts in the Czech Republic and Slovakia. Co-operative transformation was closely tied to the career of its chairman, NM. NM was somewhat unusual in that he had been in office since 1962. Less unusually, but of significance for the development of the co-operative, he had also pursued a party career through first the district and then the county organisations of the single (communist) party of the country, a career that had given him privileged access to information about policy and funding, which had helped the co-operative prosper. He was thus reluctant to see the creation of thirty years of his working life fall apart, not least because he had no second economy venture to fall back on. Furthermore, because the co-operative had prospered under socialism, the majority of villagers were predisposed to accept his judgement; they re-elected him as chairman in 1992.

Committed to the survival of the co-operative, he expelled from membership those who wanted to secede. This was illegal, and when the injured parties took him to court, they invariably won; but it had the desired effect of keeping the number people withdrawing assets from the co-operative to a minimum. Thanks to NM's tough management, his continued good contacts within the agricultural administration and with banks and suppliers, and his ability to bully creditors into paying up, the co-operative survived into 1996 remarkably unscathed. Some 23 members were sacked for not renting their land back to the co-operative, but the co-operative had made no redundancies for economic reasons. Members continued to get benefits in kind (feed for their animals at cost price, vouchers for subsidised lunches and so on), and the co-operative continued to contribute generously to village life. By this time it farmed only 2,700 hectares rather than the former 4,046 hectares of the socialist years, but it still retained a large livestock sector with 2,100 cattle and 560 sows; it made a profit of 80 million forints in 1995 from a turnover of 850 million, owned eight combines and 40 tractors, and continued to provide employment for a total of 200, not all from Szálfa.

Not all were convinced the co-operative's future was rosy however. NJ, the head of the cattle section since 1977 received 70 hectares of land under restitution. Initially he was happy to leave it in the co-operative, but in 1993 he was already expressing concerns about overstaffing levels of up to 30 per cent and questioning the long-term viability of his unit; by 1996 he had started (in somebody else's name) his own private venture on rented land. HJ, head of the cereal unit since 1980, received around 80 hectares and was also initially happy to leave it in the co-operative. But even in 1993 he was talking about moving into private farming, and in 1994 he bought a tractor so that the following year he, in partnership with another manager, could rent 200 hectares from a neighbouring co-operative. He did so in his own name, and NM immediately sacked both of them, forcing HJ's hand. He became a private farmer, although his own land remained with the co-operative because it was tied into a five-year rental contract that was too costly to break.

The Non-Farm Economy

Small family businesses—contrasting fates in Pakucs and Tabar

In Pakucs, the careers of NB and BF illustrate some of the problems that entrepreneurs in non-agricultural sectors faced. Both had resources of social capital, yet their fates differed. NB started out as self-employed craftsman (a plumber and central heating engineer) in the late socialist years. In 1986 he married the daughter of KJ, then still chairman of the General Co-operative, and set about building a house. He overestimated on the building materials, and, with the surplus and an investment of only 50,000 forints, built a 'boutique' on an adjacent plot which he rented from the council; the idea was for his wife to run the boutique after her maternity benefit had expired. But NB quickly realised that it would be difficult to make a living from fashion clothes in a small and relatively poor settlement like Pakucs. From his contacts with the surrounding factories he realised that there was a market in protective clothing and shoes for workers, and soon this made up 50 per cent of the shop's turnover; he also began trading in building supplies. By the early 1990s he had bought from the council the land on which the boutique stood, his plumbing venture had developed to the stage where he had four employees doing the work while he concentrated on finding new business and managing the outfit, and a bank manager friend of his in Zalaegerszeg had suggested that he apply for a loan from the new government-supported business start-up scheme (Start credit, i.e., soft credits funded ultimately by the German government).

NB's original idea for expanding his business was to build a sales outlet, half of which would be a business that he owned selling electrical goods and household chemicals, while the other half would be rented to another business, ultimately a greengrocer, which would help defray his costs. But while they were drawing up plans, new government schemes were introduced to support rural tourism. NB amended the plans with the help of a friend who worked in planning to include extra storeys where he located a guest-house (*panzió*). He secured the necessary bank loans by a mortgage on the new buildings, his other business interests and his sister-in-law's flat in Budapest. The shop and guest-house business began operations in 1993 employing two staff and a student from a retailing college. Initially he ran both the shop *cum* guest-house and plumbing businesses in tandem, but by 1995 had given up on the latter, and focused on the former which had increased in volume and now employed 5 people. The success of the guest-house opened up for him the possibilities of rural tourism and he was developing plans to set up a campsite and open a new shop; and he had long term plans to take over some of the sports facilities from the council, particularly the automatic bowling alley that had been half-finished for more than half a decade. NB's ventures certainly benefited from the social capital of his father-in-law's contacts, but he was always responsive to changes in the market and sources of funding.

BF started his career with the General Co-operative run by NB's father-in-law, but in 1984 joined COOPKER, a Budapest-based company which opened a unit in Pakucs. Although not a co-operative itself, it plugged into Hungary's co-operative network. In 1988, following the sacking of the managing director, it became clear that the company was beginning to fall apart, partly because of declining markets. BF together with the manager of the Zalaegerszeg unit of the company began to think of an escape route and in December 1989 registered a company, Hanig Ltd, which would work in a similar area. At this point they took no further action, but in January 1990, there was discussion of dividing COOPKER up into a series of limited liability companies based round the regional units, and the management and workers of the Pakucs and Zalaegerszeg units discovered that a limited liability company to run a business of this kind already existed—Hanig Ltd. They pressurised BF, his partner, to take them all into the business, and the partners felt obliged to do so because they needed the buildings and the lorries of the two units.

The original Hanig Ltd registered in December 1989 had 18 shareholders, the two partners, some of the employees who had the spare cash to buy the 50,000 forint shares, and some of their customers. After the change of plan, the old company joined as a 19th shareholder, bringing a contribution in kind valued at 1.5 million forints. This would have made the old company a majority shareholder, but all agreed to cap its shareholding at 46 per cent. Until 1993, Hanig Ltd carried on basically the same business as Coopker, but with a reduced labour force. In 1991, however, ever mindful of the need for an escape route, BF calculated that he had gained sufficient experience of the retailing trade over his career and established a general store. The shop was located in an abandoned house which had a good location but was in a state of disrepair. Initially he ran it himself and opened only in late afternoon and early evening, but in March 1992 his son gave up his job as a car mechanic and became employed in the shop fulltime. Meanwhile, by 1993, it was clear that Hanig had to change tack if the business was to survive. The only product that made money was rabbits which were exported to Italy.

Hanig decided to develop the business in two ways: to start bottling and selling honey, and to develop a bakery. They had sufficient resources from their income to fund the honey plan and spent half a million forints arranging for jars to be manufactured and labels produced. The bakery, however, required investment and a strategic partnership with the Croatian company which would provide the baking equipment. Although they toyed with raising more money from the shareholders, it was clear that the company needed a bank loan; and this proved to be its downfall. The bank first said that it would only lend them sufficient funds if they owned the building in which they operated and then offered it as security. Hanig therefore sunk its cash into buying the building, only to discover that the bank still refused to fund the venture. They tried to sell the building again to raise cash, but could not find a buyer. Hanig was declared bankrupt and the bank auctioned off the buildings. BF was left with nothing except the family shop. His wife, who had first worked as a clerk for the council and then in BF's state and private companies, opted for disability benefit. Despite the extensive social capital that BF and his partner enjoyed, it proved insufficient to overcome the hard economic realities of a business with too much baggage from the past and a disappearing market.

In Tabar, the business career of DJ, whose involvement in the restructuring of the agricultural co-operative was considered above, was linked with the non-agricultural activities of the Szerencs agricultural co-operative. He began work as a driver for the chief engineer of a state company, did his military service and then joined the secret service of the Ministry of the Interior until 1972, but he was obliged to resign because his bride-to-be had relatives who lived in the West. He then worked for 13 years in various pubs and restaurants owned by the General Consumer and Marketing Co-operative before, in 1985, joining the Szerencs agricultural co-operative as head of an autonomous unit in the co-operative renting out small-scale machinery. At the same time, together with his wife, who had a similar background in the restaurant and pub trade, he established a private 'pub' (beer-drinking restaurant) as a second job. By the end of the 1980s and the 'change of system', but before the Szerencs co-operative underwent transformation, he realised that his job there had no future. Rather than become unemployed, he turned his second job into his first and to supplement it rented a lorry from the Tabar co-operative and began a haulage business which transported workers locally by bus and goods locally and internationally by truck. Not satisfied with these two ventures, DJ later set up an agricultural machinery and car repair business on property formerly owned by the co-operative which he planned to develop with a car wash, and the farming business which fronted for the former co-operative farm chairman. Because he had the courage and experience to jump early, he ended up as one of the most successful entrepreneurs in the village, yet his labour force fell from 15 in 1990–91 to only six in 1993, and he acknowledged that his pub, the only business that he knew well, was subsidising his other ventures.

Larger-scale new business success—Károlyháza and Zádorpuszta

Social capital inherited from the socialist era was central to the success of RA, the biggest post-socialist entrepreneur to emerge in Károlyháza. Like NB in Pakucs, his origins lay in the private sector, but his 'second economy' venture was more substantial. RA came from a nearby village and his uncle, whose entrepreneurial spirit he felt he had inherited, had been a businessman in inter-war Hungary. He studied in an agricultural technical school and began his career on an agricultural co-operative where he spent a decade or so climbing the ladder so that, by the end of the 1960s, he had become the Number Three on the farm. He then had a 'difference of opinion', which resulted in his being thrown out of the party, and he decided to go private. He acquired a tractor and a mechanical saw and gradually built up a carpentry business, employing on occasion as many as five people. The 1970s was a decade of extensive house-building in Hungary's villages, and he found plenty of work. His relations with the local authorities improved after he did work on the local party secretary's house; and there was always household plot tobacco growing as a supplementary source of family income. In 1983 he decided to move in a different direction—fattening chickens. He established a 'specialist group' and sold the chickens on contract to the Hajdúnánás 'New Life' agricultural co-operative.[14] But in order to run the chicken business successfully he needed more space, and it was the possibility of buying a large house with extensive grounds that brought him and his wife to Károlyháza.

They combined chicken fattening (five and a half seven-week cycles a year of 8–10,000 chickens per cycle) with a side-line in pig fattening (around 120 pigs per year), and made enough money over seven years to raise a family and amass a useful amount of capital. But by the early 1990s market conditions were changing again. The massive increase in oil prices which accompanied the 'change of system' reduced profitability, and their only customer, the co-operative, was beginning to have problems with the abattoir to which it sold; it ultimately went out of business. RA decided to capitalise on the demise of the local abattoir and invest the proceeds of his chicken fattening business into a new chicken slaughtering venture.

He gave up the chicken fattening business in 1991, but it was almost 18 months before the slaughterhouse started operation, during which time he and his wife negotiated with the local council and co-operative over acquiring the necessary land, arranged a bank loan, and toured the country looking for ideas about how to operate it profitably, both in terms of technology and practical organisation—ensuring that they had a constant supply of live chickens and a steady market for dead ones. They had to buy their land from the agricultural co-operative, which exercised its influence with local council to have the land reclassified as 'internal' (commercial or housing use) rather than 'external' (agricultural use) land, so increasing its price. Neither party was surprised when the land was reclassified again as 'external' once the purchase had been made. The total cost of the investment was

---

[14] The 'specialist groups' were one of the many new forms introduced in 1982 to incorporate forms of 'second economy' activity into the official economy. See Swain, *Hungary*, 175–7.

36 million forints, of which 16 million was a bank loan, 7 million a job-creation subsidy, and 13 million the family savings.

At both the supply end (an army of 40–50 individual fatteners for whom he provided feed and baby chicks) and the marketing end, RA's contacts built up over two decades as a socialist entrepreneur and almost a decade in the chicken industry itself proved invaluable. All the key chicken fatteners had been involved in the former specialist group scheme, as had the companies from which he acquired chicks and his main market outlets. Socialist social capital of this kind was also important in obtaining staff, many of whom had worked for his previous business. In particular, through his contacts, RA knew that a person with the sorts of skills that he needed worked for a similar abattoir, specialising in ducks, located in a nearby village. RA managed to recruit him, and he brought with him a small army (22 in all) of friends and relatives who were willing to work for the new venture. The bulk of these workers lived in RA's home village, but it was specialist labour requirements, rather than a preference for his home village, that led RA to recruit there. RA was in fact not liked in Károlyháza, something that he and his wife put down to jealousy, but the villagers explained in terms of his low wages. His status as an outsider and his reliance on non-village labour did not help his esteem. When he stood for the local council in 1994 he was not elected.

Károlyháza villagers nevertheless did benefit from RA's investment and the 7 million forint job creation funding that he received. The first to do so were the 13 Károlyháza residents who were employed building the factory. Three of these retained their links with RA and became drivers for him. In fact they had asked originally for jobs as drivers and he had told them to work first on the building phase of the project, gaining a degree of trust and commitment which was important because the drivers were well placed to spot new market opportunities while carrying out their standard delivery roles. In early 1993 RA employed approximately 40 people, but by the end of the year this had doubled to 80 and an increase to 110 was planned for January 1994. Although, and partly because, most of the chicken abattoirs in the region had gone bankrupt, RA's proved competitive thanks to his careful planning and the high level of through-put that he achieved. In 1995 the business remained on approximately the same scale, but he had brought to fruition the plans that he had had in 1993 to buy shares in a refrigerated warehouse in Debrecen where he could store chickens and ease some of the pressure on the marketing side of the business. A business of these dimensions went some way to alleviate the level of unemployment in the village, but it was still registered officially as 23 per cent in 1993, and the lady mayor estimated that it was nearer 45–50 per cent if the number of women who had given up work but did not qualify for benefits was taken into account. Furthermore, the doctor reported a rather dramatic increase in the number of people claiming invalidity benefit: it tripled between 1992 and 1993 and had doubled again by 1995.

The leading entrepreneur in Zádorpuszta, located almost within the Budapest agglomeration, also had his origins in the non-agricultural activities of an agricultural co-operative. ST, who had graduated in organic chemistry from Budapest's technical university after a vocational–technical secondary education, followed by part-time study and night school courses, became manager of the plastic bottle and container manufacturing venture of a mammoth agricultural co-operative which farmed in the environs of Budapest. The plant was very run down but within two years he had turned it into a very profitable unit. In 1990 he tried to negotiate with the co-operative leadership to rent the business from them, but they rejected the idea and sacked him. But, having sacked him, they could not find an appropriate manager, and they eventually resorted to re-appointing the person that ST had replaced. He was no more successful than he had been before, and the unit veered towards bankruptcy again.

ST had the satisfaction of taking his employers to the labour relations court and winning a judgement that his dismissal had been unjust. But he did not wait for the wheels of justice to turn and went into business for himself. At the time of co-operative transformation, ST went back to the top management and explained that he still had 1.8 million forints worth of shares in the co-operative and would like to offer them in return for the plant. His proposal was rejected outright. But ST had read up on the provisions of the Co-operative Transformation Law. In the face of intense hostility from the co-operative management, he approached as many people as he could who had also lost their jobs in the failing co-operative unit to join in his venture. His idea was for them to pool sufficient shares to acquire the unit, shares which he would eventually buy back if the others so desired. When this did not realise sufficient shares to buy the unit, he persuaded some of the better workers still employed in the unit to join the venture on the same terms. In the event, they pulled together a total of 35 million forints worth of shares, more than enough to buy the plant which was officially valued at 25 million forints.

Having taken over the venture, which was officially registered as a co-operative, ST realised that so much investment would be necessary if it were to operate at a 'European level', that all available funds should be used to develop the business rather than buying out the shareholders. Luckily he was able to convince his colleagues that this was the correct course and set to work laying on gas and re-plastering the walls. He then set about disposing of unnecessary layers of middle management. The business had previously had six managers, but ST ran it on his own, with a secretary and a person in charge of the warehouse. On the other hand, he kept on the bulk of the twenty-strong manual labour force, 80 per cent of whom lived in the village. ST did not take a penny out of the business for three months, and promised monthly 10 per cent wage increases so long as profits could cover them. After a few months, sales were good enough for ST to consider taking on 10 more staff.

ST was also at pains to maximise his return on his assets. An office building was converted into a supermarket which employed three people, and, needing bricklayers to help renovate his buildings in any case, he developed a small builder's business too. Meanwhile his order book for plastic products stabilised. They exported via an agent to the Czech Republic, and ST had friends in Italy, Austria and Germany who acted as unofficial agents, bringing in various items of business, such as plastic water bottles for bicycles for a German company. Three years later the business appeared to be flourishing. Employment had doubled to 40, three quarters of whom came from Zádorpuszta.

'Socialist personal services gap' family businesses—Korcona

Post-socialist change in the retail sector in Korcona perhaps best illustrates the general trend of plugging the socialist personal services gap, mostly by people who were force-of-circumstances entrepreneurs of one kind or another. None of them was created after the 'heroic' era of new business creation following the change of system. By 1996 most had stabilised; some had developed further, although not dramatically, particularly those run by people capitalising on skills learned in the socialist years.

A typical example was PS. She had originally worked as a sales assistant in the village food shop that was owned by the Győr-based General Co-operative, but had not returned to work after maternity leave. Years later she accepted the offer of a private company to establish a 'boutique' in a garage on the ground floor of her house. She would be an employee of the company, although her 'remuneration' consisted of only an allowance for renting the space in her house and three percent of her turnover. The business was not a success. The clothes that were provided for the boutique were attractive, but village demand was rather restricted, and Korcona suffered not only from its proximity to Győr as a shopping centre, but also from the fact that the 'Polish market' was located on the Korcona side of Győr. Meanwhile, her son had trained as a car mechanic but could not find employment. PS therefore closed the boutique, registered for unemployment benefit (for which she qualified because she had had an employment relationship), and used a period of unemployment to restructure the shop as a general store. She did not need to take out a loan for any of this because the family always had the security of her husband's income from his job as a repairman in the council-run old people's home, and they could generate relatively large sums of money by rearing pigs. Mother and son ran the shop together; the mother served in the shop (12 hours a day, every day except Sunday when they were open in the mornings only), and the son bought supplies in a nine-year-old Lada car with a trailer. In 1993, PS expressed pleasant surprise at how successful the venture seemed to be; and by 1996 the business had developed further. She had begun renting the General Co-operative shops located in a separate part of the village where the former estate-worker dwellings had been. Her son now managed these, and her husband had given up his job and taken over the role of obtaining supplies.

Another new shopkeeper, KB, used to work as a horticultural expert in a nearby agricultural producer co-operative (not the village one) and lived with his wife, who was a teacher in Korcona, in the service accommodation that she was due as a teacher. From 1988 onwards he had started growing flowers in three polythene tents in the yard of their house, which he sold at the local market. When his wife had children, it was KB who took maternity leave, and after he had returned to work for two months he decided to give up his job and become a flower-seller fulltime. Permission was sought to convert a room on the ground floor of the schoolhouse (which they were negotiation with the council to buy in any case) into a shop, and he established a business selling his own flowers and gifts. In addition to the polythene tents in the yard, he had a small plot of land where he grew open field vegetables. KB had no grand development plans in 1993, being content with a village-based family business, a business which was still prospering at that level three years later.

ZJ was also content with a village-based, family business. He gambled on the absence of any outlet for buying fresh meat in the village to set himself up as the village butcher. He had worked in a state-owned butcher's shop all his career and had wanted to set up his own business for many years. Encouraged by the complaints of some villagers about the need to go into Győr to find a butcher's, he left his job in 1992 and obtained for himself a year's unemployment benefit. He made use of this cushion to plan carefully and establish the business. On the physical side he converted a room on the ground floor of his house into the shop. On the commercial side, he conducted what he termed 'market research'. Mindful of the need to have a solid customer base, he approach the village institutions which cooked—the school, the nursery school and the old-people's home—and negotiated a deal which undercut their existing suppliers. On the financial side, he purchased the necessary equipment from savings, with no need to take out a loan. He ran the business almost entirely as a one-man operation, and his wife retained her job in the Co-operative Savings Bank. He provided fresh meat every day, travelling to his suppliers in the morning to choose meat and either having them deliver it or persuading his wife to pick it up for him, her only contribution to the venture. His gamble paid off, and in 1996 his local family business was prospering.

PZ, together with his brother PA, had ambitions beyond a single family shop. PZ had been manager of the Győr-based General Co-operative's 'midi' supermarket in Korcona. In 1990 he was operating it on a sub-contracting basis, and in January 1993 he bought it for 2.3 million forints. He was not the only person interested in making the purchase, but the competitors somehow obtained misleading information and when they realised just how much they would need to bid, they withdrew. PZ had had to borrow 1.4 million forints from a bank on a four-year loan at 29 per cent interest to finance the purchase. He had no intention of being burdened by debt for the full four-year period, however, and planned to pay it back within two years, from income generated by selling sauerkraut and potatoes from his and his brother's agricultural plots. His brother was a 'silent partner' in his businesses and, initially at least, concentrated on the agricultural side of things. The shop had three employees.

PZ had a keen eye for competition. When he learned that Mrs F was opening a shop he convinced brother PA that he should convert his garage into a shop which his wife could run to compete with Mrs F. They did this so quickly that their shop was ready about three months ahead of the competition. But his competitive instincts did not stop there. Mrs F had a stroke of luck. Because of a divorce, a house came up for sale in the development zone of the village. Her mother bought it and opened a shop on the ground floor, seemingly away from competition. But this state of affairs did not last long. PZ immediately rented a shop close by that had once been a hairdressers and set up business in direct competition again. In 1995, by mutual agreement, PA bought out his brother's share of the shop in his garage, and his wife took out an entrepreneurs licence. PZ continued to operate two shops, concentrating on the former 'midi' market which was the biggest shop in the village. He also continued to sell the sauerkraut and other vegetables produced from the family plots. Throughout all this, PZ's wife maintained her administrative job in the council offices.

Mrs F, PZ's chief competitor, was born in Korcona, although her husband hailed from Győr. She had worked as a shop assistant in a supermarket in a nearby village and become concerned about her future employment prospects. Her pessimism was not improved by the fact that her husband, who had been operating as a private haulier since 1984, had had hardly any work for a year. In 1991, therefore the two of them decided to set up in business and opened a general food shop in a purpose-built wooden kiosk. She worked behind the counter and her husband was in charge of getting supplies. Despite PZ's competitive reaction, business considerations were not the primary motivation behind the opening of their second shop. Their daughter was about to finish school and had few prospects of employment. The family therefore persuaded the paternal grandparents to sell their flat in Győr, buy the house that had become available because of a divorce, and establish a second shop which the daughter could run in its garage. The grandparents agreed with the plan and supplemented their pensions by working occasionally in the family businesses. By 1996 it seemed as if they had decided to focus their activities in the shop in the garage, which was relatively distant from PZ's 'midi' store. They had bought a plot opposite the garage shop and had laid the foundations for what was planned to be new and bigger one.

LOCAL GOVERNMENT AND LOCAL DEVELOPMENT POLICY

As discussed in Chapter 1, local government developments in Hungary were similar to those in the former Czechoslovakia in that there were demands for villages that had been merged in the socialist years to regain their independence, but Hungary differed in that it awarded genuine autonomy to these entities, especially in the field of education. This is perhaps best illustrated by events in Kissikonda which gained independence from its neighbour Dombház.

Independence, control of schooling and promoting tourism unsuccessfully—Kissikonda

The first issue that the local authority of newly independent Kissikonda had to address was the viability of an independent school in the village. Until 1978, the school had taught all four initial primary years before sending the children to Dombház to complete their elementary education. In 1978, however, because of the Kissikonda school's inability to cover foreign language teaching, the fourth year too was moved to Dombház. The early 1990s witnessed an impending crisis, however, which threatened the very future of the school. Kissikonda's school role fell to 11, painfully close to the figure of ten which would make the school officially unviable. With the connivance of the Ministry of Education, the fourth year was transferred back to Kissikonda for 1994 and the German teacher was persuaded to commute from Dombház to Kissikonda to hold the German lessons there. With this government-supported sleight of hand, the village school was saved and the Kissikonda teacher found herself in a position of unprecedented freedom after Hungary's devolution of education budgets to local authorities. Because Kissikonda now had its own budget for education, she no longer had to wait in line but could spend as she chose, so long as she remained within the budget. The mayor told her to 'order what she needed'; and she did. The school received new flooring, a new coat of paint, new black-out curtains, new cupboards, and a new tape-recorder. The teacher also promoted community life in the independent village, organising a carnival dance and celebrations on 23 October, 15 March, Mothers' Day and St Nicholas' Day. A Christmas play was also planned. All in all, she relished her increased autonomy and what was perhaps only a temporarily increased absolute level of funding.

The mayor, an independent but former member of the communist party, established a four-year plan which began by addressing issues of conflict with Dombház. A doctor's surgery was built, so that the doctor, originally from Transylvania, who served the village four days a week did not have to operate from a variety of ad hoc premises. A proper village dump was established outside the village, and the services of a self-employed driver were engaged to remove the rubbish containers to the dump on a regular basis. In 1992 they worked on improving the roads and beginning work on the water supply and drilling new wells. At the time only 17 per cent of village houses had all modern conveniences, and 55 per cent had no modern conveniences at all. Both main streets in the village were paved, as was an area for the bus to turn around in. Gas pipes were laid in 1995, but by 1996 it was clear that sewerage was too costly for the village's meagre resources. The council nevertheless managed to find funds to renovate the mayor's office, replace the roof on the school, and renovate the culture house and library. Like Dombház, the village also benefited from the new road linking them to Salgótarján, and from the new digital telephone exchange in Ózd. In 1994 the village had only one phone, located in the mayor's office; villagers were summoned to it over a loud-speaker system.

The mayor was keen to promote business development and an early move was to claim back from the General Consumer organisation the grocery and general store that it operated in the village but which was council property. The council felt that by reclaiming it and then renting it themselves to a private business, as they did, the council would get a little extra income (although it charged a lower rent than the co-operative had been paying), and, more important, might be able to exercise a greater influence on what goods and services were available in the village.

There were five further possible village business ventures in which the council played some sort of a promotional role, some considerably more successful than others. The first of these was a small slaughterhouse. The mayor offered a free site and said that it would probably be possible for the council to pay for a road leading up to it. But nothing came of the venture: the two individuals concerned did not have sufficient capital. The second also came to nothing. Four former steel works employees tried to set up a business selling metal items such as swings and wrought iron work. The mayor tried to help promote their wares by activating his personal contacts amongst the managers of the steel works (where he had been employed). The council also paid for photos to be made of the products and for the mailing costs to send brochures to potentially interested parties. There was no interest in metal products in this former metal working area. The mayor's active role was not unrelated to the fact that one of the individuals concerned, KB, was a relation by marriage: the dividing line between public council policy and the mayor's private interest was a little hazy, as it was in the case of the Lesovice mayor in the Czech Republic.

The third related to rural tourism, but it too remained in the realm of possibilities rather than realities. Budapest people had come to both Kissikonda and Dombház with plans to develop tourism. One aspect of the plan, which was dependent on the developments in Dombház, was to convert the sheep fold near one of the co-operative's manor buildings into a stable for horses. Kissikonda would become the equestrian centre for rural holidays in the Dombház–Kissikonda region. The mayor was interested in other options too for the 3–400 square metre building (proposals for rearing snails and creating a furniture workshop), but this tourism idea had an attractive air of concreteness about it. However, nothing could be done in 1994 because land issues still had to be resolved, and later the moment was past.

By 1996 the mayor was thinking more in terms of establishing a honey-bottling venture, because many villagers kept bees. He had conducted some preliminary negotiations with entrepreneurs in Miskolc and Ózd, but nothing concrete emerged. More positively, the council had been successful winning PHARE money to renovate a hunting lodge located at the edge of the village and create three rooms in it, one with three beds, one with two and one with five. The next step on this front was to apply for a further grant from PHARE to build a wooden house on the same plot so that the facility could accommodate 25 tourists. Despite this small success, the mayor was not convinced that rural tourism was the solution to the village's problems. He felt that too few villagers had the necessary initiative or capital to improve a bedroom and a bathroom to western standards, which was the minimum necessary for such a strategy to succeed. In his view, the village had seen a mere trickle tourists, mainly Dutch (whereas the Smallholder Party's leader reported that they had had 'lots of tourists'), and that the village also had a future in timber processing using facilities formerly owned by the co-operative.

Ambivalent links with private business— Károlyháza and Kissikonda

The lady mayor of Károlyháza, elected in 1990 in a race against the co-operative chairman, was Mrs N, who had initially considered running as a Christian Democrat. The party would not have her, so she ran as an independent and succeeded thanks to the efforts of her extended family. She had never figured in village politics during the socialist years, and had been employed as a middle-level white-collar worker in the co-operative before being briefly unemployed. But her family was probably the wealthiest in the village and its various members had been significant land-owners in the inter-war years; some of them figured amongst the village's relatively high number of successful private farmers. She was easily re-elected in 1994. Reflecting the *modus vivendi* described above between the co-operative and the private farmers, this time the co-operative chairman was elected to the council. But despite this association with agricultural businesses and the fact that the mayor's husband ran his own business, the council had no substantive policies aimed at stimulating enterprise and no single council official whose job it was to liaise with local businesses. It was, however, prepared to rent or sell land or buildings cheaply to entrepreneurs who wished to set up businesses in the village, it did endeavour to grant licenses and carry out the necessary paper work quickly and efficiently, and it permitted entrepreneurs like RA to use the village sewerage system rather than make their own provision. It also always informed new entrepreneurs of the numbers of similar businesses already located in the village, and in one case dissuaded a potential investor from establishing yet another food shop when the village already had, in the minds of the council, too many. But the council had not promoted the idea of a club for entrepreneurs, and neither had this idea emerged from the local community. Business families such as RA's reported that they were too much wrapped up in their own affairs to involve themselves in a forum of this kind. Their worlds remained separate.

Károlyháza was nevertheless lucky that RA had taken over some of the services previously performed by the co-operative. It had provided the kindergarten with cheap vegetables; RA supplied chickens at cost price. He was also persuaded to help in the construction of the kindergarten by transporting equipment, providing shutters and removing rubbish. Indeed he felt not only that it was expected of him, but that it was so natural that he did not mention it when asked. In his account, the council had 'not yet' asked entrepreneurs to take on the role previously performed by socialist economic institutions and help with the upkeep of the village. He was contemplating, but did not bring to fruition in the years under consideration, a major contribution such as building a sports hall for the village.

There was one glimmer of success amongst the gloom of mass unemployment and unfulfilled attempts to create alternative employment in Kissikonda: KB, the baker. KB trained as a locksmith and smith and followed his father in the metal works. In 1983 he moved his family into a block of flats in Ózd because both he and his wife worked there and they thought it would be better for their children's education. But they never really got used to town life, and spent all of their summers back in the village with the parents. In 1985 KB was moved to a new unit in the factory and made foreman. As a foreman in the late socialist years he earned a good salary and, despite occasional conflicts with his superiors, he stayed in the job until 1992 meanwhile saving sufficient money to build a family house in the village.

KB did not wait to be sacked. He could see the way things were going and decided to combine moving into their new home in the village with a complete new start. His first idea was to set himself up as an 'entrepreneur' in the trade that he knew, metal working, and he was one of the four involved in the failed wrought iron venture considered above, for which the mayor had provided considerable support. KB then thought about working in Germany as many other villagers did. He went as far as organising the paperwork before deciding that he should stay with his family and resolve things in the village. The one secure point in his life at this stage was the fact that his wife still had a stable, fulltime job with the post office.

It was at this point that family contacts built up over the socialist years came to his aid. Some years previously a Mr F, mindful of the radical restructuring that would inevitably take place in a region like Ózd so closely tied to a declining industry, had established the small business development company that had opened information offices in both Dombház and Kissikonda. KB had known Mr F as a family friend for some twenty years: he had started his career as a lawyer on the co-operative farm where KB's elder brother worked as a driver. Mr F offered two very concrete pieces of help. First, he informed KB of one of his company's intensive courses which was to take place in a nearby village very soon. Second, knowing that KB's dilemma was that he wanted to be an entrepreneur but could not be one in his own field, he pointed out that a very good baker lived in Kissikonda, but that he commuted to work in Ózd. Perhaps there was an opportunity for establishing a bakery in the village itself. He consulted with the baker who said he was willing to give the venture a go, but he wanted to restrict his involvement to the baking rather than the business side of things. They agreed on 80:20 participation, the majority of the baker's participation being in terms of his own labour.

KB attended the intensive course organised by Mr F's company, the costs of which were covered by the Ózd employment company which also paid, retrospectively, a small salary conditional on him registering as self-employed within 6 months of completing the course. Both partners participated on the course and, by the end of it, had their business plan ready. The course proved to be an invaluable success, not so much for the content as for the contacts that they built up, both in terms of the experts—bankers, tax advisors and so on—who lectured to them and the fellow participants on the course, 60 per cent of whom went on to establish their own businesses. He also learned what grants to apply for, and successfully obtained money from the Labour Office and a Start credit (see above). In addition, the family ties between the mayor and KB notwithstanding, the council voted to either invest in the business itself on a commercial basis, or provide a one-off job-creation grant of 40,000 forints per employee. The bakery duly benefited from 200,000 forints for its five new jobs. Over and above these loans KB's personal contribution came to 2–300,000 forints.

Thanks to the efforts of the two partners, their success in winning financial support, and the strength of the family ties that underpinned them, not least the wife's stable job, the venture was successfully established. This represented no little achievement given that a prospective baker from Dombház had been on the same course and had given up declaring that it was impossible to set up a small bakery in the region. The business initially employed two women in the bakery itself and a third woman who cleaned and looked after the store. The baker initially worked alone but soon took on a young assistant. All had previously been unemployed, and none were family members, although one of the two women was related by marriage to KB, and his wife occasionally helped out. The book-keeping was carried out by Mr F's company.

The name of the bakery spread by word of mouth and it was soon supplying shops in 10 surrounding villages and eight in Ózd. By 1996 its labour force had expanded to seven, and KB was planning a further investment in September 1997 which would create a further 2–3 jobs. One of the reasons for this expansion, however, was the failure of a competitor. The formerly state-owned Ózd 'bread factory' had closed down. Since nine villagers had worked in this factory in 1993, the net effect on village employment of KB's venture was barely positive; but the former state company would probably have closed in any case and without KB there would have been no new jobs at all.

The emergence of a business block— Székhely, Korcona, Tabar, Zádorpuszta

Nearby Székhely differed from Károlyháza in that the bulk of its pre-socialist population had been estate farm servants. The villagers had a reputation for being hard-working but in need of direction. There was no equivalent to Károlyháza's clan of former rich peasants; nor were there significant indigenous businesses: all of the businesses on the main road to Ukraine that runs through the village—a new restaurant, a vegetable stall and a grocer's shop—were owned by 'outsiders'. Newly independent administratively since 1990, Székhely witnessed first a continuity of socialist paternalism and then a take-over by 'outsider' entrepreneurs. The mayor elected in 1990 was the school teacher and former party secretary. He had only stood for the post reluctantly, and he insisted that he would only do it on a part-time basis, on the basis of an honorarium rather than a salary. He would work in the school until 1pm and then take up his mayoral duties. At 55 he was a generation older than most of the councillors, which meant he had been the teacher of many of them. Many referred to him inadvertently as 'teacher, sir' rather than 'Mr Mayor', so it was not difficult for him to dominate proceedings. His role as a teacher also explained, according to the Reform Church pastor, his popularity with the Roma population of 40–50 adults (all unemployed, but only one in receipt of unemployment benefit) and 110 children. He had been the teacher of the separate Roma class and was seen as 'their' teacher.

He was easily re-elected mayor in 1994, although this time, as predicted by the Reform Church pastor, he was opposed; and this time things did not go his way. The new council, which had been reduced to seven because of the difficulty of getting people to stand at all, was not as compliant as the old one. Four new people had been elected, all of them entrepreneurs, and, although they lived in the village, all were newcomers in that they had arrived in the last 10–15 years. These four formed an alliance with the deputy mayor, a middle manager in the Nyíregyháza water authority, to counter the influence of the mayor. A power struggle developed between these 'outsider entrepreneurs', who 'took their profits away from the village', and the 'original Székhely residents', who were 'soft on the Roma and too generous with social benefits'. It was the attempts of the entrepreneurs to take a tougher line on the distribution of social benefits that brought matters to a head. The mayor was obliged to resign 'on health grounds', and the deputy mayor stepped into his shoes.

The emergence of a business block within local government was also a feature of Korcona politics. Korcona's mayor had worked as an engineer and then plant manager for a construction company based in Győr during the course of which he had joined the party. In

1986, the former chairman of the council in Korcona retired and he was approached by the party secretary of the agricultural co-operative. It was made clear to him that the party thought that he would make a good mayor and it was his duty as a party member to accept the post, which he did in 1987. He embarked on three programmes, introducing piped water, paving all village roads and building a kindergarten. Because the first two of these had been completed, he was easily re-elected in 1990; and he was re-elected overwhelmingly again in 1994, not least because he had acted nimbly to attract a German investor who established a textile factory which employed 22 (12 from Korcona) by 1996. He had quickly bought land from the co-operative in order to offer a location, and had given them the use of one of the council's own telephone lines.

But what distinguished the 1994 elections was the emergence on the council of an entrepreneurial bloc. The agricultural entrepreneur who had attempted to expose the underhand dealings of SGy and KGy in the socialist years, NFJ, was re-elected, as was KGy, the leading light in KZZ Ltd the co-operative successor company. He became deputy mayor. They were joined by KF, the owner of a farm supplies shop, PA who by this time owned the shop in his garage which he had previously run with his brother PZ, and KT, a smaller-scale farmer with a disability pension. The entrepreneurs tended not to vote in favour of expenditure on social services, or complained bitterly if they did, and KGy ensured that more money was spent than in surrounding villages on his favourite pass time, the football team. The entrepreneurs were still finding their feet, but they were beginning to form a business interest to influence council policy.

Tabar council was perhaps noteworthy because it had used its autonomy with respect to education to act generously toward the sector. It increased teachers' salaries to the average level in the surrounding area; it always accepted the budget that the school presented, including items like a photocopier and computer equipment; it found sufficient funds to help the children of the unemployed buy school books with a grant of 1,200 forints; and it made a contribution to the cost of school meals to maintain prices at their previous level. Such generosity was partly because the council was in the unusual situation in 1993 of being cash rich having just sold a property. But Tabar was also of interest for the political changes brought about by the 1994 elections. A somewhat oversimplified characterisation of the two local administrations in Tabar in the early 1990s might be that a cleric-dominated regime was replaced by a business-dominated one.

A brief discussion of the position of the church in Tabar is required to clarify this characterisation. The socialist history of Tabar had been characterised by the dominance of a village elite that transcended conventional socialist-era divides. It consisted of the primary school headmaster, the party secretary, the chemist, the reform church pastor, the vet and Uncle L, a former rich peasant who since regaining some land in 1957 had become well known for the quality of his wine. They met regularly to celebrate one another's name days and to play cards together. This informal association did not survive 'the change of system', but its demise was not related to politics. It had been in decline in any case in the late socialist years, mainly because of the age and infirmity of the participants, especially Uncle L, but also because of problems of a personal nature. When the party secretary formed a liaison with a younger woman and began co-habiting with her, the reform church pastor felt he could not be seen to be condoning such behaviour by continuing to socialise with him. Nevertheless elements of the old elite was still able to exert some influence in the early post-socialist years to the extent that the Reform church pastor helped an elder of his church get elected as mayor and became himself a member of the council with the highest number of votes.

Whilst all agreed that church attendance had remained constant since 'the change of system' (beyond the appearance in church of a number of well-known communists, which outraged some members of the congregation), the church's standing in the community increased in two rather different ways. First, its role as a spiritual and social insurance policy increased. This manifested itself in a substantial increase in the number of baptisms, although the number of all other life-milepost ceremonies remained the same. People who were either not religious or worked in professions where being religious had been frowned on, such as teachers and agricultural engineers, were having their children baptised in their older years. To some extent this was for spiritual reasons; but it was also a factor of social advancement. The popular Reform Church grammar school in Sárospatak would only take children who had been baptised. The church also increased its profile in the community following the 1990 elections, with a religious mayor and a cleric on the council. Church representatives were regularly invited to attend and make speeches together with other dignitaries at civic ceremonies of one sort or another, such as the unveiling of a war memorial or the unveiling of a memorial for the 'For Tabar' Foundation.

The issues that often caused tension in post-socialist church-local authority relations were all amicably resolved. The churches were happy with what they received under restitution, even though, because the school had its kitchen in the building concerned, the Reform Church had to accept a former gendarme barracks as a substitute. Religious instruction in schools was also accepted readily, with two thirds of children attending, not least because it had only ended as late as 1978 after the primary school teacher (and member of the village's old elite) had retired. But the 1990 mayor was widely seen as being too old for the job, and the entrepreneur DJ complained that the council had no backbone and was made up of the 'same old gang'. In the 1994 elections the incumbent mayor withdrew and there were seven candidates to replace him, a teacher, the former co-operative chairman and now private farmer, two disability pensioners, two unemployed people, and a 38 year-old agricultural engineer who used to work for the Wine Corporation. The latter was elected. Although four of the existing councillors were re-elected, the Reform Church pastor was not amongst them. The clerical interest diminished, and, by contrast, a business interest came into being. The biggest group on the council (four of the seven council members) was now made up of entrepreneurs.

Finally, Zádorpuszta, which also gained independence in 1990, witnessed a similar emergence of a business elite. The council was made up entirely of independents, both in 1990 and 1994. But whereas these independents had included two members of the socialist administration in 1990, by 1994 the majority of the independents were entrepreneurs. The village also benefited somewhat from the fact that ST felt a moral responsibility to replace some of the services provided in the socialist years by socialist employers such as the agricultural co-operative. He could not duplicate such services exactly, but he did support the kindergarten by providing it with milk from his shop at cost price, a shop which he had established partly at the suggestion of the mayor who wanted a second shop in the village to introduce competition. The village also gained financial advantage from its proximity to Budapest. It did a deal with Budapest to erect a rubbish dump on its land for which Budapest was paying a sum equivalent to 430 million forints at 1995 prices. The site was located five kilometres away from the village, beyond a hill, so did not constitute a particular eyesore for villagers.

The council's main development aim was not to promote local business, nor tourism, but to increase the village population and create an attractive dormitory settlement, like Nezávislice in the Czech Republic. To this end it set about promoting the building of new houses. It bought land from private individuals, the agricultural co-operative and a local state farm, and subdivided them into building plots already provided with electricity, water, gas and telephone. These they sold at well below the current market rates, less than a tenth of the price of local authority land a few miles closer to the Budapest agglomeration. Some 20 new houses had already been built and settled in 1991–92. The majority were either skilled workers or technical graduates. This policy continued in subsequent years: 24 building permits were granted in 1994, and twelve in the months up to October 1996. The village authorities were hopeful that a planned new exit from the M1 motorway would make the village even more attractive to such newcomers. The net effect was considerable. A population of 712 at the time of the 1990 council elections had increased to 830 by 1996, and the future viability of the school and kindergarten seemed to be guaranteed because the majority of incomers were in their child-bearing or child-rearing years. Nevertheless, in 1996, the long-standing goal of bringing back to the village the top four years of elementary education, which since 1978 had taken place in the former commune centre, had still not been achieved.

HUNGARIAN SPECIFICITIES IN SUMMARY

What is striking in Hungary's agricultural transformation is the great variety of outcomes and the different paths, both 'first economy' and 'second economy', to large-scale private farming. The winners in this process were not so much 'green barons' who kept their co-operative farms together, but rather those who became private farmers, people like TR and SzI in Pakucs, KGy and SGy in Korcona, TI and DJ in Tabár. Such individuals capitalised on their human, social and cultural capital advantages from the socialist era, not necessarily from their positions at the top of the socialist pecking order, to manipulate bankruptcy and co-operative restructuring regulations to create post-socialist successor farming companies. Perhaps the most dramatic losers were the villagers of Dombház who put their faith in a new village dairy conceived on the basis of a Smallholders' Party-inspired social, rather than a business, rationale, only to see it fail because of the implacability of market forces.

In the post-socialist rural non-farm economy, the most successful new business was that of RA in Károlyháza who built on an extensive late-socialist, 'second economy' legacy. ST in Zádorpuszta capitalised on under-utilised socialist-era assets from an agricultural co-operative's non-agricultural side-line to create a business on a slightly smaller scale, while NB in Pakucs was beginning to move beyond the confines of a purely family business by 1996. The similarly successful KB from Kissikonda was the only new entrepreneur of this kind to benefit from measures designed to promote the creation of new businesses, yet he too relied on family resources—the security offered by his wife's permanent employment while developing the business, and the family ties of an interventionist, socialist mayor with a fuzzy sense of the public-private divide. Local councils suffered the same 'fiscal stress' of increased responsibilities and reduced resources as their counterparts elsewhere, but teachers in Kissikonda and Tabar benefited in the short term at least from improved conditions when responsibility for schools was devolved to councils. The pattern of local politics in Hungary suggested more clearly than elsewhere that new business interests were beginning to extend their influence in the political sphere. In Tabar a cleric-dominated council was replaced by a business-dominated one in 1994; in Zádorpuszta and Korcona businessmen constituted the majority of councillors by the same time, while in Székhely a business interest engineered a coup to get rid of the socialist mayor who was too committed to social expenditure on the Roma poor.

Map 7.1. Research sites, Poland

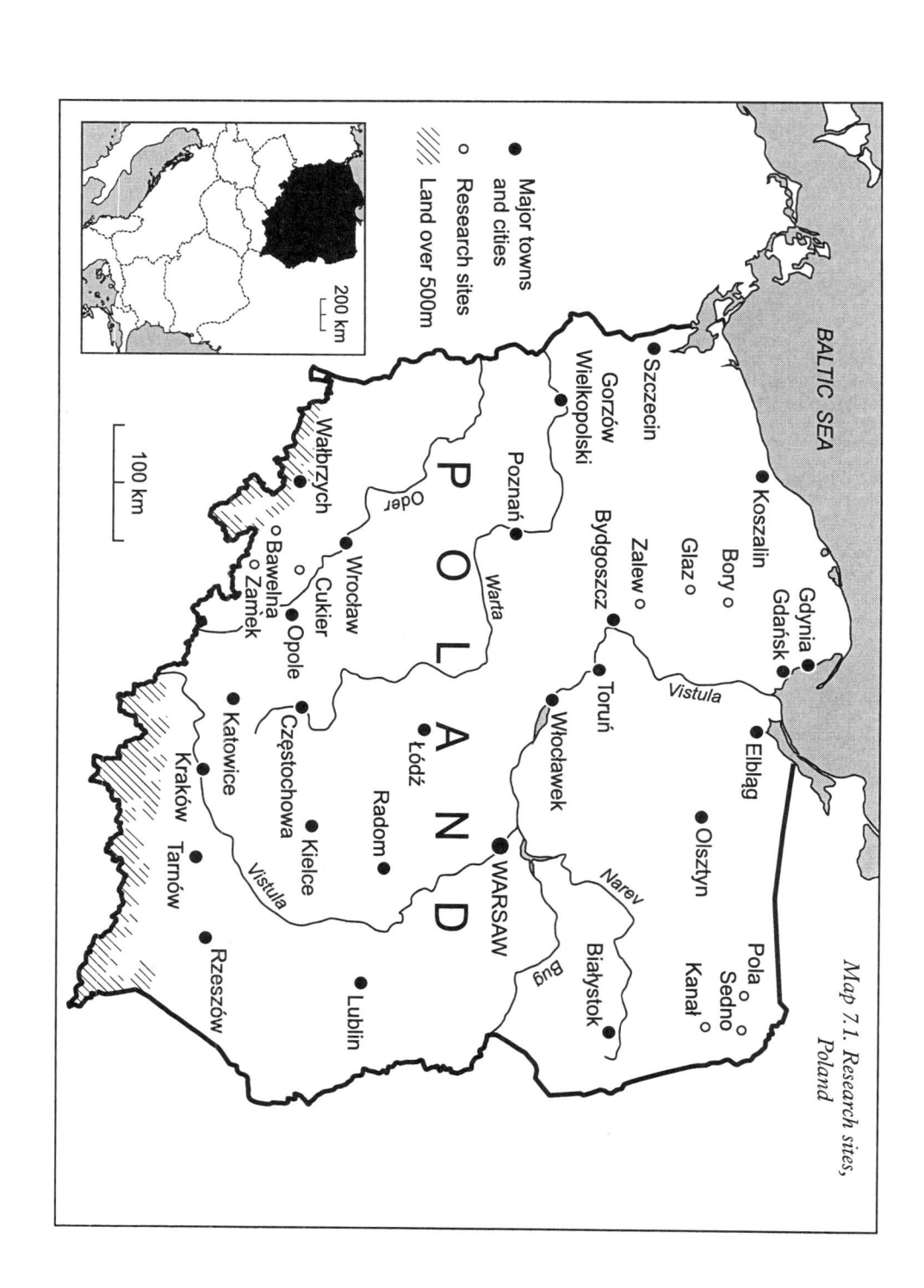

CHAPTER 6

Poland

Poland's abandoning of collectivisation in 1956 meant that it lacked one of the central features of the rural post-socialist transformation elsewhere: the restructuring of agricultural producer co-operatives. But if this major drama for rural actors did not take place, restitution issues emerged in relation to the state sector in farming nevertheless, even though the Polish government failed to pass restitution legislation before Poland's entry into the EU. The absence of agricultural producer co-operative restructuring necessarily resulted in greater continuity of, and variety in, farming structures, but the main developmental trends were broadly in line with the rest of the region. State farms, rather than agricultural producer co-operatives, were taken over mainly by their managements who became large-scale private farmers, predominantly on rented land, but land rented from the state rather than the 'inverted pyramid' of *de facto* new private owners. Some of the 'specialist' private farmers of the later socialist years also became large-scale private farmers mainly by participating in the state farm privatisation process, while the majority of small-scale farming continued on the same limited scale as before. There were thus similar 'first economy' and 'second economy' paths to private farming, although the 'second economy' path was both more common and in a sense more visible because of the formal status that 'specialists' had enjoyed in the socialist years. State farm privatisation differed from co-operative restructuring in another important way. Most co-operative members had some land to fall back on, the land that they or their parents had contributed to the co-operative. State farm workers were landless. If they lost their jobs under privatisation, as most did, because state farm labour forces, like those of the agricultural producer co-operatives, were also reduced by between a half and two-thirds, then they had no land to fall back on; and they often lived in apartment blocks which were not conducive to even subsistence farming.

The formal status of 'specialists' reflected another important difference between Poland and the rest of the region. Elsewhere successful practitioners in the 'second economy' in the socialist years were outsiders—by definition. In Poland, specialist farmers were part of the socialist establishment, with their own political party, the satellite party of the communist party which 'morphed' almost seamlessly into the post-socialist peasant party, the PSL, as discussed in Chapter 1. In Poland therefore, unlike other countries in the region, in the local political struggles that developed during the transition, the advocates of private peasant farming could be representatives of the 'old guard' and the status quo. There were two further specificities of the Polish transition. One was the rather more interventionist role of the Catholic Church; and the other was the legacy of its one-time ally, Solidarity. The latter's influence in privatisation was reflected in an emphasis on worker-companies and in employment conditions being imposed on privatisation projects, both in the case of state farms and non-agricultural companies. The policy of 'shock therapy', initially endorsed by the first Solidarity-led government, and the unemployment that it entailed also forced Polish local authorities to engage actively in job-creation projects. These were present in every country under consideration, but they figured more prominently in the minds of our Polish interlocutors.

Before turning to developments in our Polish villages, it is appropriate to present the variety of state and socialist sector agricultural actors that existed in the Polish countryside, for Polish agriculture was more complex than the conventional picture of private farms and state farms and all figure in this account. In addition to the once standard agricultural producer co-operative (RSP—Rolnicza Spółdzielczość Produkcyjna) which all but disappeared after 1956 (although some existed in some of the villages covered by our communes) the co-operative sector consisted of the general Commune Co-operatives (GS—

Gmina Spółdzielnia), other marketing co-operatives such as commune dairy co-operatives (GSM—Gminne Spoldszielnie Mleczarska), and Co-operatives of Agricultural Circles (SKR—Spółdielnie Kolek Rolniczych). The latter had been created in 1970, as successor to Farmers Circles which in 1956 had succeeded the Peasant Self-Help co-operatives, and they gradually took on communal production as well as providing machinery for private farmers. In addition to the State Farm (PGR—Państwowe Gospodarstwa Rolne), the state sector consisted of State Centres for Pedigree Breeding (POHZ—Państwowy Ośrodek Hodowli Zarodowy), subdivided into Pedigree Breeding Farms (GHZ—Gospodarstwo Hodowli Zarodowe), and State Machinery Centres (POM—Państwowy Ośrodek Maszynowy).

AGRICULTURAL TRANSFORMATION—STATE FARM PRIVATISATIONS AND SPECIALISTS

From manager to owner—Zalew and Lusowo

Zalew is a small market town in north-central Poland, the administrative centre of 34 hamlets, one of the larger of which is Lusowo (population of 570). The town itself had a population of 10,000 in the mid-1990s (the surrounding villages 12,000) and it was oriented at the end of the twentieth century towards agriculture and tourism. The Tuchola forest had been popular for tourism between the wars and retained this role in the post war period. A dam built in the 1960s created a lake which added further to the tourist potential; and Zalew's narrow-gauge railway attracted railway enthusiasts. A wide range of socialist agricultural units graced the Zalew of that era: a POM, a smaller state farm of 841 hectares in the settlement of B, a state-owned Fruit Growing Centre which covered 237 hectares, three SKRs which farmed 2,097 hectares in total, and the PGR of M which farmed 3,637 hectares. The latter had been created from eight previously independent state farms which had been merged over the course of the socialist years, especially in the 1970s. The consumer and marketing co-operative (GS) was founded in 1945 and took over the activities of a pre-war Agricultural Co-operative Society. By the end of the socialist period it employed 130 people in a distillery, a bakery and an abattoir as well as its sales and purchasing activities. In the post-socialist agrarian economy, the POM was privatised, but the three SKRs continued to exist and created a joint agricultural machinery services and repair company. The privatisation of the fruit farm was complicated by the Church's attempt to reclaim land, which, in the view of the chair of the town council, would result in the loss of about 60 jobs. The GS was still operative and profitable; it had plans to divest itself of some of its assets in 1993, but had not done so by the mid-1990s.

The privatisation of the PGR of M, and particularly its branch in Lusowo, which covered some 500 hectares, illustrates the importance in the transformation process of both the human and social capital advantages enjoyed by former socialist sector managers—human capital in the form of the scientific knowledge necessary to research how to cultivate certain products with higher value-added than conventional agricultural crops, social capital in the form of the contacts inherited from the socialist world. By 1991, the PGR consisted of seven agricultural units and two manufacturing works, and it had debts of around 30 billion złotys, a sum that it had no chance of paying back. The privatisation plan, to break the farm down into a number of units of 100–300 hectares and have the bigger ones transformed into 'worker's companies', while smaller plots would be sold or leased to private farmers, was devised by the head of the Lusowo unit of the PGR, a married man, whose wife was a qualified agricultural engineer and who was also deputy head of the commune council and a Peasant Party parliamentary candidate.[1] Responsibility for PGR entities which had significance for the community, such as the sports centre, sewerage systems and roads was to be handed over to the commune. Because of possible restitution claims, in only one case could the land be sold, the rest was allocated on 15-year leases. Zabłocki notes that in the early 1990s, 15 times more former state farm land was rented rather than sold because of possible restitution claims and the absence of restitution legislation.[2] Although sale of the farm was at a public auction,

---

[1] For the mechanics of state farm privatisation, see Grzegorz Zabłocki, 'Privatization in Polish agriculture: Determinants and effects', *Eastern European Countryside* 1 (1995): 67; and Psyk-Piotrowska, 'State-owned and co-operative farms', 155–8.

[2] Zabłocki, 'Privatization', 65.

there were no counter bids to seven of the eight successor farm proposals (including the unit in Lusowo). For the eighth unit, however, competition was fierce, because this was the only one where there was no possible restitution claim. The farm was bought by two private farmers, one of whom had been a member of parliament and had a background as a PGR manager. This new farm was entirely arable, and did not employ a single former PGR employee. Five of the successor farms were run as 'workers' companies', and all were headed by their former management. The remaining two were private farms, bought by women, one of whom had previously worked as a PGR manager.

The 'workers' company' of Lusowo operated on a much smaller scale than its predecessor, 280 hectares rather than 500, with a work force of 12 rather than the 46 of 1980. They kept cows and engaged in arable farming, but specialised in pigs, as did the big private farmers in the village. Although it was established as a 'workers' company', the former unit director owned 98 per cent of its shares. In the spring of 1995 he was speculating that it might be better to buy the farm outright, because it would then be easier to transfer funds back and forth between it and the private venture (0.42 hectares owned, 1.4 hectares rented concentrating on mushroom growing) that he ran on the side. By the December of that year, he had bought up all the outstanding shares, but had not yet taken over the farm as a private individual, that is to say, he owned 100 per cent of the shares in what was still legally an independent 'workers' company'. On the other hand, despite having to lay off some staff, the prospects for the farm looked brighter and tax arrears had been paid off.

Two years later, in December 1997, the 'workers' company' had formally been wound up and the former PGR manager ran it as a private individual. He still farmed roughly 280 hectares, but, not only had he now merged the mushroom business with the former state farm, this had given him an idea for a new venture which was proving quite profitable: the production of compost for mushroom growing. He had ignored the mushroom business for a bit because of the work involved restructuring the former PGR, but once that was more stable, he studied ways of improving his production and manufacturing compost. Thanks to good contacts inherited from the socialist years with a poultry farmer and a farmer who kept horses, he established a deal whereby he provided them with straw in return for the horse and poultry droppings. This new business, together with an increase in his pig stock to 1,000, meant that he was employing eleven outsiders in addition to himself and his wife, two more than he had in 1995, despite having given up dairy farming entirely. He had finally finished paying for the machinery that he had acquired under privatisation and was considering investment in new equipment. On the other hand, because the restitution issue had still not been entirely settled, his prospects when the lease ran out were uncertain. First, he felt that the income that he had gained from agriculture would nevertheless be insufficient for him to purchase the land. Second, although legally he could now purchase the land because the claim against the land was now fully documented, the State Agency in practice was reluctant to sell. Finally, if he took on a loan to buy the land, he felt that he could not afford to employ his current quota of staff.

Elsewhere in the commune there were very few commercial farmers. There was little interest in buying land because, to the chagrin of the local bank manager, few could afford commercial loans. The bulk of the 150 farming families in Lusowo, for example, produced essentially for self-supply and occasional sale. Only three families (besides the successor to the PGR) farmer commercially. The first was regarded locally as the 'wealthiest farmer in Poland', but his wealth came from his factory not his farm which specialised in pigs. The other two were also pig farmers, but they were both financially insecure because they had been hit by the interest rate hike of the early 1990s, of which more below.

Other privatisations—Głaz, Bawełna, Zamek

'Workers' companies' also figured in post-socialist developments in Głaz, also located in the Tuchola forest region, which in the mid-1990s had the status of a town, despite being no bigger than many villages. Its population was only 2,200, and the total commune population of the 13 villages and hamlets it covered was around 7,000. Socialist agriculture in the commune consisted of a PGR, an SKR and a state beef cattle farm, based in one of the commune's outlying hamlets. The PGR had been merged with many similar smaller state farms to become the centre of a large socialist farm which encompassed seven production units, a mechanisation and repairs unit and a construction unit and employed a total of around 800, farming 8,500 hectares in eight separate villages, with 1,300 cattle, 10–12,000 pigs and 5,000 sheep. But it had debts of six billion złotys and was adversely hit by the 'shock therapy' interest rate hike. The seat of the SKR which operated in the Głaz commune was located in the neighbouring commune, but in the Głaz commune's village of P it had a pig farm and associated arable land. In all, the SKR farmed a total of 1,000 hectares, mainly for fodder, in three separate units; it kept 3,000 pigs, 30,000 chickens, 100 dairy cattle and 150 beef cattle, and it employed around 240 people, 40 of them in administrative jobs. It also ran a saw mill.

The state beef cattle farm within the Głaz commune did not survive into post socialism and was bought by an entrepreneur from Tuchola. In 1992, the PGR was taken over by the State Treasury Agency. Employment was immediately reduced; but, as a local teacher wryly remarked, the managers were all unaffected: they became administrators for the State Treasury Agency. The bulk of the former PGR's property was leased by two 'workers' companies', but because of uncertainties about restitution (the Church had submitted a claim for 100 hectares, although it had previously owned much more) no land could be sold. Both 'workers' companies' were headed by former managers, but they were different in style. The one based in the village of R was very much 'post-socialist'. It was headed not just by a manager but by the former director of the PGR (who had also stood as a parliamentary candidate) who leased the bulk of former PGR land, had 200 shareholders and 350 employees. The second was a smaller operation, based around a single unit. It employed 50 and had only eight shareholders, six former managers of the unit and two of its employees. In addition to these larger farms, some 500 hectares was rented to private farmers under the privatisation project, a further 500 hectares were rented to the SKR which was beginning to specialise in pigs and had made an attempt at vertical integration by constructing an abattoir and a butchering unit, 400 hectares were transferred to a newly established State Potato farming plant, and the two non-agricultural units (the machinery unit in Głaz itself and the construction unit based in an outlying village) were wound up. The State Farm flats were sold off. All former employees availed themselves of the opportunity to buy their flats at concessionary prices, but 50 per cent of them failed to find employment in the successor companies. Many could not find employment on state job creation schemes either and, in the view of the local priest, 'drag[ged] out a wretched existence without even a minimum income and no prospects of change'. Buchowski also records the closure of a state farm in 1992 leaving much of its workforce abandoned and workless in blocks of flats outside the village. They had originally been attracted by the promise of housing and the small income that went with it.[3] Karwacki has described the 'culture of poverty' that emerged on the state farm housing block in Lesk.[4]

The average unit size on the 5,900 hectares of private farms in the commune was generally on a different scale—8.6 hectares, although there were pig and dairy 'specialists' with 10 to 40 hectares, and the biggest farmer, who ran a mixed farm, had 72 hectares. There was little interest in buying land, except from the former state farm; but this could only be possible once restitution issues had been cleared up; and few farmers were in a position to contemplate long-term bank loans. In the view of one commune council member, 'most are now autarkic farms'. The head of the GS also noticed a 'remarkable fall in the demands for fertilizers and agricultural equipment generally'. The co-operative no longer distributed such things and had almost stopped buying from local farmers, because they preferred to sell to private middle men rather than state companies or co-operatives, concentrating instead on retail activities and its bakery.

In Bawełna, a small Silesian textile town with a large rural hinterland in the Sudety Hills, the main unit of state agriculture during the socialist years, a 319 hectare GHZ, had been passed into the hands of the State Treasury Agency by 1996, but its ultimate fate was unclear; neither was that of the small RSP which farmed some land in the commune. The SKR, which had been created in 1970 and was relatively successful in the socialist years and had been responsible for building the House of Culture, broke up and its dairying activities were converted into a commune dairy co-operative. Agricultural restructuring was more dramatic in Zamek, another settlement (of 4,500) in the foothills of the Sudety Hills. The commune which it headed in the

---

[3] Michal Buchowski, 'Redefining social relations through work in a rural community in Poland', Working Paper no. 58 (Max Planck Institute for Social Anthropology, Halle-Saale, 2003), 9.

[4] Arkadiusz Karwacki, 'The culture of poverty in the post-state farm community', *Eastern European Countryside* 8 (2002): 79–92.

mid-1990s covered 15 settlements in all, with a population of 9,000, most of whom came from territory lost to the Soviet Union after the war. By the end of the socialist years, socialist agriculture consisted of an SKR, which had inherited some assets from earlier RSPs, and a POHZ which had developed out of a failed PGR but operated profitably. It had a young management and specialised in sheep and cattle breeding, with approximately 800 hectares of land on which to grow fodder; it operated profitably during the socialist years. In 1993, the POHZ was yet to be privatised and operated as a body under the supervision of the State Treasury Agency; by 1996, it had been privatised and operated as an independent limited liability company. Its staff had fallen dramatically from 560 to around 120.

The SKR in Zamek fared worse. Even before the end of the socialist period, its position had been weakening because many farmers had their own machinery; indeed, some were providing machinery services themselves and undercutting its rates. It was wound up early in the post socialist period, before 1993. Private farmers took over and farmed the land that it had itself cultivated, mainly on a rental basis. As in Głaz, at the end of the socialist era, there were very few individuals within the private sector who could be described as commercial farmers however. In 1993, locals estimated that there were only about 15 good farmers in the commune; by 1996, the estimate had fallen to four or five, although the understanding of what constituted a 'good farm' had increased to 300–400 hectares. There was little market in land, but rather more leasing of land from older peasants who could no longer cope. In general, as the clerk to the council noted, small farmers did not sell their land, even if they had other sources of income, a reluctance related to land's security function, a backstop if all other sources of income disappeared. Its consequence was that, if the more commercial farmers did buy or lease any land, they generally did so from formerly state land made available by state farm privatisation. Slawomira Zbierski-Salamek notes too, on the basis of her study of 'Rolnicy' in Wielkopolska that the expected post-socialist organic consolidation of land holdings did not take place,[5]

---

[5] Slawomira Zbierski-Salameh, 'Polish peasants in the "valley of transition": Responses to postsocialist reforms', in *In Uncertain Transition: Ethnographies of Change in the Postsocialist World*, ed. Michael Burawoy and Katherine Verdery (Lanham, MD and Oxford: Rowman and Littlefield, 1999), 189–205.

while Hann notes no trend towards specialisation even after the introduction of EU subsidies.[6]

From socialist specialist to commercial farmer— Zamek and Bawełna

RB, a 'specialist' farmer of the socialist years in Zamek, quickly became a large-scale, commercial farmer. His case illustrates well how, in the Polish context, people who followed what elsewhere in the socialist world would have been a 'second economy' path to commercial farming, could do so in Poland while being firmly embedded in the agricultural establishment and capitalising on all of the social capital advantages that a successful socialist career gave. RB's father had come from a part of what is today Ukraine and had received eight hectares of land as part of the settlement, slightly more than the average. Over the course of the years, he slowly built the farm up to 20 hectares, which, on his death in 1980, passed to RB. RB, who had attended an agricultural secondary school, built the farm up rapidly so that by 1993 he owned 80 hectares and rented a further 80. He employed two full-time farm labourers, who lived in houses that he owned in the village (effectively tied cottages), and ran a mixed farm of arable crops (sugar beet and rape seed) and livestock (either pigs or cattle depending on market conditions). In addition to his farm, he had established with a partner a company to manufacture animal feed, which employed ten people, and to which he sold his own produce. He had also become active politically alongside his farming, and was: a member of the local council, president of the supervisory board of the local consumer co-operative and a member of the control commission of the SKR. He even stood for parliament (unsuccessfully, although with strong local support) as a candidate for the former communist party. By 1996 he had expanded his farm to over 300 hectares, by purchasing some land and buildings from the former POHZ, and renting the land that he could not buy. He had also moved more strongly into livestock farming acquiring the necessary facilities in villages outside the one in which he lived. His 'cherry-picking' of former socialist sector assets

---

[6] Hann, 'Not the Horse', 122.

was not restricted to agriculture. He had further developed the feed-mixing company too by buying mixing equipment from the former GS co-operative.

A case from Bawełna also illustrates the socialist-era 'specialist' turned post-socialist large-scale farmer pattern, although his success was curtailed by one of the unanticipated consequences of 'shock therapy' on the agricultural sector. RM's father had been active locally in the Peasant Self-Help co-operative (becoming its chairman) and in politics, (becoming, in 1964, deputy chair of the local organisation of the ZSL, precursor to the PSL). RM inherited his father's three hectare farm in 1971. He already had a job in a state-owned factory making machinery for the textiles industry and initially he continued the family farm only on a spare-time basis, as he progressed to become director of the firm. But he gradually took farming more and more seriously, especially after 1988. By this time, he had joined the PSL himself and attended a course on developing agriculture. Through piecemeal purchase, he increased the farm to 20 hectares and he started renting a further 50 hectares from the commune, with the intention of buying it eventually. He employed one fulltime farm-hand and seasonal labour, owned his own combine harvester, kept detailed records of which crops grew best on which pieces of land, took an annual holiday and considered himself a 'farmer' rather than a 'peasant'. But even so he was hit by the dramatic increase in interest rates of the end of the socialist period which proved the ruin of many 'specialists' and formed the back drop of the many peasant demonstrations against the regime of the early 1990s.[7] The latter are discussed briefly by Gorlach and Mooney[8] and more fully by Foryś and Gorlach,[9] where they are critical of the writings of Ekiert and Kubik

---

[7] Zabłocki, 'Privatization', 66.
[8] Krzysztof Gorlach and Patrick H. Mooney, 'Defending class interests: Polish peasants in the first years of transformation', in *Theorising Transition: The Political Economy of Post-Communist Transformations*, ed. John Pickles and Adrian Smith (London and New York: Routledge, 1998), 262–83.
[9] Grzegorz Foryś and Krzysztof Gorlach, 'The dynamics of Polish peasant protests under post-communism', *Eastern European Countryside* 8 (2002): 47–65.

on popular protest.[10] Although RM survived in the end, he had to sell some of his machinery in order to be able to pay back his loan.

LOCAL AUTHORITIES AND REGIME CHANGE

From a clerical to a commercial regime—Bawełna

The Catholic Church had always played a stronger role in Poland than elsewhere in the socialist bloc and it is not surprising that it took on a more prominent and vocal role as socialism collapsed. In Bawełna, for example, a somewhat over simplified characterisation of post-socialist developments in the local authority would be that over the course of the first half decade or so of the post-socialist era, a pro-clerical regime was replaced by a secular and pro-business one.

Despite a reluctance on the part of those concerned to speak openly, there appear to have been three groups on the council. One of them, the 'opposition' on the council board, was mainly made up of former communists and fought in the name of the 'average person' to defend jobs and traditional industries, in particular the textile industry which had suffered dramatically in the post-socialist recession pushing unemployment up to 30 per cent. The other two groups promoted new directions for the community, but ones in which they were not disinterested. The first, the power-holders of the first post-socialist administration, had strong links with the Church and Solidarity. The priest of the 'low parish' in particular had helped Solidarity organisationally, although it was claimed by those active in Solidarity that the Church had withdrawn to its traditional role after the collapse of socialism. Its enemies claimed that this group wanted influence over the privatisation of commune property and contracts for municipal works in the direction of companies in which they had shares. Indeed, it was alleged that the town development plan was drawn up by the mayor and deputy mayor without the participation of the rest of the council, and that it reflected their business interests. Accusations were directed at the deputy mayor, for example, a former electrician in the POHZ, later a Solidarity activist

---

[10] Grzegorz Ekiert and Jan Kubik, *Rebellious Civil Society: Popular Protest and Democratic Consolidation in Poland, 1989–1993* (Ann Arbor, MI: University of Michigan Press, 2001).

in 1980, who had been in the USA between 1984 and 1986 and who then developed his own electrical wiring business. The council's activities in relation to privatisation in particular so incensed the 'opposition' that it organised a referendum in an attempt to unseat the council. Turnout was under 10 per cent, however, far too little to succeed.

The 1994 elections brought a change of political direction. The new majority force, the 'Self-governmental Forum', was a collection of members of the Freedom Union (Unia Wolności—a strongly pro-market party created in 1994 by a merger of two post-Solidarity parties) and business groups united in their opposition to the former administration. They claimed that they would take more account of the citizens' own opinions, and they introduced a new image by arranging in September 1994 for all council members to attend a course to develop more effective co-operation. In particular this regime was more distant from the Church. The priest complained that co-operation had been better under the previous mayor; the mayor explained that he was a firm believer in the separation of the Church and the state, and that he would insist on there being both religious and secular versions of all celebrations and anniversaries. The Church had requested a channel on the town's cable television system, for example, but the mayor, with council support, had turned it down. The new regime focused on improving efficiency and cutting waste. The official car was disposed of; a computer-controlled telephone exchange was introduced, minor taxes were increased, leases were renegotiated, arable land was sold, and rents on flats were increased so that they at least covered maintenance costs. In its self-image, the new ruling group was interested only in developing the potential of the village, whereas the earlier group had only been interested in using office to make itself rich. Yet the new group was not without business interests of its own, which were well served by the newer focus on developing the tourist potential of the community. The mayor, for example, was executive president of the Tourist Foundation of the Sowie Mountains Board. He was also a member of the board of the Together in Europe Foundation, an organisation that linked many of the town's new business community.

A key figure in the Together in Europe Foundation was JC, who had worked in Germany in the 1980s and had a German wife. He had made sufficient money, and learned enough about business to want to return to his native town and invest there before the 'change of system'. He quickly established two businesses, a butcher's shop, which bought meat direct from local peasants, and an alcohol wholesaling business. The latter quickly flourished and soon employed a staff of twenty. JC applied his 'can do' dynamism to both his business and his work as a councillor. In his business life, he overcame the problems of the poor telephone system by using two-way radios instead; for the council he was a leading light amongst those promoting a change of direction towards rural tourism rather than textiles. In the latter, he made much use of his German contacts, contacts which eventually developed onto an institutional level when a former resident of this once-German town came to visit. A twinning arrangement was established with the German town, in the far west of Germany, where this former resident now lived.

Ultimately it was links with Germany that would be the core of JC's business activities. Even in 1993 he was very aware of competitive pressures. His had once been the only butcher's shop in the community, but by 1993 there are lots of them and he felt the need to specialise or move into something else. Within two years, partly because his wife sustained a serious injury in a car accident, he had changed direction radically. He handed the butcher's business over to his sister, sold the alcohol distribution business, and invested in a hotel, which for a long time remained empty because he could not afford to fit it out. In the interim he made a living by acting as a consultant and intermediary for German firms wishing to invest in the area.

Clerical influence and intrusion—Pola, Bory and Cukier

In Pola, a village located close to Sedno which will be discussed at length below, the Church had been active in charity work in the 1980s. But the new priest who arrived in the early 1990s saw no reason to continue the practice because the state and commune council already provided support. The commune Social Aid Centre thus cared for 27 families in 1993 and 28 in 1995. The children of 14 families qualified for free school meals paid for by the council, and in 1993 the council also financed the funerals of three of the commune's poor. There were twenty households in the commune where no family member had a job of any kind; furthermore, the mayor ruefully recognised that in some of the outlying villages children did not complete more that elementary schooling.

Pola's priest was a man of decided views. In addition to seeing no need for charity in post-socialist Poland, he had faith in Poland's 'Catholic majority' but feared that the former communists were still well organised and active in the village (a fear that no other villager shared). His belief in 'self-help' was further reflected in his unembarrassed ownership of a Japanese car which he had managed to purchase from savings made during his previous post. On the other hand, he was happy for the Church to receive the help of others. As soon as he arrived, he set about repairs to the church and building a centre for young people from Catholic organisations. These investments cost more than was available in church funds, so he asked for contributions from the parishioners. When these proved insufficient, he went to the local savings bank and found out details of villagers' accounts. Having calculated that a sum of 0.1 per cent of these savings would cover the costs required by the church, he made pointed remarks to this effect from the pulpit in an attempt to shame the villagers into paying up. This and other comments from the pulpit about parishioners resulted in a decline in church attendance. Nevertheless the mayor remained loyal to the priest. (A fellow councillor and former head of the consumer cooperative complained that the mayor listened to the priest but not to the inhabitants.) And perhaps this loyalty paid off, certainly when there was a Solidarity government in power nationally. The priest was well connected with Solidarity and claimed, and almost certainly with good reason, that it was he who got the commune the money necessary to build the new school—a single well-connected phone call did the trick.

The priest in the village of Wiejce, part of the Bory commune, was also forceful and forthright. He had particularly strong views on the role of women, contraception, and 'living in sin', which probably explained the tension between him and the (female) head of the commune council in 1993, a tension exacerbated by his refusal to let a teacher rent an unused house in the community. He had also initiated a dispute with the headmaster of the Wiejce school by trying (ultimately unsuccessfully) to have prayers said at the beginning of every lesson. These forthright views, according to one councillor, had stopped some from attending church altogether, but bullied others into doing so, so that overall attendance had remained roughly the same. The prayers incident inflamed an already tense relationship between the priest and the headmaster following the introduction of compulsory religious education in the schools. Relations between the Church and the school in Wiejce at least remained 'cool', as they were in Cukier where there was a dispute over the location of a new cemetery. Although the context is very different, the resolve of sections of the Roman Catholic Church to pursue their interest in post-socialist uncertainty is reflected in the tense relations between Roman and Greek Catholics and their restitution issues described by Hann.[11]

Continuities, innovations and the PSL—Głaz, Pola, Kanał

The most remarkable feature of local politics in Głaz was the mayor himself. He had first entered local government in 1965, after training as a tailor and then heading a tailors' co-operative; and he had been the key politician in the commune ever since, serving as mayor continually from 1973 onwards. He survived the initial post-socialist upheavals, and proved his ability to lead in the post-socialist climate by being re-appointed in 1994. A key figure in the community, he was also chairman of the sports club and president of the Union of Volunteer Fire Brigades, and he remained a (former communist) party member. Embedded as he was in the old establishment, he used his experience to navigate the bureaucracy and gain access to grants for infrastructure development and job-creation schemes (cleaning streets, redecorating schools, digging sewers, laying gas pipes, cleaning the water supply and so on), partly a consequence of the fact that Głaz was located in a region 'threatened by structural unemployment' for which special assistance was available. A total of 300 such jobs were created between May 1992 and May 1993. The problem for the mayor was how to maintain them, as the Ministry realised that it had been over generous and cut back its funding. Nevertheless, he still managed to create 260 jobs in 1995, although it had fallen to 180 in 1996, despite being well aware that these were not 'real jobs'.

Unemployment in the commune was very high: 24 per cent in 1993 and 29 per cent in 1995, which represented 240 individuals in the village itself and 500 in the surrounding commune villages; some 240 of the latter no longer qualified for benefits. The problem

---

[11] Hann, 'Not the Horse', 184–7.

of unemployed youth was not unique to Głaz, but it was a particularly prominent issue in the minds of villagers. The deputy head of the Labour Agency was concerned about the growing problem of alcoholism, and an increase in prostitution, both casual and organised, something that was only reported in Głaz in Poland (but was an issue in Bárov in the Czech Republic). The local police chief was similarly concerned and reported a 32 per cent increase in crime between 1993 and 1994.

The commune's Social Aid Centre struggled in face of reduced funding and the increased need that such unemployment caused. In 1995 it asked the council for a budget of 500 million złoty based on its estimates of its needs: it was given 200 million. In 1993 it provided assistance for 190 families, 703 people; by 1994 this had increased to 274 families, 1,134 people. The Church provided a degree of limited additional support in that it asked the social workers in the health care centre for a list of villagers who might be in need of charitable works, and, in conjunction with the Society of Catholic Families, it also occasionally organised collections of second hand clothes to support the Elizabethan Sisters. The latter organisation, which ran two charitable institutions, one catering for the elderly, the other for mentally disabled children, collaborated with the commune Social Aid Centre. It had been active in the commune for 180 years and in earlier (socialist and post-socialist) times had received charitable donations from abroad, but this had ceased by the mid 1990s. The bulk of the burden of looking after the poor of the commune thus fell on the under-resourced local authority.

Głaz looked to tourism as a potential source of development, in particular the lake located nearby. The council had inherited from a socialist-era factory its leisure facilities, holiday cottages and other facilities, which were located by the lake. Some of these it was breaking up into plots and selling, others it was developing itself. In 1993 most of the plots had already been sold, some 40 per cent of them to people living in the nearby town of Chojnice. By 1995 the council was moving beyond what it could develop directly to encouraging others to move in the direction of tourism. It had developed links with the 'Kashub' society in Chojnice whose business was the promotion of rural tourism, and some 40 farmers in the commune had begun to offer holiday accommodation on their farms.

Głaz decided to jump before it was pushed on the policy of taking over responsibility for schools, in the expectation that it might benefit from additional subsidies. It took over responsibility for the commune's eight primary schools (over 1,200 children) and three kindergartens in January 1992; education became over night the biggest expenditure item in the council budget, 52 per cent of the total in 1993. Two years later, however, the climate had moved beyond the early enthusiasm witnessed in Kissikonda and to some extent Tabar in Hungary. 'Biggest' was not big enough and the council was feeling the pinch of falling school rolls: government subsidies were provided *per capita*, yet operational costs remained constant or even increased. Autonomy had come with the cost of accepting a funding system that did not suit them.

A defining problem for policy-makers in Głaz was the stranglehold that the 'farming lobby' had over taxes, a vested interest that even a man of the stature of the mayor struggled to overcome. There were fourteen farmers on the twenty-person (all but four male) council, and farmers made up the majority on the all-male, five-person management committee. Raising significantly taxes related to agriculture was *de facto* impossible. The mayor complained that land taxes were so low as to be meaningless, and contributed a mere billion złoty to the budget. He was obliged to sit and watch as, in 1993 for example, the council members actually reduced the agriculture tax from 200,000 złoty per quintal to 180,000 złoty per quintal. Given the impossibility of raising land taxes, the council's only real economic lever was to reduce other tax obligations, yet, with employment being such an issue in the commune, this was a policy used more to forgive liabilities of existing and struggling companies, such as the communal co-operative, than to attract new businesses.

The mayor of Głaz was not the only one to be frustrated by the conservative influence of farmers and their political representation via the PSL, and it might be noted in passing that Buchowski claims that in his village in the Wielkopolska region practically all farmers voted PSL.[12] When he came to office, Pola's mayor had drawn up a plan for the economic development of the commune which included both

---

[12] Buchowski, 'Redefining social relations', 15.

tourism (a hotel) and food processing (a slaughterhouse and bakery). Furthermore there were local initiatives in the field of tourism. In one of the outlying villages there was a former estate building that had formed part of the state farm. The local villagers, mobilised by the head of the local fire brigade, wanted to renovate the property and then sell it to private buyers; they even went as far as establishing a committee for the preservation of the estate. But the project depended on the council providing an adequate infrastructure, and it was unable to do this. Council members too expressed the desire to develop tourism, but inevitably followed such comments with the rider that there was no money for it. The mayor was keen to develop the area that bordered on Lake Wigry for tourist purposes, and certainly there was some interest in purchasing recreational plots within the commune, as the accountant noted. In addition, there were outstanding natural features (a deep gully near one of the villages in the commune) and sites of cultural interest (a collection of work by a local painter and archaeological museum in Pola itself). But in 1993 the mayor was aware that this could only be developed with the help of an outside investor, and there was none; while, in 1995, he recognised that the area's status as a nature reserve (on the basis of legislation passed in 1992) made significant development of tourism impossible. Nevertheless, by 1995 the mayor could describe the infrastructural developments with a degree of pride. The cultural centre, already started in 1993, had been built to replace the room used in the council building. Some 14 kilometres of water pipe had been laid (a third of the costs having been covered by the council), a new primary school had been built to replace a very old one, thanks to a grant from the state budget (and, perhaps, the political influence of the priest), and a 500-subscriber telephone exchange had been opened. Furthermore, thanks to judicious juggling of funds, it had not proved necessary to close any of the smaller schools. The next big infrastructure project was a five-year plan to build a water treatment plant, fifty per cent funded by the provincial environment agency.

Despite these relative successes, both the mayor and the accountant felt that the agricultural tax was too low. But it was simply impossible to pass a budget in a community like Pola that was unfavourable to agriculture. Farmers, or those with a significant farming element to their family income, made up the majority of the council, both in

1993 and, following the 1994 elections, in 1995. The composition of the personnel on the council changed radically between the two elections, although the mayor remained in place. Only five people were re-elected, and there were 13 new faces. But a farmers' majority remained, and with it a veto on radically increasing the land tax and thus the commune's revenue. The limited horizons imposed by this farming veto were well reflected in the fact that the mayor felt able to state in 1993, with some pride, that he had managed to persuade the councillors of the need to provide a service as rudimentary as decent street lighting in the centre of Pola in the vicinity of the cultural centre.

Kanał is a tiny and relatively young settlement in the middle of the forest, very close to the 'green border' with Belarus. It owes its origins to the Augustów canal, built in the 1830s, which linked the Vistula via the River Narew to the River Niemen in Lithuania, crossing what is now Belarus on the way. Villages were established along its course to develop forestry; lumber was floated down the canal to urban markets, a pattern that continued to the 1990s. The Kanał commune too sought to tackle its educational problems head-on by becoming, like Głaz, one of the first communes in the country to take over the running of schools, but, as in Głaz, it was far from clear that this ambitious policy had paid off. Taking responsibility for education had given the commune an overall subsidy of 30 billion złotys for education, but it turned out that this was insufficient to cover maintenance costs, and a further 5 billion złotys had to be found from the communal budget. Part of the problem, as in Głaz, was that the new system did not recognise the increased costs of education in a low density, highly dispersed commune like Kanał, which encompassed 16 hamlets large enough to have a *sołtys* (see Chapter 1), but numerous other smaller ones, and had a population of only 2,700 on a total area of 37,000 hectares, the bulk of it state-owned forest. The commune had a total of six schools, but only an average of 67 pupils per school and a staff-pupil ratio of 1:9. One school was scheduled to be closed because, though it covered the full 8 years of elementary education, it had only 17 pupils. Furthermore, the commune had to report that a not insignificant number of children (10 per cent in the mayor's estimate) did not go on to secondary education at all. Augustów, the nearest town with a secondary school, was 15 kilometres away from the closest part of the commune, and as many as 40 kilometres away from its more distant hamlets. Transport costs were increasing as subsidies were reduced, and few children benefited any more from government grants to cover the costs of boarding. Indeed, since 1990 the government had stopped subsidising all school meals.

The PSL's influence was to be felt in Kanał too, as in Głaz and Pola. The first post-socialist, 16-person commune council was dominated by farmers, and few decisions were taken that contradicted their interests. It was also entirely male. The young, female head of the social welfare centre in the commune was scathing about its lack of vision and a focus which was restricted to matters that affected the councillors personally. The original post-socialist mayor was almost certainly guilty of focusing on his personal interests to the detriment of those of the community. He had been dismissed prior to 1993 for what one councillor, in a vocabulary of an earlier era, called 'voluntarism', and others hinted was an abuse of power. Certainly there was a lack of trust, despite the fact that he came from the commune, unlike the person who replaced him. Despite all the talk of developing tourism, one of the village administrators, not a council member, noted that the council wanted farming to be the engine for growth in the community. The council taxed leisure plots and holiday homes to the maximum permitted by the regulations, but kept property taxes and land taxes low.

'Teachers', 'farmers' and rural tourism—Bory

It is clear from the studies so far that many Polish villages based their development strategy on tourism, and Bory was particularly successful in this regard. The commune had begun to prosper when socialist tourism developed from the 1970s onwards. But there was parasitic aspect to socialist tourism. It was organised entirely by the enterprises based in Bydgoszcz and Gdańsk which maintained their recreational facilities in the village. When these enterprises experienced difficulties or were closed down, the village did not have the expertise to market itself. There was no industry of significance within the commune, and the bulk of the forestry workers, even seasonal ones, were not local.

Perhaps because of Bory's greater dependence on tourism (it provided the council with an income identical to that from agriculture,

500 million złoty), Bory differed from other villages in that it had a particularly clear conception for the direction in which it wanted this branch to develop. Providing the infrastructure alone was not enough. Key figures in the development of this strategy were women and, although they lost power in 1994, their tourism strategy was not abandoned by their successors. As the woman head of the commune council put it, western tourists wanted to come to the area, but they needed different kinds of facilities. Big, socialist rest homes were no good, and in any case the companies that used to run them had gone bankrupt. Westerners preferred self-catering holidays, or holidays on farms; but the majority of local farmers were not geared up for that.

In order to promote tourism in its preferred way, the Bory council established a special committee for Tourism and Environmental Security which established links with a tourism agency based in Gdańsk, encouraged co-operation with neighbouring communes, and published a brochure advertising the tourist potential of the commune. In addition, the secretary of the council, who had been on a course in Bremen, came back with a plan to promote tourism by promoting traditional customs and ceremonies, such as the elements of local culture that are connected to the ethnic minority of Kashubians in the region. The council accepted the scheme, and gave her one fulltime employee; moreover the project was retained by the new council which took office in 1994, although the latter tended to highlight the material results associated with cultural activities such as the Cultural Centre and facilities associated with it. Although when socialism collapsed, the common complaints that the community was passive and self-interested were to be heard here as elsewhere, the continued support of the Cultural Centre as part of the commune tourism strategy kept it vibrant; it even attracted young people from Bydgoszcz. The instructors ran puppet shows for children and organised amateur dramatic groups for young people and adults. There were clubs for bridge, chess and draughts, table tennis, and embroidery; there were foreign languages groups and a dance group, a sculpture studio, an international boat race on the lake, and volley ball, football, water sports and dance competitions.

Although party political organisations were of little significance in Bory, politics was acrimonious, under the first administration at least, and that tension remained with the second administration when the balance of power shifted. It is tempting, as some locals did, to categorise the dispute on the council as being one between 'teachers' and 'farmers', but in reality it was between teachers and farmers allied with businessmen. Furthermore, there was an 'old guard' versus 'new guard' dimension to it too in that most of the 'farmers' had been in local government in the 1980s, while the 'teachers' were newcomers, and seen by the 'farmers' as representing Solidarity, part of whose purpose, one councillor acknowledged approvingly, was to 'take revenge on the old nomenklatura'. Despite the acrimony, the dispute was not about the most important element in the council's strategy, the tourism plan, although it did provide part of the pretext that led to the first administration's downfall. The issue which divided the 'teachers' (and there were only three actual teachers, all women) from the rest was social expenditure. The 'farmers' and businessmen, not surprisingly, wanted to keep this to a minimum; the 'teachers', in greater daily contact with cases of need within the community, were keen to increase it. The commune secretary in 1995 estimated that 95 per cent of the commune's population lived 'on the edge of poverty and misery'. Despite the normal extreme pressures on its finances, such as free school meals for 30 children provided by the Social Aid Centre, the council bought a bus to transport children to school, although it was under no legal obligation to do so. The council was also keen to collaborate with the Social Welfare Centre in opening a hostel for the homeless.

Both 'farmers' and businessmen accepted the tourism plan; but they made their acceptance of it conditional on the plan for the hostel for the homeless being dropped. The 'teachers', recognising the value of tourism to the commune as a whole, reluctantly accepted. Ironically it was to contribute to their downfall. One of the contested elements in the 1994 elections was the allocation of concessions to sell drinks and run catering establishments around Lake Wiejce, the centre of the tourism project. The 'farmers' called foul and claimed that it had favoured friends of the 'teachers'' administration. The 'farmers' won the elections, but tourism remained central, although because the new mayor had a background in forestry perhaps, he also stressed the importance of light industry related to timber processing. The new mayor was energetic chasing funding from every conceivable source, and proudly reported in 1995 that he had already raised as much in subsidies as the previous administration had done in four years.

The Non-Farm Economy

Solidarity-influenced privatisation—Cukier

Events in Cukier reflected the influence of the Solidarity legacy particularly clearly in so far as it was manifest in the privatisation of non-farm businesses, although in this particularly agricultural commune, all of the entities concerned were related in some way to agriculture. The privatisation of the POM was protracted and reflected many of the tensions involved in coming to terms with the dominance of market forces, especially in a climate created by Solidarity's ambiguous status as a labour union and a political party favouring radical reform. The POM had been founded as late as 1981 and employed 120. In addition to providing machinery services for agriculture, it also earned an income from a contract with the 'Star' truck factory to service its vehicles. With the 'change of system', both the agricultural services and the truck-servicing businesses collapsed. In 1992, with the active participation of the mayor, there was an attempt to rescue what could be salvaged from the enterprise by converting it into a fifty-strong private 'workers' company'. However, fearful of losing further jobs in the market environment, and unwilling to accept the redundancies that this strategy entailed, the majority of the workforce went on strike. The result was stalemate: the POM was effectively closed; but the strike was doomed to failure in the post-socialist economic climate. Even Poland, the first country to return to post-socialist growth, was languishing in recession.[13] Eventually, in 1993, the acting director of the company leased the assets to a company which wanted to establish a business manufacturing large plastic refuse bins for export to Germany. The business was a success, and by 1995 it had assembled a reasonable order book. But its labour force, thirty in all, many of whom had previously worked for the POM, was a quarter of the latter's socialist peak.

The biggest employer in the commune, by contrast, was its sugar refinery, which was considered to be one of the best in Lower (western) Silesia, which employed 250 people, 90 per cent men, mostly aged between 35 and 55. Its privatisation was less traumatic

---

[13] See Swain, 'A post-socialist capitalism', 1673.

because of the refinery's technological advantage; it was the only refinery in the country to produce one specialist type of sugar. By 1993, employment at the sugar factory had fallen, but only by 50, as the enterprise was restructured. It continued to operate profitably, paid off its loans and invested in new technology so that it could refine its product further and sell direct to the market, finding it more profitable to sell refined sugar in Poland than the semi-finished product to Germany and Belgium.

Insiders and outsiders in the face of disappearing socialist certainties—Kanał

If Poland's particular 'Solidarity legacy' made itself felt in privatisation projects even at the local, rural level, new business development faced similar challenges to those of the region as a whole. In many contexts, such as in Kanał, it tended to be outsiders who saw business opportunities that locals missed. There the key element in the post-socialist transition was not the restructuring of agriculture so much as the 'cold shower' of market realities and the removal of subsidies. In a fashion analogous in some respects to the destruction of a particular remote socialist way of life in Blagun and Chala in Bulgaria, in Kanał a secure, government-supported, pluriactivity based on tobacco-growing and employment in forestry became an insecure pluriactivity based on an agriculture in which tobacco-growing was no longer possible and forestry employment which was far from certain. With a reduction in the price of tobacco by a factor of three, its production became loss-making over night. The area planted for tobacco throughout the commune fell from 250 hectares to 15. Two years later, tobacco prices had increased to more acceptable levels, and tobacco imports had been restricted, resulting in an increase in the area sown with tobacco again. The State Forestry Inspectorate, on the other hand, was six billion złotys in debt and was forced to rationalise and abandon water transport in favour of conventional road transport. The more market-oriented Forestry Inspectorate no longer allowed local farmers to use forest land for pasture. This resulted in a roughly three-fold fall in livestock holdings, exacerbated by a drought in 1992, as farmers reverted to keeping animals to meet family needs only, despite the continued presence of two dairy co-operatives in Sedno and Augustów which were willing to buy, and a slight general increase in the profitability of dairy farming.

Two years later, employment in forestry was even more insecure following a move towards casualisation and the introduction of a system based on sub-contracting work gangs made up of its former employees. The latter could provide more or less fulltime employment for only a fraction of those formerly employed by the state. By mid-decade, the State Forestry Inspectorate's work force had fallen to 50 administrators, 15 fulltime employees and 10 part-time casual employees, the latter being employed for two months in the summer to look after its campsites. The Forest Inspectorate had initially run more campsites, but they barely covered their costs and were leased out to outsiders. It also owned numerous holiday houses which could be put to tourist use, but by the mid-1990s they were in need of renovation and their potential could not be realised. The decline in fulltime forestry jobs resulted in an increase in migrant working as far afield as Germany and the United States, in more casual employment in forestry, in greater reliance on harvesting berries, mushrooms and other 'fruits of the forest' for sale, and in increased part-time trading and smuggling (see section on Sedno below). Unemployment rose from 300 in 1992 to 400 in 1993, and would have been much higher but for the opportunities provided by smuggling, which, according to the estimates of one council member, was indulged in by fifty per cent of the commune youth. The Council Secretary in 1993 estimated that every second person in the commune was either an old-age pensioner or a disability pensioner.

Despite job loss, retreat to subsistence farming and casualisation, some new ventures did emerge. Three private saw mills were already in operation by 1993, one with the participation of German capital; and a fourth was under construction in another hamlet. One of the Kanał businesses was run by two 35-year-old men, both with higher education, one a former white-collar worker on the council and the son of a canal worker, the other with his own business already. They acquired the assets of the former SKR and with it the rudiments of four businesses: a wood-processing business, a small bar, a haulage business, and a petrol station. However, despite the fact that the petrol station was the only one for 20 kilometres, they could not make money from it and wound it down. They concentrated rather on the wood-processing business, despite intense competition from eleven competing companies in the region. The business began to operate profitably a year or so after the privatisation, and gradually expanded, eventually employing ten people. Outsiders, one with business skills already, and both well educated, had seen potential in assets that were about to be written off.

The privatisation of one of the holiday complexes in the commune was less straightforward and reflected tourism's capacity to bring external agents into a local economy. This complex of campsites, wooden cabins and small hotels accommodating a total of 200 had been the holiday centre of a Warsaw-based company. The obvious purchaser was the sitting tenant, the person who had run the complex on a leasehold basis since 1986. But he had let the complex run down, partly because of a lack of resources, partly in a deliberate attempt to let the value of the property fall so that it could be bought more cheaply when it was finally auctioned. This ploy seemed to be bearing fruit, and in the first round of the auction he even gambled on not putting in a bid in the hope that the asking price would fall still further. But, at the very last moment, in the second round of the auction, a competitor submitted a rival, and higher, bid. This competitor was a company that had been established for the express purpose of making the bid, by a man who was based in Warsaw, but who had come to the region regularly as a party lecturer and hunter, and had even managed the complex briefly, between 1984–86, when he had taken a career break for health reasons. His company was set up in conjunction with 'friends who liked hunting', fellow company directors and an official in the Ministry of the Environment. The new owner then hired as his agents a family who had worked for him in 1984, used his contacts in high places to renegotiate the lease on the land from the Forest Inspectorate, and began investing heavily in renovating the site. He engineered a loan from a Euro-region project operating in the area and developed plans to co-produce a guide book to promote the region. The local actor was out-manoeuvred by an outside investor with better business and political contacts.

Kanał also illustrated how outsiders could identify a totally new tourist market. Kanał's origins, as noted above, stemmed from the canal which runs through its territory. With the exception of floating logs, the canal had long since lost its commercial rationale. But holiday-makers from Warsaw and Augustów saw its potential for canoeing and it became a regular stop-over point on organised canoeing holidays offered, in the main, by 'alternative' groups of one kind or another in Germany, the Netherlands and Scandinavia. The mayor complained in the mid-1990s that the organisers of the canoeing holidays had not created a single new job in the village, but their business prospered and it must, at the very least, have introduced additional expenditure into the community.

An old new business hostile to the socialist mayor—Głaz

Głaz witnessed the development of a Polish 'second economy', private sector non-agricultural venture to post-socialist success. Unlike similar developments in Hungary, it had no links with the co-operative sector. Elder-Pak began operations manufacturing buckets as early as 1974, the private business (on a sole trader basis) of the elder of two brothers. The brothers came from Bydgoszcz, but the elder brother had married into Głaz. In 1981, the company became a partnership and they began to produce a variety of metal goods and containers. Their first stroke of luck came in 1982 when they participated in a tender offer for a contract to supply a huge production run of small water tanks for Polish State Railways (PKP). They won the tender, received loans from PKP for purchase of materials and employment of staff and enjoyed three to four years profitable production. By the time that the contract ran out Elder-Pak had bought new machinery and established itself as a rather different business, producing tins for paint and glue. By the 1990s, the company employed 16 (the vast majority from Głaz or other commune villages), had built a new plant, and was turning over six billion złotys shipping its produce to customers in a 400 kilometre radius; it was one of only three manufacturers of such products in the country, producing a million tins a year in sizes ranging from half a litre to 20 litres, and had secure contracts with a major paint producing company.

The impact of post-socialism on Głaz's non-agricultural economy was harsh. The biggest non-agricultural employer in Głaz had been a branch of the Bydgoszcz-based Automatic Turning Lathe Company (FATO), but it had only arrived as late as 1985, was restructured in 1988, by 1990 was employing 50 villagers, but was dependent on the Soviet market for profitability. FATO fell victim to the collapsed Soviet market and finally closed down in 1992. The municipality's services company reduced jobs from 77 to 35 in 1993, as it teetered on the verge of bankruptcy with debts of 80 million złoty. The local Forest Inspectorate also shed 50 per cent of its jobs. Meanwhile opportunities for commuting workers were also reduced. Some 100 villagers who had commuted to factories in nearby Chojnice and Wapno were made redundant following the decision of those companies to sack their commuting workers first. The GS similarly reduced staff, from 140 in 1981 to 37 in 1993, but remained operation.

Elder-Pak suffered too from the recession associated with the collapse of Soviet trade because it imported superior quality Russian steel, but this had no effect on employment. In fact it took on four former FATO employees to push its labour force up to 20. In addition to this, a further ten were employed on a seasonal basis for the summer (for 6–9 months) when demand was higher. The demise of FATO provided a further opportunity for Elder-Pak. FATO's buildings in the village had passed into the property of the commune. Relations between council and company had always been tense. The socialist mayor referred to Elder-Pak's boss simply as a 'person from Bydgoszcz', and the council felt that the company contributed rather little to the commune budget because, the main local tax related to the size of the property, which in Elder-Pak's case was quite small. The boss of Elder-Pak, by contrast, had served twice on the local council and was frustrated by its policy of focusing on short-term job creation measures (at which it was successful as we have seen), rather than promoting 'real jobs'. Despite this mutual antipathy, Elder-Pak acquired the former FATO site and, in addition to the investment grants available to companies in regions 'threatened by structural unemployment', exploited a concession offered by central government, for the employment of disabled workers. The bulk of the workforce in this expanded operation, which would employ up to 100, was to be disabled workers.

THE PECULIARITIES OF A NON-EU BORDER COMMUNITY—SEDNO

Sedno shared many of the features discussed so far in terms of agricultural restructuring, non-farm employment, new businesses and local authority autonomy, but all were magnified by its peripheral status in the far east of Poland—a small town located on the historic trade route to Grodno, Vilnius and the Baltic States and close to Poland's current border with Lithuania. The border offered particular opportunities for legal and illegal sources of additional income—a perverse variant perhaps of the 'border effect' that has been noted elsewhere, although the erotic club in the Czech Republic's Bárov reflected a seamier side to the EU border effect.

State farm privatisation—with a little help from the border

Within Sedno in the socialist period there operated a PGR, an SKR and a POM which employed 130 and provided services for farmers as well as operating a dairy and a spare parts business for a Warsaw company. The SKR had branches in three commune hamlets and neighbouring Pola, and had begun agricultural production in 1970 on land that it received from the State Land Fund. The PGR was established in 1946 on land formerly owned by agricultural estates, Germans and Jews—the interwar population had been 24 per cent Jewish. In addition to Sedno itself, it operated with centres in three commune villages, including one which immediately before World War II had been the seat of an estate of about 180 hectares which employed 14 full time workers and additional seasonal workers. The Sedno PGR had been relatively small until the 1970s when it was obliged to merge with two others in two nearby communes. The resulting farm covered 1800 hectares and five per cent of Sedno commune land. In the 1980s it employed 189, of whom 32 worked in management and administration. Labour efficiency and discipline were low; the workforce suffered from absenteeism, drunkenness and theft. It was a mixed farm and also had a construction and building works brigade which employed 24 workers and 40 technical staff. It built housing (high-rise flats) for its workers, which the building brigade renovated, and also ran a marginally profitable distillery producing 160–200 hectolitres of alcohol a year. Furthermore, it took its role as exemplar of the future of Polish agriculture seriously and organised extension courses for the surrounding farmers. In fact, despite initial conflicts, private farmers and the PGR co-operated successfully, the latter buying some produce from the former (mainly potatoes for the distillery) and also providing seasonal work for farmers whose holdings were too small to provide an adequate income. It also hired equipment out to private farmers, rented them small parcels of land, and provided them with potato seed at no cost, if they contract-sold to the distillery. PGR workers also raised pigs on a contract basis for sale via the farm. There was interaction and mutual support between state and private not dissimilar from that which existed between co-operative and private in collectivised countries.

The person entrusted with the task of privatising the State Farm in Sedno was JR, a young man in his late thirties, who had graduated from an economics 'high school' (a college of higher vocational education) and worked on the farm, progressing up its ranks to become a deputy director. He was given the task of privatising the PGR because he was a relatively highly placed but politically untainted manager; and he realised quickly that only a rather radical restructuring could work. By his calculations (figures borne out by the scale of subsequent redundancies), there was two-thirds over-employment on the farm, and the scale of its debts meant that its break-up was inevitable. But this put JR in a difficult position. His chances of finding a job for which he was qualified would disappear with the farm. Furthermore, his chances of finding work of any kind would be very low given redundancies on the scale that he knew was inevitable. His only course of action was to seize the time and become a private farmer using the PGR as his springboard. He could not do this without money, however; and he obtained this 'from the border', by exploiting the manifold smuggling opportunities discussed more fully below.

Like others entrusted with the privatisation of a PGR, he was first sent to Warsaw to attend a training course explaining principles and practices before returning to put this knowledge to use. The centre dictated the principles, but the actual solutions were left up to the local person responsible, in consultation with the regional (*województwo*) branch of the State Treasury Agency. Privatisation plans were then sent to Warsaw for final approval. JR was pleased with the speed with which he accomplished his task, just a year, from November 1992 to November 1993; the planning took about six months, and the sales a further six. Although privatisation could in theory have taken the form of selling the farm as a 'going concern', the size of its debt precluded such an option. By selling off all of the machinery and animals, the bulk of its liabilities could be met. Luckily there were plenty of takers for the agricultural machinery because local farmers were hungry for the bigger tractors that they had been prevented from buying under socialism.

A unique feature of agriculture in socialist Poland was that the dispersal of holdings so typical of the private sector was true for the socialist (state and co-operative) sectors as well. PGRs and later SKRs were under a duty to buy land offered by peasants who opted to swap their land for a state pension, or land for which there was no living owner. In no sector was there the sort of consolidation of land holdings that had been an integral part, indeed an underpinning rationale, of collectivisation elsewhere. Even PGRs, although they did farm consolidated parcels, were the owners of a patchwork of tiny plots. PGR privatisers such as JR were thus faced with the problem of splitting a mixture of large and small plots into saleable units. His solution was to divide the farm three ways. Five big farms of 100–150 hectares were created out of the consolidated land, located, where possible, adjacent to existing farm buildings; some 700 hectares were split into small plots of between one and fifteen hectares, and 200 hectares of forest was returned to the State Forestry Commission. The distillery was established as a separate limited liability company and was leased by a private farmer who also leased some 'tens of hectares' from the PGR. Of the five 100–150 hectare plots, in the absence of any genuine initiative from the labour force itself, three were leased to former managers, including JR himself who obtained 160 hectares and associated farm buildings, and two plots (of around 170 hectares) were sold to local private farmers with 'good reputations'.

One of the private farmers 'with a good reputation' was Mr W, a member of the local council. In partnership with a friend he rented (on a ten year lease) 174 hectares together with some workshops from the former PGR. They employed a staff of four, compared with the eleven of PGR days. Mr W's case reflected the socialist 'specialist' farmer career path observed in the cases of RB in Zamek and RM in Bawełna. He had begun in 1972 when he took over the 12 hectares owned by his parents. He rented an additional 18 hectares and, by the 1980s, had created a successful dairy farm. But dairy farming ceased to be sufficiently profitable in the 1980s, so he switched to beef, in which he was also successful selling to Italy as well as domestically. But, because of what he saw as bad luck and an unfavourable climate, by 1996, he felt that he was unable to expand further. The lessee of the distillery also commented that his large investment in former PGR assets might not have been a good move. Specialisation had its costs, especially the high interest rates which could not be avoided when farming on that scale.

Two of the successor farms run by the former management followed the more normal route of setting up 'workers' companies'. JR adopted a different approach. Having decided that, if he was to farm successfully he should go after one of the bigger units, he realised that, on his own, he could neither afford one, nor did he have the requisite knowledge to farm it. But he was also acutely aware of the degree to which the farm was overstaffed. He therefore went into partnership with two slightly younger colleagues, who had qualifications from agricultural mechanical schools. He was the 'brains' behind the organisation, supplying an understanding of economics and, more important, the contacts with banks and marketing companies that he had made over his career in socialist agriculture; they supplied the technical know-how and practical experience. Indeed, unlike his partners and their families, he and his wife did not even live in the village where the farm which they eventually bought was located. The day-to-day running of the farm was in the hands of the partners and their wives, aided by two fulltime employees and some seasonal staff.

Like the other new purchasers, JR and his partners benefited from relatively generous conditions for the purchase of state farm machinery: a 20 per cent down payment with repayment of the remainder over seven years. But the conditions for getting land were not at all advantageous. Because restitution issues had not been resolved, state land could not be bought outright. Rather, it had to be held on a ten year lease in the expectation that it would be bought at a later date when restitution issues were resolved. In addition, because the possibility of successful restitution by a private owner remained, the lease had to contain a clause allowing for its abrupt curtailment. Indeed, in JR's case, a former owner was endeavouring to prevent the sale of the land. JR was obliged to stake a lot of money, money that he had obtained by exploiting the opportunities (on the fringes of legality) offered by the newly opened eastern border, for land which he might never own and might be obliged to relinquish at very short notice. By 1996 still only about 30 per cent of the former PGR land had been sold, the rest was still leased.

Town and village councils and the border tax

Local government in Sedno shared the same qualities of inexperience and impotence as elsewhere, but here the tensions were resolved in an unusual way which capitalised on unanticipated opportunities proffered by the border. Local politics in Sedno was rendered complex by the split that developed between the town and the village councils. The history of the division into two councils went back to 1991. The original post-socialist council had 12 representatives from Sedno town, and ten from the surrounding villages. The former could therefore always outvote the latter, and by 1991 the feeling on the village side of the council was that it was losing out, that all resources were being devoted to the town. It was more interested in keeping taxes low and improving the infrastructure, while Sedno town inevitably had a wider agenda. The village representatives first boycotted the council sessions, and then insisted on the establishment of a separate council, which began operations in January 1992. Relations might not have got as far as a split had the village council not had the chance of access to a considerable source of independent funding in the form of legislation dating from 1933. This legislation, never subsequently repealed, allowed the commune to levy a tax on all those who crossed the border from Lithuania onto its territory. With the help of a local lawyer, they had resurrected this moribund right and defended it in the courts; and, after the commune split, Sejny village took over the rights to this income which reduced the 'fiscal stress' of increased responsibilities but reduced resources. But, of course, it only served to fuel the ongoing tensions since, as the town mayor was keen to point out, it was not only the outlying communities that suffered from the impact of the border traffic. The heavy trucks drove through Sedno town too.

Other border benefits

What rescued Sedno from profound decline was the border with Lithuania and the new border post that had been built as this previously closed border was opened up. The border provided secure jobs which paid good salaries. But, much more important, it offered opportunities for smuggling, a business from which, according to many, the customs officials and police also benefited by taking their 10 per cent cut. The income achievable from a customs job was so high that, in one case recounted by a member of the local council, a former student of his, who had gone to a prestigious college and graduated successfully, returned to the village to work as a junior customs official rather than pursue a more glittering but less remunerative career. For those who were unemployed and did not have relatives or contacts in Germany who could help them find jobs, or whose farm was too small, smuggling, mainly of cigarettes, represented a more than viable alternative—in stark contrast to the border communities of Blagun and Chala in Bulgaria where smuggling was not reported at all, not least because the border with Greece remained closed. 'Everyone is involved in smuggling, except the mayor', quipped the mayor. Other more modest estimates put it at 20 per cent of the population, and restricted it to the communities located in the immediate vicinity of the border. For students it was a form of summer job, and one council member complained that children sometimes did not turn up for school because they were on a 'smuggling tour'.

There was also a whiff of illegality to some of the more dynamic new businesses in the community, which plugged the socialist personal services gap, but perhaps not at the essential end of the spectrum. A private individual, who already operated a Mercedes dealership, bought a local rural transport co-operative. The individual purchaser of the privatised GS hotel also took over a restaurant, a night club in one of the commune's outlying villages, and the hotel's currency exchange office. In fact, Sedno quickly spawned seven foreign exchange offices, an unusually high number for a settlement of some 5,000 inhabitants, prompting the head of the council to complain about what he called Sedno's 'grey zone'. Those more heavily involved in smuggling invested their earnings in local front businesses such as bars or the exchange offices, whose turnover suggested that they were scarcely viable businesses on their own. The realities of the 'grey zone' were confirmed by the difficulties the team encountered tracking down such individuals. Between 1993 and 1995, not only did our enquiring researchers discover that one such bar-keeper had disappeared, his colleagues maintained that he had never even existed.

For those unemployed who did not, or could not, resort to the grey economy, life could be exceptionally grim. In one of the former state farm settlements within the community, where all of the former workforce was unemployed, an eleven-year-old boy twice tried to commit suicide because his school-mates made fun of him. They did so because he always wore the same hand-me-down clothes that his mother, who struggled with almost no income and a tiny agricultural plot, made for him.

POLISH SPECIFICITIES IN SUMMARY

The structure of agriculture in Poland in the early-to-mid-1990s was more variegated than in other countries because of its abandonment of collectivisation forty years previously. Nevertheless the socialist sector (in this case mainly state farm) manager 'green barons' who privatised some of their former farms to themselves, as described in both Zalew (Lusowo) and Sedno, constituted a significant subset of the winners in agricultural restructuring. But in Poland, some former socialist-era specialists also successfully developed their holdings into large-scale commercial farms, such as those of RB in Zamek and RM in Bawełna. Large-scale though they were, they were nevertheless generally rather smaller than their equivalents elsewhere (with the exception of Romania—see Chapter 7). It is noticeable too that there was no evidence of an organic consolidation of holdings. Those with land clung to it for security; farmers who wanted to expand bought or leased from the former state sector.

In the non-agricultural rural sector, Elder-Pak in Głaz was transformed from a socialist era private sector anomaly into a large-scale private company employing around one hundred in a manner that had no parallels elsewhere: it had contracted to the socialist sector but had never been part of it. Non-farm new businesses in Kanał confirmed the importance in stimulating entrepreneurship of wider horizons than the local community. The rural poor who had been pushed back to subsistence farming lost out everywhere, but in Poland 'shock therapy' hit hard. Social welfare and job-creation schemes figured higher on local council agendas, as did rural tourism, and Solidarity-inspired labour-retention clauses were attached (unsuccessfully) to privatisation contracts. Prominent amongst the rural unemployed were former employees of state farms, such as those in Sedno where a child attempted suicide, who had only the tiniest of plots to fall back on and often lived in high-rise flats poorly suited to agriculture of any kind. In addition, in very remote rural communities like Kanał, unrelated to the devolved responsibility for education which proved to be far from unproblematic, there was evidence of children being withheld from secondary schooling—schools were too distant, difficult and expensive to get to, and the children's labour was needed on the farm. The mayor of Głaz exemplified continuity with roots way back in the socialist years; in Bory and Bawełna pro-business regimes came to the fore, in Bawełna replacing a clerical regime, in Bory one dominated by Solidarity-influence 'teachers'. In Sedno, councillors latched onto moribund legislation to boost their coffers drained by 'fiscal stress', while the proximity of a non-EU border offered opportunities to the enterprising, but not the inward investment facilitated by EU border proximity.

Map 7.1. Research sites, Romania

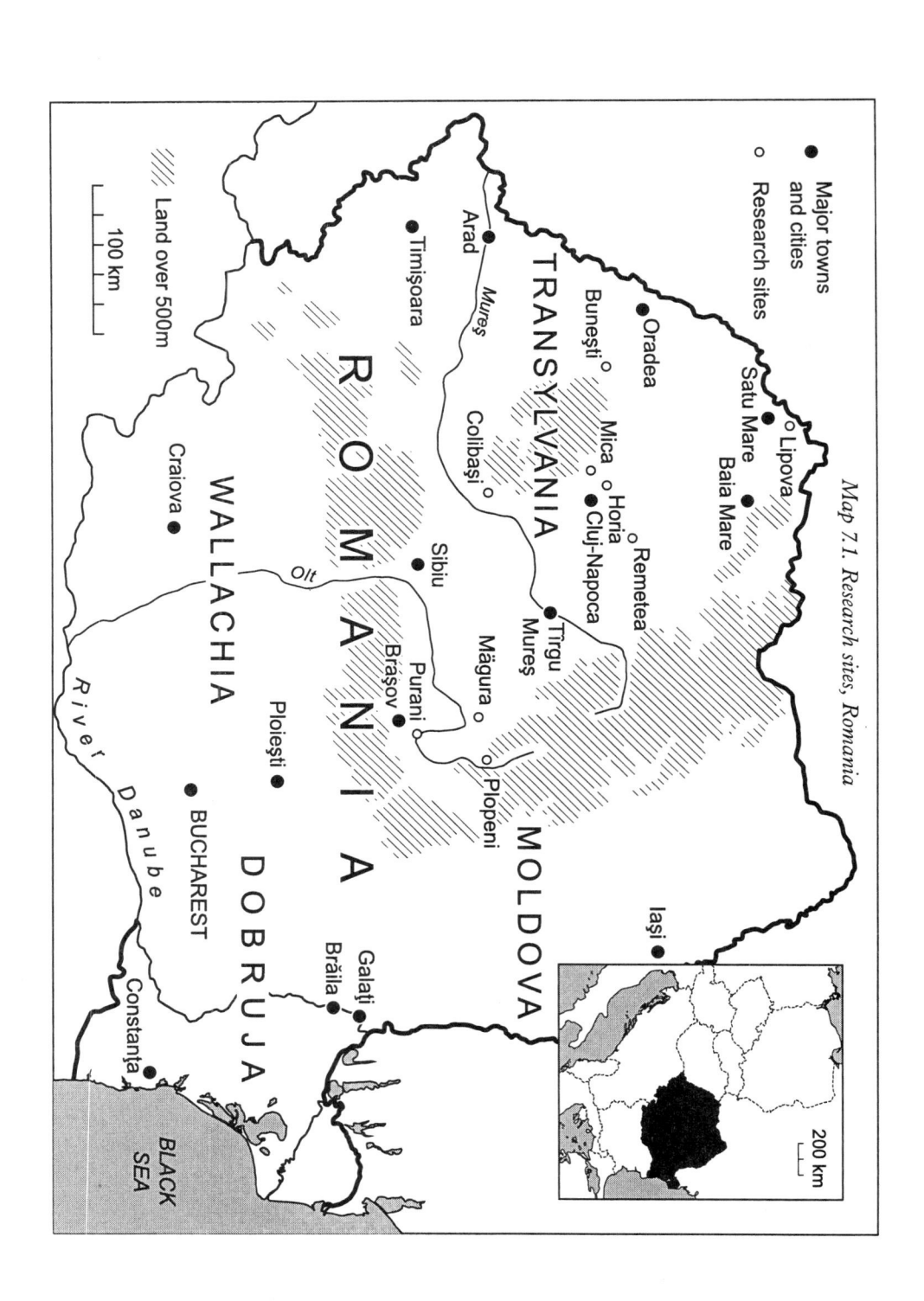

CHAPTER 7

Romania

Village-level developments in Romania were structured by the legacy of its unreformed Stalinist policies. This was manifest both in agriculture and in the extreme dependence and impotence of local authorities who struggled with a particularly severe socialist public services gap. In agriculture, collective farms were spontaneously destroyed because they had delivered no benefits to their members, while the continuance of Stalinist Machine and Tractor Stations (Agromecs) meant that agricultural producer co-operatives had very little machinery that might form the basis of post-socialist agriculture. Post-socialist co-operatives shunned the term 'co-operative' in favour of 'association', which covered a variety of organisational forms along the Bulgarian 'red co-operative'–'blue co-operative' spectrum. Furthermore, their membership was often dominated by pensioners and thus had to take on employees to carry out their agricultural activities. In regions where no, or only a rather weak, large-scale post-socialist farm emerged, pre-socialist land-holding proved to be a key factor in which families prospered initially in the post-socialist world. But such prosperity could only be on a limited scale because access to machinery was much more difficult than elsewhere: Agromecs were not privatised until later in the 1990s.

The post-socialist impotence of local authorities in Romania was extreme and their task enormous. One tactic to increase access to scarce funds that continued to be distributed in a politicised manner was 'political migration', ensuring that local politicians were of the same political stripes as the power-brokers at county level. But there were also frequent examples of circumventing the standard channels of resource distribution altogether by relying on external charities, and these could operate in a poorly targeted manner. Where communes did intervene economically, it tended to be in agriculture in defence of poor, small-scale farmers. Romania's rather slow structural adjustment and relatively low national rates of unemployment resulted in a mixed employment picture. Generally unemployment was lower in villages located near major industrial cities. New business, as elsewhere, plugged the 'socialist personal services gap'.

As noted in Chapter 1, by the time that our interviews took place, the land re-allocation associated with restitution and co-operative restructuring had already taken place. This process has tended to take centre-stage in much writing on Romania. Andrew Cartwright discusses it in his *Return of the Peasant* and elsewhere and cites the mayor of Moldovenesti who stresses the need for land to be 'elastic' in order to cope with the conflicting claims put upon it.[1] Verdery uses the image of elastic land in her seminal article in *Slavic Review*[2] and reprises the theme in Chapter 3 especially of *The Vanishing Hectare*.[3] There she cites a villager from Vlaicu, her research site, who pithily sums up the issues thus: 'Mrs Bora's family had five hectares, of which she has recovered six.'[4] As Verdery and Cartwright make plain in their different studies, the problem with returning land to 'historic boundaries' is that it is an intrinsically difficult process in any case in the absence of accurate maps and a landscape that does not remain static; it is not helped by reliance on verbal agreements, a common feature of rural communities, nor by the fact that peasants were economical with the truth about how much land they contributed to the co-operative, nor by manifest corruption, nor by conflicting claims of insiders, new-comers, Germans

---

[1] Cartwright, *The Return of the Peasant*, 194; Andrew Cartwright, 'Against "decollectivisation": Land reform in Romania, 1990–1992', Working Paper no. 4, Max Planck Institute for Social Anthropology, Halle-Saale, 2000); Andrew Cartwright, 'In from the margins? State law and the recognition of property in rural Romania', Working Paper no. 10 (Max Planck Institute for Social Anthropology, Halle-Saale), 2000.
[2] Verdery, 'The elasticity of land'.
[3] Verdery, *The Vanishing Hectare*, 116–57.
[4] Ibid., 139.

(deprived of their lands at the end of the war) and those who received land under Decree 42 which allocated land to those who had not originally contributed any to the co-operative.[5] All this uncertainty was compounded by the high cost of registering land formally[6] and the fact that in 1997 some 60 per cent of rural land was owned by people resident in urban areas.[7] Land re-allocation was a painful and frustrating process. Nevertheless, by the time our teams were investigating, it was no longer in the forefront of the minds of our interviewees, although it had not been legally finalised, as noted in Măgura.

AGRICULTURAL TRANSFORMATION

Smooth progression from co-operative to association— Lipova and Purani

In Lipova, close to the border with Hungary, the agricultural co-operative, which had merged with that of a neighbouring village in 1970, split in 1990 to its pre-1970 structure. In 1992, it underwent transformation and the association that emerged also operated in Lipova only. Transformation was described by one involved as 'rough', and another commented that 'people stole everything they were not ashamed of taking ... it is a wonder the association was left with any machinery at all'. These words echo the comments of a sixty-two-year-old man in Budieni, Gorj country, reported by Rus, who stated the following:[8]

> Everybody took whatever they could. Nobody thought about others. Some took irrigation pipes, others even took all the materials from the cooperative buildings. The engineers were luckiest because they organised an auction and bought the cooperative's machinery at a very low price.

---

[5] Cartwright, *The Return of the Peasant*, 131–7; Cartwright, 'In from the margins', 11.
[6] Cartwright, 'In from the margins', 6–7.
[7] Cartwright, 'Against "decollectivisation"', 20.
[8] Alin Rus, 'Rural development versus traditionalism and synergy versus poverty in rural Romania', *Eastern European Countryside* 10 (2004): 121–36.

Cartwright notes how in Plăieşti villagers literally dismantled the co-operative,[9] while Verdery provides photographic evidence of the destroyed co-operative buildings in Geoagiu, although those in Vlaicu were preserved.[10] In Lipova, at the request of the members of the former co-operative, no auction was organised during the course of the transformation process in order to prevent strangers obtaining co-operative assets. The management had wanted to carry out the transformation in accordance with the law, but all of the animals were simply taken by the villagers—'calves were put in bags and taken home'. Despite this, only six former co-operative members decided to farm privately. The association attracted fewer managers, however. Of the co-operative's seven managers, only two opted for the association; four left agriculture altogether and set up private companies of various types, and the fifth became a private farmer with 50 hectares of land. The leader of the association had previously been an agronomist in the co-operative and had served briefly as mayor between 1990 and 1992. Under his leadership, the membership quickly increased to 274 members and a total of 420 hectares, and it farmed profitably in both 1994 and 1995, partly because of the tax-free status enjoyed by associations for the first five years of their operation. Other villagers expressed an interest in joining, but their parcels of land were too small to be cultivated by machinery; the association soon decided to admit as new members only those who could put together at least five hectares in a consolidated form.

The Lipova association took over several properties from its predecessor; one was rented out as a general shop, others were sold, yet others became the objects of a legal dispute with the council. The association obtained one tractor from the co-operative, and bought, from a distributor in Satu Mare, two more, as well as two trailers, a seeder and other equipment, paid for with the help of a loan (repaid on time) from the Agrobank. But it also needed to rent machinery from the Agromec. In 1995, it had 17 employees (including an agronomist, a bookkeeper, a secretary and tractor drivers), all of them local. When needed, at harvest time, it also took on temporary staff at 6,000 lei per day, or,

---

[9] Cartwright, *The Return of the Peasant*, 171–7.
[10] Verdery, *The Vanishing Hectare*, 125–7.

in the case of the potato harvest, 25 kilos of potatoes per day. The chairman earned around 400,000 lei a month, the bookkeeper 200,000, the secretary 150,000 lei and the tractor drivers between 150–200,000 lei, a figure that was based on the salaries paid by Agromec to tractor drivers. Because the majority of the owner members were beyond retirement age, the bulk of the field work was carried out by landless workers from outside the village, including Roma. Members' incomes were paid in kind, unless special arrangements were made to the contrary (for those no longer resident in the village for example)—800 kilos of wheat, 100 kilos of potatoes and 15 litres of cooking oil for each hectare of land, the basic principle being a 30:70 split between member and association. Both the chairman and the bookkeeper also farmed privately, from which they earned a good income.

In post-socialist Purani, by contrast, more than one association emerged and there were echoes of the Bulgarian distinction between 'red' and 'blue' co-operatives in the differences between them. Co-operative transformation proceeded relatively smoothly in the village, and was conducted in accordance with the legal requirements: assets were distributed according to the amount contributed to the co-operative at the time of formation, and the amount of labour contributed to it during its years of operation. But, like Lipova and as was common in Bulgaria, livestock farming was abandoned entirely, and the animals were distributed to the members in a 'chaotic way'. Some 1,000 pedigree dairy cows 'disappeared', either slaughtered or sold, and the stables remained empty in 1995. The bulk of the sheep ended up in the hands of only three or four shepherds, each with 1,500 to 3,000 sheep, who dominated the village's pasture and made it difficult for other villagers to keep cattle. But the 'chaos' was not accompanied by vandalism, mainly because the co-operative was succeeded by as many as ten, mainly small-scale family associations. Two larger associations also emerged, neither the creation of the co-operative's top management, and their membership appears to have been based on personal sympathies with certain leaders and local loyalties, rather than issues of principle.[11] The Infratirea association was created by the manager

---

[11] But there may well have been other issues in the background. Compare the comments made by our interviewees in Venets and Kaneff's discovery of political motivations in Talpa discussed in Chapter 3.

of the co-operative's fodder store, whose wife had worked as a stockkeeper. His primary motivation had been to ensure employment for himself and his wife, so he ended up as its manager, while his wife acted as cashier. Most of its members were villagers from poorer backgrounds, some of whom, like CD, who eventually became the association's accountant, joined because they, like the manager, had moved to the region from Moldavia. The association was obliged to take over three million lei of debt from the co-operative, but the accountant did not see this as a burden. Its right to some of the co-operative's assets, however, was disputed by the council, in particular two of its buildings, one of which it wanted to sell, the other, equipped as a piggery, figured in its ambition to re-start large-scale livestock farming. It also farmed 35 hectares of land reclaimed by the village's Saxon community, most of whom were too old to farm it.

The second larger association in Purani, the BAA, was a more typical successor body in that it farmed the bulk of the land formerly farmed by the co-operative, and it had taken over many of its assets. But there was no continuity of personnel at the top level. Of the former co-operative's agronomists, one became a teacher, another worked for the Chamber of Agriculture, and the third opened a shop in a nearby town. The leading figure in BAA was the former managing director of the local state farm, who had been sacked in 1989 for political reasons. The association consisted of 367 landowners, mainly heirs to smaller plots of land, 80 of whom were not local. Many in fact had had such little interest in their land that they had asked the association management to buy it from them; but the association could not own land in its own name, and its managers were not in a position to buy it privately. The membership owned around 1,000 hectares of land in all, of which some 800 hectares of arable land was rented by the association, 300 producing wheat, 200 producing malting barley, 150 producing maize and 50 producing potatoes; hay fields were left in the possession of the members. The labour force in 1995 was much smaller than it had been in socialist days; the number of employees that it engaged had been reduced to eight tractor drivers, four other drivers, and five workers in administration—the chairman, a works manager (the former chief engineer, who was already a pensioner but could not live without farming), two bookkeepers (compared with four in the socialist years) and the deputy chairman of the management committee. The deputy chairman was local, as were the bookkeepers, but the tractor drivers were not. Locals preferred to find jobs in industry, in the association manager's view because life as a tractor driver was hard. The members received their incomes mainly in kind—wheat, potatoes and sugar—related to the amount of land farmed by the association. As in the socialist co-operative, every family retained land for its own use, on which it normally grew potatoes; in 1995, the size of this plot stood at between one and one and a half hectares, rather than the 0.15–0.25 hectares plus a cow and up to ten sheep of the socialist days. As in the socialist co-operative too, they focused their attention on the land that they kept for themselves rather than that which was farmed communally. Because most of the younger villagers had jobs and only the elderly were available to work, the association faced a labour shortage for seasonal work, as had its predecessor. To solve this, they employed a team to work the land which came from a village 22 kilometres away. They came for a week, were collected and taken home by bus, and were paid in sugar beet.

Unlike Infratirea, BAA was mechanised sufficiently well no longer to need to use the services of Agromec. It had taken over three functioning tractors and three cars (only one of which worked) from the co-operative, and bought three second hand tractors from Agromec with a state loan. In 1992, with the support of the members, it had bought two more, large capacity tractors and another smaller capacity one from the tractor factory in Braşov. It had also bought two sowing-machines, two harrows, five ploughs and a serviceable second hand combine. In 1995, it further benefited from the PHARE programme to purchase additional agricultural equipment. Like the Infratirea association, it was keen to develop into livestock farming, if only because the managers felt that the soil needed natural manure rather than artificial fertilizer, and mixing fodder crops with the cereals and potatoes would also improve the productive capacity of the soil. Unlike Infratirea, it had the buildings that it needed, which were fully equipped, but a bank loan would be necessary to buy the animals and get livestock farming started, and it did not want to take out another loan. It was already making high interest payments on a loan which was denominated in dollars. The chairman was proud of the association's achievements: 'Our lands are less fertile than those owned by peasants outside the association including the people in the land allocating committee.

However we proved that we are able to achieve good results even in such soil.' Villagers with three or four hectares of land clamoured to join because they could not afford the costs of ploughing, harvesting and spraying the land that they had.

A failed association—Colibaşi

Not every association was a success. Cartwright, for example, reports the bankruptcy of the Plăieşti association in 1998.[12] By the 1980s, the co-operative in Colibaşi, with a population of just over one thousand, always produced a good crop and, despite its investments in the late 1980s, was relatively unencumbered by debt. With the collapse of socialism, the popular will in Colibaşi was to sack all the co-operative staff, disband the co-operative and take home all the animals. The management saw a crowd of 80–100 angry members gathering for a meeting to decide the fate of the farm and took fright: they got into a car and drove away. MB, a 52-year-old local woman, took the initiative after ten minutes of fruitless argument. From a relatively wealthy family, she had worked in agriculture since the age of 14. In 1969, when the farm was merged with that of a neighbouring village, she became the Colibaşi agronomist. After studying at evening classes between 1978 and 1985, she became an economist and worked in this capacity until the collapse of socialism. Her overwhelming concern was that the property of the co-operative should not simply be lost. In her recollection, she requested the floor, and began: 'None of you has more land in the communal property than I do. It hurts me too to see what is happening to these assets. If you dismiss the leaders, someone will have to be responsible for this property. I accept that responsibility.' Her intervention at least meant that co-operative transformation was carried out in accordance with legal requirements. A committee was established to draw up an inventory of assets and assess the value of the animals. Individual shares of these assets were calculated according to the legal requirements: 60 per cent based on labour performed and 40 per cent based on the land brought in the co-operative. The process took three days, during which time a hundred or so

---

[12] Cartwright, 'In from the margins', 11.

members waited patiently outside the door. In the end, there were no complaints, people took their animals home, and large-scale livestock farming was abandoned. Many animals were immediately slaughtered, and the co-operative stables were carefully dismantled and sold off for building materials. The farm's small non-agricultural units were also wound up and their equipment auctioned off.

MB's goal was to do more than insist on the legal winding up of the co-operative. She wanted to use the remaining capital to set up an association for those who did not want to farm privately. But, in this, she ultimately failed. Some 270 land owners, with a total area of 320 hectares (250 hectares of it arable), pretty much the size of the Colibași part of the co-operative, were interested in farming jointly. Ten of these owned around ten hectares, a further six had between four and five hectares, four people owned about three hectares; but the rest, the vast majority, owned less than one hectare each. These holdings were greatly dispersed and in small parcels: the average size was 0.25–0.5 hectares, too small for a tractor to be used effectively, and they could be as far as 20 kilometres apart. The disparity in holding size proved ultimately to be the association's undoing. The first issue concerned a tractor. It made sense to buy a tractor if fields were pooled. But villagers with little land, the majority, complained that they did not want to buy equipment from which only the well-to-do would benefit.

In the end, because there was no desire to purchase property, no formal association was established (although what emerged was referred to as an 'association' by villagers). The balance of co-operative assets was distributed amongst the members, and the 'associates' began to cultivate the land jointly on the basis of Law 39/1991, which allowed everyone to grow what they wanted on their own parcel of land, but required an agreement about crop rotation on communal land, for which five large fields of 20–60 hectares were identified. At its peak the 'association' employed four people: MB as chairperson and caretaker, a woman bookkeeper, a driver and a tractor driver. The association members kept 80 per cent of their shares of all crops, except sugar beet (all of which was sold), and they paid cultivation costs when they were incurred, since it was mainly carried out on a contract basis by a local agricultural services entrepreneur. This solution worked for a time, although MB complained about the lack of institutional support (although a nearby state farm gave encouragement and hired them equipment) and the 'association' benefited to an extent from Law 83/1993 on subsidies which guaranteed them support for the purchase of artificial fertilizers for wheat and sugar beet, and pesticides for potato production.

But in the long run the association collapsed. Five farmers had left the association by 1995, and by the spring of 1997, as MB had herself had predicted in 1995, even this form of minimal collaboration proved impossible. Members could not agree on the pattern of crop rotation; in particular, they found it difficult to accept the fact that in some years this required that their land must grow less profitable crops. The 'association' collapsed, although MB still farmed for a few people on a private basis, and she kept hold of the lorry and some store rooms in case people wanted to recreate it.

The story of the rise and fall of the Colibași association bears direct comparison with the similar rise and fall of the Vlaicu association described in Chapter Six of Verdery's *The Vanishing Hectare*.[13] There too, the role of strong, professionally trained women with an extensive social network (in Vlaicu Anda the accountant and Nica the agronomist) were central to the struggle to form the association and keep it going. MB was perhaps slightly better placed than Anda (who, as Verdery explains, came from a humble background) in that she had both co-operative experience and came from a relatively wealthy family.[14] But a second common feature proved to be the fatal flaw for both: the short-term horizons of the members and a lack of commitment to the commons.[15] The words of the Vlaicu association president with which Verdery begins the chapter were equally apposite for Colibași:[16]

> [T]hey wanted this land so much for so long, and now they have it, but they can't work it as they'd want to. So they give it to the

---

[13] Verdery, *The Vanishing Hectare*, 229–72.
[14] Ibid., 236.
[15] In this respect see also Alexander Thomka, 'The informal economy and viability of small family farms in Romania', *Eastern European Countryside* 11 (2005): 100–2.
[16] Verdery, *The Vanishing Hectare*, 229.

Association, but they can't conceive of letting us actually work it as a long-term proposition without seeing that as 'More collective farm!'

Pre-socialist landholding *vs* machinery— Horia, Lipova and Măgura

The verdict of the Reform Church pastor on agricultural restructuring in Horia, just seven kilometres from Cluj-Napoca, was that 'Here everyone stands on two feet.' The co-operative fell apart and there was no attempt to create a successor. Of the five stable buildings that the co-operative had owned, two remained intact and were in 1995 in the process of being sold for a new mill and other new ventures; another was rented to a livestock farmer. The others were abandoned and had been gutted: their tiles and anything else of value had been stolen. A total of 60 families managed to acquire a tractor, and two families acquired a combine. The L family came away with a tractor, a combine and 40 head of cattle; MT had ten dairy cows; the policeman was reputed to own 30 pigs; the young man who rented the former co-operative stables owned 70 pigs and 'hundreds of' sheep. But even the biggest farmers in Horia had rather small holdings and farmed on a part-time basis.

For example, KI was a 75-year-old widower whose wife had worked in the co-operative but had died in 1994. He had run a joiner's shop, the only one in the village in the 1950s, and when the shop was taken over by co-operative, he also became a co-operative member, so qualifying for a small co-operative pension of 10,500 lei a month. His only daughter, the 38-year-old SG, was a medical assistant who lived in the village with her husband, who worked as a white-collar commercial supervisor, and her children. SE an 87-year-old widow and the mother-in-law of SG was also part of the extended family. KI lived separately, but SE lived with her daughter-in-law and they cultivated the family land jointly. Between them they owned ten hectares of land and had three old oxen and three or four pigs. But they had no equipment, so they had to either borrow or hire machinery from neighbours, or do what they could by hand. They would sometimes sow manually, and always weeded and hoed by hand in order to save money; and they baked their own bread to save money, for machinery work was expensive: ploughing their land cost more than SG's monthly salary. In addition, KI had revitalised his former trade and ran a small business, still the only one in the village, in his (once the co-operative's) joinery workshop. Clients brought their materials, often stolen from the surrounding forests, for him to work with.

One of the only two villagers in Horia who specialised in agricultural services was LA, a 38-year-old from a family of co-operative members, who was a qualified engineer with a degree from Cluj Technical University. Prior to the collapse of socialism, he had worked in an engineering enterprise locally, but he had been made redundant. His response had been to buy a tractor and a threshing machine when the local Agromec auctioned off all its machinery to take on a new role as a repair centre; he then offered agricultural services to his neighbours. His wife, five years his junior, was also made redundant from a textile co-operative in Cluj and was, in 1995, a housewife, although still in receipt of her unemployment benefit. His mother also contributed her small co-operative pension of 6,000 lei to the family budget. The family raised fifteen pigs, but owned only a few square metres of land. He was, by approximately a generation, the youngest person involved fulltime in agriculture-related activities in the village.

The villager that all recognised to be a 'good farmer' was BI, who was 63 years old in 1995. He was the son of 'middle peasant' parents; but he had also been the last chairman of the co-operative and so enjoyed both pre-socialist and socialist-era advantages. He concentrated on livestock (six cows, ten pigs and some horses), had his own tractor, and kept two 'servants' (poor and landless). The family was not without other resources: his 40-year-old daughter lived in Cluj and owned a restaurant there.

In Lipova, beyond the association, but also including some who had put much of their land in the association, part-time farming and pluriactivity was also the norm. 'People cannot make a living from factory wages. If they do not have any land, they are dead. They do not leave their factory jobs for the land, because everyone wants to get a pension.' Or, in the words of the deputy mayor, 'You must work two shifts to live'. True to his word, the deputy mayor, who had been council secretary for 28 years, had a job as an administrator in the school where his wife was the secretary, also farmed on a considerable scale. He fattened pigs commercially and sold them to the state purchasing company; and he had the courage to take out a loan and buy two tractors. Having known extreme poverty as a child, he was content to work his 'double shift' to make a living for himself and his family, although he doubted whether younger generations would be prepared to make such a commitment.

MG had the reputation of being one of the best farmers in the village. He was one of the heirs to a larger pre-war farm and he became a more significant post-socialist private farmer. His family had owned 18 hectares before the socialist years and his father had been condemned as a 'kulak' to perform forced labour on the Danube canal. His parents had refused to join the co-operative on their return and made a living hiring themselves out as agricultural labourers. MG worked for the doctor's office and as a carter thereafter, because the family land had been taken by the state rather than the co-operative and they had been allowed to retain a horse and cart. He received back roughly six hectares of good quality land in 1990, but did not put it into the association. He started farming privately, together with a total of eight family members, on 10 hectares plus livestock: cows, horse and pigs. He had a contract for the wheat with Romcereal, the state cereals monopoly which also provided operating credits for those who contracted with it, but sold maize and animals in the Satu Mare market and delivered his milk to the dairy.

The extended SM family, ten adult members in all, represented another example of a pluriactive, part-time farming from a relatively wealthy background, although inherited wealth played only a minor role in its overall success; income came from a multiplicity of sources, and the family was already embarked on a 'second economy' path to private sector success by the end of socialism. SM was about 60 in 1995, with nine years of schooling. She was from a relatively rich peasant family and had married into the village in 1952, into a family which farmed roughly 13 hectares. After collectivisation, she had worked as a co-operative member for a time, while her husband also worked briefly on the farm as a shepherd, and then as a publican. SM also worked as a seamstress on an outworker basis prior to the 1980s. But the family fortunes looked up in the 1980s, when she established a wreath-manufacturing business; and, in 1983, the family started intensive greenhouse production of vegetables in addition.

When the co-operative dissolved, SM and her family fared well in the land re-distribution process. All of the arable land that they received was of good quality, although, of course, not in a single location. SM did not rent land in the village on a commercial basis, but had come to a mutually convenient agreement with neighbours who had land, but no tractor. Both of her sons gave up their factory jobs to work on the farm, and both learned how to operate farm machinery in order to avoid having to use outside contractors. The normal division of labour within the family was that the male family members worked in the fields while the women stayed at home and worked in the wreath-manufacturing business. Their ten hectares was worked with their own tractor, plough, disk-harrow, seeder and combine harvester, bought from an Agromec auction locally. They had three Holstein cows, four heifers, a horse, 19 pigs, geese and chickens. Five or six pigs were sufficient to keep them in meat for a year, so the rest were sold in Satu Mare market. In addition to family labour, they hired additional workers for four to five days at a time during peak periods. Neighbours also helped SM with planting and harvesting, in return for SM undertaking the machine work on their land. She was also willing to carry out machinery work for other villagers, for a fee, an area in which she competed with the owners of the other 15 privately owned tractors in the village and the association. Over 80 per cent of total family income came from farming.

Another considerably larger-scale, private farmer from a rich peasant background was GI, the mayor. His parents had been co-operative members, but his own background was in commerce, and it was socialist-era wealth rather than his pre-socialist inheritance that explained his success. From his background in commerce he had acquired a bar in the village which brought in a significant income; and this provided the capital that he needed to obtain machinery when the co-operative dissolved. By 1995, he owned, jointly with his wife, 37 hectares, some of it recently purchased; and he was the possessor of two tractors, a combine harvester and all other necessary machinery.

The precariousness of the economics of pluriactive farming for those whose pre-socialist legacy did not permit farming on this scale was illustrated by the case of the pensioner JJ and his wife in Măgura. After land redistribution in 1991 he received 10 hectares of land, two hectares less than his parents had owned. Of this land, seven hectares were arable and three hectares were hay-fields. In 1995, he and his wife farmed only two hectares of arable land, and all of the hay fields. But the income that they derived from agricultural production was insufficient to cover the costs incurred cultivating their land. In the autumn of 1995, for example, they planted wheat on 0.5 hectares, incurring the following costs: 45,000 lei for seed-corn, 15,000 lei for sowing, 17,000 lei for harrowing, 33,000 lei for transportation and 125,000 lei for the transportation of farmyard manure, a total of 235,000 lei, to which had to be added the cost of chemicals (about 60,000 lei) and harvesting (about 100,000 lei), so that the total production costs for the 0.5 ha of wheat was likely to be 395,000 lei. If yields were good, they might produce 1,000 kilos of wheat, from which 700 kilos of pure wheat would remain. But at the market price for wheat they could buy almost twice as much, 1,300 kilos, for the almost 400,000 lei that it cost them to produce 700 kilos. Farming his patrimony made no economic sense. JJ would happily have put his land into an association in return for ten to twenty per cent of the crop. But there was no association, and no private individual locally willing to take it on. The only way to reduce the costs was to work the land manually themselves. As JJ noted poignantly, 'In the old days 70-year-old people did not go out to the fields and work. Now eighty and ninety year-olds do, because they have to'.

The importance of gaining access to machinery for success in larger-scale farming is well reflected in the case of Mr D from a village in the Cluj district (not one of our main research sites). Mr D ran a farm of 100 hectares, ten hectares of which (unusually located in the same place) was his own land that he received on the basis of the 30 hectares that his grandfather had contributed to the co-operative; the remaining 90 hectares were rented from those unable or unwilling to farm themselves. He came from a wealthy farming family, but he could farm on this scale not because of inherited land but because he had been able to obtain agricultural machinery in the post-socialist agricultural world. He had struck a deal with the director of the local Agromec to rent two tractors and a combine on an annual contract which ultimately resulted in purchase. The director of the Agromec entered into an arrangement of this type, which went against the spirit of the institution, because he liked the financial security of a long-term contract; because he was in any case planning to go into business for himself and build a hotel; and because, according to local whispers, he had had contacts with the security services, which was a common suspicion in the case of individuals who had good contacts in the political structures and maximised them to pursue business interests. By contrast, in Budieni, Gorj county, Rus reports the words of an elderly woman who complains that 'we had our fields in the cooperative and it what paid was a mockery. Today we have the land but we don't have agricultural machines to work it.'[17] The general problem was expressed particularly succinctly by one of Verdery's 'supertenants': 'Property restitution failed because Law 18 gave people land without equipment, and then the land rental law [of 1994] prevented Agromecs from renting land. In this way the equipment was blocked.'[18]

Most rural restructuring in our villages either where no association emerged or outside the association suggests that former land-holding was important in post-socialist outcomes—in the absence of the sorts of machinery that Mr D gained access to. In general terms it is true, as Andor and Kuczi argue[19] and Chris Hann confirms that the 'idea of kulak continuity is not supported', despite the individual successes of some sons of kulaks.[20] But in the Romanian case of redistribution to historic boundaries in the absence of significant machinery that could be acquired from the socialist sector, a situation was created in which the only valuable asset available was land, and in this situation a 'kulak' past clearly helped. That this was not universally the case however is suggested by Tatjana Thelen, who, in her comparison of a Romanian and Hungarian village, found the exact reverse to be true—the consequence, she argues, of the greater degree of arbitrariness in Romanian collectivisation.[21]

Agromec as farmer—Mägura

The Agromec was central to the early years of the transition in Mägura too, but in a rather unconventional manner. The closure of the cooperative in Mägura was protracted and bitter. Attempts to create an

---

[17] Rus, 'Rural development', 126.
[18] Verdery, *The Vanishing Hectare*, 354.
[19] Andor and Kuczi, 'What happened', 86–91.
[20] Hann, *'Not the Horse'*, 10, 67 and 69. See also Swain, 'From kolkhoz to holding company', 164.
[21] Tajana Thelen, 'Violence and (dis)continuity: Comparing collectivization in two East European villages', *Social History* 30, no. 1 (February 2005): 25–44.

association failed because of pressure from outsiders resident in towns; co-operative buildings were sold or left derelict and looted. Much of the livestock was sold or slaughtered immediately, since the villagers had no fodder with which to feed them. The former co-operative leaders had themselves appointed to the land claims committee and, it was claimed, redistributed land unfairly and to their advantage. People from the towns, who had taken back their land, then lost interest and left it uncultivated. By 1995, one former agronomist calculated that 60 per cent of commune land was uncultivated. Others discovered that they were too old to start a new career that required manual labour, for the deputy mayor's estimate was that 95 per cent of those who got their land back were aged over 65. Furthermore land redistribution was far from finished, dogged, in the view of one council member, by the 'elastic land' problem—discrepancies between what people remembered and what the documents stated, compounded by the fact that people had registered less than the actual amount of land that they owned in order to pay less tax and lower compulsory deliveries.[22]

Although the co-operative in Măgura disbanded with no successor organisation, the Agromec took over the role of large-scale agricultural producer despite the fact that the land rental law of 1994 was aimed at preventing Agromecs from doing precisely that.[23] In the new world, the Agromec now found itself with few people to serve, because there was no association and no one who farmed (and needed machinery) on the scale that Agromec was geared up to. Cartwright also notes that Agromecs were reluctant to service small farmers with dispersed strips of land.[24] The Măgura Agromec therefore tried to survive by renting land and farming on a large-scale itself as had its equivalent in Cartwright's Mirşid.[25] At one point, it had farmed up to 700 hectares locally, but, by 1995, it had given much of it up because it was marginal land which could not be farmed profitably; it reduced its activities to 300 hectares

---

[22] See the Verdery and Cartwright literature discussed above.
[23] Verdery, *The Vanishing Hectare*, 354.
[24] Andrew Cartwright, 'Private farming in Romania: What are the old people going to do with their land?" in *The Postsocialist Agrarian Question: Property Relations and the Rural Condition*, ed. Chris Hann and The 'Property Relations' Group (Münster: LIT Verlag, 2003), 179.
[25] Cartwright, 'Private farming', 179.

in Sînpetru (part of the Măgura commune), where land holdings had been consolidated at the time of its redistribution, but only 100 hectares in Măgura, where it had not. It also continued its traditional work for private customers as well as associations and state farms, its most distant customer being a state farm 70 kilometres away.

A large-scale private farmer—Remetea

Remetea witnessed a radical change in farming relationships and the emergence of a private farmer on a grand scale. The co-operative based in the village had been one of the best in the county; it even received medals for achievement from Ceauşescu himself. The mature socialist farm covered a total of 2,000 hectares, some 1,200 hectares of it arable, and was divided into two cropping units which produced cereals, a vegetable farm on 100 hectares, two livestock farms with 1,500 cattle, and a 150 hectare intensive fruit orchard (70 per cent apple trees, 30 per cent plum trees); there was also a 0.3 hectare greenhouse together with five hectares of polythene tents. Around 100 people worked in the two cropping units, mainly on a 15–20 per cent share-cropping ('accord global'—see Chapter 1) basis, and there were, in 1989, 40 permanent employees on the vegetable farm, although it had once employed 110. Around 80 per cent of workers in the livestock farm, who received an income in money rather than kind, were not local people but Roma who had moved to the village 'from the hills', in the words of one of the agricultural engineers. The orchard was also operated on an 'accord global' basis: two hectares of orchard was rented out per family (mainly to pensioners), thus providing an income for seventy to eighty families; and payment was either in kind or for 15 to 30 per cent of the price of the produce. It also ran non-agricultural activities, a fruit processing unit and a smithy, both established as half-hearted responses to directives from on high that non-agricultural activities should be established. The co-operative management consisted of a chairman, a chief engineer, four farm managers, a chief accountant, three bookkeepers and three warehousemen. There were also two tractor drivers, one coachman and the drivers of other farm vehicles; but it depended on Agromec for all other machinery. Despite the prizes that it won, only the horticulture farm generated a profit; and the livestock farm ran at a loss. In Remetea too members regularly had to steal from the co-operative in order to survive; and managers connived by turning a blind eye.

Despite its celebrity, the Remetea co-operative simply dissolved in 1990, and, despite abundant agricultural land, no association emerged to replace it. The membership had no loyalty to an institution that had given them nothing over the years, and the management, especially the former chairman, had lost all commitment to the co-operative idea. The latter described himself by 1989 as 'a communist boss but not a communist'. Much of the property was looted, the livestock was stolen, and the stables were pulled down. The village's former stock of 1,000 cattle was reduced by three quarters. The rest of the property was sold at auction, but everything went for allegedly low prices, the bulk of it (as we shall see) to just two or three people. The co-operative office building was converted into a bar; but the water tower and pumping station remained unused. The bulk of the orchards were given back to their original landowners, with the exception of 50 hectares of apples and 17 hectares of plums located in the co-operative's original orchard from 1963. Situated in the hills, the latter was effectively abandoned: by 1995, no one was tending the trees and the fruit was regularly pilfered. The posts and wires surrounding the other horticultural areas were sold off at auction.

In the land distribution that accompanied the winding-up of the co-operative, 290 villagers received back 428 hectares, while 325 heirs of former owners, 200 of them resident outside the village, were granted 493 hectares, although full title to land had only been given in 15 per cent of cases in 1995. But, as already noted, agricultural assets were much more important than land for those with ambitions to farm seriously. The larger part of the co-operative's agricultural assets were acquired by the former co-operative chairman, ChI, and his main competitor in local private farming, the local vet (KA), whose wife (KI) had managed the horticultural unit since 1982. ChI bought the glass-houses, its irrigation system, heating system and associated warehouses, that is to say the bulk of the profitable horticultural farm.

ChI, in 1995, was 47 years old, the son of co-operative farm members from a poor peasant background. He had gained only a technical education at school and worked as a tractor driver, before attending agricultural university and becoming an agricultural engineer. During the course of this career he had been obliged to join the party, and from 1982 to 1989 he was chairman of the co-operative. He started with five hectares of inherited land and 100,000 lei. He took out a 20 million lei bank loan to buy the vegetable farm for a total of 30 million lei, and began to rent additional land from the new owners. By April 1997, the farm was worth 1.3 milliard lei and he had become by far the biggest farmer in the area. He had expanded his private land holding to 30 hectares, but farmed 105 hectares in all, centred around the greenhouses, next to which he had a small office. He owned five tractors, two cars, and one lorry with trailer, and employed 14 full-time workers (up from eight in 1995), thirty to forty seasonal workers and 200 occasional workers, sometimes recruited from the local jail. Although he concentrated on horticulture, he also kept around 45 pigs which were farmed non-intensively—they roamed the greenhouses when they were not in use. At one time he had as many as 200 sheep, but gave them up after he lost money on them. He also grew wheat, maize and fodder crops, mainly to pay the owners in kind for the rental of their land. He owned five houses in the village and also a four-room flat in a desirable district of Cluj for his daughter who studied there.

Although the word in the village was that ChI and the others bought co-operative assets at knock-down prices, he felt that he had paid a high price for the unit, had been obliged to take on a risky bank loan to fund it, and was providing a service to the community by giving employment to some of the former co-operative's labour force. He was 'the only person who could do it, the only person people trusted. It was a very big risk, especially in the first two years'. The secret of his success appeared to be his marketing strategy, for which he needed both his network socialist-era contacts, but also business acumen. That he used prison labour says something about his networking ability: only someone with excellent contacts would have had access to such sources of labour. That said, it is striking that Toma Mezei, one of Verdery's 'supertenants' in Vlaicu, also had access to prison labour.[26] His wife's job as a medical assistant in the local orphanage also gave ChI access to long-term customers. The bulk of his produce was sold to state bodies such as the army and hospitals. He claimed not to trust private companies; public institutions, on the other hand, paid. Again

---

[26] Verdery, *The Vanishing Hectare*, 311.

there is a parallel with Vlaicu. A second of Verdery's 'supertenants', Ion Olaru, also established contracts with hospitals and canteens,²⁷ as in deed did the ZJ the butcher in Hungary's Korcona. ChI acknowledged that he was helped getting his first contract by the fact that he was well known in the region. But in order to secure his markets he behaved with a shrewd business sense. First, he offered prices 10 per cent lower than his competitors, and, second, he delivered fresh produce every day, free within a 150 kilometre radius. Because he was the largest producer in the region, he could afford to offer these generous terms; and he was well aware that such generosity need not continue forever. He was happy to work with reduced profits for a time in order to squeeze out the competition. Then he planned to increase his prices. Even his charitable acts had a commercial edge. He helped the villagers build a church, and then they helped him get the contract to supply the local hospital.

ChI in Remetea and Verdery's 'supertenants' in Vlaicu, all of whom came from the same collective or state farm management stock,²⁸ suggest that the strong emphasis on returning land to historical boundaries in Romania and the concomitant destruction of cooperative resources, had the result of delaying a more or less common post-socialist transformation rather than creating a new trajectory for it. Chapter 4 in Verdery's *The Vanishing Hectare* describes the painful process by which most village dwellers, predominantly old, with minimal resources, were forced to the decision that, despite their often protracted struggles to get their land back, after all the only future was to rent to a 'supertenant'.²⁹ All faced the same economic realities as JJ in Măgura which did not add up. Chapter 7 of *The Vanishing Hectare*, by contrast, takes the perspective of the 'supertenants' and their nurturing of their businesses to large-scale success,³⁰ with numerous parallels to ChI's experience. That said, 'large-scale' in all of these cases, including ChI in Remetea, remained rather modest compared with their counterparts in the other countries under consideration, where assets were not destroyed and rental to post-socialist, corporate 'super-

---

²⁷ Ibid., 327.
²⁸ Ibid., 199.
²⁹ Ibid., 158–83.
³⁰ Ibid., 273–309.

tenants' occurred over night. Most of Verdery's supertenants developed their businesses while continuing to be employed elsewhere,[31] although ChI farmed full time; and their farms covered the odd hundred rather than the odd thousand hectares.

THE NON-FARM ECONOMY—MODEST DEVELOPMENTS

Purani had been in many respects a socialist dormitory village to Braşov, and the impact of the early post-socialist recession there was modest. Braşov companies appeared to be weathering the transition rather successfully in 1995 and had not been obliged to introduce wide-scale redundancies, even after privatisation. Thus, although their number had dropped a little since 1989, the vast majority of younger Purani villagers continued to work in industry and commute to Braşov. The village did, it is true, also include a socialist-era factory and distillery and a pre-socialist cloth factory which was operating at only 50 per cent capacity by 1995, but a new unit of a Braşov-based factory had been set up which employed 500–600 people, and there was a new bakery and a new brewery (a joint venture with an Israeli) which together provide about 30 new jobs. A small, locally based construction, milling and repairs company, the successor to one of the co-operative's non-agricultural ventures, offered 10–15 jobs, and its joinery and furniture unit continued under another guise. There were also a small number of public sector jobs in the mayor's office and the schools, including the hostel and canteen of the specialist agricultural school which had been located in the village in 1981, and the local branch of the Credit Bank also provided some white-collar jobs, its presence alone testifying to the relative affluence of the village. The consumers' co-operative was in crisis however, although it struggled along with a repair workshop, a hair salon and tailor's shop. Some state farm, non-agricultural units also remained, but with scaled down operations. The slaughterhouse continued to produce salami for sale in Braşov; the dairy still produced some cheese, and the repair workshop,

---

[31] Ibid., 334–5.

which had once employed 45, continued to provide employment for 30 fitters and mechanics. Post 1989, thirty or so families had started running private businesses, providing employment for a further forty to fifty.

Horia in the early 1990s was a village that had lost the same sort of dormitory role that Purani had, but had not yet found a new one. Severe job cuts in Cluj had destroyed most of the previous commuting opportunities. New businesses tended to be family businesses only and were mostly located in areas which plugged socialism's personal services gap, such as a thriving non-stop bar in the centre of the village, owned by a young couple who also ran two other businesses in Cluj where they lived.[32] The village also boasted: a general food store, the owner of which (a woman of about 45) was also from Cluj, but employed an assistant from the village; a smaller food shop which also ran a buffet, owned by a 45 year old woman who lived in the village; and an ice-cream bar. The owner of the latter, CV, was a 32-year-old woman who also engaged in farming part-time and produced the ingredients herself which she then froze. In total six shops replaced the single general store of the socialist years, which had been little used in any case because most villagers bought what they needed in Cluj on the way to or from work. In addition to these commercial ventures, mainly run by a younger generation of women, often from outside the village, self-employed craftsmen in traditionally male trades had also been established: carpenters, cobblers, mechanics and panel beaters. Of the three car mechanics, two serviced the village, while the other worked mainly for a Cluj clientele.

Mica, also in commuting distance from Cluj, saw by contrast some modest new business development, despite a similar reduction in commuting and an increase in unemployment. The largest business in the village, in the view of the commune centre mayor and others (including its owner), was that of AT; and it provided at least some employment beyond the family circle. AT, husband of the village head-

---

[32] Davis, 'Sustainable non-farm', describes the collapse in industrial employment and provides figures suggesting the tendency of new businesses to plug the socialist personal services gap. He also stresses the importance of, yet inconsistency in accessing, credit, and the importance of a managerial background.

mistress and cousin of KT, a part-time farmer and village notable, was born in 1957 into a family with a kulak background. Despite this, AT's success did not come from agriculture. In partnership with a friend, who was a member of the folk dance group that AT and his wife ran, he headed a business which assembled and installed aluminium radiator systems from a former co-operative cowshed rented from the commune council. They worked to order and employed eight workers. In 1995, they had just taken on another employee, a graduate, whose job it would be to take orders and represent the company in the showroom that they had established in Cluj. They had a well-filled order book and were planning to enlarge the company.

In Măgura, the new business community was equally small, but some enjoyed social capital advantages and influence on the local council. Socialist Măgura had offered few opportunities for non-agricultural employment. The consumer co-operative operated small-scale industries, such as a sewing workshop, a shoemaker's workshop, employing four or five people and a wool-combing workshop, employing three. The council operated a construction team, which also ran a woodworking workshop. Commuting to work outside the village had begun in the early 1960s with collectivisation, and the retired headmaster estimated that, at one time, as many as two hundred villagers commuted to the nearest town, where there was a clothes factory, a smelting works, a machine-tool factory and a yarn factory.

After 1989, the number of regular commuters collapsed to around ten, the small consumer co-operative businesses did not survive, and most co-operative non-agricultural units closed down when the co-operative was wound up. One irony of post-socialist developments was that, while agricultural restructuring had pushed many back to farming with horses and carts, the traditional skills necessary to maintain this type of farming had disappeared. There was no blacksmith in Măgura; the blacksmith in nearby Corod, who also worked as a cartwright and did welding and machining, was sixty years old and had no apprentice. The Măgura bakery was bought by three private entrepreneurs, one of whom had moved back to the village from the nearest town and reputedly received financial help from a relative in Germany. But the entrepreneurs found it difficult to make a go of the business. Villagers were happy to have the bakery as a kind of social service: to convert their flour into bread. But they farmed on such a small scale that they could not provide the bakers with sufficient flour for it to be worth their while heating the oven for commercial activity.

PK became one of the village's most successful businessmen, albeit on a modest scale. He had worked since 1949 in commerce as a shopkeeper in a series of co-operative shops in the surrounding villages and in the regional Union of Consumers' Co-operatives (where his two sons had also worked) until his retirement. In 1994, he decided to start his own business and set up a mixed-profile shop in premises rented from the consumers' co-operative selling textiles, shoes, kitchen utensils, and, predominantly, second-hand clothes. One of his sons, who lived in the local town, had opened a restaurant in a nearby village even before 1989 and then took over the running of a restaurant in Măgura itself, which was owned by the other brother who had emigrated to Vienna. In 1995, they only sold drinks and cigarettes and cold food in the restaurant in Măgura, and restricted their cooking to special occasions such as confirmations, weddings or funerals, when the cook from the other restaurant would come over, and PK's wife would also lend a hand. PK began helping with the restaurants and then bought the petrol station which had belonged to the co-operative, where he eventually planned to open a buffet and sell spare car parts, using money provided by the son in Vienna. His various businesses together employed eleven people including family members. Despite these wide-ranging business activities, PK maintained that his main source of income was his pension, and that he had to work, because he had to help his three children and seven grandchildren. But he was well aware that his years of experience in the socialist commercial sector, his familiarity with the rules and regulations, his contacts, and even his experience dealing with customers, gave him an advantage over force-of-circumstance entrepreneurs; and his family gradually established a role in local politics. His son was elected mayor in June 1996. In Verdery's Vlaicu, there was similar tentative evidence of businessmen entering local politics in that one of the 'supertenants', Toma, had been elected to the commune council.[33]

The importance of outsiders in recognising business potential where locals failed to see it was reflected in Bunești. A variety of new

---

[33] Verdery, *The Vanishing Hectare*, 312.

small-scale, mainly family businesses quickly plugged the Buneşti personal services gap (twenty shops and catering units and 14 private businesses, mostly engaged in trade or transport) but the most significant private employer in the village was an outsider—a Syrian businessman, who had studied medicine in Bucharest but not returned home. He bought the key object of socialist tourism, the formerly state-owned motel (with about 24 employees and 600 rooms) located by a local beauty spot. To be on the safe side, he also bought two campsites in the area as well, since locals could not afford the prices charged by the motel. Buneşti's natural resources also offered various opportunities for casual employment in addition to tourism. There was plentiful day labour in the forestry industry, and in the summer, there was hay making, while mushroom collecting had become particularly profitable in the 1990s. Italian companies had established themselves in the village and, during the six-week season in the autumn, bought and dried specialist varieties of mushroom for 15,000 lei per kilo. Villagers also collected raspberries and other fruits of the forest; but this was only for either family consumption or private sale, as there was no commercial buyer. In the view of the Orthodox priest, some young people were attracted to this life-style and did not even look seriously for work.

In Remetea, post-socialist, small-scale businesses were mostly established by people maximising socialist-era experience and plugging the socialist personal services gap: a pharmacist opened her own pharmacy, a baking industry worker set up a bakery. The background of bar-owners was mixed. One was the 31-year-old CF, a member of the village's Roma community which, in the view of the Reform Church pastor, was 'mainly' unemployed by the mid-1990s. This community was so excluded from the mainstream that was no consensus even about its size. The clerk of the council put the number of Roma in Remetea itself at 885; the mayor put the figure at 230, while the agricultural entrepreneur ChI estimated two thousand. With such uncertainty on the part of the majority community about something as basic as numbers, it seemed unlikely that the single Roma representative on the commune council would be in a position to do much to represent the interests of his community. CF was sensitive about this degree of social exclusion and was understandably reluctant to give too much away about his activities or the sources of his capital. His parents and grandparents had worked on the co-operative and thus qualified for a few tenths of a hectare of land, and he had worked in the private sector as a trader before 1989, but he failed to mention the fact that he also owned a bus and a second bar. He had opened the bar that he admitted to in 1993 and employed two young barmaids; he made 'satisfactory' money, and they received 'satisfactory' remuneration. CF's business interests though substantial did not match those of the Roma entrepreneur BJ in Slovakia's Krížava (see Chapter 8).

EXTREME IMPOTENCE AT THE LOCAL LEVEL
The Catholic priest and the doctor—Plopeni

Verdery, when explaining corrupt practices in relation to the reallocation of land and in particular the behaviour of mayor Lupu of Vlaicu, stresses that Law 69/1991 gave mayors significant new powers and lessened their dependency on the county prefect.[34] This, in conjunction with the absence of effective sanctions if local officials failed to implement the law, a point also emphasised by Cartwright,[35] meant that the decisions of mayors and land commissioners could not effectively be challenged.[36] This legal independence certainly increased their autonomy with respect to land claims; but such decisions did not cost money. Perhaps the most characteristic feature of the local authorities in our Romanian villages was their inability, despite the formal greater independence of mayors, to meet their communities' needs from their own resources and their reliance on external sources of support in the form of charities, political patronage, external funding, or the resourcefulness of key individuals.

Strategic thinking in Plopeni appeared to come from the 51-year-old Catholic priest (who had been in the village for 14 years)[37] and his

---

[34] Ibid., 145.
[35] Cartwright, *The Return of the Peasant*, 151.
[36] Verdery, *The Vanishing Hectare*, 146.
[37] Monica Heintz, 'Romanian orthodoxy between the urban and the rural', Working Paper no. 67 (Max Planck Institute for Social Anthropology, Halle-Saale, 2004), 16, stresses the importance of personality over institutional factors when assessing the role of the Church in post-socialist Romania.

associates (the doctor and the vet), rather than the 14-person council (on which the doctor also served). The priest was full of plans to develop the village. An early initiative had been to attract young people by restoring an old building and converting it into a guest house. The village had ample potential for rural tourism, and the priest had plans to establish traditional tourist houses and campsites. Given the level of infrastructural provision in 1995 (no paved roads at all, no mains drainage, no running water), their initial market could only be younger tourists who were prepared to 'rough it'. Similarly he sought to breathe new life into the kindergarten and House of Culture which had been closed down because of a shortage of funds. The kindergarten eventually re-opened as private body, operated by the (Hungarian) Catholic Church, against the initial opposition of perhaps 90 per cent of the villagers. The Catholic Church was keen to take over the House of Culture too, but was experiencing staunch opposition from the (Romanian) Orthodox community, amongst whom rumours were spreading that once it belonged to the Catholics, they would not be allowed to use it. Others, perhaps, opposed the idea because of what the vet described as a spirit of 'jealousy and spite' in the village: 'let's just prevent others from profiting from anything at all'.

Further initiatives in the field of economic development included converting a building that had belonged to the Agromec into a factory for making sacks (it would be 60 per cent owned by locals and 40 per cent by three associations in the local area), and creating a western-style 'machinery circle', for which German assistance might have been forthcoming. The chances of such projects coming to fruition increased after the 1996 elections, when a new mayor was elected who was a former employee of a nearby Agromec, but more importantly a protégé of the priest and his associates. Interviewed in the summer of 1996, he stated that his priorities were: the infrastructure, roads, bridges, the House of Culture, and telephones. His predecessor, a former tractor driver, had been criticised for both lacking vision and incompetence; in particular for having signed away rights to mineral water in the village, because he did not read a document properly before putting pen to paper.

Medical provision in the village also relied on external and private sector contributions. There were two permanent doctors in the close core of villages which made up the commune centre. One of these,

Dr S, had been born in the village, left it with his parents at the time of collectivisation, but moved back with them in 1977; he qualified locally, and had written extensively about the village and its problems. There were also two permanent medically qualified assistants, a team of four nurses (funded by a Swiss grant specifically to support the sick, elderly and disabled) and a midwife. Dr S had also opened a private clinic, which was stocked with the contents of western aid parcels. The local pharmacy had closed in 1992, and some speculated that this worked in Dr S's interests, in that he effectively acted as a pharmacist with his access to western drugs. Indeed, some argued that he had prevented a new pharmacist from setting up after the first one had closed.

The village had received significant amounts of foreign aid, from Belgium, France and Switzerland. But it was by no means always the case that the village had benefited from the aid, and by 1995 the foreign links were weakening. Furthermore, potential generosity from foreign friends was on occasion turned down because of the limited horizons of the locals. Five years earlier, the Belgian partners had offered to help improve the water supply, but with the proviso that the village cover 30 per cent of the costs itself. No one was prepared even to try to raise the money to fund it at the time. By 1995, however, the new shops in the village were demanding a better water supply, and there was no such generous offer on the table.

The Reform Church pastor and political patronage—Mica

Mica, an ethnically Hungarian village in a predominantly Romanian commune, was left to its own devices in the early 1990s and relied on foreign charities, political patronage and its 68-year-old Reform Church pastor to provide direction and support. The socialist years had done little to improve Mica's infrastructure. There were no paved roads, and the three-kilometre access road between the main road and the village was in an extremely poor condition. Nor was there mains drainage, and although there was running water to a lot of the village (110 of 400 farms according to the mayor's 1992 statistics), and 70 per cent of houses had baths, the springs that fed them were drying up and there was a severe water problem. (Most houses had wells in their yards as an alternative.) There were only two telephones in the village, in the post office and in the doctor's surgery, both of which shared the same party line to the manual exchange. It was not surprising, therefore, that improving the infrastructure was the council's main priority. Five million lei was allocated for road improvements generally in 1995, and, in 1995 and 1996, an additional 185 million lei was allocated to repair the bridge on the access road, a project that all agreed was essential and long overdue. Gas was the next priority. It had already been introduced in the commune centre and there were plans to extend it to Mica and two other commune villages, although one of the Mica representatives on the council did not expect it within five years.

But there was little evidence of a fuller development strategy on the part of the council. The mayor's office had not tried to initiate discussions with local entrepreneurs, and, although entrepreneurs were obliged to become members of the Chamber of Industry, in the view of AT, they felt that they had no organisation acting upon their behalves and that they were acting alone. The Reform Church pastor, by contrast, had an eye for possible developments in the field of rural tourism. With a little investment, he thought that the warehouse that had been rescued from the co-operative could be converted into a motel with a café and space to sell embroidery and other folk art.

Shortage of funds meant that the community centre had to be run on a voluntary basis, and the pastor had to take the initiative to organise activities such as language classes. Furthermore, the village no longer benefited from the limited assistance that the agricultural co-operative had provided in the socialist years, contributions in kind to pensioners of approximately 30 kilos of wheat and 40 kilos of maize per year. In the view of a village-domiciled teacher, who was also a member of the council and active in the UDMR (see Chapter 1), 'the budget is so little that there isn't anything to distribute'. The absence of the local authority from the field of social welfare was partially compensated by the church, which had some funds to spend on welfare thanks to the generosity of its Dutch partner. But it was not sufficient to meet demand, and aid from the Netherlands was falling off by the mid-1990s as donor fatigue set in. Such aid had also sometimes been misdirected. The village, or rather its church, had received a small mill from a Dutch fellow congregation, which was located in a warehouse that the church had rescued from the co-operative when it underwent transformation (that the pastor wanted to turn into a motel). But the villagers found little use for it. The reason was simple: it only produced flour suitable for wholemeal bread. The pastor had difficulties explaining to the villagers of Mica that wholemeal bread was healthier than the white bread to which they were accustomed. Furthermore, when the pastor had first gone to Holland, they had offered him to equip a dairy plant for the village for free; all that was necessary was the provision of a building; but the idea was rejected because of village antipathy to any form of 'communal' venture.

The pastor had been more successful with the combine harvester. One of the six privately owned combines in the commune was collaboratively operated by the church, which the pastor had persuaded some villagers to buy:

> I could see as early as 1992 that the village could not rely on the two rickety harvesters of the Agromec. Everyone was waiting, but no one was acting. They were all waiting for someone else to take care of things. So I called a meeting and said to the lads: 'We need to sort things out for ourselves, let's pull together and buy a harvester.'

Some 25 villagers agreed to contribute 200,000 lei each, the church put in two million lei, and they succeeded in buying a machine in Bucharest at four million lei below the list price, one that had already been invoiced but then rejected by the customer. It was registered in the pastor's name, and the income that it generated was split 35 ways reflecting their original contributions, one share each to the 25 participants and 10 to the church. Discounting inflation, everyone got their investment back within two years.

Village 'intellectuals', particularly in the later socialist years,[38] had helped create a vibrant cultural life for the village, which boasted a successful dance troop (organised by the school headmistress and her husband, the radiator entrepreneur) and a church choir (organised by the pastor, but directed by a colleague from Cluj). The dance troop had established an international reputation, and had been filmed by

---

[38] The role of cultural tourism in the later post-socialist years is addressed in Bernadett Csurgó, 'Urban pressure—A recent phenomenon: The Valley of Arts', *Eastern European Countryside* 10 (2004): 155–65.

Japanese film-makers, and, more significantly, studied by Hungarian ethnographers investigating Transylvanian Hungarian customs. It had performed in Hungary many times, and in Switzerland, Germany and France. The choir was a more recent formation, the successor to one that had folded in the 1970s. Recreated in 1993, it had already performed in national events and in Holland and Switzerland. The headmistress also strove to keep regional identity alive by organising subscriptions to the regional paper. Yet some villagers complained that, despite these activities and the existence of the village's community centre, there was little cultural life: the young people preferred to go to the disco which one of the pubs organised on Saturday and Sunday evenings. The teacher also complained that parents were even less concerned about encouraging their children to study hard at school than they had been in the past, and none of the traditional annual balls took place any more. Pensioner JJ reflected a similar malaise when he bemoaned the lack of collaboration in the village: 'We do not believe anyone or trust anyone anymore.'

The only political party to have a presence in Mica was the UDMR, which, in 1995, managed to retain a relatively large membership on paper of 500. Mica's two representatives on the commune council were both members. But the leaders of the transformation years of 1989 and 1990 had gone, and the new leaders did nothing, not even collect membership fees. In the 'heroic' transformation years the UDMR had wanted to change everything: the party secretary, shopkeepers, agricultural engineers, anyone associated at all with the former regime. Its leader had stormed into the mayor's office in Criş and spoken only in Hungarian, although he had always spoken in Romanian in the past. Dramatic gestures of this sort only alienated Mica's representatives from other council members; they gradually toned down their stance, but without gaining much for the village. In this climate of shortage, the party itself took on a role as distributor of largesse, in return for political patronage. The regional organisation of the UDMR saw an opportunity and promised Mica a telephone exchange in return for revitalising the moribund local party branch. The village organisers agreed and generated a paper membership of 500. The party duly handed over to the village its exchange. Unfortunately, when the telephone company tested it, it turned out to be wholly inappropriate for their needs, only usable by a small company not by a village.

A vibrant community culture under threat—Măgura

Măgura, like Mica, enjoyed a rather vibrant ethnic minority culture despite a gaping socialist public services gap. There was no mains drainage in the village, only the main roads were paved, there were places where telegraph poles had fallen down and not been replaced, rendering all telephone contact unreliable. The village's fiscal crisis in the mid-1990s was severe. Only 37 per cent of the budget came from state support; but roughly a third of the budget was taken up paying local administration salaries; school maintenance and supplies had become a local responsibility. Within this tight budget, the scope for autonomous decision-making was extremely low, although it did allow the mayor's office to buy a photocopier so that villagers could get copies made easily of their official documents. This gave the office a small additional income, although the mayor had to do the copying himself. The council further used some of its income from forestry to bolster the inadequate school repair budget. The Măgura co-operative's rather limited contribution to the commune ceased after 1990, and little replaced it, although PK's restaurant-owning son and future mayor had been persuaded to sponsor the local water polo club. The village had also received charitable aid from a Hungarian village in 1989 and 1990, although this had developed into mainly cultural ties thereafter. Aid from a 'twin' village in England allowed them to complete a project laying water pipes. There was an old people's home in one of the commune villages, which had been built in the 1980s, but outside assistance was necessary too for its survival: by the mid-1990s, it had been taken over by 'one of the churches' which functioned using western aid.

Despite this fiscal crisis, the council was able to provide some funding to support the community's cultural life, which developed significantly after 1989, partly because it had firm traditions on which to build. In the 1970s, the village had had a four-part choir in which old and young sang together, but it had folded in 1980. The village's tradition of amateur dramatics had continued however. A play had been produced every year by a group which was run by the school maths and physics teacher in Sînpetru, who, after 1989, became a leader of the UDMR. It continued into the 1990s, and was complemented by two other groups. Groups of villagers put on cabarets too, including a political cabaret on 17 December 1989. After 1989, the villagers tried to develop cultural activities further. On the initiative of a prominent older village resident, in 1992, an annual festival was re-established on the last Sunday in May, recreating a tradition of fifty years before. In its new guise choirs and dancers performed on an open-air stage, attracting hundreds of visitors and both local television and radio. One of the other commune villages had managed to maintain its festival, on the first Sunday in June, for the last 37 years. A series of annual art camps was also established.

On a smaller scale, the manager of the Cultural Centre, a thirty-year-old former music and singing teacher and single mother, had managed to organise a small choir of 15 to 20 young people; and she was in the process of establishing a choir for pensioners. There was a folk dance troop and an orchestra which played both classical and folk music, and they held dances and fancy dress balls. In the Easter of 1995, the then newly appointed manager of the Cultural Centre herself and some others sang the Matthew Passion in the centre, and then performed it in other commune villages. Needless to say, there were financial problems in organising cultural activities of this scale. In addition to the commune council, the county educational inspectorate, a local company, and the local forestry office (headed by the father of the manager of the Cultural Centre, and where her brother also worked) all supported educational activities such as festivals. The commune council made a further contribution in kind to culture in that it did not charge for use of the cultural centre. On a more prosaic level, the Cultural Centre had a colour television and satellite dish, which pensioners watched some evenings. It also contained a 30-year-old library, which had briefly closed but then re-opened, although, in 1995, it had not yet acquired any new books.

In the early post-socialist years, the role of intellectuals in the village increased dramatically, not least because the ability to speak a foreign language was important when aid began to arrive. The Unitarian Church minister, who had studied English and had many English contacts, was instrumental in creating an ecumenical International Youth Centre, which attracted many foreign visitors. But he then emigrated to Hungary in the mid-1990s. Agronomists left the village when the co-operative disappeared, as did teachers, once they could freely choose where they wanted to work. Many of the initiatives of the heady days of 1990 floundered, such as the public education association (set up by teachers, engineers and the doctor) and a philanthropic association (set up to tackle health and social problems). With the departure of the minister, none of the congregations in Mägura enjoyed the services of a fulltime officiate, so making religious instruction in schools problematic. Curiously, despite all the choirs in the village, there were no permanent church choirs. What is more, the Unitarian church's four annual tea evenings (one in each of the four parishes), which had begun in the 1980s and at which entertainment was always provided and large sums were collected for the church, died out after 1990; people were no longer interested.

There was recognition that the village had agro-tourist potential, but also that it could only be developed properly when the people were a little better off financially. The cultural festivals had developed independently of the local authority (apart from its funding of the Cultural Centre and its employees), and they were not part of a commune-led, tourism-development strategy. The commune's concrete support measures towards the community related to agriculture. One of these was the attempt to get an agricultural entrepreneur to take on the commune's uncultivated land. But entrepreneurs of this kind did not exist. In 1993, an outsider had taken on some land in one commune village, but he did not do it again, because the land was too poor to make it worthwhile. The council also had a pasture policy and employed two guards to look after it, charging nominal fees to cover the cost of drinking troughs and sheep dips. Other council members pressed for the creation of some sort of large-scale farming, either within an association or on a private basis, and for the promotion of food processing industries, such as fruit juice bottling. The mayor in 1995 commented that, he would have liked to be able to hand some of the village's uncultivated land over to the landless poor to help them make a living for themselves. They had indeed tried to do this once, but the owner of the land had immediately appeared and refused to let them use his land. The council also supported farmers to a limited extent by giving the Farmers' Circle space on the notice board in front of the council building, so that chairman of the Circle could post notices advising what was in season, what chemicals should be used and so on.

In mainly Hungarian Mägura, the UDMR formed a party branch with 300 members in 1990, and it was very active until the land had been redistributed. After that, its membership dropped drastically as in Mica, and, after 1992, nobody paid their membership fees. In 1994, it reorganised itself anew with only 30 members, and remained the only political party in the village—all members of the commune council belonged to it. But the members were not universally happy with the way in which the party was organised, and the fact that its treasurer had previously been the village's communist Party Secretary suggested how little criteria other than ethnic identity mattered. The comments of the Cultural Centre manager also reveal something about expectations of the party. When she said pointedly that the UDMR had not supported financial activities such as the festivals that she organised, her expectation was clearly that it should have, that it should have distributed political patronage to a kindred organisation.

Patronage, incompetence and despair— Buneşti, Colibaşi and Horia

Reliance on foreign charities was not restricted to villages with large ethnic minority populations. They also contributed to village welfare in Buneşti, where they also proved to be a mixed blessing. Buneşti had developed links with villages in France, Belgium and Switzerland, and an English group worked fulltime with handicapped children. But the Orthodox priest refused the task of distributing the aid, and passed it on to the mayor's office; and in the end they had to ask their partners not to send clothes, but rather school equipment and medicines, because the latter in particular were expensive, and the nearest pharmacy was in Atid. The links with the Belgians nevertheless became so institutionalised that the mayor had had a small house built for them where they could spend holidays, and the council was in the process of equipping and furnishing it. Buneşti also opted for 'party homogenisation' as a means of courting patronage. The mayor at the time of the majority of our interviews came from a local family, had a background in socialist local government, and had stood as an independent. The first post-socialist council was made up of councillors from three parties, the Democratic Convention, the Agrarian Party and the Liberal Party. However, in the 1996 elections things changed dramatically. The county prefect was a member of the nationalistic Party of Romanian National Unity (PUNR). The result of the 1996 elections in Buneşti was that suddenly the PUNR became the strongest party; a new PUNR mayor was elected, and the former mayor both changed his allegiance to the PUNR and accepted demotion to the post of deputy mayor—100 per cent party homogenisation.

Buneşti too witnessed an example of inexperience as well as impotence. An issue which particularly exercised the priest related to piped water. A company had been engaged to lower the level of the river bed, a procedure that required blowing away a section of rock. But this also lowered the water table. Wells ran dry, and they could not be deepened because this required boring through the rock. While it was working on the project, the contracting company concerned had pumped up water to its building site, and permitted villagers to tap into this supply. But when it left, it took the pump away, and the wells ran dry. The priest was not the only villager who thought that the company should have been obliged to provide a permanent water supply for the villagers as part of the contract. But because of incompetence or inexperience with the world of competing commercial contractors (no one suggested corruption), the contract had failed to do so. The commune, of course, did not have the funds to resolve the problem itself.

Colibaşi, like Mica, was not a commune centre although it had been in the early socialist period with responsibility for three other villages, a status it lost in 1968. There was talk in 1990 of restoring the old administrative boundaries of the village, an idea which the residents of Colibaşi supported. But the other villages in the commune overruled them; the villages that used to be part of Colibaşi commune prior to 1968 had no desire to belong to it again; and Colibaşi could not survive on its own. By the mid-1990s, Colibaşi felt totally abandoned. It was effectively without a local authority since it had no representation on the commune council, which was made up entirely of the inhabitants of the small town where it was based. 'There is no regional development strategy and no conception of village policy' was the judgement on the council's activities of MS, the former head of the viticulture association and unsuccessful agricultural entrepreneur. There was no mains drainage, most water came from wells, and only the main road and two cross streets were paved. Gas was provided for the village however, but this was the result of a citizens' initiative. The primary mover in this was a local factory worker and former political activist. Fed up with council inactivity, he took the initiative, mobilised villagers to sign up, and made all the necessary arrangements for gas to be installed. But such local initiative was only partially successful in the end. They managed to get the gas mains laid, but they did not raise sufficient subscribers or donations to install all of the necessary lateral piping. The organisers were conscious that almost half of the village residents were pensioners with only a small co-operative pension who would find it difficult to put up the necessary cash to finance this, and had hoped therefore to supplement the private subscribers with institutional contributions, from the school and the kindergarten. But neither of these had access to monies for unofficial expenditure of this type, even if they would benefit from it. Without their contributions, bringing gas to every villager's door in the first instance proved impossible.

The extreme impotence of local authorities, the extent of the socialist public services gap and their consequent reliance on outside forces resulted in some throwing in the towel. In Horia villagers indeed asserted that the 13-member council only existed on paper and did nothing. Certainly, by 1995, it had become totally dependent on links with western villages, especially Holland, for its basic medical supplies. Prior to that, the medical centre did not even have a decent blood pressure set or a set of scales for weighing babies. The mayor, a teacher who had settled in the village because his wife was a kindergarten teacher there, was in fact keen to give the job up and return to teaching. He felt that his salary was far too low for the responsibilities that it entailed; he had lost interest. With no personal commitment to the job beyond the inadequate income that it provided, it was not surprising that the mayor had lost the support of the villagers. Nor is it surprising that no one could identify the existence of any kind of development strategy for the village. The mayor was voted out of office in 1996, but the scale of the task remained daunting. The mayor of Lipova had likewise announced that he did not wish to stand in the next elections because he felt the job not sufficiently well paid and that his work was not properly appreciated.

In Poland in the case of Kanał it was reported that some children from outlying villages and hamlets were missing secondary school. This phenomenon appeared to be more extensive in remoter communities in Romania. In Horia teachers reported that, especially in the outlying villages, children often missed school in order to do jobs around the farm; and in Măgura, teachers reported that absenteeism was on the increase, particularly in the cases of children living in the more outlying villages, or outside the villages altogether. In Buneşti, although funds were still sufficient to provide a minibus to bring most of the children from outlying areas to school, some parents, in the Orthodox priest's view, were beginning to take the view that there was no point in giving their children an education because they would not find jobs in any case. The deputy mayor also commented on the trend, as did a pensioner. The deputy mayor linked it with the fact that there was no longer a legal obligation to complete ten years' schooling; the pensioner lamented rather the birth of a new illiterate generation: '[T]he mountain people cannot educate their children because they are poor. There will be illiterate people again.'

ROMANIAN SPECIFICITIES IN SUMMARY

Our research identified only one large-scale private farmer in Romania, ChI, the former co-operative chairman in Remetea who privatised the most commercially viable parts of his farm to himself, but even this large-scale farm was of relatively small dimensions compared with equivalents in Hungary or the Czech Republic (or some relatively uncommon cases in Slovakia identified by Námerová),[39] or the Bulgarian *arendatori* identified by Giordano and Kostova in Bulgaria.[40] His farm was nearer the dimensions of the 'supertenants' identified by Verdery. Even such success stories were building on the ruins rather than the achievements of socialist agriculture. Some associations transformed smoothly and seemed to be destined for success, although most could only afford to provide remuneration in kind and many, like the successor co-operatives in Bulgaria, had to abandon livestock farming. Others like that in Colibaşi and Verdery's Vlaicu, failed because of the short-term horizons of their members. In contexts where no association emerged, not least because machinery remained locked up in Agromecs, pre-socialist land holding was often important

---

[39] See Námerová, 'Private farmers', and the case of PR.
[40] See the discussion in Chapter 3.

determining post-socialist, small-scale success than elsewhere in the region. But, as the case of JJ in Măgura makes clear, the economics of farming alone on this scale made no sense and, as the villagers of Verdery's Vlaicu also painfully realised, the future lay in renting to people like ChI or 'supertenants'.

The effect of the post-socialist recession on commuting jobs was uneven. Purani, near Braşov, was not badly affected, but Horia and Mica, near Cluj, were. Although no substantial non-agricultural rural businesses developed in any of our post-socialist Romanian communities, businesses that did somewhat more than plug the socialist personal services gap emerged in the form of the radiator business in Mica and the interlocking business interests of PK in Măgura. The key figures driving our Romanian rural communities were not members of local authorities or mayors, who tended to be impotent in the face of an overwhelming challenge; indeed, in some cases, they gave up entirely, faced with a socialist public services gap that was wider than anywhere else as a consequence of Romania's Stalinist policies in the socialist years. Yet, while the level of need was certainly as great as in Poland, issues of social welfare figured much less prominently on the local authority agenda because of the absence of resources from which to address them. Concrete council strategies, as in Bulgaria, tended to relate to agriculture, and in Romania too, in Buneşti, Horia and Măgura there were reports of children from the more outlying communities being kept out of school. The driving village forces tended rather to be individual local actors, mainly clerics (endowed with greater human, social and cultural capital than their flocks), some of whom had access to external, charity funding. The inequities, real or imagined, associated with confessional-based (and therefore also ethnicity-based) support were keenly felt in Plopeni. The dangers of reliance on individual initiatives as the dynamo for rural development were revealed in Măgura in the 'routinisation' of community life when those key individuals left. Nevertheless, despite this extreme impotence of Romanian local authorities, in Măgura the son of the dominant local business family saw the advantages of exerting influence locally and found himself elected mayor in 1996.

Map 8.1. Research sites, Slovakia

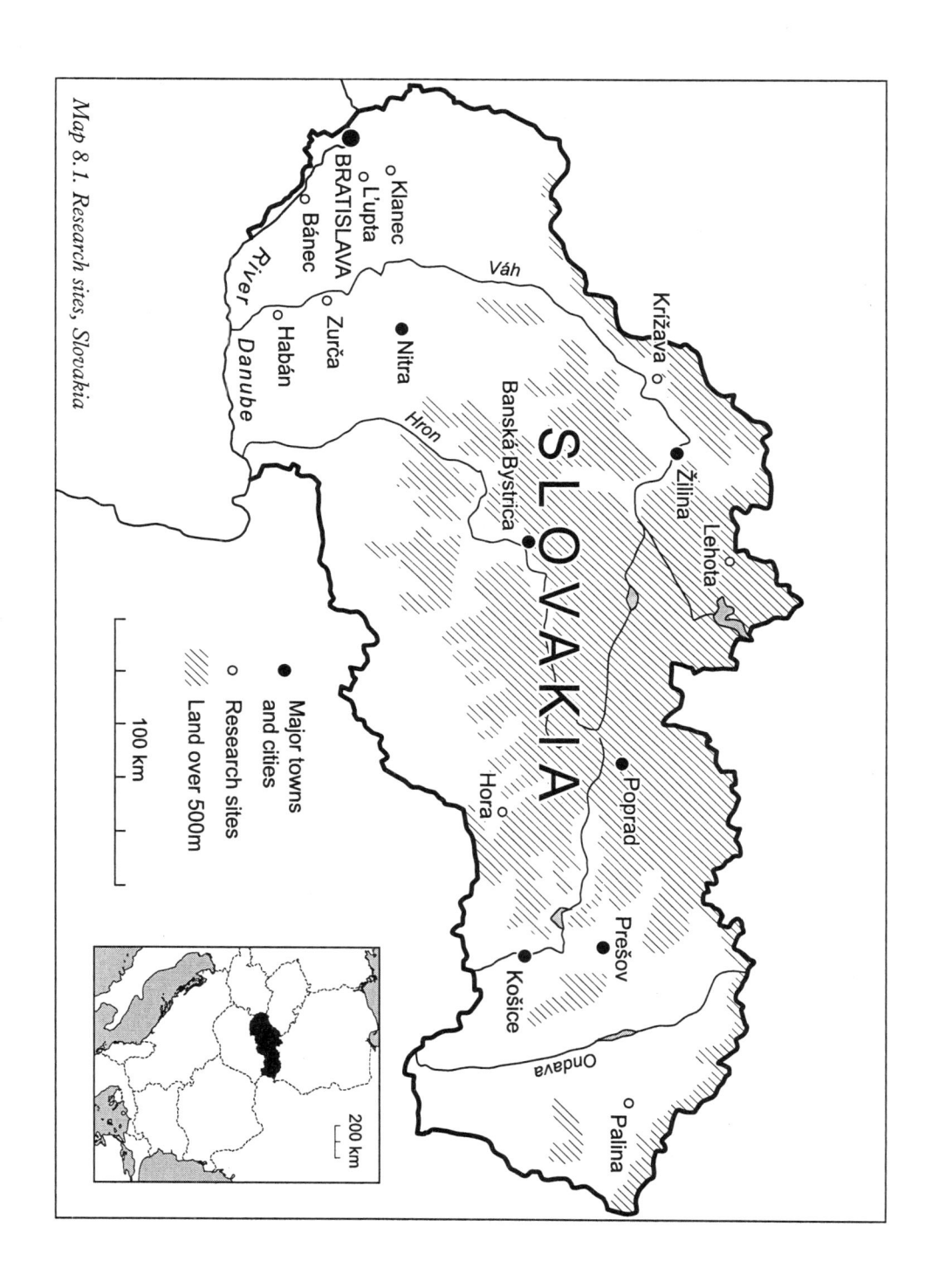

CHAPTER 8

Slovakia

As discussed in Chapter 1, Slovakian politics in the early-to-mid 1990s was dominated by the rise of Mečiar, and this left its mark on rural restructuring and local rural politics. As in the Czech Republic, agricultural co-operatives underwent restructuring but, to an even greater extent than in the Czech Republic, tended to stay in place. It was, however, more common for them to demerge to their constituent parts prior to the mergers of the 1970s.[1] Whereas Czech governments were somewhat embarrassed by the continuity of socialist entities and always stressed that co-operatives were a form of private ownership, co-operatives in Mečiar's Slovakia became a feature of Slovakia's special path to post-socialism and were promoted. Slovak farm managers were more likely to say that nothing had changed, when in fact it had, while Czech managers were keener to report how they had adapted to the market. Decentralising initiatives were discouraged; essentially private company initiatives continued to call themselves co-operatives; and co-operative legislation was amended to reflect just this: institutions that were nominally co-operative abandoned the principle of 'one member, one vote'. The pro-co-operative climate

---

[1] Gejza Blaas and Axel Woltz, 'Economic situation and structural changes in Slovakian agriculture', *Eastern European Countryside* 4 (1998): 99–116, confirm the greater propensity of co-operatives to demerge in Slovakia, although they suggest it was far from uncommon in the Czech Republic too.

did not encourage private farming, an option which made less sense in Slovakia than its former partner because of its historical structure of extremely small-scale subsistence farming. Blaas and Wolz remind us that the average pre-socialist land holding was only five hectares.[2] Indeed land of such dimensions was of so little interest to many Slovaks that large swathes of land remained unclaimed. In Hora for example, as much as 40 per cent of the land farmed by the co-operative had no identifiable owner; in Torsello's Királyfa the ratio was somewhat lower: 10 per cent of the 60 per cent of village land farmed by the co-operative land had no owner.[3] And most co-operatives continued their traditional forms of assistance, not unlike Bulgaria's red co-operatives and the continuing Hungarian co-operative in Szálfa.

In the non-farm economy, 'full, direct and specific' restitution played a minimal role, because, to a far greater extent than in Bohemia and Moravia, industrial development in Slovakia was a phenomenon of the socialist era. On the other hand, unemployment levels were consistently higher in Slovakia than in the Czech Republic, reflected in the rural sector in the attractiveness of returning to subsistence farming and the persistence of commuting across the border to the Czech Republic for work. The Slovak rural economy under Mečiar suffered extremely from the problem of circulating debt and unpaid bills, as noted in Chapter 1, and this impacted in many cases on the relationship between cash-strapped councils and indebted but still functioning and politically supported agricultural co-operatives. A certain ambivalence concerning market structures might also have been a factor in the greater willingness of local authorities in Slovakia to intervene directly in the economy. In the Balkans, local authorities did not have the resources for such an approach, even if they shared ambivalence about the market. Although 'party homogenisation' along Romanian lines was not a feature noted by commentators, there is no doubting the dramatic swing of support at the local level from the KDH to Mečiar's

---

[2] Ibid., 106–7.
[3] Davide Torsello, 'Trust and property in historical perspective: Villagers and the agricultural co-operative in Királyfa, Southern Slovakia', in *The Postsocialist Agrarian Question: Property Relations and the Rural Condition*, ed. Chris Hann and The 'Property Relations' Group (Münster: LIT Verlag, 2003), 108.

HZDS, nor the difficulties in attracting funding experienced by mayors who belonged to parties that opposed the HZDS.

AGRICULTURAL TRANSFORMATION—VARIATIONS ON THE THEME OF CONTINUITY

Co-operative demergers—Hora, Habán, Zurča, Ľupta, Bánec

In five of our nine Slovak villages, the co-operative de-merged prior to 1992, while transformation itself was characterised by continuity. In Hora, for example, a village which nestled in the mountains on an ancient trade route between Poland and Hungary, with exquisite traditional wooden houses (albeit topped by satellite dishes), and traditions of shepherding, iron ore mining and smelting and only latterly agriculture, the co-operative demerged in 1991 to its pre-1970s units before undergoing transformation in 1992. The latter process was uncontested; there was minimal interest in private farming; the workforce was halved; and the successor co-operative was blessed with managers who adjusted activities to nature of the mountainous landscape and changed market conditions. In Habán (in southern Slovakia between the River Váh and River Hron), there was a similar demerger (although only one of three became independent) and the management at the time accepted that this would necessitate increased investment in buildings which were almost complete at the time of transformation. This proceeded smoothly with little change in the co-operative's activities, although some adjustment to market conditions and extensive job loss. By 1995, however, it was beginning to regret the demerger and lost economies of scale, and some argued that the membership had been unduly pressurised towards demerger by representatives of Public Against Violence.

In Zurča, demerger was associated with most managers abandoning the farm. By the end of the socialist period the co-operative operated profitably in five villages and almost all spheres of agriculture, although it was saddled with a sizable debt for investments in a new hay loft, irrigation systems, a tobacco drying unit, cattle and pig units, and a non-agricultural unit, which produced slippers for the Bata shoe enterprise based in Zlín in Moravia. Given its size, it is perhaps not surprising that it de-merged again into its five pre-1975 component parts; and slipper production ceased in 1990 with the loss of all 130 jobs. Many managers, men in their forties with university degrees and outsiders to the village, abandoned agriculture at this time, in favour of banking, the law and agribusiness. In 1992, as part of the uncontested transformation process, the co-operative settled the claims of the 801 'entitled persons', including only 114 active co-operative members and 72 inactive members, and became, with a smattering of new members, a Shareholders Agricultural Co-operative. Its board of directors represented interests very different from the past; it was dominated by pensioner former rich peasants. It appointed a new 15-strong management made up of people who had grown up in the village, aged between 30 and 40. But the new management, burdened with old debt and 20 per cent interest rates, could do little more than continue in the same way, while attempting to adjust to market conditions by, for example, liquidating twenty of the farm's thirty hectares of unprofitable vineyards, and abandoning its support for community activities. Two years later, the general view of the co-operative was that it was still 'in decline', although it had fared better than the other former components of the larger socialist farm, two of which had folded completely. The co-operative continued to offer services and equipment to its members for their household plot cultivation. Interest in the village in private farming as a fulltime commercial venture was minimal. The only success was a villager who began growing medicinal herbs as the basis for an ointment for rheumatism on only 0.15 hectares of land. The business provided a livelihood for himself, his wife and five casual workers, which, by 1995, had expanded by adding a new building for producing and packing the ointment, and had sales mainly to chemists in Western Slovakia.

In Ľupta too, a village with favourable agricultural conditions situated close to the Bratislava agglomeration, a demerger (of the second of the politically inspired mergers of the 1960s and 1970s) was associated with management abandonment of the farm and stagnation. The chairman, the chief agronomist, the chief economist and the heads of the non-agricultural units all left to start new private businesses outside the region; the co-operative to the south and east broke away, but the one to the north and west remained with Ľupta. Thereafter the co-operative's non-agricultural units began to close and the labour force fell by 93 in 1991, 71 in 1992 and 31 in 1993. Co-operative transformation itself went smoothly, creating a total of 950 shareholders. The remaining managers tried to adjust to the market by reducing some of their livestock holdings, closing the social fund and giving up sponsoring the local sports club (although it retained the holiday cottage in the Tatra Mountains), but, two years later, its inexperienced management struggled. In the view of one manager, there was no one in the village capable of running the farm. It continued to give members their income in kind (1,200 kilos of maize for the pigs and poultry that most kept still on their household plots), but it had no funds to replace old equipment; labour discipline had worsened; tractor drivers arrived late in the fields; pilfering of crops and equipment had become a severe problem; people who hired equipment from the co-operative did not pay for it; and the tenants of co-operative flats did not pay rent, partly because the farm did not have the money to make the necessary repairs. There had initially been little interest in private farming (four people registered as private farmers, but all 'farmed' less than a hectare each), but by 1995 a former manager from the co-operative in nearby Klanec had decided to quit the stagnating co-operative sector. He rented 42 hectares from relatives in Ľupta and the surrounding area, concentrating on fruit and vegetables in addition to cereals.

In Bánec, too, the co-operative first demerged into its pre-1976 components, and because the farm had been wealthy and had accumulated a significant reserve fund, there was little conflict over the distribution of assets. Some managers also moved out of agriculture entirely, and even those who stayed, including the chairman, developed independent private business interests, usually in the name of another family member, suggesting an ambivalent commitment to the co-operative. The post-transformation co-operative management was particularly hostile to secessionists (of whom there were very few) because it felt that it needed a farm of about 2,000 hectares in order to justify the irrigation equipment that had been installed in the socialist years. Pensioners who wanted to get back their land and rent it to private entrepreneurs rather than the co-operative claimed that they were 'bamboozled' into renting to the co-operative by threats that they would lose their pensions if they did not rent to the co-operative. A machinery manager who left complained that he had been forced to give up his co-operative membership, although the law did not require him to do so, that he had only received 4.26 hectares from the co-operative when he expected more, and that the 44,341 crowns that he received in cash represented only 30 per cent of his total share. The view was common that 'The bosses are the same party members as before. The co-operative has not been transformed.'

Two years after the Bánec transformation, the co-operative was still operating profitably, but the management was pessimistic about the future. Its structure of production had scarcely changed; the co-operative had not invested for four years, although in 1995, partly thanks to the good contacts that the agronomist had with the bank, they had received bank loans and other funding and had invested 15 million crowns in machinery and buildings; and the membership had fallen to 226 plus 22 management. It retained a social fund for subsidised holidays, contributions for weddings or funerals of members; but it had given up is sponsorship of the sports association, doing no more than occasionally lending it its bus for transport to away fixtures. It also offered services to the members and private farmers, but the latter felt that their prices were too high and preferred to use the services of private entrepreneurs from other villages. Furthermore, over the years from 1993 to 1995, there was an increase in the numbers taking out land for subsistence farming. Although the mayor and co-operative leaders referred to tiny numbers, the official figures revealed tiny quantities of land per person, but quite significant numbers of individuals: 91 in all, taking out a total of 127.5 hectares, hardly a vote of confidence in the co-operative. The bulk of the villagers continued to be 'pluriactive' in that they rented most of their land back to the co-operative and combined small-scale agriculture with a job, a business, a pension or unemployment benefit. The former machinery manager continued to farm privately; with his wife he owned six hectares, he rented a further five, and he was about to inherit a further 6.5 hectares. But his income from farming was insufficient to live from and he had to supplement it when possible working as a machinist on the co-operative's irrigation equipment.

Continuity without demerging—Palina and Krížava

By the time of post-socialist co-operative transformation in Palina, in the far east of Slovakia, the co-operative was a rather distant institution for the bulk of the villagers. In 1971–72 the co-operative had merged with six others and the co-operative centre moved outside the village. Most of the only twelve villagers who worked for the co-operative fell into either the unskilled category or were workers with livestock; they were all between 40 and retirement age and worked mainly to receive their pension rights and a small income in kind, chiefly in potatoes. Nevertheless, the co-operative did not demerge and, following its formal and uncontested transformation in 1992, it continued to operate as before. No organisational changes took place except for the non-agricultural pallet producing unit which employed 25–30 which was privatised (see below); the co-operative continued to rely on subsidies for survival; it had given up all social provisions it had once made, and it shed some 70 jobs. No one left the co-operative to embark on private farming, and six hectares only were reclaimed by 15 people. The co-operative chairman contemplated renting one of the dairy units to himself as a private business, but decided against it. Two years later, despite assertions that 'nothing had changed', the co-operative had adjusted marginally to market conditions. It had restarted chicken farming, because a customer had offered the facility in lieu of payment of its debt, and it proved profitable; and it had moved extensively into growing poppy seeds which had not previously been a major crop.

In Krížava, located in the wide flat valley of the River Váh on the main road from Poland to Italy, the co-operative did not demerge either, but it did introduce radical decentralisation before co-operative transformation. There had been discussion of demerger immediately after 1989, but eventually Krížava and its neighbouring village down the valley agreed to stay, on condition that the director, appointed in 1988, were sacked. But, partly in anticipation of the expected split, the management of the farm was decentralised into the former six independent co-operatives, each of which had its own chief agronomist and livestock specialist and overall head. There was consistent job-loss over the 1989–92 period. In the first two years, this affected mainly the non-agricultural units as they were scaled down to meet the immediate needs of the co-operative only. The space in former poultry sheds, which had been converted into an engineering unit in 1988, was let first to a company which failed to pay the rent, and then to another which assembled agricultural machinery and was somewhat more successful (although it sometimes paid its rent in kind, in agricultural equipment, rather than cash). But in 1991 agricultural jobs were also lost. Across all branches of the farm, in 1990 there was a net reduction of six; in 1991, it was 211; in 1992, it was 70, and in 1993 it was 46. By 1993, the co-operative employed 329.

The co-operative in Krížava transformed itself according to legal requirements, but not without some complications and confusion because the land register was not up-to-date. Some 50 cases proved hard to settle, with owners as far afield as the Czech Republic and the United States, and management reported apocryphal cases of the value of some pieces of land being less than the price of the postage stamp needed to notify the individuals concerned of their holding. As in some of our Czech villages, the membership fee of 10,000 crowns in the transformed co-operative proved too expensive for some younger members with no land and few years of service, and they left. With the exception of the non-agricultural units, the structure of the farm and its management did not undergo radical change. Not a single co-operative member left the farm to start private farming. Nevertheless, a total of 150 hectares was allocated to claimants, the average claim being 0.5 hectares; only two claimants asked for plots significantly larger, and these were only for 2.8 hectares and 2.6 hectares respectively. Two years later, although the initial reaction of co-operative management was that everything was the same, here too the structure of production had changed to reflect changed market realities—orchards had been cut from 80 hectares to only 30 hectares, partly because fruit was no longer profitable, partly because the co-operative could not afford either to fertilise them properly or to fence them off securely; sugar beet and open-field vegetables were converted to pasture; the cattle stock was reduced, by around 50 per cent. The labour force had more or less stabilised by 1995, at around 300; despite this, some saw the co-operative in severe decline and commented on the dramatic fall in labour discipline.

Continuity, secession and one private farmer—Lehota

In Lehota, remote in the hills on marginal agricultural land, not far, as the crow flies, from the Polish border, but also quite close to the Czech border, the co-operative did not demerge either and the effect of the 1992 co-operative transformation was minimal. But the impact of the changing economic climate between 1989 and 1992 had already been catastrophic. Its labour force had been reduced to 70; all of its non-agricultural units had closed down; the transport unit was effectively closed; livestock jobs were cut as herds were reduced; tractor-drivers had to be laid off for the winter with only the promise of re-employment in the spring. By 1992 the co-operative was dependent on subsidies simply to reduce the size of its loss (from 19 million to 5.6 million crowns), and in mountainous areas subsidies were based on the overall area farmed: it was existentially interested in maintaining its size, even if only on paper. There was no interest amongst the co-operative membership in taking out land and assets in order to farm privately, although there was considerable interest in getting some land, the land with the best quality soil. Villagers wanted plots of one or two hectares, not the basis for a fulltime family farm but rather a continuation and slight extension of the household plot farming of the socialist years. A total of 350 hectares was returned to previous owners or their heirs on this basis, and the co-operative continued to offer its traditional services: ploughing, transport and occasionally construction.

Three years beyond legal transformation, the situation had changed little: co-operative organisation remained the same; the membership and number of fulltime employees remained the same, although the slight switch of emphasis which had begun in 1990 was continued (beef and sheep farming were reduced in favour of pigs and poultry); but there had been a significant defection. Mrs R, the economic manager, a 35 year-old divorcee with no children, from a working class family (only one grandmother was a peasant), had left the co-operative in the autumn of 1994. Although she had not proposed such a move at the time of transformation, she now suggested a 'holding co-operative' strategy as a solution to the continuing financial problems. When her advice was ignored, she decided to mirror the co-operative's move towards poultry on the basis of a private venture, with three other women from the co-operative. Things started well when they succeeded in getting a special Ministry grant for the purchase of Dutch poultry-rearing technology that the ministry was promoting. They rented six halls from the co-operative in which to install the technology and bought 120,000 chickens. The day after they commenced production, however, under circumstances which were never satisfactorily explained, the new unit burned down; and Mrs R was not insured. Despite no longer having the technological edge over local competitors, she continued her business on a smaller scale, using much cruder technology. The business initially operated with a staff of 20, mostly paid for by local job creation schemes, but numbers had to be reduced to 12, working 12 hour shifts, because prices had fallen and she was dependent on a single major customer. All staff had remained members of the co-operative, although they were contemplating taking out their shares.

Although no locals had been interested in establishing significant private farms in Lehota, a father and son partnership from a small town just beyond the immediate vicinity was. The father, aged roughly 60, had a peasant background, while his son, aged roughly 30, had been an electrical engineer. In the socialist years they had already operated as a small-scale business subcontracting to a nearby co-operative. This had begun as breeding sheep and rabbits, but in 1985 they took over an entire dairy herd and the necessary pasture to support it. In this respect they represented a Slovak variant of the more common Hungarian 'second economy' path to commercial farming. With the fall of socialism the couple wanted to turn this into a wholly private venture and buy land locally; but no one would sell to them. So they had to be satisfied renting land and some disused barns from the Lehota co-operative and set up an operation specialising in dairy farming, producing both milk and cheese. Two years on they continued in the same premises and employed three men and one woman; but they were experiencing problems. Their customers were questioning the hygiene of their operations, but they could not make the necessary investment in new technology to improve it because their contract with the co-operative remained on an annual basis and could be cancelled before any investment paid off. So they reduced their dairy activities and changed to fattening bullocks and weaners from 100 sows. Their contract with the co-operative was also restrictive in that it stipulated less land than they actually farmed. The co-operative could not afford to rent them on paper the full amount of land that they actually used because it needed to maintain its nominal area in order to retain its area-based mountain subsidies. A further two years later still, pig production had increased to 600 pigs (in addition to 106 cows), but they had resolved to move the farm away from Lehota. They had had enough of the co-operative and its discriminatory policies—annual contracts for the buildings and the charade of renting less land than it actually used just so the co-operative could keep its subsidies. Námerová's study of private farmers in Slovakia would place this partnership among the middling farmers on the borders of profitability and success. In her study the most successful private farmers were those who came from top or middle co-operative management.[4] For the Lehota father-and-son private farm to expand, it needed clarity and transparency, not fuzzy conditions imposed by a politically more powerful partner.

Client and co-operative privatisation—Klanec

In lowland Klanec, quite close to the Bratislava agglomeration, the co-operative did not demerge, nor did it decentralise prior to transformation, but decentralisation at the time of transformation was reversed over time in favour of a particular co-operative vision. The Klanec co-operative had been recognised as a 'success' at the end of the socialist years and it was even visited by Gorbachev in the 1980s. By then it farmed around 2,500 hectares, mainly cereals and especially maize. Its livestock activities focused on dairy cows (1,600 in 1988) and pigs (9,000 in 1988). The dairy herd was located in a single facility; pig farming, on the other hand, took place in three separate locations. The total membership in 1988 was 750, of whom 477 were employed full-time, and 77 worked in management and administration. Under transformation 1,596 entitled persons accepted the transformation project submitted by the chairman. No counter strategy was proposed by any group at this time, membership fell to around 560, and the number who were employed to around 200. The most significant aspect of the transformation project, the brainchild of the co-operative chairman, was to develop a form of 'internal privatisation' within the co-operative, analogous but not identical to the Hungarian 'holding co-operative' approach. Each operation was rented out to individuals, usually their former managers, who bought the inventories and stock (but rented

---

[4] Námerová, 'Private farmers', 63–9. Statistical evidence on this 'heterogeneous group' is provided by Blaas and Woltz, 'Economic situation', 112–5. Gejza Blaas, 'Privatization of the rural sector in Slovakia', *Eastern European Countryside* 1 (1995): 91–8, gives an early report on the state of the agricultural transformation in Slovakia.

the sites), usually with the help of a loan from the co-operative; they then operated them as private entrepreneurs. The machine workshop, transport unit, construction unit and a pig unit in Klanec itself were 'privatised' in this way in 1992; other units, including the two cropping units followed suit from the beginning of 1993. The dairy unit, however, together with one cropping unit and the feed-mixer unit remained fully within the co-operative. Part of the rationale of the 'internal privatisation' solution was to generate additional income so that the co-operative would be better placed to repay property shares to outside owners. A further element of their post transformation strategy was to reduce the potential influence of members (especially outside members) by buying them out. Co-operative membership fell further to 480 by the end of 1992 and 194 by the end of 1993. By the end of 1994, the co-operative itself employed 68 fulltime and it had recorded a loss, although its high level of reserves meant that it could begin 1995 debt-free. It was becoming clear that the 'internal privatisation' was not proving as beneficial for the co-operative as might have been expected.

It was at this point that Mr M, who had become chairman of the village HZDS organisation, came onto the scene. At the time M was not a member of the co-operative. He had left it in 1992 and worked for two years in Germany. His original plan upon return had been to establish a private beef farm in the area, and he had entered into discussions with officials within the Ministry of Agriculture. But they did not look favourably on this proposal, and, anxious about developments in Klanec, suggested rather that he take the co-operative over. Capitalising on the discontent within the Klanec membership, and criticising the previous management for selling co-operative livestock in order to settle the property shares of outsiders, M initiated a general meeting to evaluate co-operative performance. At this meeting, in May 1995, a new board was elected and M became general manager. His policy priority was to improve the situation in the dairy farm, and this required undoing some of the earlier decentralisation. In order to do so, unilaterally, without compensation, and in the middle of the agricultural year, he cancelled the leasing arrangement with the Klanec cropping unit. The work force was persuaded to accept the change by the promise of higher salaries, achievable by providing them with alternative dairy jobs in the slack season. The former lease-holder was re-employed as unit manager, retaining control of all production decisions; but financial responsibility reverted to the co-operative, which was thus able to transfer profits to balance the loss-making dairy farm. In the knowledge that he was operating with the approval of the Ministry of Agriculture, M invested heavily in 1995: he liquidated 10 million crowns from the reserve fund, took out a bank loan for 5 million crowns and received one million crowns in government subsidies. The Klanec pig unit was refurbished and brought into operation with a plan to increase its stocks to the 9000 pigs of the socialist years. The co-operative cut its loss to 1.5 million crowns in 1995, made a small profit in 1996, but was hardly more than breaking even in 1997. Despite his high investments, despite visits around the globe in search of the perfect dairy herd, and despite regular lengthy visits to his patrons in the Ministry (less than an hour away by car), M's management of the co-operative was far from successful.

In this situation of financial uncertainty, his decision to accede to the desire of the lease-holder of the cropping unit based in a neighbouring hamlet to set up an entirely independent business was reasonable. The lease-holder, its former manager in socialist times, had long complained of problems with the rental agreement. Neither lessor nor lessee was interested in maintaining, let alone improving, the buildings and infrastructure, and they were falling into disrepair. The increasingly cash-strapped co-operative recognised that sale of the assets represented a means of generating cash and pressed a hard bargain: the asking price was four times higher than its valuation in 1992 at the time of co-operative transformation. The lease-holder accepted because it meant that he was finally free of co-operative influence. But the organisational form of this new business was unusual. First, it was nominally a co-operative, not a private company, even though it was effectively a one-man business. Torsello notes too that co-operative remained the 'safe option' at that time in Slovak history;[5] Námerová and Swain concur,[6] although Námerová also identifies former co-operative chairman who did opt for the private company form, taking over his whole co-operative as his own private farm.[7]

---

[5] Torsello, 'Trust and property', 111.
[6] Námerová and Swain, 'Co-operative transformation'.
[7] Námerová, 'Private farmers', 70.

The second important feature of this business was that it was a co-operative of a rather unusual form in that the traditional co-operative principle of 'one member, one vote' did not obtain. The minimum compulsory contribution for each member was 100,000 crowns, payable over two years after an initial deposit of 5,000 crowns, and this entitled the member to one vote. An investment of 200,000 crowns gave two votes, and so on, up to a maximum of ten votes. Furthermore, the co-operative itself did not employ anyone. All employment was on the basis of individual private contracts. In theory all co-operative members were at liberty to set up businesses as part of the co-operative, and employ insiders and outsiders as they saw fit; the co-operative was a form of capital umbrella. In reality, it was only the former lease-holder and socialist boss who employed anyone; as a registered private farmer, he employed all of his former staff, on a fulltime basis. But in Mečiar's post-socialist Slovakia, it was important to retain the co-operative label.

The Non-Farm Economy

A brand new big business in a village of pensioners and Roma—Palina

The most significant new rural non-farm business in our sample emerged in Palina, although it was in a way curiously marginal for a village which, because of extensive out-migration in the socialist years, was made up of pensioners and Roma, very roughly 220 'Slovaks' and 440 Roma. The elderly 'Slovaks' inhabited the inner village; the Roma lived in a large settlement with no facilities outside the inner village boundary. The first and biggest blow to the job market for the inhabitants of Palina came when the Humenné-based chemical works was privatised and sold to a French company. The number of commuters from the village more than halved between 1990 and 1993, from 124 to 57, and unskilled workers, including many Roma, were the first to go. By 1995, only ten villagers commuted, still predominantly to Humenné, and half of them still to the chemical works. In the face of this assault on employment opportunities, six new village businesses emerged, but only one of them made significant use of labour beyond the immediate family. Two former colleagues in a state company established a TV and electrical repairs business. The village pub was privatised to the woman (the mother of the mayor) who used to run it. It was still in business in 1995, as was the new general store, although there were fears by that time that the Jednota co-operative shop would finally close down. Two brothers-in-law, who had both married into the village, established a stone-cutting business. One had the necessary craft qualifications and had worked for a state company that had gone bankrupt, the other had a technical qualification and left a state sector company to start the venture. By 1995, the business had expanded to provide seven jobs for members of the two families. Finally, as noted above, the pallet-making unit of the agricultural co-operative set itself up as an independent venture.

The sixth business was BSS, a manufacturer of glass pellets for the costume jewellery trade. The leading figure in this business was PB, who had been brought up in Palina in a 'kulak' family (in this region meaning that his family owned six hectares of land) and whose parents still lived there. After graduating from the Technical University in Košice and a period working in a machine tool plant, he moved to the glassworks in nearby Medzilaborce and worked his way up to become deputy director. Conscious that the future for socialist industry was not rosy and that redundancy was a possibility, he decided to jump first. He established BSS with two childhood friends, brothers, both with ties to Palina (their grandfather had been miller in the village, and one of them had been born there). One of the brothers was also a deputy director of the glass works, the other lectured in the Technical University of Košice. There was also a fourth partner, a lawyer who had been born in Humenné but was now resident in the Czech Republic. He took charge of the marketing side of the operation, the University lecturer remained an outside investor, and the two former deputy directors ran the day-to-day business.

The four owners, all with extensive experience of the glass industry in the socialist years, realised that the manufacture of glass pellets was a discrete aspect of the glass industry, which under socialism had been centralised along with everything else, but which could easily be separated out and conducted in an area of low labour costs and low rents, and with low technology. They saw the opportunity for a much cheaper mode of production, yet they retained, because of their years of experience in the industry, extensive market contacts, and they were prepared to pursue new ones in Western Europe and the Middle East. But there was the issue of where to locate the business. It had to be in the general area of Medzilaborce, which is where PB lived and where a major customer was situated, but this covered a wide area. PB chose his home village partly out of sentiment, but partly because of inside knowledge; he knew the village very well because his parents still lived there, and they knew that the building that had once housed the elementary school and then the kindergarten and which had been returned under restitution to the church (which had owned it before the war) was currently available for rent. PB (university educated with years of experience as a manager in socialist industry) had both the marketing knowledge of the wider world and the insider knowledge of the resources available in an otherwise unremarkable rural community. He had unrivalled human and social capital courtesy of his socialist upbringing and employment.

The business was established in 1993 and developed rapidly. From the start it applied for government grants which promoted job-creation in disadvantaged regions. Partly because of this support, employment trebled from 15 to 45 between August and December 1993, 18 of the employees coming from Palina. By this time it had already outgrown the former school building and had rented a second site from the cooperative in a neighbouring village where the sorting of the pellets took place. In 1994 one of the original partners, the second former deputy director, decided to leave and establish his own business in the same field. But this had no negative impact on BSS. It found an alternative investor, an electrical engineer from a Ukrainian family, and PB and his marketing active partner hired two managers to help run the business. BSS continued to develop rapidly: by 1995 it was employing 106 (46 men maintaining and running the equipment and 60 women sorting the glass) 72 of them in the Palina unit, 20 of them from Palina itself, and there were plans to develop even further and push employment up to 300.

The net effect of the presence of BSS in Palina was that the village appeared to have virtually no unemployment. The two women who were registered as unemployed in July 1993 had found jobs in BSS by that December. In 1995 the 'only villagers' without a job were seven who had not yet completed their studies. Given the rates of unemployment elsewhere, this was a remarkable achievement, yet it has to be tempered by two factors. First, those who took early retirement when the chemical industry was shedding jobs did not find living from their pensions easy, and the agricultural co-operative noted in 1995 that there was a significant increase in such pensioners looking for seasonal agricultural work. Second, these figures excluded the Roma, who lived beyond the boundary of the inner village. In 1993 it was reported that only ten of the one hundred Roma of active age had permanent jobs; in 1995 the mayor reported 88 long-term unemployed Roma. In the face of these levels of unemployment, the 3–4 job-creation-scheme posts that the mayor had been able to establish cutting grass, cleaning and tidying and helping with the construction of the priest's house, were a drop in the ocean. The fact that the mayor could refer to 'no village unemployment' in one breath and '88 long-term unemployed Roma' in the other speaks volumes for the degree of Roma social exclusion that existed in eastern Slovakia in the early post-transition years. The new venture did not alleviate local Roma unemployment. Furthermore, the village had two kindergartens, one for 'Slovak' children, the other for Roma children, and the elementary school in 1993 was divided between buildings for 'Slovak' and Roma children, who made up three quarters of the children in the school. The former followed all four elementary classes before completing their elementary education in the neighbouring village; the latter focused on the first two classes only and children were not expected to complete their elementary education. By 1995 this casual apartheid had changed to the extent that the Roma kindergarten had special classes to prepare the children for school, and Roma school children studied three rather than just two years of elementary schooling.

Co-operatives as business parks—Klanec

In Klanec no brand new business developed on anything like the scale in Palina, but two of the non-agricultural units of the agricultural co-operative turned themselves into vibrant new businesses. The co-operative privatised all of its non-agricultural ventures on the basis of the same lease-purchase agreement mentioned above. The price of the business was calculated on the basis of the full costs of the depreciated assets within the business plus a three per cent overhead. The co-operative then loaned the new owner the money to buy the business on relatively soft terms, including a two year repayment holiday. But some exploited this opportunity better than others. The transport and haulage business was dissolved immediately, and the lorries and equipment sold or leased to the former employees who were obliged to operate on a self-employed basis. The feed supplement business stagnated because of insolvency amongst its customer base, although continued to provide 14 jobs. The agricultural machinery company, Metalagro, however prospered. The new owner, who now ran the business with his two sons, was well aware that the company profile would have to change. The demand for agricultural equipment was limited. So it diversified into other equipment, particularly for forestry, and it sought out new, international markets. In order to do this they exploited links of the socialist period, in particular those with Germany. The company sought out these old contacts, and used them to make new ones. The company started out employing 30; by 1995 it was employing 140.

Metalagro spawned another light engineering business, which also prospered thanks to the market awareness of its manager and his business contacts. The manager, the son of a bus driver and housewife who was educated in a technical school and the technical university in Bratislava, had worked previously as a foreman in Metalagro. When the co-operative was transformed, rather than continue with Metalagro, he decided to branch out on his own. Because he too had worked on the co-operative, he knew that there was space available to rent and that the co-operative was ready to lend him money to start up the business. So he began operations in 1992, initially renting both machinery and space from the co-operative, although he soon bought his own machines. The company began by manufacturing metal shelving and containers for shops, mainly for the domestic market. But this manager too saw the need to diversify and also break out of the domestic market. This he achieved in 1994 through his contacts with a trading company called Slovak-Deutschland which was established by Slovak émigrés in Germany to promote German-Slovak commercial links. With their help he found a suitable partner and began to manufacture wrought-iron hanging baskets and window guards exclusively for the German market. For tax reasons he preferred to continue to operate as a sole-trader, rather than incorporate the business, and this artificially disguised the scale of his operation. As a sole trader he could employ no more than 20, and this was the number that he officially employed. But he regularly took on additional staff on a temporary basis and had a core of an additional ten temporary workers to call on. Despite his market-awareness and emphasis on labour discipline, he was conscious of his social obligations. As the company developed he provided jobs for much of his extended family: his brother, his father, his father's brother and his brother-in-law.

Smaller-scale successful new businesses— Lehota, Ľupta, Krížava

In Lehota, the official register for 1993 recorded a total of 75 entrepreneurs, the bulk of them, as elsewhere, family or self-employed businesses. Notable among them were: a timber processing venture located in sheds rented from the co-operative, which developed towards furniture production; a manufacturer of working shoes, located in other co-operative buildings; a baker's, which was established with the help and encouragement of the first mayor in a converted house and initially employed four; a joiner's business, which employed six manufacturing wooden pallets; and a pharmacy. Two years later the shoe business had disappeared; the joiner's business had expanded into co-operative buildings; and the furniture company was flourishing, concentrating on both expensive, quality items which it exported to Germany, the Netherlands, Switzerland and Croatia, and cheaper mass items for the domestic market, rough and ready products which undercut western imports. But the baker's had made a strategic retreat to family business status. The owners were dissatisfied with the quality and commitment of the staff that they could get hold of for the low salary that they were able to pay; and they were heavily dependent on the seasonal tourist trade and customers from outside the village rather than local custom because the locals, perhaps motivated by envy of their success, preferred to buy from the established village baker, part of the socialist Jednota co-operative chain.

In Ľupta, a school for agricultural apprentices was located in the village and it continued to be its biggest non-farm employer. It saw no shortfall in its students because it adjusted its curriculum to reflect changing demand (agri-business management, rural tourism), and it maximised its commercial resources. It rented out space in its buildings to a metal construction company, which was struggling to find markets, and to a group of five builders and decorators anxious to penetrate the Austrian and German markets. In 1994 a company began an egg venture with 5,000 hens in the neglected and ransacked agricultural buildings formerly used by the School's farm and the agricultural co-operative. It also rented out its under-utilised hostel to 100 students from the university in Trnava; it used its agricultural machinery to provide traditional agricultural services, such as harvesting, for villagers; and it claimed an income of 550,000 crowns from the sale of produce (confectionary and meat products especially) that the students made in their practical classes. The director of the School also embarked on entrepreneurship himself, and was one of four partners who established a company, which employed 18 in all, manufacturing wafers. The business got off to a hesitant start because their customers did not pay, and they were unable to pay their workers as regularly.

A smaller scale venture in Ľupta was the light engineering business run by JK, who had come to the village 17 years earlier and worked as a plumber in the poultry factory in Klanec, but in 1990 saw that the prospects for the business were not good and set up his own business operating from a workshop next to his house. He employed six in all, his two sons (his two daughters were still studying) and four others.

Perhaps the most noteworthy new business in Krížava, because of its rarity, was the printing business established by BJ, a 40-year-old Roma from a nearby village. BJ, who had only primary school education, had worked with his brother for a state publishing company that produced calendars prior to 1989. In 1989 he saw the possibility of establishing a small-scale venture printing such specialist items and the two went into business. They used their houses as security for a bank loan and rented a small, single storey, unprepossessing building in Krížava. Later, when its owner died, they bought the building. They also bought machines for cutting and perforating paper. Initially they employed 15 people on very low salaries. Later, once they had newer technology, they reduced the staff to eight, although salary levels remained rather low. They sold through a network of dealers throughout the country and by 1995 they were one of the biggest producers of calendars in the country, concentrating on cheap, popular products. They also took on other printing jobs, and would increase their labour force accordingly. Their biggest job of this kind was to produce voting lists for the state elections, for which they took on 300 temporary staff. Given this success, which was considerably more substantial than CF's bars in Remetea (Romania), BJ's development plans seemed rather modest, being restricted to developing the site where his works were located, creating a proper car park and building a pub. This was perhaps an element of ethnic insecurity in this modest ambition. The vocabulary used by villagers describing his business suggests continuing racial tensions: his company was described as one of the few where 'white people work for blacks'.

Mixed success plugging the socialist personal services gap—Zurča and Ľupta

Much more normal for Slovakia, as elsewhere, were businesses that plugged the socialist personal services gap. In Zurča by 1991 there were 32 business licences in the village, mostly in the retail food sectors and other retail outlets (such as the chemists run by the lady deputy mayor's family), and a smattering of locksmiths, plumbers, central heating engineers, electrical repairers, car mechanics, stone masons and undertakers—many of them successors to the defunct village Municipal Services Unit. The Jednota co-operative was rented out to a woman from a neighbouring village. But only two of these employed more than family labour: the plumber's, which employed five, and the stone mason, who employed seven. The number of new businesses in the village scarcely increased between 1993 and 1995, and, according to the deputy mayor, the most successful was the very first to be established: the small shop located in the railway station. The secret of its success was its location. It had a captive market of commuters, and a constant clientele among the, generally older-generation male, unemployed who congregated for much of the day around the shop to drink their fill. It was cheaper to buy at retail prices and stand around the station than frequent pubs and bars.

The fate of two legitimate drinking establishments in the village reflected the difficulties facing entrepreneurs in a climate of limited demand. In 1993, a couple, who originated from Zurča but had moved to Nitra, bought and renovated a building in the village and set up a 'day bar'. But by 1995 everything had gone wrong. The couple were getting divorced; they still owed 750,000 crowns on their investment and they were desperate to sell, but no one was interested in buying. The business was simply not viable. The fate of Piváreň u Notára, on the other hand, demonstrated that success could be possible if outgoings were kept low, and a niche market sought out. Piváreň u Notára was a pub (draught beer plus simple food such as goulash and a special type of pancake) established by three partners, two from the village, one from a nearby village, in the house of one of the partners. The business was family-run, except for one employee, and between 1993 and 1995 developed into a successful operation, focusing on a young clientele from Zurča and the surrounding district, providing them with a pinball table and a table tennis area in addition to the food and drink. These attractions, plus the beer garden that it operated in the summer, and the opportunities for bathing offered in the nearby lake (a flooded gravel pit) had turned it into one of the main attractions for the youth of the surrounding district.

Non-farm businesses in Ľupta beyond those mentioned above also plugged the socialist personal services gap, and, while the village was affected by the post-socialist recession that hit Trnava in particular, this did not result in exceptionally high levels of unemployment. The seven employed on job-creation schemes helped in a small way. The other employers in the village outside the public sector were the local shops (a general store and a grocer's) and the pub. In the socialist years there had also been a butcher's shop, but no one could make a go of it in the post-socialist years. Most villagers kept pigs and poultry and did not buy meat. This inability to recreate socialist-era demand was reflected too in the case of the pub owner, MH, a former village mayor, long-standing council member and a one-time member of the co-operative management team; he still lived in a co-operative-owned flat. He decided to go into business for himself early in 1990 and his first venture was to supply the Slovak army that had taken over the former Soviet army base near the village. At this time, the future of the agricultural co-operative looked more rosy than it ultimately proved to be, and his idea was to rent the cellars from the Community Centre, and persuade the co-operative to build a kitchen and dining room which he would then rent from the co-operative and operate together with a bar. The centrepiece of the plan, and it proved a major miscalculation, was that the major user of the facilities would be the agricultural co-operative. It would use them as its works canteen, and pay for its staff to take their mid-day meals there. The plan back-fired because the co-operative's financial crisis: it had to stop paying for its employees' lunches. There was insufficient village demand for a full-time restaurant; but there was enough, from villagers and students, for the bar. His market share improved a little after 1995 when the legislation on cash registers forced out of business the two private shops run from garages which allowed customers to buy bottles of alcohol and consume them on, or next to, the premises.

Protracted privatisation and commuting to the Czech Republic—Krížava and Lehota

If rural Slovakia differed from the rural Czech Republic in having a smaller incidence of full, direct and specific restitution and higher levels of unemployment, privatisation could be equally protracted. Non-agricultural employment in Krížava had been dominated since World War II by the 'Zinkfarben Fabrik', which employed around 200 manufacturing inorganic paints and putty. Privatisation was not resolved during the course of our research. In 1993 it had not shed labour and its future was considered to be secure because of full order books for domestic and foreign markets. In 1995, it continued to employ large numbers, 190 fulltime and 16 seasonally, and it paid very good wages for the area. But by then it at least faced the cloud of privatisation. The workers and the village mayor all favoured a management buy-out scenario; but twelve companies had expressed an interest, including a German one with a reputation of purchasing and then winding down entirely production in a former GDR company. Nothing final had been resolved.

Krížava had 155 registered unemployed in 1993, some 13.3 per cent of the economically active population. Employees in the council offices considered that just over half of these were actively seeking work, the remainder being happy to live from a combination of benefits and casual and seasonal work. But after a slight increase in 1994 (from 155 to 157), it fell to only 95 in 1995. Some of this decline was accounted for by job-creation schemes; five such jobs were provided by the council, five by the agricultural co-operative and a further five by private sector companies which responded to the Employment Office scheme. But the bulk of the explanation was two-fold: an increase in the number of force-of-circumstance-entrepreneurs, and the development of longish distance commuting to the Czech Republic where there was still a strong demand for cheap labour with engineering skills (the consequence of its 'ersatz shock therapy'). The main form that this took was via newly established employment agencies which organised temporary contracts with Czech companies and bussed out the necessary gangs of workers, leaving at 7 am and returning at 5 pm, paying wages considerably lower than had previously been current.

Commuting to employment in a Czech Republic which was still benefitting from 'ersatz shock therapy' was also common in Lehota, where it had had a longer tradition than in Krížava. In Krížava, long-distance commuting was a substitute for commuting to industrial employment in surrounding towns and villages in the Váh Valley as employment conditions in Slovakia worsened. In more remote Lehota, where all commuting was long distance, the Czech Republic had always been one of the destinations. The total number of registered unemployed there was 151, some 12.3 per cent of the labour force. In the view of the mayor at the time, only 20 of these were serious in seeking work, and she had difficulties finding sufficient numbers interested in the job-creation schemes that she organised. The reason for the relatively low level of unemployment was the continued relative buoyancy of the Czech labour market. The number of commuting workers fell during the post-socialist recession, but even in 1995 the mayor estimated that 50 per cent of the village's active population worked in the Czech Republic, and more than 100 still commuted to the Ostrava region.

LOCAL AUTHORITY BUSINESSES AND ACCOMMODATIONS TO CENTRAL POWER

Continuity and change—Klanec

Two features stood out in local government developments and politics in Klanec: the continuity provided by its mayor, who had first taken office in the socialist era, and its decision to engage directly in economic activity in service of community needs. The Klanec co-operative had been particularly active assisting the village. It had built apartment blocks; provided interest-free loans for co-operative members to build their own homes; built the kindergarten; helped with the establishment of the crèche; contributed in the construction of recreational facilities; donated 1.5 million crowns to the building of the village hall; had established and paid for the running of the local rural history museum based in one of the villages governed by Klanec; supported the sports club, especially the riding section by maintaining stables and other facilities for them; organised and contributed financially to holidays for children and for co-operative members; provided meals for pensioners; and it was the exclusive sponsor of the village's folklore ensemble, which had a national and even international reputation. In the cold shower of economic realism that accompanied 'system change', the co-operative gave up nearly all of these roles. Klanec's mayor complained of a 'continuous fiscal stress'. It was not so much that the village's own revenues were reduced (in fact, he reported that tax revenues from the commune had increased considerably in 1993), but rather that the central government component was being reduced. The first substantial casualty of the fiscal crisis was the crèche, which had been in operation since 1982; it was closed for good a decade after opening.

Despite the 'fiscal stress', the commune managed to find the funds from its own resources to take over from the co-operative the costs of providing lunches for pensioners, a service it was still providing in 1995, and it continued its sponsorship of the folklore ensemble, which it took on for a fixed term of a further three years. By 1995 too it had managed to find a tenant for the sports centre (which included tennis courts, a swimming pool, a restaurant and accommodation, and was a popular venue for parties and weddings), but there was no interest in the cinema and it was closed down. The post-socialist years also saw the introduction of cable TV in the village and the completion of the cultural centre. The Klanec council had no economic development plans as such for the village. Its Programme for Municipal Development focused on the infrastructure: completing the water supply and drainage networks, providing a gas supply for the whole village, and building a new kindergarten in one of the smaller villages administered by Klanec (which was nearing completion in 1995). Although the council stressed that it supported all business development, it had no active policy for attracting investment, and noted that investors were few and far between. Rather than do nothing, however, the council tried to develop some entrepreneurial activities of its own, in catering, and particularly in baking. Its bakery was particularly successful, employing fifteen, mainly women, and was still operating successfully in 1997.

The mayor of Klanec had already held that position for two cycles in the late socialist years; he stood as an independent in 1990 to be elected again, and was re-elected in 1994. As this career suggests, what was central to local politics in Klanec was reputation and a track record rather than a party label. Party organisations existed in Klanec: both the former communists and the KDH had local branches there, both of which had members on the council. But the national party policies had little impact on local political developments, and one surprising feature of the local situation, given the long agricultural history of the village, was the failure of distinctly 'rural' parties. They did not make it onto the eleven-person council at all in 1990, and in the 1994 election only two representatives of the Agricultural Movement were elected. Unusually, the HZDS was not more successful, with only four elected in 1994. The former communists fared better with eight, but the plurality was held by the KDH. Although it was generally agreed that the village public took little interest in local politics, this was not true of those with interests that the council could influence. Most of the councillors on the first post socialist council were managers of or representatives of local business entities, and the mayor talked enigmatically of the existence of bases for clientelism. In the second post-socialist regime, the council member responsible for finances noted that, while the commune office did not experience any pressures from political parties, it was 'possible to notice the pressure of entrepreneurs who protect their own interests'. Local business people were beginning to realise that local government could be made to work for them.

A new non-market business elite—Krížava

In Krížava, early post-socialist conflict between the local authority and the agricultural co-operative was gradually transformed into compromise as each side adjusted to real world conditions. As in other villages, the Krížava agricultural co-operative had reduced its contribution to communal services. By 1993 the only minor way in which it helped was by allowing co-operative pensioners to purchase corn from the co-operative at the same reduced price as the active members. Yet the council's need for some sort of assistance was all the greater because, in the mayor's estimation, total municipal revenue in 1993 was 50 per cent lower than its 1989 level, and this despite the council having introduced new fees and increased existing ones. Only the sports club was successful in finding a private sponsor to replace the co-operative, but even so it needed continued help from the council, which also found funds to support the volunteer fire brigade. The council's contribution to social care was restricted to looking after the elderly, for which it received a degree of assistance from religious organisations, although the churches themselves concerned themselves more with their pastoral roles and the occasional one-off charitable donation to members of the congregation. Although in 1993 care for pensioners included providing them with subsidised lunches, by 1995, after a further reduction in the state grant, the council had to abandon the service. The money available amounted to no more than two crowns per person, more of an insult than a service. The overall climate was perhaps best reflected in the words of the secretary to the commune council when explaining the declining birth rate (which had resulted in spare capacity in the kindergarten): 'It is a luxury to have children today. Why have children if you cannot give them what they deserve? Why produce beggars?'

Yet despite this climate of gloom, the new regime that came into power in 1994 was rather more effective than its predecessor in squeezing something out of the scarce resources available. The first post-socialist regime, under the influence of the KDH mayor, had refused to allow the cash-strapped co-operative to pay off its outstanding tax liabilities and other financial commitments in kind. This was understandable as a principled rejection of the cosy, hand-in-glove relationship of the socialist past. Yet, given that the council was unable in the pro-co-operative climate of Mečiar's Slovakia, to impose the ultimate sanction of the capitalist present (namely to force the co-operative into bankruptcy), it was something of a short-sighted stance. The second post-socialist regime consisted of many who were less negative about the socialist past, and more willing to make compromises. Payment in services to the community was seen as better than no payment at all, and by 1995 the co-operative had already paid off some 800,000 crowns of its 1.2 million crown debt by carrying out such tasks as digging excavations for building projects, removing refuse, and helping build a new bus-stop. The new mayor's pragmatic approach was also reflected in his dealings with the business community generally. In 1995 he established what was referred to as a Businessmen's Club. The club was made up of representatives of the six biggest companies in the village and a deputy mayor. Its chief goal, beyond generally promoting relations between village and the council, was to extract corporate sponsorship rather than promote the interests of the business community, to remind local economic actors how important the local council was for them, and how important it was for them to support it actively. In this the mayor chalked up a considerable success: commitments to help clear snow in winter, a new bus stop, a new cemetery fence, and from the 'Zinkfarben Fabrik' a grant of half a million crowns to be spent as the commune pleased. It was spent on promoting events in the Cultural Centre and poaching a music group, which had a considerable local reputation, from the neighbouring village.

Flexible political allegiances—Krížava, Zurča and Ľupta

Local politics in Krížava reflected both the collapse of the KDH vote noted nationally, and the return of an 'old structure', a term the second mayor used about himself. The KDH had won the overwhelming majority of seats in the 1991 elections, eleven of twelve. But by 1994, the KDH badge had disappeared from the scene entirely, and the seats were shared between the majority Party of the Democratic Left (SDĽ), the former communists (seven seats), and the HZDS (five seats). The reason for this radical change of fortune was explained variously by the local population. There was dissatisfaction with the politics of the KDH as a party at the national level, and individual councillors changed their allegiance to the HZDS long before the 1994 elections. Locally, there was an impression that many of the KDH representatives had used their new office for personal profit, although concrete cases were not cited. The mayor was criticised by old and new structures alike. In the view of the former manager of the co-operative, 'it was horrible to work with the last one, who was from the KDH. The current mayor is better... He is a builder... and there is a great deal of construction to do in the village'. An agricultural entrepreneur noted more acidly: '[H]e was an ass. He wanted me to pay tax on a crop from a greenhouse that had not been built yet.' In 1994, the villagers wanted a return to a more familiar world: an individual who had worked in local government since 1976, and had been mayor from 1981 to 1990, was given another chance.

The elasticity of party political support in rural regions of Mečiar's Slovakia was also apparent in Zurča and Ľupta. In the former, there appeared to be huge swings in political support, despite the fact that the mayor, who stood on both occasions as an independent, was re-elected. The 1990 council was made up of nine from the KDH, eight from the SDĽ and eight from the Slovak National Party (SNS). That elected in 1994 included ten who represented a coalition of the SDĽ and the Farmers Movement, seven from the HZDS, five from the SNS, only two KDH and a single Christian Social Union (KSU) representative. The KDH as a consequence lost its seat on the council board where it had once had three members. But the KDH candidates had simply not run in 1994; the councillors were so disillusioned by the party's declining national reputation. Much of the increased HZDS vote, on the other hand, was the result of former SDĽ and SNS councillors changing their allegiance. In Ľupta, by contrast, it was the mayor who lacked party political constancy. A 50-year-old former technician in a housing co-operative, he had originally stood as a member of the small Democratic Party, and he was its single representative on the twelve-person council where the KDH had five members, the Democratic Party, the SDĽ and Public against Violence had one each, and there were four independents. But between 1990 and 1994, he 'sailed with the wind' and joined the HZDS which established a branch in the village in 1994. He was re-elected in its colours that same year.

Fuzzy ownership and its consequences—Habán

Circulating debts and payment in services figured in Habán as in Krížava, but the central issue in the village related to the 'fuzzy ownership' of assets created in the 1970s. Habán consists of two originally autonomous settlements. The inhabitants of Jezersko were originally agricultural labourers and estate servants who worked primarily for the church estate owned by the bishop of Esztergom in present-day

Hungary; only one village peasant was rich enough to employ non-family labour. The population of Senné was mainly independent peasant, but predominantly very small-scale: 15 per cent were landless and 63 per cent had under five hectares. Both villages were incorporated into Hungary under the First Vienna Award in 1938, despite their wholly Slovak population, and it was partly as a reaction to this that Senné changed its name to the more Slovak-sounding Svätuš in 1947. The two villages were merged into a single administrative unit called Habán in 1960.

Habán, more specifically Svätuš, benefited from thermal springs and in 1974 a swimming pool was built to exploit them. Although state-owned, the village took over their operation and, in 1976, passed it over to the district recreation service. In 1979, the co-operative sought to gain further advantage from nature's resources and established a joint venture with the baths, Thermalagro, which used its steam to heat greenhouses in which it grew vegetables. Thermalagro began by employing 38 (21 of them women), but by 1990 had increased its labour force to 50 (32 of them women). The co-operative also built two blocks of flats for its staff in the village, and contributed to diverse social and cultural events; although it refused to help with the construction of a new council office in 1967, which was built symbolically on the border between the two previously independent villages. In 1974 the consumer co-operative established a buffet nearby, and the following year a restaurant to service the pool, followed gradually by a hotel with 96 beds, cottages for 64 guests and a campsite. The pool also had a knock-on effect in the private sector as villagers, some with official licences, others without, offered bed and breakfast to tourists.

As in Krížava, under the conditions of 'fiscal stress' and inter-enterprise debt, the interests of Habán's co-operative and council became more closely interlinked. The co-operative began to participate in infrastructure projects, laying the new water pipes, collecting refuse, tidying the refuse site—on the basis of payment in kind for its outstanding tax liabilities. The council was understanding of the co-operative's strained finances and did not want to pursue its debts aggressively for fear of threatening co-operative jobs: accepting payment in kind was the obvious compromise. And Habán had a need to develop its infrastructure. In 1993, the council was proud that it had already completed street lighting in the village, repaired roads, built a chapel of rest and removed illegally dumped waste. Still outstanding, and these were mostly still outstanding in 1995, were: providing Jezersko with running water; providing mains drainage for all, laying on gas for the whole village, connecting the whole village to a better electrical power supply, enlarging the school building, reconstructing the chemist's shop, and connecting the playground to the electricity supply.

In a sense, Hábán had a development strategy thrust upon it: the swimming pool and its tourist potential. All village plans had a swimming pool element, whether building a new pool or something associated with it, such as a new health centre, or a hotel, or a hairdresser's, or a massage parlour. For the first post-socialist administration, the problems centred on establishing ownership. Without clarification of ownership, the company to run the facility could not be established; but, given its original state ownership, its operation by first the village and then the district council, and the complications of the joint venture with the co-operative, ownership was opaque. Furthermore, the Ministry of Health was also slow in issuing a certificate confirming that the Hábán water was 'curative'. The first post-socialist mayor, a retired former librarian who had earlier worked as a secretary in the council office and supported the post-socialist SDĽ although she had stood as an independent, had devised a scheme whereby ownership of the complex would remain with the state, obviating the duty of the council to pay tax on it. But she had problems implementing anything because 10 of the 12 councillors represented the KDH. Her successor, who beat her by just 19 votes, was a representative of the KSU, a young man and a former soldier, with no experience of local government, who had married into the village 14 years earlier. His council was more amenable because the KDH representation had disappeared entirely in 1994. Despite his predecessor's critical comments that for the first six months the new council 'just celebrated their victory' and left the gas and water projects to stagnate, much of the essence of her policies in relation to using a council-owned swimming pool to boost the local economy remained in place. But rather than state ownership, his administration opted in favour of the Slovak solution of embarking on entrepreneurial activity in its own right and establishing full council ownership. In August 1995 the swimming pool complex (including the restaurant, the buffet, the hotel with 96 beds, and the cottages with beds for 64) passed into the hands of a company wholly owned by the council. Occupancy rates in late 1995 were reported to be up on the preceding year, which included large groups from the Ukraine and Poland, and the council endeavoured to promote the centre regionally, in Žilina and Poprad.

Problems of football sponsorship, tourism and promoting a hotel—Bánec

In Bánec the local council also strayed into direct participation in an economic venture, and it learned to its cost that private sector solutions to sponsorship problems did not always function smoothly. In the socialist years, the Bánec co-operative had taken a considerable interest in community affairs, spending, at the end of the 1980s, around 2.5 million crowns a year on social and cultural programmes, and giving the council use of its machinery for public works, maintaining parks, clearing rubbish and so on. In particular, not only had it been the Sports Club's sponsor, but it had built the football stadium in the neighbouring village administered by Bánec and the sports hall in Bánec itself where the handball team played. With the ending of socialism, the main facilities of the Sports Club, the stadium and the sports hall, passed from co-operative to local council property. The council took over some financial commitments towards the club, but the main sponsorship was taken over in 1991 by a trading company based in nearby Nové Zámky. Although this seemed to be a perfect solution, market realities proved to be fickle. By 1995 the trading company was in financial difficulties, and in an attempt to overcome them, it used the facilities of the sports club, the stadium and the sports hall as security against a 10 million crown loan. The loan did not help, and company went bankrupt in any case. As a consequence, not only did the sports club find itself without a sponsor, but the creditor bank claimed ownership of the village's stadium and sports hall. The council thus had to use some of its scarce resources pursuing a court action asserting that the company had had no right to raise a loan against the property, that the contract between the bank and the company was thus invalid, and that the assets should therefore remain council property.

Despite 'fiscal stress', the council managed to maintain quite a full social welfare policy of its own. In addition to the provision of lunches for poorer pensioners and Christmas bonuses, it had a special programme of food aid for diabetics; it helped with the travel costs of those prescribed treatments in a spa; and it was building social housing in the form of 15 single-room apartments, for which there were already 40 applicants in 1993. It also found money to increase the staff of the Culture Centre by two over the 1989 level, and by 1995 had had to commit itself to additional expenditure to support bus services. When providing additional support for poor pensioners, the council enlisted the help of the appropriate pensioners' club because of their familiarity with the individuals concerned. But discretionary benefits of this nature inevitably led to disputes. One woman saw her request for a 3,000 crown loan to buy coal turned down, while another family was given 10,000 crowns, notionally to buy school books and equipment, even though it 'was spent on alcohol'.

But it was less successful strategically. In the mind of the mayor, the village's development strategy was based on agriculture; the development of light industry, in particular food processing; and the development of tourism. The strategy remained unchanged between 1993 and 1995, but it also remained an ideal only. As the mayor admitted, 'these are all just plans. The council has no money for them'. Although the council claimed that it supported entrepreneurs by selling or renting them property from which to run their businesses, it offered no services for entrepreneurs other than farmers, on the pretext that their profits taxes went to the district level. Further, there was a case of the council refusing to sell land to a local businessman for reasons that were hard to explain in terms other than those offered by the locals: 'envy', dislike of the local who had become disproportionately wealthier than the rest. The businessman wanted the plot for a shop, and use of the land as a shop conformed to the village's spatial development plan; yet it was turned down. In terms of industry and food processing, the mayor had mentally set aside land for a business park, on land that the council actually owned. He was convinced that in the long term there would be interest in food processing in the area, especially juice production. There was more fruit grown locally than existing manufacturers could process, and there was a ready market, the mayor was convinced, both domestically and in the Czech Republic.

Like other local authorities in the post socialist countryside, the Bánec mayor was aware of the link between improving the infrastructure and tourism. What they had to offer tourism was fishing in the Danube and their hot springs. But this required a solution to their waste water problem, particularly tricky in this area of water protection. This was too big a project for the council to even consider without government support; and, even with a National Environment Fund grant, the council would have had to produce 50 per cent matching funding. The other big environmental issue affecting tourism was a new refuse dump. This was slightly less costly, and by 1995 plans were in hand to introduce a German system of separating rubbish. The council also set aside a nature reserve in order to promote tourism. Infrastructure investment was not without success, if not the quantum leap necessary to ready the village for tourism. In 1993 all streets were paved, all houses had running water, most had bathrooms and central heating, and there were perhaps 150 satellite dishes. Between then and 1995 the council had completed a cable television system, so reducing the number of satellite dishes, and provided gas for the whole village, even connecting the school to the system despite it being the responsibility of the district. The social housing for fifteen had been completed, and the cinema and culture house renovated. The sewage system remained at the planning stage, although it was scheduled for 1997–98. While the processing industry was a development for the future, and tourism was stalled because of the infrastructural investments required, agriculture was the here and now. The council remained committed to the continuation of the co-operative and to preventing it from going bankrupt. It also refused to rent its own land to anyone but the co-operative itself or people who had contributed land to its creation.

Finally, there was a further strand to the council's tourism policy: it decided to take a small share in a hotel that was built in 1994. The mayor was instinctively opposed to such a measure. In 1993, he had argued that the law prevented it, and in 1995, despite the investment in which the majority owners were described as trade unions and other companies, he explained that 'people will not be as motivated working for a community enterprise as they would be working for a businessman'. And his misgivings were perhaps justified. By late 1995 there was something of an air of mystery, not to say a lack of transparency, about the venture. The 'owner' lived some distance away in Nová Baňa and kept no contact with the staff; they did not even know his telephone number. If he needed to visit, he stayed with his father in Bratislava. Nevertheless, the receptionist reported that it did good business, with a holiday trade in the summer and sufficient year-round business from businessmen, mainly Austrians, visiting Dunajska Streda. Its net contribution to the village in terms of employment was half a dozen new jobs, receptionists, waiters, a cook, a plumber and a cleaner.

Developing a village 'with no development prospects'—Hora

Hora, too, embarked on a local-authority-run venture, but it also had to rejuvenate itself as a community. By the end of the socialist years it had suffered from a declining and aging population despite retaining its own independent local authority throughout, and it had been designated a village 'with no development prospects'. Its commuting and local jobs were badly hit by the post-socialist recession. Registered unemployment represented 22.6 per cent of the population of working age in 1993 and 32.5 per cent in 1995, two thirds of them Roma who lived in a separate shanty settlement a kilometre or so away from the village. Perhaps not surprisingly in a village with a severely ageing population, there was little entrepreneurial activity. Villagers relied on their pensions and retreated into the household, supplementing their meagre cash income with their small plot farms and the fruits of nature that surrounded them. Some of the women in the village (15 by 1995) went back to traditional forms of income supplementation—producing embroidery and hand-woven carpets, which they sold via the state folklore company.

Hora had huge, but scarcely tapped, tourist potential beyond the women embroiderers and five male pensioners who supplemented their pensions by producing traditional shingle roofing tiles, an activity that the mayor was keen to encourage and have taught to a younger generation. A Bratislava businessman spotted an opportunity and bought the village pub under privatisation. But, by 1995, he was having second thoughts. Developing the tourist trade was a longer term prospect than he had anticipated and he was contemplating selling up and returning to Bratislava. Some of the local elite, on the other hand, had already responded to its attractions and potential, such as the teacher, the co-operative chairman, the co-operative agronomist, and the chairman of a neighbouring co-operative. But the villagers in general either did not see a tourist potential, or wanted to keep their village's charms for themselves; and the village's first post-socialist regime admitted to not having a policy for the economic development of the village, only a series of pragmatic responses to changing conditions. Yet these responses added up to a strategy of sorts. Its first goal was to improve the technical and social infrastructure. Although running water had been provided for the village in 1974, it still lacked mains drainage, and telephone provision was limited. Its second goal was to stabilise the population. To do this, it planned first to promote the use of existing housing stock as second homes, to get new blood into the village, even on a part-time basis, but then to create the conditions which would encourage people to move to the village permanently. It therefore supported new house building, which had been prohibited previously because of its status as a village 'with no development prospects'. The three houses built in the village between 1989 and 1993 and the six more under construction in 1993 were destined for, amongst others, the local elite listed above; and by 1995 net outward migration had come to an end.

The second post-socialist regime continued these policies, but in a slightly more pro-active and articulated way. First, it planned to involve itself in entrepreneurship by creating a community enterprise which would provide services such as glazing, manufacturing shingle roof tiles, and buying and processing fruits of the forest. Second, it declared a policy of promoting traditional crafts, such as lace making and fashioning simple wooden tools and utensils. Third, it supported the development of tourism. In addition to these local level policies, it had ambitions to promote the creation of some sort of development fund for the region as a whole, and support the activities of the Horný Gemer Community Union, a regional body which already had one employee of its own based in the nearest sizeable town Rožňava.

A change of mayor and perhaps a change of prospects—Lehota

Lehota, by contrast, never contemplated the possibility of intervening directly into the economy. The fundamental problem facing those who entered post-socialist local government in Lehota was that the mayor in the socialist years had not been up to the job. He had been 'passive' and had not chased the rather more plentiful sources of finance then available. Thus at the end of the socialist period the village found itself still with no running water, no sewage system (and hence a polluted river that could no longer support fish), no village hall or community centre, and no chapel of rest for its cemetery. Furthermore, and not unconnected, the links between the co-operative and the council had not been particularly strong. The village thus faced a more than averagely difficult investment task when 'fiscal stress' hit. The village's good fortune was that it was managed by local politicians with a clear sense of what needed doing and how to set about doing it.

The first post-socialist administration was headed by a mayor who was a 30-year-old woman, an unmarried economics graduate from Bratislava and member of Public Against Violence with religious convictions, who decided to return to her home village to do the best for it that she could. Her council was made up of seven KDH, four Public Against Violence (which included the Greens), and independents, but she also worked with a group of local businessmen. Under her regime, running water had been provided to about to about three quarters of the community in 1993; a sewage system was still at the planning stage, but, with the help of external funding, a new road to the cemetery had been built in 1992. As far as tourism was concerned, the first post-1989 administration was somewhat laissez faire in approach. It was hopeful that the potential would reveal itself more or less spontaneously as the open air museum (Skanzen) run by the Ministry of Culture in the neighbouring village became more popular, and as a direct link to the Polish border (never realised) was built through the village. On the other hand it did intervene directly to try to bring jobs to the region and in 1993 had negotiations (ultimately unsuccessful) with a Czech company in the hope that it might invest in the region.

By 1995, there was a new mayor, another economics graduate, who was also a member of the local KDH party organisation and was developing numerous contacts in the party machine. He had worked as a deputy director for social development in a state company, moved briefly to Austria, and by the 1990s ran his own construction business. In fact, he had been a member of the group of businessmen who had advised the previous mayor and was responsible for finding the funding that built the road to the cemetery. There was also a new council in which the KDH unusually retained all of its seven council seats, but

Public Against Violence disappeared in favour of two HZDS, one Union of Slovak Workers (ZRS) and one SDĽ.

The new mayor could point to a detailed and costed plan for the development of the community, with slightly changed priorities: improving the electricity supply and providing a gas supply, because these two together would allow villagers to move away from coal-fired heating which would significantly reduce pollution; completing the water supply and a sewage system; and finishing the Cultural Centre. The chapel of rest also still figured in the plan, although it had been pushed back to 1996–97. In addition, the village hoped to build a small manufacturing centre with units that could be rented out to different potential investors; whilst, in relation both to developing tourism and the village's own cultural facilities, a new sports arena was under construction, with an almost completed football pitch and plans for a swimming pool and tennis court. What is more, in the even longer term, the mayor had plans to tidy the village, to finish off the pavements, to start an ecologically friendly dump, to build a water treatment plant, to begin a system of separating waste, and to develop tourism by building recreational areas for skiing (including building a ski lift), hiking, cycling and fishing (including stocking the lake with fish) and hunting.

But actual achievements by 1995 were modest. Permission had been given to start work on the gas and water supplies; the village had landscaped a small park in an area of waste land opposite the hotel; it had altered the course of the river at a cost of 300,000 crowns; work had started on a new bus stop; and it was continuing on the Community Centre. By late 1997, gas had been provided and the electrical generator upgraded; the football stadium had finally been completed; and running water had been supplied to the lower part of the village. With the help of additional funding from the State Fund for Slovakia, the Cultural Centre was 'nearing completion', much to the relief of the two village teachers who had resurrected the village's interwar tradition of amateur dramatics as well as its folk music ensemble; while, again with external funding from a private foundation, the chapel of rest was under construction.

No funding had yet been found for the sewage project, however. In 1995, the mayor had still been hopeful of attracting foreign investors to the village and he had had discussions with Belgian companies, but by 1997 he was more resigned to this not happening. There was some interest on the part of both locals and people from Bratislava in building houses in the village, and not just as second homes, and the mayor was keen to encourage this. Plots were being identified that could be sold reasonably cheaply. The new mayor continued to see his main task as mobilising funding for the village, and to do this he lobbied constantly, both within his party hierarchy and using whatever other contacts he could think of. He joined the Slovak–Egypt Friendship Society because it gave him the opportunity to rub shoulders with the great and the good, and he estimated that he was lobbying in Bratislava (over 200 kilometres away) at least once a week. He was constantly fearful that his projects would be rejected for the simple political reason that he was a member of the KDH not the nationally dominant HZDS. The water pipes project was submitted to the HZDS-controlled regional office of the Environment ministry, and they were granted only half the amount they asked for, enough to supply the lower village only. The reasons might not have been political, but in the politicised climate of the Mečiar years it was a deduction that was easy to make.

SLOVAK SPECIFICITIES IN SUMMARY

Rural developments in Slovakia revealed much in common with its partner successor state, except that in Slovakia the serendipity factor of restituting pre-socialist industry was not present and the entirely new BSS business in Palina developed rapidly beyond the dimensions of plugging the socialist personal services gap, as did the printing venture of BJ, the Roma businessman in Krížava. 'Ersatz shock therapy' in the Czech Republic also provided something of a safety valve for unemployment. The winners in the agricultural transformation were 'green barons', sections of the former co-operative management and the few of their number who set up private businesses (albeit retaining the co-operative brand). The Lehota co-operative's insistence on maintaining a fuzzy ownership fiction about just how much land the private father and son business actually farmed eventually forced them to move away. Uniquely in the region, many councils opted to intervene directly in economic life, but, as the experience in Habán made clear, this had to be on the basis of clear local authority ownership not socialist imprecision. The local authority in Bánec had to go to court to protect itself from a third party trying to exploit such imprecision to its advantage.

As in the Czech Republic, leading local figures in community development came from the public sector, such as: the constantly re-appointed mayor of Klanec with roots deep into the socialist past; the new old socialist mayor of Krížava who engineered a 'post-socialist' or Mečiar-style *modus vivendi* with his business community; and the Christian Democrat mayor of Lehota, who battled at the local, regional and national levels to find funds for his community and drove 500 kilometre round trips to lobby in Bratislava. Others preferred to sail with the wind and shift parties in a process analogous to Romanian 'party homogenisation' as was the case in Ľupta and less clearly in Zurča and Krížava. In Mečiar's Slovakia, business and politics were intermingled, as we saw in the case of Mr M, the new agricultural co-operative leader in Klanec. It is perhaps not surprising therefore that there was less evidence of a specifically business interest beginning to dominate local government structures, although there were perhaps glimmers of this on the Klanec council.

Conclusion

This project in contemporary comparative history has investigated agency and large-scale social change in rural communities in Eastern Europe undergoing what, for most of the countries concerned, was the fourth radical restructuring of agricultural relations in the twentieth century, a fourth restructuring that was also part of a historically unprecedented trajectory from socialism to capitalism. Conscious of all of the methodological compromises that it had to make (see Introduction), it attempted to recapture a moment in the early, pre-European Union phase of the formation of post-socialist capitalist democracy. By using case studies it sought to achieve a balance between providing a range of experience and achieving sufficient depth of analysis to recover meanings and intentions.

It is appropriate to return to the quotation from Marx with which we began, in particular to the phrases 'not in conditions of their own choosing' and 'make their own history'. This work has examined the interaction of legacy elements of 'not in conditions of their choosing', both structural, in terms of different staring points, and personal, in terms human, social and cultural capital, and the exercise of agency (individuals 'making their own history') in a number of dimensions. At the level of national politics, it has considered the roles of the strength and nature of the socialist-era opposition and reform communist wing within the communist party in determining post-socialist political pathways. Where both were strong, regimes committed to the post-socialist capitalist project emerged; where they were not, clientelistic, 'nomenklatura' capitalist regimes took power—until the promise of EU membership and EU-conditionality forced them to change in the new millennium.

In the sphere of agricultural transformation, legacies of collectivisation created different degrees of loyalty to the collective farm, which in turn, interacting with differing national political preferences, resulted in greater or lesser degrees of continuity of a dualist agrarian structure. The deadweight of history ensured that the Western European model of family farming would not be introduced as the regional norm, and the policy-priorities of national governments (except in the case of Romania) determined whether new structures would be built on the achievements or ruins of socialism and how quickly the postsocialist model would emerge. More nuanced elements of the agricultural legacy explained why Hungarian restructuring often took place in the context of bankruptcy and why more Hungarian farm managers had an alternative private venture to fall back on, why *arendatori* were absent from our Bulgarian villages, and the different reasons for so much destruction in the Balkans—collective farms were destroyed in Romania because the members hated them; they were destroyed (less completely) in Bulgaria because the regime hated them.

In the rural non-farming economy, it is striking how many of the new businesses in Hungary emerged from the non-farming, industrial and commercial activities of agricultural co-operatives.[1] This legitimate, semi-entrepreneurial sphere had no real equivalent elsewhere, although many Czechoslovak agricultural co-operatives did diversify beyond agriculture: the (less typical) successful co-operative 'business park' ventures in Klanec were examples of this. The biggest non-farm business from our Polish villages was, by contrast, the result of a quintessentially Polish legacy in that none of the other countries under consideration would have awarded a state contract to a wholly private company in the early 1980s. The serendipity element of Czech 'full, direct and specific' non-agricultural restitution reflected a pre-socialist legacy however. The same legislation applied to Slovakia where it was not observed.

---

[1] See also Swain, 'From kolkhoz to holding company', 151–2.

At the local government level, the interplay of legacy and agency broadly mirrored national priorities, reflected in extreme centralisation in Bulgaria, the differential identification of socialist 'wrongs' in Central Europe and the role of external agents and political homogenisation in Romania. Co-operative destruction elements in the Romanian and Bulgarian legacies provided the context for local authorities' greater focus on agricultural issues; the socialist public services gap lay behind the universal focus on improving services; 'shock therapy' (together with greater disposable resources than Romania) underpinned the greater salience of social welfare and job-creation on Polish local government agendas, while their greater concern with rural tourism may have reflected generations of wanting to find an alternative to agriculture in rural communities. Slovak clientelism and circulating debts provided the context for the emergence of a specific form of non-market collaboration between business and political elites in Krížava and the Slovak 'third way' perhaps explains rural Slovakia's unique phenomenon of direct intervention in the economy.

Post-socialist regimes faced a common project with relation to their rural communities: to reintroduce private ownership of land as a reality (because in most countries it had not been abolished on paper); to reintroduce private ownership of non-land assets, both by restituting objects from the past and allocating a share of co-operative assets in the process of co-operative transformation; to make possible at least more radical transformation towards private family farming, although in the event the trend was towards private corporate farming; and to make genuinely democratic local government structures that had never previously enjoyed real autonomy (except perhaps in interwar Czechoslovakia). But they approached this common project 'not in conditions of their own choosing'; they had different starting points—different socialist and immediately post-socialist histories, and political elites with differing commitments to the project and differing interpretations of the project. There were therefore both common elements in the rural transformation process and yet examples of considerable divergence and difference.

The common elements in these processes constitute the basis of Chapter 2 and aspects of divergence and difference are summarised in the final sections of Chapters 3 to 8; they need not be repeated here. Similarity and difference in rural transformation has structured this book, but general issues of agency and change have been addressed and these will be reprised here. To return to the surfing metaphor used in the Introduction, our research revealed many who were able to exercise agency, who could 'seize the time' in the agricultural economy, in the non-farm economy and as servants of their communities; and this despite the dead weight of extreme post-socialist recession. But the majority of those who were able to 'make their own history' also 'rode the wave' rather than swimming against the tide. Most found opportunities in socialism's legacies, the personal and public services gap (the result of socialist over industrialisation) or, in the case of BSS in Palina, socialist industry's over centralisation. They exercised agency, but under the constraint of structures created by the weight of dead generations. They were agents, but their options were not infinite. Like the mayor of Rodáky, they recognised changed realities and built a strategy around them, and in the case of some their analysis proved to be correct. The contrasting fates of small-scale entrepreneurs in Pakucs, Korcona and Zurča for example suggest how fine the line was between getting the analysis right and getting it wrong.

Furthermore, the key resources that they had at their disposal were similarly part of the weight of dead generations. Socialist-era mayors who had already used their socialist education and experience for the benefit of their communities often stayed in place; even the clerics who substituted for mayors as leading community actors in Romania benefitted from a socialist-era, if not socialist, education, as did the new capitalist and larger entrepreneurs in agriculture or the non-farm rural economy. In Chapter 7 it was striking that in the accounts of the failed association in Colibași and the parallel case in Verdery's Vlaicu, the leading figures were professionally trained women. But this is not surprising. Socialism was good at educating and employing women, certainly to the level of the actors in these stories. That there were women available with the necessary skills to seize the time in this case is explicable by the dead weight of the previous generation.

In the Introduction it was claimed that there was a particular virtue in selecting rural communities as the lens through which to investigate post-socialist social change. Two arguments were advanced. First, it was argued that there was a particular value in examining small-scale, face-to-face communities because the interconnectedness of complex relationships (that can remain hidden in larger-scale social formations) can be revealed in such communities. Second, it was contended that socialist agricultural producer co-operatives were quintessentially socialist in that they encapsulated two essential features of the socialist economy (the interrelationship between 'first' and 'second' economy, and the unequal powers between management and labour with the socialist production unit) and that the transformation of such quintessentially socialist entities would tell us something about the nature of the world that followed.

To take the second of these first, post-socialist developments make it unambiguously clear that the symbiosis of 'first' and 'second' economy was something that could only exist under the non-market relations of a socialist economy and it disappeared with the arrival of the market. That is not surprising. But our case studies also make it clear that what made possible the symbiosis of 'first' and 'second' economy was the security of employment that the socialist sector provided. Incomes from the 'second economy' could afford to be marginal because the socialist sector guaranteed a basic minimum and social security entitlement. This lesson was perhaps not self-evident because literature on the 'first' and 'second' economy tended to focus on the interrelated nature of the two sectors, rather than the dependence of the second on the first for its very existence. When market forces were introduced and co-operatives shed between a half and two thirds of their labour forces, supplementary agriculture in a member's 'marginal labour time' became subsistence farming.[2] You were either employed, or you were not; and if you were unemployed, the options were self-employment (force-of-circumstance entrepreneurship) or living from (inadequate) benefits. Managers were no longer constrained by obligations to employ labour. They no longer needed to manipulate labour inputs to maximise their bonuses, they simply needed to maximise profits.[3] Labour became just another factor of production with no special privileges; Marxists would say that labour power became a commodity again.

Our rural research further confirmed that sections of collective and state farm management provided the new indigenous capitalists

---

[2] Swain, *Collective Farms*, 9.
[3] Ibid., 11–20.

for post-socialist capitalism, those who in some way were motivated to build on the human, social and cultural capital that they (along with many others) had garnered from a socialist education and management experience in socialist industry and launch into new business. It has also confirmed that such people did not necessarily come from the very top of their previous institutions. A simplistic picture of 'nomenklatura captialism' is rejected.[4] In the non-farm economy, the non-competitiveness of the 'first economy' and its relatively unattractiveness to major foreign investors in the post-socialist era was also reflected in rural communities in the closure of socialist industries in the commuting area and the villages themselves, although the border effect that we noted suggested that smaller western companies were attracted by cheap labour and laxer environmental standards. In Sedno the border provided opportunities too, but of dubious legality. Our few successful, large-scale indigenous businesses were 'exceptions that prove the rule', and they too tended to exploit elements of the socialist legacy. Employment beyond the family business was thus dependent on foreign investment in the more reforming countries and the extent to which market forces were subordinated to political interests further east, both features of the distinctly post-socialist form of capitalism.[5] The prevalence of 'force-of-circumstance entrepreneurs' (described most fully perhaps in the case of Korcona) presages almost certainly the weak small and medium enterprise (SME) sector in post-socialist capitalism that economic analysts have noted.[6]

Turning to the positive virtue of conducting research in rural, multi-faceted communities, much was revealed in the arena of local politics. Our village studies demonstrated, as might have been expected, that party labels have little significance at the local level, and, indeed, that the philosophical priorities of different parties carried little weight when there was almost no scope for discretionary spending in a local authority's budget, and key issues were of the nature of whether or not to repair the football club's roof. But they also revealed some characteristics of early post-socialist democracy that might cause

---

[4] Swain, 'A post-socialist capitalism', 1679–80.
[5] Ibid., 1672–5; see also references in Chapter 1 to clientelistic capitalism in this period in Bulgaria, Romania and Slovakia.
[6] Swain, 'A post-socialist capitalism', 1675–7.

concern to anyone who imagined a smooth progression from socialist dictatorship to liberal democracy. The unimportance of party labels in small-scale rural communities is not surprising. The impermanence of political allegiances and wholesale switching of support to the party that held the purse-strings, such as witnessed in Slovakia and especially Romania, reflected a degree of political patronage that has no place in liberal polyarchies—but then both countries were acknowledged to be clientelistic at the time and such patronage is characteristic of clientelist regimes. Our findings in countries where the political regime was less centralised revealed, by contrast, the contradictions of granting autonomy without the resources to support it. Under conditions of 'fiscal stress', granting autonomy in educational policy, for example, devolved few decisions of substance, although the teacher in Hungary's Kissikonda enjoyed her autonomy, which was likely to be short-term on the basis of the experiences of Poland's Głaz and Kanał. The starting-point for our mayors and councillors was the impotence of increased responsibilities and reduced resources.

Focus on the interrelatedness of multi-faceted rural societies was also suggestive of class dynamics. An 'ecologist' and a 'business' lobby vied for influence in Rodáky in the Czech Republic, as did 'teachers' and 'farmers' in Bory in Poland. Relations in Głaz between the major businessman and the mayor from the socialist era were tense; in Károlyháza, where the lady mayor came from a family of large-landowners, they were also ambivalent; but, in four villages in Hungary and at least one village each in the other countries covered by the research, a business elite appeared to be taking over local politics, irrespective of the party badge that it wore. Despite the relative impotence of local government, groups of constituents strove to make their interests felt, and in particular, a business interest sought political as well as economic power to secure its interests. Furthermore, interconnectedness extended in some cases well beyond the local community. The Catholic priest in Pola had links with Solidarity at the national level; the Dombház clerk of the council had a brother who was a Smallholder member of parliament; the mayor of Nezávislice had a parallel career in national politics; the mayor of Lehota engaged in 500 kilometre round trips to lobby in Bratislava.

Our case studies revealed the resilience in adversity of human kind as villagers struggled to make ends meet in the early post-socialist recession. It was recognised that 'Here everybody stands on two legs' and 'You must work two shifts to survive', so people did. But they reveal much too about the contradictions of large-scale social change, about the paradoxical sense that many experienced, namely that everything had changed, and yet so much had remained the same. Labour became an unprivileged factor of production almost overnight; equally rapid was the opening of the 'personal services gap' to nascent entrepreneurs, and the 'public services gap' as a problem for those struggling to serve the interests of rural communities under conditions of 'fiscal stress'. Polish 'specialist' farmers were suddenly hit by market interest rates and many went bankrupt or took to the streets to protest. Two uniquely socialist livelihood patterns were radically changed overnight, both by chance linked to subsidised tobacco prices (although at opposite ends of Europe)—the logging cum tobacco farming communities around Kanał in Poland, and the tobacco farmers of Blagun and Chala in the Bulgarian mountains. Bulgarian peasants responded to the sudden disappearance of socialist marketing channels by setting up informal roadside markets. The villagers of Dombház saw their faith in the Smallholders Party-inspired Dombmilk project shattered as the logic of the market unforgivingly pushed it towards bankruptcy.

Yet in other dimensions, change was more protracted. Labour might have become an unprivileged factor of production again, but labour is an abstraction from groups citizens, and citizens have votes; citizens can engage in social and political action; citizens have needs which they feel should be addressed even if from a macro-economic perspective this entails 'living beyond their means'; and citizens have life-cycles which means that those needs continue long after they cease to labour or be economically active. Politicians, national and local, have to take account of citizens as human beings because they vote and provide their rule with legitimacy. If they lose that legitimacy, they lose everything, as their socialist predecessors had learned to their cost less than a decade before. The social and material worlds are intractable at the best of times. Perversely, periods of large-scale social change can encourage inertia in the interests of social harmony.

It is not surprising that Polish politicians quietly abandoned the strict tenets of 'shock therapy' as soon as workers and peasants began to demonstrate. The Polish government, like all of the local authorities in our villages, pursued defensive, 'fire-fighting' strategies to keep things ticking over and avoid social unrest. As noted frequently above, tough bankruptcy legislation, the ultimate form of market discipline, only existed in Hungary during the period under consideration and in all other countries was not introduced until the second, EU-dominated phase of post-socialism in the new millennium. In the former Czechoslovakia in particular, post-socialist co-operatives struggled with unpaid bills and circulating debts and privatisation was often a protracted process; in the Czech Republic 'ersatz shock therapy' reigned until the crash of 1997; in Slovakia, Bulgaria and Romania variants of clientelist state capitalism remained in force throughout our research period. In Bulgaria, as we have seen, the 'red' co-operatives continued to provide traditional social benefits to their members, as did Slovak co-operatives, Romanian associations and the untransformed Hungarian co-operative in Szálfa. Furthermore, almost everywhere socialist and post-socialist enterprises alike continued to provide subsidised lunches for village pensioners. The cash-nexus took time to destroy this feature of everyday socialism because vulnerable lives depended on it. Pensioners everywhere qualified as 'deserving poor' whatever the prejudices of the local policy makers (Chapter 2). In this respect, it is noteworthy that welfare systems in Eastern Europe retain strong state involvement and are closer to European than North American norms.[7] Meanwhile others gradually realised that the world had changed fundamentally and adjusted accordingly, the budding entrepreneurs of course, but also local activists such as the woman responsible for rural tourism in Bory who recognised that a radically different conception of tourism was required by the new realities.

It is not just a question of large-scale change being introduced at periods of 'fiscal stress' when defensive policies are safest. As the references throughout the book to the moral economy of socialism and the quotation from Katherine Verdery used in the Introduction suggest, the discipline of an economy based on exclusive property rights, limited liabilities and the 'cash nexus' has to be learned. Some of our mayors (most dramatically in Lesovice in the Czech Republic) took time to understand the public-private divide on which, in theory at least, the market economy and liberal polity are based. Forty years

---

[7] Ibid., 1687.

experiencing 'actually existing socialism' generated a cynicism towards co-operation and the principles of mutual support generally. 'Co-operatives' were either oppressive or provided material rewards despite rather than because of the democratic principles according to which they were supposed to (but did not) operate. Even if community cohesion and identity proved surprisingly resilient, as the experiences of some of our villages suggest, community support groups were rather uncommon. At this early stage in post-socialist capitalism, civil society was weak and many commentators argue that so it has remained.[8] In addition, the mindsets of large sections of our rural societies remained sceptical of rewards based on anything other than labour and regarded the newly successful with 'envy', even in commercial, 'optimistic' Bárov in the Czech Republic. Post-socialist labour could become an unprivileged factor of production overnight as market forces were introduced, yet national and local politicians would simultaneously continue with unchanged defensive policies, while all gradually adjusted to a world in which labour alone no longer determined value. Fundamental things changed, but much that was important remained the same.

In the end, the conclusion of this analysis is perhaps frustratingly mundane and can be summed up in two statements: 'Change is complex and can be simultaneously radical and protracted' and 'Nothing comes from nothing'. Market conditions relating to the employment of labour and sky-high interest rates can be introduced over night, but political considerations related to the fact that the extent to which labour can be treated as a mere commodity is limited ensure that concessions are made to soften the blow. Labour becomes a commodity over night, but not everyone is obliged to experience it immediately. Irrespective of the speed with which economic realities change, it takes longer to change mindsets: vestiges of a moral economy of socialism remain, as do uncertainties about the divide between the private and public spheres. In the context of such change, certain individuals are able to 'seize the time' and act as agents of history; some establish the embryo of a new class, yet this ability does not come from nowhere and the choices on offer are not infinite.

---

[8] Ibid., 1688–9.

The agents are a subset of those with certain skill sets inherited from the past who are able to use them in the present, but they make their own history, in the main, in areas where the legacy of the past has provided certain opportunities which can easily be exploited, they do so by manipulating elements of the dead weight of past generations. But they are active agents nevertheless; in conditions of severe economic recession, they struggle against enormous odds to realise their visions, whether it is in relation to private business interests or the well-being of their communities.

This book began with a discussion of comparative history and its usefulness in separating the causal from the contingent when considering 'plausible' counterfactual history. It has not been an exercise in counterfactual history; nevertheless some caveats emerge for those who wish to use the past to inform policy-making in the present. First, there would seem to be no plausible scenario for the development of Western European family farming in the region. Even former specialists in Poland grew at the expense of the state sector and not the organic consolidation of family holdings characteristic of market societies. Second, our comparative research revealed that the same outcome can have different causes. As noted above, socialist agriculture was all but destroyed in Bulgaria and Romania, but for diametrically opposed reasons; in Slovakia and the Czech Republic the dimensions at least of socialist agriculture were retained, but, the political regimes which oversaw that continuity could not have been more different. There are pathways from socialist to post-socialist, but they are not straightforward. Establishing the direction of causation is complex; yet rural development policy for the region is unlikely to be effective if it is ignorant of such complexity.

Bibliography

Andor, Mihály. "The terrain of local politics in Hungary." Rural Transition Series Working Paper no. 22, Centre for Central and Eastern European Studies, University of Liverpool, 1994. http://liv.ac.uk/history/research/cee_pdfs/WP22v2.pdf.
——— and Tibor Kuczi. "What happened in Hungarian agriculture after 1990?" *Eastern European Countryside* 4 (1998): 83–98.
Baldersheim, Harald, Gejza Blaas, Tamás M. Horváth, Michal Illner and Paweł Swianiewicz. "New institutions of local government: A comparison." In *Local Democracy and the Process of Transformation in East-Central Europe*, edited by Harald Baldersheim, Michal Illner, Audun Offerdal, Lawrence Rose and Paweł Swianiewicz, 23–41. Boulder and Oxford: Westview Press, 1996.
Bauerkämper, Arndt and Constantin Iordachi. *The Collectivization of Agriculture in Communist Eastern Europe: Comparison and Entanglements*. Budapest, London and New York: Central European University Press, forthcoming.
Bell, John D. "Democratization and political participation in 'postcommunist' Bulgaria." In *Politics, Power and the Struggle for Democracy in South-East Europe*, edited by Karen Dawisha and Bruce Parrott, 353–402. Cambridge: Cambridge University Press, 1997.
———. "Populism and pragmatism: The BANU in Bulgarian politics." In *Populism in Eastern Europe: Racism, Nationalism, and Society*, edited by Joseph Held, 20–61. New York: Boulder East European Monograph, distributed by Columbia University Press, 1996.
Berend, Ivan T. "Agriculture." In *The Economic History of Eastern Europe 1919–1975. Volume I: Economic Structure and Performance between the Two Wars*, edited by M.C. Kaser and E.A. Radice, 148–209. Oxford: Clarendon Press, 1985.

Bezemer, Dirk J. "Micro-economic institutions and the transformation of agribusiness: Evidence from the Czech Republic." *Eastern European Countryside* 5 (1999): 85–97.

——. *Structural Change in the Post-Socialist Transformation of Central European Agriculture: Studies from the Czech and Slovak Republics.* Amsterdam: University of Amsterdam, Tinbergen Institute, 2001.

Bird, William A. and Lin Qingsong, eds. *China's Rural Industry: Structure, Development and Reform.* Oxford: Oxford University Press for the World Bank, 1990.

Blaas, Gejza. "Privatization of the rural sector in Slovakia." *Eastern European Countryside* 1 (1995): 91–8.

——, Stanislav Buchta and Iveta Námerová. "The economic, legislative, political and social policy contest of Slovak agriculture." Rural Transition Series Working Paper no. 23, Centre for Central and Eastern European Studies, University of Liverpool, 1994. http://www.liv.ac.uk/history/research/cee_pdfs/WP23v2.pdf.

—— and Axel Woltz. "Economic situation and structural changes in Slovakian agriculture." *Eastern European Countryside* 4 (1998): 99–116.

Blažek, Jiří and Sjaak Boeckhout. "Regional policy in the Czech Republic and EU accession." In *Transition, Cohesion and Regional Policy in Central and Eastern Europe,* edited by John Bachtler, Ruth Downes and Grzegorz Gorzelak, 301–17. Aldershot and Burlington, VT: Ashgate: 2000.

Blum, Jerome. "The rise of serfdom in Eastern Europe." *American Historical Review* 62, no. 4 (1957): 807–36.

Bőhm, Antal and György Szoboszlai. *Önkormányzati választások 1990* [Local government elections 1990]. Budapest: Magyar Tudományos Akadémia Politikai Tudományok Intézete, 1992.

van den Bor, W., J.M. Bryden and A.M. Fuller. "Rethinking rural human resource management: The impact of globalisation and rural restructuring on rural education and training in Western Europe." Mansholt Studies no. 10, The Graduate School Mansholt Institute, Wageningen Agricultural University, 1998.

Bridger, Sue and Frances Pine, eds. *Surviving Post-Socialism: Local Strategies and Regional Responses in Eastern Europe and the Former Soviet Union.* London and New York: Routledge, 1998.

Brown, David L. and László Kulcsár. "Rural families and rural development in Central and Eastern Europe." *Eastern European Countryside* 6 (2000): 5–23.

Buchowski, Michal. "Redefining social relations through work in a rural community in Poland." Working Paper no. 58, Max Planck Institute for Social Anthropology, Halle-Saale, 2003. http://www.eth.mpg.de/cms/de/publications/working_papers/wp0058.html.

Bugajski, Janusz. *Political Parties of Eastern Europe: A Guide to Politics in the Post-Communist Era.* New York: ME Sharpe Center for Strategic and International Studies, 2002.

Campbell, Adrian. "Local government in Romania." In *Local Government in Eastern Europe*, edited by Andrew Coulson, 76–101. Aldershot and Brookfield, VT: Edward Elgar, 1995.

Canning, Anna and Paul Hare. "The privatisation process—economic and political aspects of the Hungarian approach." In *Privatization in Central and Eastern Europe*, edited by Saul Estrin, 176–217. London and New York: Longman, 1994.

Capková, Sona. "Basic information on local governments in Slovakia." In *Local Governments in the CEE and CIS, 1994: An Anthology of Descriptive Papers*, edited by The Institute for Local Government and Public Services, 189–202. Budapest: Institute for Local Government and Public Services, 1994.

Cartwright, Andrew. "Against 'decollectivisation': Land reform in Romania, 1990–1992." Working Paper no. 4, Max Planck Institute for Social Anthropology, Halle-Saale, 2000. http://www.eth.mpg.de/cms/de/publications/working_papers/wp0004.html.

———. "In from the margins? State law and the recognition of property in rural Romania." Working Paper no. 10, Max Planck Institute for Social Anthropology, Halle-Saale, 2000. http://www.eth.mpg.de/cms/de/publications/working_papers/wp0010.html.

———. "Private farming in Romania: What are the old people going to do with their land?" In *The Postsocialist Agrarian Question: Property Relations and the Rural Condition*, edited by Chris Hann and The "Property Relations" Group, 171–88. Münster: LIT Verlag, 2003.

———. *The Return of the Peasant: Land Reform in Post-Communist Romania*. Aldershot and Burlington, VT: Ashgate, 2001.

——— and Nigel Swain. "Finding farmers in Eastern Europe: Some issues." Rural Transition Series Working Paper no. 60, Centre for Central and Eastern European Studies, University of Liverpool, 2002. http://www.liv.ac.uk/history/research/cee_pdfs/WP60.pdf.

Cellarius, Barbara A. "Property restitution and natural resource use in the Rhodope Mountains, Bulgaria." In *The Postsocialist Agrarian Question: Property Relations and the Rural Condition*, edited by Chris Hann and The "Property Relations" Group, 189–218. Münster: LIT Verlag, 2003.

Central Statistical Office. *Az élelmiszer-gazdaság 1994. évi fejlődése* [The development of the food economy in 1994]. Budapest: Central Statistical Office, 1995.

———. *A mezőgazdaság 1996. évi fejlődése* [The development of agriculture in 1996]. Budapest: Central Statistical Office, 1997.

Chan, Kenneth Ka-Lok. "Poland at the crossroads: The 1993 general election." *Europe-Asia Studies* 47, no. 1 (January 1995): 123–45.

Chang, Chun and Yijiang Wang. "The nature of the township–village enterprise." *Journal of Comparative Economics* 19, no. 3 (December 1994): 434–52.

Che, Jiahua and Yingyi Qian. "Insecure property rights and government ownership of firms." *The Quarterly Journal of Economics* 113, no. 2 (May 1998): 467–96.

———. "Institutional environment, community government, and corporate governance: Understanding China's township–village enterprises." *The Journal of Law, Economics and Organization* 14, no. 1 (April 1998): 1–23.

Cielecka, Anna and John Gibson. "Local government in Poland." In *Local Government in Eastern Europe*, edited by Andrew Coulson, 23–40. Aldershot and Brookfield, VT: Edward Elgar, 1995.

Coffee, John C. Jr. "Institutional investors in transitional economies: Lessons from the Czech experience." In *Corporate Governance in Central Europe and Russia. Volume 1: Banks, Funds, and Foreign Investors*, edited by Roman Frydman, Cheryl W. Gray and Andrzej Rapaczynski, 111–86. Budapest, London and New York: Central European University Press, 1996.

Coman, Pena, Eugen Crai, Monica Radulescu and Gabriella Stanciulescu. "Local government in Romania." In *Stabilization of Local Governments*, edited by Emilia Kandeva, 351–416. Budapest: Central European University Press, 2001.

Creed, Gerald W. "Deconstructing socialism in Bulgaria." In *Uncertain Transition: Ethnographies of Change in the Postsocialist World*, edited by Michael Burawoy and Katherine Verdery, 223–43. Lanham, MD and Oxford: Rowman and Littlefield, 1999.

———. *Domesticating Revolution: From Socialist Reform to Ambivalent Transition in a Bulgarian Village*. University Park, PA: The Pennsylvania State University Press, 1998.

———. "Economic crisis and ritual decline in Eastern Europe." In *Postsocialism: Ideals and Practices in Eurasia*, edited by Chris Hann, 57–73. London and New York: Routledge, 2002.

———. "An old song in a new voice: Decollectivization in Bulgaria." In *Eastern European Communities: The Struggle for Balance in Turbulent Times*, edited by David A. Kideckel, 25–45. Boulder, CO and Oxford: Westview Press, 1995.

Csurgó, Bernadett. "Urban pressure—A recent phenomenon: The Valley of Arts." *Eastern European Countryside* 10 (2004): 155–65.

Davey, Kenneth. "The Czech and Slovak Republics." In *Local Government in Eastern Europe*, edited by Andrew Coulson, 41–56. Aldershot and Brookfield, VT: Edward Elgar, 1995.

———. "Local government in Hungary." In *Local Government in Eastern Europe*, edited by Andrew Coulson, 57–75. Aldershot and Brookfield, VT: Edward Elgar, 1995.

Davidova, Sophia, Allan Buckwell and Diana Kopeva. "Bulgaria: Economics and politics of post-reform farm structures." In *Agricultural Privatisation, Land Reform and Farm Restructuring in Central and Eastern Europe*, edited by Johan F.M. Swinnen, Allan Buckwell and Erik Mathijs, 23–62. Aldershot: Ashgate, 1997.

Davis, Junior. "Sustainable non-farm rural livelihood diversification in Romania during transition." *Eastern European Countryside* 7 (2001): 51–67.

Dobreva, Stanka. "The family farm in Bulgaria: Traditions and changes." *Sociologia Ruralis* 34, no. 4 (1994): 340–53.

―――. "The farm production co-operative as a support for the rural household in Bulgaria." *Eastern European Countryside* 7 (2001): 81–90.
Donáth, Ferenc. *Reform és forradalom: A magyar mezőgazdaság strukturális átalakulása 1945–1975* [Reform and revolution: The structural transformation of Hungarian agriculture 1945–1975]. Budapest: Akadémiai Kiadó, 1977.
Draganova, Marianna. "New social actors in Bulgarian private sector agriculture." In *The Bulgarian Village and Globalisation Processes: XVIIth Congress of the European Society of Rural Sociology*, edited by Veska Kozhuharova, 45–56. Sofia: Bulgarian Society of Rural Sociology, Institute of Sociology, 1997.
Ekiert, Grzegorz and Jan Kubik. *Rebellious Civil Society: Popular Protest and Democratic Consolidation in Poland, 1989–1993*. Ann Arbor, MI: University of Michigan Press, 2001.
Erdei, Ferenc. *A magyar társadalomról* [On Hungarian society]. Budapest: Akadémiai Kiadó, 1980. (This includes the text of "A magyar paraszttársadalom" [Hungarian peasant society], Budapest: Franklin, 1942.)
Faltan, Lubomir and Vladimir Krivy. "Slovakia: Changes in public administration." In *Decentralisation and Transition in the Visegrad: Poland, Hungary, the Czech Republic and Slovakia*, edited by Emil J. Kirchner, 102–31. Houndmills: Macmillan, 1999.
Farcas, Mihai. "Basic information on local governments in Romania." In *Local Governments in the CEE and CIS, 1994: An Anthology of Descriptive Papers*, edited by The Institute for Local Government and Public Services, 159–71. Budapest: Institute for Local Government and Public Services, 1994.
Fekete, Éva, Mihály Lados, Edit Pfeil and Zsolt Szoboszlai. "Size of local governments, local democracy and local service delivery in Hungary." In *Consolidation or Fragmentation? The Size of Local Governments in Central and Eastern Europe*, edited by Paweł Swianiewicz, 31–100. Budapest: Local Government and Public Reform Initiative, Open Society Institute, 2002.
Ferge, Zsuzsa. "Welfare and 'ill-fare' systems in Central-Eastern Europe." In *Globalization and European Welfare States: Challenges and Change*, edited by R. Sykes, B. Palier and P.M. Prior, 127–52. Houndmills: Palgrave Macmillan, 2001.
Ferguson, Niall. "Introduction. Virtual history: Towards a 'chaotic' theory of the past." In *Virtual History: Alternatives and Counterfactuals*, edited by Niall Ferguson, 1–90. London and Basingstoke: Macmillan, 1997.
Foryś, Grzegorz and Krzysztof Gorlach. "The dynamics of Polish peasant protests under post-communism." *Eastern European Countryside* 8 (2002): 47–65.
Fowler, Brigid. "Concentrated orange: Fidesz and the remaking of the Hungarian centre-right, 1994–2002." *Journal of Communist Studies and Transition Politics* 20, no. 3 (September 2004): 80–114.
Frydman, Roman, Andrzej Rapaczynski and John S. Earle. *The Privatization Process in Central Europe*. Budapest, London and New York: Central European University Press, 1993.

Gallagher, Tom. "The Balkans since 1989: The winding retreat from national communism." In *Developments in Central and East European Politics 3*, edited by Stephen White, Judy Batt and Paul G. Lewis, 74–91. Houndmills: Palgrave Macmillan, 2003.

———. "Nationalism and Romanian political culture in the 1990s." In *Post-Communist Romania: Coming to Terms with Transition*, edited by Duncan Light and David Phinnemore, 104–24. Houndmills: Palgrave, 2001.

———. *Theft of a Nation: Romania since Communism.* London: Hurst, 2005.

Giatzidis, Emil. *An Introduction to Post-Communist Bulgaria: Political, Economic and Social Transformation.* Manchester and New York: Manchester University Press, 2002.

Giordano, Christian. "Multiple modernities in Bulgaria: Social strategies of capitalist entrepreneurs in the agrarian sector." *Eastern European Countryside* 16 (2010): 5–24.

——— and Dobrinka Kostova. "Social production of mistrust." In *Postsocialism: Ideals and Practices in Eurasia*, edited by Chris Hann, 74–91. London and New York: Routledge, 2002.

——— and Dobrinka Kostova. "The unexpected effects of the land reform in post-socialist Bulgaria." *Eastern European Countryside* 7 (1999): 5–18.

Gomułka, Stanisław and Piotr Jasiński. "Privatization in Poland 1989–1993: Policies, methods, and results." In *Privatization in Central and Eastern Europe*, edited by Saul Estrin, 218–51. London and New York: Longman, 1994.

Gorlach, Krzysztof and Patrick H. Mooney. "Defending class interests: Polish peasants in the first years of transformation." In *Theorising Transition: The Political Economy of Post-Communist Transformations*, edited by John Pickles and Adrian Smith, 262–83. London and New York: Routledge, 1998.

Hajdú, Zoltán. "Local government reform in Hungary." In *Local Government in the New Europe*, edited by Robert J. Bennett, 208–24. London and New York: Belhaven Press, 1993.

Hann, Chris. "Introduction: Decollectivisation and the moral economy." In *The Postsocialist Agrarian Question: Property Relations and the Rural Condition*, edited by Chris Hann and The "Property Relations" Group, 1–46. Münster: LIT Verlag, 2003.

———. *"Not the Horse We Wanted!" Postsocialism, Neoliberalism, and Eurasia.* Münster: LIT Verlag, 2006.

———, ed. *Postsocialism: Ideals and Practices in Eurasia.* London and New York: Routledge, 2002.

———. "Second economy and civil society." In *Market Economy and Civil Society in Hungary*, edited by Chris Hann, 21–44. London: Frank Cass and Company, 1990.

——— and The "Property Relations" Group (eds.). *The Postsocialist Agrarian Question: Property Relations and the Rural Condition.* Münster: LIT Verlag, 2003.

——— and Mihály Sárkány. "The great transformation in rural Hungary: Property, life strategies and living standards." In *The Postsocialist Agrarian*

Question: Property Relations and the Rural Condition, edited by Chris Hann and The "Property Relations" Group, 117–41. Münster: LIT Verlag, 2003.
Harcsa, István. "Privatisation and reprivatisation in Hungarian agriculture," Acta Oeconomica 43, nos. 3–4 (1991): 321–48.
Harris, Francis. "How Mr Klaus cooked the budget: Black hole." Business Central Europe 6, no. 49 (March 1998): 58–9.
Hawthorn, Geoffrey. Enlightenment and Despair: a History of Sociology. Cambridge: Cambridge University Press, 1976.
———. Plausible Worlds: Possibility and Understanding in History and the Social Sciences. Cambridge: Cambridge University Press, 1991.
Hayashi, Tadayuki. "'Neo-liberals' and the politics of economic transformation in the post-communist Czech Republic." In Democracy and Market Economics in Central and Eastern Europe: Are New Institutions being Consolidated? edited by Tadayuki Hayashi, 129–47. Sapporo: Slavic Research Center, Hokkaido University, 2004.
———. "Politics of the agricultural transformation in Czechoslovakia: 1990–1991." In The New Structure of the Rural Economy of Post-Communist Countries, edited by Osamu Ieda, 25–42. Sapporo: Slavic Research Center, Hokkaido University, 2001.
Heintz, Monica. "Romanian orthodoxy between the urban and the rural." Working Paper no. 67, Max Planck Institute for Social Anthropology, Halle-Saale, 2004. http://www.eth.mpg.de/cms/de/publications/working_papers/wp0067.html.
Heywood, Andrew. Politics (2nd edition). Houndmills: Palgrave, 2002.
van Hoven, Bettina, ed. Europe: Lives in Transition. Harlow: Pearson Education, 2004.
Hudečková, Helena and Michal Lošťák. "Privatization in Czechoslovak agriculture: Results of a 1990 sociological survey." Sociologia Ruralis 32, nos. 2–3 (1992): 287–304.
Hudečková, Helena, Michal Lošťák and Sandie Rikoon. "Reflections of 'late modernity' in land ownership in the Czech Republic." Eastern European Countryside 6 (2000): 93–110.
Hungarian Ministry of Agriculture. Vidékfejlesztési politika: Strukturális és környezetvédelmi intézkedések [Rural development policy: Structural and environmental measures]. Budapest: Hungarian Ministry of Agriculture, May 1996.
Ieda, Osamu. "Local government in Hungary." In The Emerging Local Governments in Eastern Europe and Russia: Historical and Post-Communist Developments, edited by Osamu Ieda, 85–129. Hiroshima: Keisuisha, 2000.
Illner, Michael. "Territorial government in the Czech Republic." In Decentralisation and Transition in the Visegrad: Poland, Hungary, the Czech Republic and Slovakia, edited by Emil J. Kirchner, 80–101. Houndmills: Macmillan, 1999.
Illyés, Gyula. Puszták népe [People of the puszta]. Budapest: Szépirodalmi Könyvkiadó, 1967.
Ivanov, Stefan, Guinka Tchavdarova, Emil Savov and Hristo Stanev. "Does larger mean more effective? Size and the function of local governments

in Bulgaria." In *Consolidation or Fragmentation? The Size of Local Governments in Central and Eastern Europe*, edited by Paweł Swianiewicz, 167–217. Budapest: Local Government and Public Reform Initiative, Open Society Institute, 2002.

Ivanova, Radost. "Social change as reflected in the lives of Bulgarian villagers." In *Eastern European Communities: The Struggle for Balance in Turbulent Times*, edited by David A. Kideckel, 217–36. Boulder, CO and Oxford: Westview Press, 1995.

Jepson, David, Valerie McDonnell and Belin Mollov. "Local government in Bulgaria." In *Local Government in Eastern Europe*, edited by Andrew Coulson, 102–14. Aldershot and Brookfield, VT: Edward Elgar, 1995.

Jin, Hehui and Yingyi Qian. "Public versus private ownership of firms: Evidence from rural China." *The Quarterly Journal of Economics* 113, no. 3 (August 1998): 773–808.

Juhász, Pál. "Az agrárértelmiség meghasonlása" [Discord within the agrarian intelligentsia]. In *Juhász Pál—Emberek és intézmények: Két zsákutca az agráriumban*. [Pál Juhász—Men and institutions: Two dead-ends in the agrarian sphere], edited by József Marelyin Kiss and Tibor Kuczi, 182–94. Budapest: Új Mandátum Könyvkiadó, 2006.

Kalb, Don. "Afterword: Globalism and postsocialist prospects." In *Postsocialism: Ideals and Practices in Eurasia*, edited by Chris Hann, 317–34. London and New York: Routledge, 2002.

Kára, Jan and Jiří Blažek. "Czechoslovakia: Regional and local government reform since 1989." In *Local Government in the New Europe*, edited by Robert J. Bennett, 246–58. London and New York: Belhaven Press, 1993.

Karlík, Jiří. *Questions of Ownership and Use of Land and Other Agricultural Means*. Prague: Ekonomický Ústav Československé Akademie VĚD, 1991.

Karwacki, Arkadiusz. "The culture of poverty in the post-state farm Community." *Eastern European Countryside* 8 (2002): 79–92.

Kaneff, Deema. "Private co-operatives and local property relations in rural Bulgaria." *Replika* (Hungarian Social Science Quarterly) (Special Issue 1998): 161–72.

———. "Property, work and local identity." Working Paper no. 15, Max Planck Institute for Social Anthropology, Halle-Saale, 2000. http://www.eth.mpg.de/cms/de/publications/working_papers/wp0015.html.

———. "Responses to 'democratic' land reform in a Bulgarian village." In *After Socialism: Land Reform and Social Change in Eastern Europe*, edited by Ray Abrahams, 85–114. Providence and Oxford: Berghahn Books, 1996.

———. *Who Owns the Past? The Politics of Time in a „Model" Bulgarian Village*. New York and Oxford: Berghahn Books, 2004.

———. "Why don't people die 'naturally' any more? Changing relations between 'the individual' and 'the state' in post-socialist Bulgaria." *Journal of the Royal Anthropological Institute* 8, no. 1 (March 2002): 89–105.

Kelemen, Eszter, Boldizsár Megyesi and Ildikó Nagy Kalamász. "Knowledge dynamics and sustainability in rural livelihood strategies: Two case studies from Hungary." *Sociologia Ruralis* 48, no. 3 (July 2008): 257–73.

Keliyan, Maya. "Agriculture and rural development in Bulgaria and Japan: A comparative perspective." In *Rural Potentials for a Global Tomorrow: 9th World Congress of Rural Sociology*, edited by Veska Kozhuharova, 30–4. Sofia: Bulgarian Academy of Sciences, Institute of Sociology, 1996.

Kideckel, David A. *The Solitude of Collectivism: Romanian Villagers to the Revolution and Beyond*. Ithaca, NY and London: Cornell University Press, 1993.

Kimura, Makoto. "An analysis of local government in Bulgaria." In *The Emerging Local Governments in Eastern Europe and Russia: Historical and Post-Communist Developments*, edited by Osamu Ieda, 333–62. Hiroshima: Keisuisha, 2000.

Konrad, Gyorgy and Ivan Szelenyi. "Social conflicts of under-urbanisation." In *Urban and Social Economics in Market and Planned Economies: Volume I*, edited by Alan A. Brown, Joseph A. Licari and Egon Neuberger, 206–26. New York: Praeger, 1974.

Kostova, Dobrinka and Christian Giordano. "The agrarian elite in Bulgaria—Adaptation to the transformation." In *Rural Potentials for a Global Tomorrow: 9th World Congress of Rural Sociology*, edited by Veska Kozhuharova, 54–64. Sofia: Bulgarian Academy of Sciences, Institute of Sociology, 1996.

———. "Reprivatization without peasants." *Eastern European Countryside* 1 (1995): 99–112.

Kovács, Katalin. "The 1997 'Peasant Revolt' in Hungary." *Eastern European Countryside* 5 (1999): 43–58.

———. "Rescuing a small village school in the context of rural change in Hungary." *Journal of Rural Studies* 28, no. 2 (April 2012): 108–17.

———. "Strengths, controversies and a show-case of failure in Hungarian agricultural restructuring: The case of the Hollóföldje co-operative." *Replika* (Hungarian Social Science Quarterly) (Special Issue 1998): 173–89.

———. "Szuburbanizációs folyamatok a fővárosban és a budapesti agglomerációban [Suburbanisation processes in the capital and in the Budapest agglomeration]. In *Társadalmi-gazdasági átakalukás a budapesti agglomerációban* [Socio-economic transformation in the Budapest agglomeration], edited by Gy. Bartha and P. Beluszky, 91–114. Budapest: Magyar Tudományos Akadémia Regionális Kutatások Központja, 1999.

———. "The transition in Hungarian agriculture 1990–1993: General tendenceis, background factors and the case of the 'Golden Age'." In *After Socialism: Land Reform and Social Change in Eastern Europe*, edited by Ray Abrahams, 51–84. Providence and Oxford: Berghahn Books, 1996.

——— and Zsuzsanna Bihari. "State and co-operative farms in transition: The Hungarian case." In *Rural Societies under Communism and Beyond: Hungarian and Polish Perspectives*, edited by Paweł Starosta, Imre Kovách, and Krzystof Gorlach, 115–50. Łódź: Łódź University Press, 1999.

——— and Nigel Swain. "Agricultural politics and the 'Peasant Revolt' in Hungary." Rural Transition Series Working Paper no. 46, Centre for Central and Eastern European Studies, University of Liverpool, 1997. http://www.liv.ac.uk/history/research/cee_pdfs/WP46v2.pdf.

Kovela, Galina. "How to be an entrepreneur in a village." *Eastern European Countryside* 7 (2001): 91–100.
Kowalczyk, Andrzej. "Basic information on local governments in Poland." In *Local Governments in the CEE and CIS, 1994: An Anthology of Descriptive Papers*, edited by The Institute for Local Government and Public Services, 145–57. Budapest: Institute for Local Government and Public Services, 1994.
Kurtán, Sándor, Péter Sándor and László Vass, eds. *Magyarország politikai évkönyve* [Political yearbook of Hungary]. Budapest: Demokrácia Kutatások Magyar Központja Alapítvány, 1993.
Kyutchukov, Stephan. "Basic information on local governments in Bulgaria." In *Local Governments in the CEE and CIS, 1994: An Anthology of Descriptive Papers*, edited by The Institute for Local Government and Public Services, 37–53. Budapest: Institute for Local Government and Public Services, 1994.
Lacina, Karel. "Basic information on local governments in the Czech Republic." In *Local Governments in the CEE and CIS, 1994: An Anthology of Descriptive Papers*, edited by the Institute for Local Government and Public Services, 55–71. Budapest: Institute for Local Government and Public Services, 1994.
Ladas, Stephen P. *The Exchange of Minorities: Bulgaria, Greece and Turkey*. New York: Harvard University and Radcliffe College, Bureau of International Research, 1932.
Laki, Mihály and Júlia Szalai. „The puzzle of success: Hungarian entrepreneurs at the turn of the millennium." *Europe-Asia Studies*, 58, no. 3 (May 2006): 317–45.
Li, David D. "A theory of ambiguous property rights in transition economies: The case of the Chinese non-state Sector." *Journal of Comparative Economics* 23, no. 1 (August 1996): 1–19.
Majerová, Věra. "Reconstitution of private farm family households in the Czech Republic." In *Economic Behaviour of Family Households in an International Context*, edited by James Cécora, 100–8. Bonn: Society for Agricultural Policy Research and Rural Sociology, 1993.
Mandelbaum, Michael. "Introduction." In *Making Markets: Economic Transformation in Eastern Europe and the Post-Soviet States*, edited by Safiqul Islam and Michael Mandelbaum, 1–15. New York: Council on Foreign Relations Press, 1993.
Marx, Karl. "The Eighteenth Brumaire of Louis Bonaparte." In *Marx Engels: Selected Works in One Volume*, edited by Karl Marx and Friedrich Engels, 97–180. London: Lawrence and Wishart, 1968.
Mason, David S. "Poland." In *Developments in East European Politics*, edited by Stephen White, Judy Batt and Paul G. Lewis, 36–50. Houndmills: Macmillan, 1993.
Meurs, Mieke. *The Evolution of Agrarian Institutions: A Comparative Study of Post-Socialist Hungary and Bulgaria*. Ann Arbor, MI: The University of Michigan Press, 2001.

Millard, Frances. "Poland." In *Developments in Central and East European Politics 3*, edited by Stephen White, Judy Batt and Paul G. Lewis, 23–40. Houndmills: Palgrave Macmillan, 2003.

———. "Poland's politics and the travails of transition after 2001: The 2005 elections." *Europe-Asia Studies* 58, no. 7 (November, 2006): 1007–30.

Myant, Martin. *The Czechoslovak Economy 1948–1988*. Cambridge: Cambridge University Press, 1989.

———, Frank Fleischer, Kurt Hornschild, Růžena Vintrová, Karel Zeman and Zdeněk Souček. *Successful Transformations? The Creation of Market Economies in Eastern Germany and the Czech Republic*. Cheltenham and Brookfield: Edward Elgar, 1996.

——— and Simon Smith. "Regional development and post-communist politics in a Czech region." *Europe-Asia Studies* 58, no. 2 (March 2006): 147–68.

Nakajima, Takafumi. "Local government in Romania." In *The Emerging Local Governments in Eastern Europe and Russia: Historical and Post-Communist Developments*, edited by Osamu Ieda, 187–265. Hiroshima: Keisuisha, 2000.

Nalewajko, Ewa. "Political parties and agriculture in Poland." Rural Transition Series Working Paper no. 17, Centre for Central and Eastern European Studies, University of Liverpool, 1994. http://www.liv.ac.uk/history/research/cee_pdfs/WP17v3.pdf.

Námerová, Iveta. "Private farmers in Slovakia: Genesis, composition, conflict." *Eastern European Countryside* 5 (1999): 59–74.

——— and Nigel Swain. "Co-operative transformation and co-operative survival in Slovakia." *Replika* (Hungarian Social Science Quarterly) (Special Issue 1998): 207–21.

Neményi, Ágnes. *Erdélyi falvak—gazdasági, szociális struktúrák és folyamatok* [Transylvanian villages—economic and social structures and processes]. Cluj-Napoca: Alsand, 1997.

Neuburger, Mary. *The Orient Within: Muslim Minorities and the Negotiation of Nationhood in Modern Bulgaria*. Ithaca, NY and London: Cornell University Press, 2004.

O'Dwyer, Conor. "Reforming regional governance in East Central Europe: Europeanization or domestic politics as usual?" *East European Politics and Societies* 20, no. 2 (May 2006): 219–53.

OECD (Organisation of Economic Co-operation and Development). *Review of Agricultural Policies: Bulgaria*. Paris: Organisation of Economic Co-operation and Development, 2000.

———. *Review of Agricultural Policies: Czech Republic*. Paris: Organisation of Economic Co-operation and Development, 1995.

———. *Review of Agricultural Policies: Hungary*. Paris: Organisation of Economic Co-operation and Development, 1994.

———. *Review of Agricultural Policies: Poland*. Paris: Organisation of Economic Co-operation and Development, 1995.

———. *Review of Agricultural Policies: Romania*. Paris: Organisation of Economic Co-operation and Development, 2000.

———. *Review of Agricultural Policies: Slovak Republic*. Paris: Organisation of Economic Co-operation and Development, 1997.
Păun, Nicolae, Georgiana Ciceo and Dorin Domuţa. "Religious interactions of the Romanian political parties. Case study: The Christian Democratic connection." *Journal for the Study of Religions and Ideologies* 8, no. 24 (2009): 104–32.
Pickles, John. "'There are no Turks in Bulgaria': Violence, ethnicity, and economic practice in the border regions and Muslim communities of postsocialist Bulgaria." Working Paper no. 25, Max Planck Institute for Social Anthropology, Halle-Saale, 2001. http://www.eth.mpg.de/cms/de/publications/working_papers/wp0025.html.
——— and Robert Begg. "Ethnicity, state violence, and neo-liberal transitions in post-communist Bulgaria." *Growth and Change* 31, no. 2 (Spring 2000): 179–210.
Pilichowski, Andrzej. "Land in the Polish agrarian system." In *Rural Societies under Communism and Beyond: Hungarian and Polish Perspectives*, edited by Paweł Starosta, Imre Kovách and Krzysztof Gorlach, 66–79. Łódź: Łódź University Press, 1999.
Pine, Frances. "Retreat to the household? Gendered domains in postsocialist Poland." In *Postsocialism: Ideals and Practices in Eurasia*, edited by Chris Hann, 95–113. London and New York: Routledge, 2002.
Pospisil, Frantisek. "Czech agricultural political parties and movements 1992." Rural Transition Series Working Paper no. 11, Centre for Central and Eastern European Studies, University of Liverpool, 1994. http://www.liv.ac.uk/history/research/cee_pdfs/WP11v3.pdf.
Pryor Frederic L. *The Red and the Green: The Rise and Fall of Collectivized Agriculture in Marxist Regimes*. Princeton, NJ: Princeton University Press, 1992.
Psyk-Piotrowska, Elżbieta. "State-owned and co-operative farms in Poland during the transformation process." In *Rural Societies under Communism and Beyond: Hungarian and Polish Perspectives*, edited by Paweł Starosta, Imre Kovách and Krzysztof Gorlach, 151–72. Łódź: Łódź University Press, 1999.
Racz, Barnabas. "The Left in Hungary and the 2002 parliamentary elections." *Europe-Asia Studies* 55, no. 5 (July 2003): 747–69.
———. "Political pluralisation in Hungary: The 1990 elections." *Soviet Studies* 43, no. 1 (1991): 107–36.
——— and Istvan Kukorelli. "The 'second generation' post-communist elections in Hungary." *Europe-Asia Studies* 47, no. 2 (March 1995): 251–79.
Ramchev, Kolio. "The personality split as a factor towards market development of the Bulgarian village." In *The Bulgarian Village and Globalisation Processes: XVIIth Congress of the European Society of Rural Sociology*, edited by Veska Kozhuharova, 85–90. Sofia: Bulgarian Society of Rural Sociology, Institute of Sociology, 1997.
Ratesh, Nestor. *Romania: The Entangled Revolution*. New York and London: Praeger with the Center for Strategic and International Studies, Washington DC, 1991.

Redfield, Robert. "The part-societies with part-cultures." In *Peasants and Peasant Societies: Selected Readings* (2nd edition), edited by Teodor Shanin, 60–1. Oxford and New York: Basil Blackwell, 1987.

Regulski, Jerzy. *Local Government Reform in Poland: An Insider's Story*. Budapest: Local Government and Public Service Reform Initiative, Open Society Institute, 2003.

Ronnas, Per. "Turning the Romanian peasant into a new socialist man: An assessment of rural development policy in Romania." *Soviet Studies* 41, no. 4 (October 1989): 543–59.

Roper, Steven D. *Romania: The Unfinished Revolution*. London and New York: Routledge, 2000.

Roszkowski, Wojciech. *Land Reforms in East Central Europe after World War One*. Warsaw: Institute of Political Studies of Polish Academy of Sciences, 1995.

Rus, Alin. "Rural development versus traditionalism and synergy versus poverty in rural Romania." *Eastern European Countryside* 10 (2004): 121–36.

Rychlík, Jan. "The possibilities for Czech–Slovak compromise, 1989–1992." In *Irreconcilable Differences? Explaining Czechoslovakia's Dissolution*, edited by Michael Kraus and Allison Stanger, 49–66. Lanham, MD and Oxford: Rowman and Littlefield, 2000.

Ryšavý, Dan. "Changes in the local political elite in small towns and rural areas: Does revolution devour its children?" *Eastern European Countryside* 12 (2006): 51–65.

Sampson, Steven. "Beyond transition: Rethinking elite configurations in the Balkans." In *Postsocialism: Ideals and Practices in Eurasia*, edited by Chris Hann, 297–316. London and New York: Routledge, 2002.

Sarris, Alexander H. and Dinu Gavrilescu. "Restructuring of farms and agricultural systems in Romania." In *Agricultural Privatisation, Land Reform and Farm Restructuring in Central and Eastern Europe*, edited by Johan F.M. Swinnen, Allan Buckwell and Erik Mathijs, 189–228. Aldershot: Ashgate, 1997.

Schafft, Kai A. "A network approach to understanding post-socialist rural inequality in the 1990s." *Eastern European Countryside* 6 (2000): 25–39.

Schülter, Achim. "Institutional change in transition: Restitution, transformation and privatisation in Czech agriculture." Paper presented at the KATO Symposium, Berlin, Germany, 2–4 November 2000.

Sengoku, Manabu. "Local government and the state: Change and continuity of the local system in Poland." In *The Emerging Local Governments in Eastern Europe and Russia: Historical and Post-Communist Developments*, edited by Osamu Ieda, 55–84. Hiroshima: Keisuisha, 2000.

Shafir, Michael. "The Ciorbea Government and democratization: A preliminary assessment." In *Post-Communist Romania: Coming to Terms with Transition*, edited by Duncan Light and David Phinnemore, 79–103. Houndmills: Palgrave, 2001.

———. *Romania: Politics, Economics and Society*. London: Frances Pinter, 1985.

——— and Dan Ionescu. "Romania: A nebulous political shift." In *Building Democracy: The OMRI Annual Survey of Eastern Europe and the Former Soviet Union*, edited by the Open Media Research Institute, 161–9. Armonk, NY and London: M.E. Sharpe, 1996.

Shanin, Teodor. "Introduction: Peasantry as a concept." In *Peasants and Peasant Societies: Selected Readings* (2nd edition), edited by Teodor Shanin, 1–11. Oxford and New York: Basil Blackwell, 1987.

Siani-Davies, Peter. *The Romanian Revolution of December 1989*. Ithaca, NY and London: Cornell University Press.

Slicher van Bath, B.H. "Agriculture in the vital revolution." In *The Cambridge Economic History of Europe. Volume V: The Economic Organization of Early Modern Europe*, edited by E.E. Rich, 42–132. Cambridge: Cambridge University Press, 1977.

Small, Lee-Ann. "Agriculture-based livelihood strategies in Bulgaria and Southern Russia: Implications for agrarian change." PhD diss., University of Aberdeen, 2005.

Stryjan, Yohanan. "Czechoslovak agricultural co-operation: The vagaries of institutional transformation." Berliner Heft zum Internationalen Genossenschaftswesen no. 5, Institut für Genossenschaftswesen an der Humboldt Universität zu Berlin, 1994.

Sun, Laixiang. "Ownership reform in the absence of crisis: China's township, village and private enterprises." In *Small and Medium Enterprises in Transitional Economies*, edited by Robert J. McIntyre and Bruno Dallago, 134–52. Houndmills: Palgrave Macmillan. 2003.

Swain, Geoffrey and Nigel Swain. *Eastern Europe since 1945* (1st edition). Houndmills: Macmillan, 1993.

———. *Eastern Europe since 1945* (2nd edition). Houndmills: Macmillan, 1998.

———. *Eastern Europe since 1945* (3rd edition). Houndmills: Palgrave Macmillan, 2003.

———. *Eastern Europe since 1945* (4th edition). Houndmills: Palgrave Macmillan, 2009.

Swain, Nigel. "Agricultural privatisation in Hungary." Rural Transition Series Working Paper no. 32, Centre for Central and Eastern European Studies, University of Liverpool, 1994. http://www.liv.ac.uk/history/research/cee_pdfs/WP32v3.pdf.

———. "Agricultural restitution and co-operative transformation in the Czech Republic, Hungary and Slovakia." *Europe-Asia Studies* 51, no. 7 (November 1999): 1199–219.

———. "Agricultural transformation in Hungary: The context." Rural Transition Series Working Paper no. 7, Centre for Central and Eastern European Studies, University of Liverpool, 1993. http://www.liv.ac.uk/history/research/cee_pdfs/WP07v3.pdf.

———. "Agriculture 'east of the Elbe' and the common agricultural policy." *Sociologia Ruralis*. Forthcoming (2013).

———. "Changing dynamics in the East European meso-area: A rural, grassroots perspective." In *Reconstruction and Interaction of Slavic Eurasia and its Neighbouring Worlds*, edited by Osamu Ieda and Tomohiko Uyama, 43–60. Sapporo: Slavic Research Center, Hokkaido University, 2006.

———. "Co-operative elites in Hungary after 1945." In *Agrarismus und Agrareliten in Mittel- und Ostmitteleuropa*, edited by Eduard Kubů, Torsten Lorenz, Uwe Müller and Jiří Šouša. In press (2013).

———. "Collective farms as sources of stability and decay in the centrally planned economies of East Central Europe." Rural Transition Series Working Paper no. 30, Centre for Central and Eastern European Studies, University of Liverpool, 1994. http://www.liv.ac.uk/history/research/cee_pdfs/WP30v3.pdf.

———. *Collective Farms which Work?* Cambridge: Cambridge University Press, 1985.

———. "Decollectivization politics and rural change in Bulgaria, Poland and the former Czechoslovakia." *Social History* 32, no. 1 (February 2007): 1–26.

———. "The ethics of agricultural transition." Rural Transition Series Working Paper no. 31, Centre for Central and Eastern European Studies, University of Liverpool, 1994.

———. "The evolution of Hungary's agricultural system since 1967." In *Hungary: A Decade of Economic Reform*, edited by Paul Hare, Hugo Radice and Nigel Swain, 225–51. London: George Allen & Unwin, 1981.

———. "The fate of peasant parties during socialist transformation." In *Bauerngesellschaften auf dem Weg in die Moderne*, edited by Helga Schultz and Angela Harre, 163–76. Wiesbaden: Harrassowitz Verlag, 2010.

———. "The fog of negotiated revolution." *In Challenging Communism in Eastern Europe: 1956 and Its Legacy*, edited by Terry Cox, 159–87. London and New York: Routledge, 2008.

———. "A framework for comparing social change in the post-socialist countryside." *Eastern European Countryside* 4 (1998): 5–18.

———. "Getting land in Central Europe." In *After Socialism: Land Reform and Social Change in Eastern Europe*, edited by Ray Abrahams, 193–215. Providence, RI and Oxford: Berghahn Books, 1996.

———. "Hungary." In *Developments in East European Politics*, edited by Stephen White, Judy Batt and Paul G. Lewis, 66–82. Houndmills: Macmillan, 1993.

———. *Hungary: The Rise and Fall of Feasible Socialism*. London and New York: Verson, 1992.

———. "Hungary's socialist project in crisis." *New Left Review* I/176 (July–August, 1989): 3–29.

———. "Inexperienced and impotent: Rural local government in an Eastern European meso-area *in Statu Nascendi*." *Acta Slavica Iaponica* 22 (2005): 1–24.

———. "From kolkhoz to holding company: A Hungarian agricultural producer co-operative in transition." *Journal of Historical Sociology* 13, no. 2 (June 2000): 142–71.

———. "The legislative framework for agricultural transition in Hungary." Rural Transition Series Working Paper no. 25, Centre for Central and Eastern European Studies, University of Liverpool, 1994. http://www.liv.ac.uk/history/research/cee_pdfs/WP25v2.pdf.

———. "Negotiated revolution in Poland and Hungary, 1989." In *Revolution and Resistance in Eastern Europe: Challenges to Communist Rule*, edited by Kevin McDermott and Matthew Stibbe, 139–55. Oxford and New York: Berg, 2006.

———. "Political parties and agriculture in Hungary." Rural Transition Series Working Paper no. 24, Centre for Central and Eastern European Studies, University of Liverpool, 1994. http://www.liv.ac.uk/history/research/cee_pdfs/WP24v2.pdf.

———. "A post-socialist capitalism." *Europe-Asia Studies* 63, no 9 (October 2011): 1671–95.

———. "The rural transition in post-socialist Central Europe and the Balkans." Working Paper no. 9, Max Planck Institute for Social Anthropology, Halle-Saale, 2000. http://www.eth.mpg.de/cms/de/publications/working_papers/wp0009.html.

———. "The Smallholders' Party versus the green barons: Class relations in the restructuring of Hungarian agriculture." Rural Transition Series Working Paper no. 8, Centre for Central and Eastern European Studies, University of Liverpool, 1993. http://www.liv.ac.uk/history/research/cee_pdfs/WP08v2.pdf.

———. "Social capital and its uses." *Archives Européennes de Sociologie* 44, no. 2 (August 2003): 185–212.

———. "The Visegrad countries of Eastern Europe." In *European Economies since the Second World War*, edited by B.J. Foley, 177–208. Houndmills: Macmillan, 1998.

———, Mihály Andor and Tibor Kuczi. "The privatization of Hungarian collective farms." *Eastern European Countryside* 1 (1995): 69–80.

——— and Mária Vincze. "Agricultural restructuring in Transylvania in the post-communist period." In *Post-Communist Romania: Coming to Terms with Transition*, edited by Duncan Light and David Phinnemore, 175–90. Houndmills: Palgrave, 2001.

Swianiewicz, Paweł. "Is there a third way between small yet ineffective and big yet less democratic? Comparative conclusions and lessons learned." In *Consolidation or Fragmentation? The Size of Local Governments in Central and Eastern Europe*, edited by Paweł Swianiewicz, 294–325. Budapest: Local Government and Public Reform Initiative, Open Society Institute, 2002.

——— and Mikołaj Herbst. "Economies and diseconomies of scale in Polish local governments." In *Consolidation or Fragmentation? The Size of Local Governments in Central and Eastern Europe*, edited by Paweł Swianiewicz, 219–92. Budapest: Local Government and Public Reform Initiative, Open Society Institute, 2002.

Szajkowski, Bogdan. "Romania." In *New Political Parties of Eastern Europe and the Soviet Union*, edited by Bogdan Szajkowski, 219–49. Harlow: Longman Current Affairs, 1991.

Szczerbiak, Aleks. "The birth of a bipolar party system or a referendum on a polarizing government: The October 2007 Polish party elections." *Journal of Communist Studies and Transition Politics* 24, no. 3 (September 2008): 415–43.

———. "Dealing with the communist past or the politics of the present? Lustration in post-communist Poland." *Europe-Asia Studies* 54, no. 4 (June 2002): 529–52.

———. "Interests and values: Polish parties and their electorates." *Europe-Asia Studies* 51, no. 8 (December 1999): 1401–32.

———. "Old and new divisions in Polish politics: Polish parties' electoral strategies and bases of support." *Europe-Asia Studies* 55, no. 5 (July 2003): 729–46.

———. "The Polish Peasant Party: A mass party in postcommunist Eastern Europe?" *East European Politics and Societies* 15, no. 3 (2001): 554–88.

———. "Testing party models in East-Central Europe: Local party organization in postcommunist Poland." *Party Politics* 5, no. 4 (October 1999): 525–37.

Szelenyi, Ivan. *Socialist Entrepreneurs: Embourgeoisement in Rural Hungary.* Cambridge: Polity Press, 1988.

Takla, Lina. „The relationship between privatization and the reform of the banking sector: The case of the Czech Republic and Slovakia." In *Privatization in Central and Eastern Europe*, edited by Saul Estrin, 154–75. London and New York: Longman, 1994.

Theesfeld, Insa and Ivan Boevsky. "Pre-socialist cooperative traditions: The case of water syndicates in Bulgaria." *Sociologia Ruralis* 43, no. 3 (2005): 171–86.

Thelen, Tatjana. "Violence and (dis)continuity: Comparing collectivization in two East European villages." *Social History* 30, no. 1 (February 2005): 25–44.

Thomka, Alexander. "The informal economy and viability of small family farms in Romania." *Eastern European Countryside* 11 (2005): 89–109.

Thompson, E.P. *Customs in Common.* London: Penguin, 1993.

Tímár, Judit and Mónika Mária Váradi. "The uneven development of suburbanization during transition in Hungary." *European Urban and Regional Studies* 8, no. 4 (October 2001): 349–60.

Torsello, Davide. "Trust and property in historical perspective: Villagers and the agricultural co-operative in Királyfa, Southern Slovakia." In *The Postsocialist Agrarian Question: Property Relations and the Rural Condition*, edited by Chris Hann and The "Property Relations" Group, 93–116. Münster: LIT Verlag, 2003.

Valchovska, Stela. "Entrepreneurship among post-socialist agricultural producers: The case of Bulgaria." PhD diss., University of Gloucestershire, 2010.

Verdery, Katherine. "The elasticity of land: Problems of property restitution in Transylvania." *Slavic Review* 53, no. 4 (Winter, 1994): 1071–109.

Verdery, Katherine. *The Vanishing Hectare: Property and Value in Postsocialist Transylvania.* Ithaca, NY: Cornell University Press, 2003.

Vinton, Louisa. "Poland's social safety net: An overview," *RFE/RL Research Report* 2, no. 17 (23 April 1993): 3–11.
Wilkinson, Henry Robert. *Maps and Politics: A Review of the Ethnographic Cartography of Macedonia*. Liverpool: Liverpool University Press, 1951.
Wolf, Eric R. *Peasants*. Englewood Cliffs, NJ: Prentice-Hall, 1966.
Woltz, Axel, Gejza Blaas, Iveta Námerová and Stanislav Buchta. *Agricultural Transformation in Slovakia: The Change of Institutions and Organisations*. Saarbrücken: Verlag für Entwicklungspolitik, Heidelberg Studies in Applied Economics and Rural Institutions, Publications of the Research Centre for International Agrarian and Economic Development no. 29, 1998.
Zabłocki, Grzegorz. "Privatization in Polish agriculture: Determinants and effects." *Eastern European Countryside* 1 (1995): 61–8.
Zaucha, Jacek. "Regional and local development in Poland." In *Decentralisation and Transition in the Visegrad: Poland, Hungary, the Czech Republic and Slovakia*, edited by Emil J. Kirchner, 53–79. Houndmills: Macmillan, 1999.
Zbierski-Salameh, Slawomira. "Polish peasants in the 'valley of transition': Responses to postsocialist reforms." In *In Uncertain Transition: Ethnographies of Change in the Postsocialist World*, edited by Michael Burawoy and Katherine Verdery, 189–222. Lanham, MD and Oxford: Rowman and Littlefield, 1999.

Index of Research Villages

B

Bánec, Slovakia, 325–326, 352–355, 359
Bárov, Czech Republic, 15, 154, 157, 179–190, 191, 257, 270, 370
Bawełna, Poland, 248, 251, 252–254, 272, 276, 277
Blagun, Bulgaria, 15, 139, 140–146, 151, 265, 275, 368
Bory, Poland, 255–256, 261–263, 277, 367, 369
Breze, Bulgaria, 124, 126–127, 133, 139
Buneşti, Romania, 303–304, 314–317, 318

C

Chala, Bulgaria, 15, 125, 140–146, 151, 265, 275, 368
Chůzovany, Czech Republic, 15, 154, 157, 179–190, 191
Colibaşi, Romania, 122, 286–289, 315–316, 317, 364
Cukier, Poland, 256, 264–265

D

Dombház, Hungary, 209–213, 226–228, 231, 232, 238, 367, 368

Dragana, Bulgaria, 115, 118–123, 138, 148–149, 150–151

G

Głaz, Poland, 246–248, 249, 256–258, 260, 261, 268–269, 276, 277, 367

H

Habán, Slovakia, 323, 349–352, 359
Hora, Slovakia, 94, 322, 323, 355–356
Horia, Romania, 289–290, 301, 316–318

K

Kanał, Poland, 260–261, 265–267, 276–277, 316, 367, 368
Károlyháza, Hungary, 196, 207–209, 218–221, 229–230, 232, 238, 367
Kissikonda, Hungary, 196, 210, 226–232, 258, 367
Klanec, Slovakia, 325, 331–334, 337–339, 340, 344–346, 360, 362
Korcona, Hungary, 74, 109, 196, 197–199, 205, 222–226, 233–234, 237–238, 299, 364, 366

Krížava, Slovakia, 94, 305, 327–328, 340–341, 343–344, 346–350, 359–360, 363
Kupen, Bulgaria, 125–126, 134–136, 140–146, 150, 151

L

Ľupta, Slovakia, 324–325, 339–340, 342–343, 349, 360
Lehota, Slovakia, 109, 328–331, 339, 344, 356–360, 367
Lesovice, Czech Republic, 156–157, 169–171, 174–176, 191–192, 228, 369
Lipova, Romania, 281–283, 290–291, 316

M

Mägura, Romania, 109, 281, 292–293, 294–296, 299, 302–303, 311, 313, 317–318
Městysov, Czech Republic, 15, 109, 161–165, 191
Mica, Romania, 109, 301–302, 307–310, 314, 315, 318

N

Nezávislice, Czech Republic, 155–156, 171–173, 178, 191, 237, 367
Nová Huť, Czech Republic, 154, 165–169, 191

P

Pakucs, Hungary, 79, 201–205, 215–217, 218, 237, 238, 364
Palina, Slovakia, 95, 326–327, 334–337, 373, 378
Plopeni, Romania, 305–307, 318
Pola, Poland, 254–255, 258–260, 261, 270, 367

Pripek, Bulgaria, 108, 114–118, 123, 137–139, 146–148, 150
Purani, Romania, 283–286, 300–301, 318

R

Remetea, Romania, 94, 296–300, 304, 317, 341
Rodáky, Czech Republic, 75, 109, 115, 155, 176–178, 191, 364, 367
Rozino, Bulgaria, 131, 137, 148

S

Sedno, Poland, 254, 365–266, 269–277, 366
Slivka, Bulgaria, 123–125, 128, 139, 149, 151
Szálfa, Hungary, 200–201, 213–214, 322, 369
Székhely, Hungary, 94, 232–233, 238

T

Tabar, Hungary, 93, 205–207, 211, 217–218, 234–236, 237–238, 258
Tvrz nad Řekou, Czech Republic, 159–161, 191

V

Venets, Bulgaria, 127–133, 138, 150, 283
Výletnice, Czech Republic, 109, 157–159, 178–179

Z

Zádorpuszta, Hungary, 221–222, 236–237, 238
Zalew, Poland, 243–245, 276
Zamek, Poland, 248–251, 272, 276
Zurča, Slovakia, 323–324, 341–342, 349, 360, 364

General Index

A

Agrarian Alliance, Hungary, 27
Agrarian Democratic Party of Romania (PDAR), 35
Agrarian Party, Czechoslovakia, 29
Agricultural Party, Czech Republic, 29, 173
Agro–industrial complex, Bulgaria, 52, 119–120, 146
Agromecs, Romania, 49, 74, 78, 82, 279, 282–283, 285, 290, 292–296, 306, 309, 317
Arendatori (Bulgaria), 78, 150, 317, 362
Augustów canal, 260

B

baking, 40–41, 119, 124, 140, 145, 150, 165, 168, 170, 217, 230–232, 243, 248, 259, 300, 302–304, 339, 346
bankruptcy, 38, 42, 54, 68, 94, 147, 161, 186, 195–214, 217, 220, 221, 238, 262, 269, 286, 335, 347, 352, 354, 362, 368–369
Barley, 119, 284
blue co-operatives, *see* Co-operatives 'red and blue' (Bulgaria)
'Bokros package', 24
'Border effect' non-EU, 97, 269–276, 277, 366
'Border effect' EU, 97, 151, 182–3, 185, 366
boutiques (fashion), 184, 215, 223
BSP, *see* Bulgarian Socialist Party
builders, 149, 165, 168, 170, 174, 190, 222, 270, 340, 348. *See also* construction
Bulgarian Agrarian National Union (BZNS), 31–32
Bulgarian Socialist Party, (BSP), 30–32, 47, 69–70, 116, 130, 135, 137, 145
BZNS
    Aleksander Stamboliski, Bulgaria, 32
    Nikola Petkov, Bulgaria, 32
    People's Union, Bulgaria, 32
BZNS, *see* Bulgarian Agrarian National Union

C

capital
    cultural, 74, 75–76, 95–96, 118, 148, 163, 191, 237, 318, 361, 366
    human, 74, 95–96, 191, 237, 244, 318, 336, 361, 366
    social, 16, 74, 75, 95–97, 109, 118, 148, 163, 176–177, 191, 215–218,

220, 237, 244, 250, 302, 318, 336, 361, 366
car repair, 95, 131, 146, 165, 168, 170, 186, 217, 218, 223, 301, 341
carpentry, 145, 147–150, 168, 186, 218, 301
Catholic Church, 28, 110, 167–168, 178, 191, 196, 242, 252–256, 257, 305–307, 367
charities, 102, 168, 254–255, 257, 280, 299, 305, 307, 311, 314, 318, 347
choirs, 309–313
Christian Democratic National Peasant Party, Romania (PNȚ-CD), 34
Christian Democratic People's Party, Hungary, 27
Christian Democrats, Czech Republic, 158, 168, 176
Christian Democrats, Slovakia (KDH), 68, 100, 322, 346–349, 351, 357, 359
Christian Social Union, Slovakia (KSU), 349
Civic Democratic Party, Czechoslovakia (ODS), 28
Civic Forum (Czechoslovakia), 28, 44, 67, 172, 174, 188
Civic Platform (Poland), 22
co-operative
　holding (Hungary), 82, 205, 329, 331
　liquidation (Bulgaria), 114–134
　'red and blue' (Bulgaria), 76, 78, 86, 113, 127–133, 150, 279, 283, 322, 369
　transformation, 15, 26–27, 29–30, 32, 43–55, 67–70, 72, 74–88, 113, 153, 154–165, 179–180, 191, 195–215, 221, 237–238, 241–242, 271, 280–300, 321–334, 337–339, 359–363
collectivisation, 1, 4, 23, 26, 31, 41, 43–54, 78, 81, 87, 89, 114, 119, 125–127, 140–142, 190, 241, 271–2, 276, 291, 294, 302, 307, 362
community associations, 2, 106, 108–109, 158, 178, 189–190, 235, 326
commuting, 88, 92, 105, 144, 146–148, 168, 171–173, 177, 182–3, 187,
205, 210, 226, 231, 269, 300–302, 318, 322, 334, 341, 343–344, 355, 366
'comprador bourgeoisie', 19
Constantinescu, Emile, 33
construction, 114, 144, 147, 148, 163, 165, 169, 174, 180, 182–184, 188, 201, 233, 246, 270, 300, 302, 329, 332, 340, 357
Coopker, 216–217
councillors, 62, 65, 189–190, 233, 236, 238, 254, 255, 260–263, 277, 314, 346, 348–349, 351, 367
cultural centres, 63, 166–168, 179, 187, 248, 259–260, 262, 306, 312–314, 345, 348, 358

C

dairy farming, 93, 114–115, 117, 119, 124–125, 131, 141, 146, 159, 202–203, 210–213, 236, 238, 243, 246–248, 265–266, 270, 272, 283, 289, 291, 300, 309, 327, 330–333, 368
dance groups, 262, 302, 309–310, 312
Democratic Party, Slovakia, 349
Dombmilk, 212–213, 368
DPS, *see* Movement for Rights and Freedom, Bulgaria

E

Education
　levels of, 74, 88, 90–93, 121, 125, 135, 141, 145, 187, 221, 260, 266, 271, 297, 317, 336, 338, 340, 364
　responsibility for, 56–64, 69, 102, 226–229, 234, 258, 260, 277, 367
'Elastic land', 118–123, 280, 295
Elder-Pak, 268–269, 276
entrepreneurs
　'force-of-circumstance', 11, 16, 89, 93–96, 149, 151, 222, 303, 344, 365–366
envy, 106–107, 181, 187–189, 339, 353, 370

General Index

erotic clubs, 185, 270
Ersatz shock therapy, 12, 38–39, 68, 154, 164–166, 182, 187, 191, 344, 359, 369
estate farm servants, 246, 290, 349
ethnic minorities, 109, 311. *See also* Roma, Pomaks
EU, 15, 20, 55, 361
Evangelical Church, 110

F

Făniţă, Triţă, 35
Farmers' Movement, Czech Republic, 29
Farmers' Movement, Slovakia, 30
FATO, 268–269
Fidesz, Hungary, 26, 202
'fiscal stress', 102, 238, 274, 277, 345, 350, 352, 357, 367–369
forestry, 168, 174–175, 179, 188, 202–203, 260–261, 263, 265–267, 272, 304, 311, 338
fruit, 94, 114–116, 119, 124, 127–129, 137, 139, 161, 198, 208–209, 243–244, 266, 296–297, 304, 313, 325, 328, 353, 356
'fuzzy' public-private divide, 37–38, 39, 103, 174–176, 238, 331, 349–352, 359

G

Golden Lion, 158–159
Greek Catholic Church, 110, 256
Greek Orthodox Church, 110
Green barons, 11, 74–76, 191, 237–238, 276, 359

H

hairdressers, 95, 115–116, 120, 146, 165, 168, 184, 225, 300, 351
Hanig Ltd., 216
honey, 217, 228
household plots, 50–54, 115, 141–142, 196, 205, 208, 210, 219, 324, 325, 329

houses of culture, *see* cultural centres
Hungarian Democratic Union of Romania (UDMR), 35, 100, 307–314
hunting, 108–109, 158, 171, 179, 229, 267, 358
Hussite Church, 110
HZDS, *see* Movement for a Democratic Slovakia

I

Iliescu, Ion, 33, 69
Infratirea, 283–285
'inverted pyramid' of land ownership, 73, 241
irrigation, 102, 114–116, 119–120, 129, 137–139, 281, 297, 323, 325–326
Islam, 31, 110, 141

J

Jagieliński, Roman, 22

K

KDH, *see* Christian Democrats, Slovakia
Klaus, Vaclav, 28, 68, 175
Kmetstvo, Bulgaria, *see* Mayors
KSU, *see* Christian Social Union, Slovakia
Kubat, Bohumil, 157
kulak, 44, 118, 159, 163, 191, 291, 294, 302, 335

L

Law and Justice Party, Poland, 23
League of Polish Families, 23
Liberal Social Union, Czechoslovakia, 29
Liquidating Committee, 47, 120. *See also* co-operative liquidation (Bulgaria)
lobbying, 178, 192, 258, 359–360, 367
local government impotence, 98, 102–104, 274, 279, 305–318, 367
local government reforms, 15, 55–71, 134, 139, 195–196, 226–229, 363
Lux, Josef, 158

M

maize, 115, 119, 129, 131–132, 205, 209, 284, 291, 298, 308, 325, 331
Maniu, Iuliu, 34
mayors, 56–59, 62–63, 65, 94, 99, 101, 102, 106, 117, 118, 121–124, 129, 130, 134–138, 147, 149–151, 156, 158, 161, 164, 167–169, 171–179, 183, 185, 187–192, 210, 212, 227–229, 231–236, 238, 252–256, 258–264, 268–269, 275, 277, 280, 282, 292, 300, 303–318, 323, 326, 337, 339, 343– 349, 353–360, 364, 367
meat and poultry, 93–94, 114–116, 118, 119, 125, 137, 141, 146–147, 156, 159, 160, 162, 163, 168, 199, 200, 204–205, 219–221, 224, 230, 245–248, 254, 271, 289–292, 298, 323, 325, 327, 329–333, 340, 342
Mečiar, Vladimír, 28–30, 36, 38, 58, 68, 83, 103, 321–322, 334, 347, 349, 359–360
Mihalache, Ion, 34
moral economy (of socialism), 106–107, 369–370
Moravčik, Jozef, 68
Movement for a Democratic Slovakia (HZDS), 28
Movement for Rights and Freedom, Bulgaria (DPS), 30–31
Movement of Farmers, Czech Republic, 173

N

National Peasant Party, Romania (PNȚ), 34
Nazis, 29, 167, 169
New Economic Mechanism (Hungary), 53

O

ODS, *see* Civic Democratic Party, Czechoslovakia

Olszewski, Jan, 21
Orbán, Viktor, 26
Orthodox Church, 110, 134–135, 140–141, 304, 306, 314, 317
outsiders, 45, 77, 79, 96, 117, 123, 127, 133, 149, 171, 179, 187–189, 198, 210, 220, 233, 242, 246, 265–268, 295, 303–304, 313, 324, 332, 334

P

Party of Romanian National Unity (PUNR), 314–315
Pawlak, Waldemar, 22
PDAR, *see* Agrarian Democratic Party of Romania
pensioners, 58, 81, 88–90, 93, 113, 116–119, 125, 129, 131, 135–138, 145–147, 156, 172, 179, 186, 201, 236, 266, 279, 284, 292, 296, 308, 310, 312, 316–317, 324, 334–337, 345–347, 352, 355, 369
Pentecostalist Church, 110
petrol stations, 147, 149, 157, 168, 171, 178, 184, 198, 207, 266, 303
PGRs, 243–247, 249, 270–273
PHARE, 122, 229, 285
PKP, Poland, 268
plumbing, 168, 215–216, 340, 341, 355
PNȚ-CD, *see* Christian Democratic National Peasant Party, Romania
Polish Peasant Party (PSL), 21–24, 25, 30, 69, 100, 242, 251, 258–261
political migration, 100, 279–280
POM, *see* State Machinery Centres, Poland
Pomaks, 31, 140–142
potatoes, 117, 119, 209, 225, 247, 270–271, 283–285, 288, 327
prison labour, 298
private farmers, 45, 51, 75–76, 81–83, 117–118, 125, 127, 128, 131–133, 144, 150, 160, 161, 196, 201, 207, 209, 214, 229, 236, 237, 241, 243–249, 270–272, 282, 291–292, 296–300, 317, 325–326, 328–331, 334

privatisation, 15, 20, 36, 35, 36–43, 49, 59, 67, 69, 74, 77, 80, 82, 97, 104, 151, 154, 161–164, 165–166, 170, 177, 181–182, 184, 191, 201, 241–242, 243–250, 252–253, 264–265, 267, 270–274, 276, 279, 300, 317, 327, 331–335, 337, 343–344, 355, 369
property, 12–13, 43–44, 49–50, 52–53, 103, 132, 155, 162, 163, 166, 188, 197, 202, 206, 208, 210, 211, 247, 252, 269, 294, 297, 332, 352–353, 369
prostitution, 18, 257
PSL, *see* Polish Peasant Party
pubs and bars, 95, 145, 147, 149, 150, 165, 170, 182, 187, 208, 217–218, 266, 275, 292, 297, 301, 304–305, 310, 335, 341, 342, 355
Public Against Violence, Slovakia, 28, 68, 323, 349, 357
PUNR, *see* Party of Romanian National Unity

R

red co-operatives, *see* co-operatives – 'red and blue' (Bulgaria)
Reform Church, 110, 205, 233–236, 289, 304, 307–310
residual estates, 72, 82, 157
restaurants (includes snack-bars, buffets, etc.), 145, 146, 149, 158, 168, 170, 208, 217–218, 233, 275, 290, 301, 303, 311, 343, 345, 350–351
restitution, 27–29, 36–44, 48, 67, 72, 82–83, 97, 185, 241, 244–248, 256, 273, 280, 294, 336;
'full, direct, specific', 11, 36–39, 44, 121, 153–154, 159–161, 163–164, 166–167, 169–171, 191, 322, 343, 362;
'historic borders', 48–49;
'partial, indirect, uniform', 11, 39–41, 199–203, 208, 211, 214, 236

Roma, 94, 127, 134, 233, 238, 283, 296, 304–305, 334–337, 340, 355, 359
Romanian Democratic Convention (CDR), 33–35

S

Samoobrona (Self-Defence), Poland, 22–23
'second economy', 3–4, 54, 81, 195–196, 199, 200–201, 215, 218, 219, 237–238, 241–242, 250, 268, 291, 330, 365
shops (including grocers, excluding supermarkets), 95, 140, 142, 147–150, 161, 164–165, 168, 170–171, 173, 175, 178, 184–185, 187, 212, 216, 223–226, 230, 233, 236, 254, 282, 284, 300–304, 307, 335, 341–343
SKR, 243–250, 266, 270–272
Slovak Agrarian Party, 30
Smallholders Party (Hungary), 25–27, 40, 54, 68, 208, 209–213, 238, 368
smuggling, 266, 271, 273–276
'Socialist personal services gap', 11, 94, 102, 145, 147, 149, 165, 168, 170, 185, 191, 222–226, 275, 280, 301, 304, 318, 341–342, 359, 368
'Socialist public services gap', 11, 102, 106, 135, 137–139, 279, 311, 316, 363, 364, 368
Sokol, 167
Solidarity, Poland, 21–22, 24, 35, 60–61, 69, 110, 242, 252–255, 263, 264–265, 276–277, 367
specialist groups (Hungary), 219–220
'Specialists' (Poland), 51, 53, 82, 241–252, 276, 371
sports clubs, 109, 183, 230, 234, 244, 256, 325–326, 345, 347, 352, 366
State Machinery Centres (POM), Poland, 243, 244, 264, 270
Stolojan, Theodor, 35
subsidiary farm, *see* household plot
subsidies
economic, 51, 59, 83, 116–118, 135, 146–148, 151, 160, 163, 175, 177,

203, 214, 220, 250, 258–261, 263, 265, 288, 327–331, 333, 368
subsidised lunches, 137, 179, 214, 261, 347, 369
Suchocka, Hanna, 21, 69
supermarkets, 222, 224, 225
supertenants, 78, 294, 298–300, 303, 317–318

T

Tlustý, Vlastimil, 44
tobacco, 119–120, 125, 127, 141–144, 209, 219, 265, 323, 368
Together in Europe Foundation, Poland, 253
Tomášek, František, 44
Torgyán, József, 25–27
tourism, 62, 103, 136, 159, 177–179, 185, 189, 215–216, 226–229, 237, 243, 253–254, 257–259, 261–263, 266–267, 276, 304–308, 313, 339, 350–358, 363, 369
Town and Village Enterprises (TVE), 103–104
transferable skills, 90, 92
Trnka, František, 29
Tyl, Miroslav, 44

U

Union of Democratic Forces, SDS (Bulgaria), 30–32, 43, 46–47, 70, 125, 129, 145
Union of Slovak Workers, ZRS, 357
Unitarian Church, 110, 312–313

V

Vlaicu, 280, 282, 288, 298–299, 303, 305, 317–318, 364

W

Wałęsa, Lech, 69
Wheat, 117, 125, 131–132, 201, 209, 283–285, 291, 293, 298, 308
woodwork and wood processing, 146, 165, 167, 168, 170, 174, 180–181, 266, 302, 339, 356. *See also* forestry

Y

Young Communist League, Czech Republic, 159